Stabilising fragile democracies

Political parties are likely to play a crucial role in the process of democratisation and the establishment of new parliamentary democracies. They often form as a result of opposition to the previous authoritarian regime and their performance during the transition to democracy and immediately after can give a good indication as to the nature of, and prospects for, the new democracy.

This book provides a systematic comparison of the democratic transition in both southern and eastern Europe. The role of the parties is a crucial determinant as to whether a new democracy will put down deep and long-lasting roots. The book is directed towards four main themes – 'coping with the past' (party identities and inheritances); the formation and performance of new democratic political elites; parties and alliances/coalitions; and their electoral behaviour. These themes are discussed comparatively with the aid of four case studies from both southern and eastern Europe. The countries covered include Italy, Spain, Greece, Portugal, Hungary, Romania, Poland and Bulgaria.

Democratisation is a very complex process because it operates on so many levels, but by studying political parties you can focus on an area that covers many of them. Students of European politics will find this an invaluable guide to recent events in eastern Europe as well as a means to understanding the process of democratisation more generally.

Geoffrey Pridham is Professor of European Politics and Director of the Centre for Mediterranean Studies, University of Bristol. **Paul Lewis** is Senior Lecturer in Government at the Open University.

Stabilising fragile democracies

Comparing new party systems in southern and eastern Europe

Edited by
Geoffrey Pridham and
Paul G. Lewis

In association with the Centre
for Mediterranean Studies,
University of Bristol, and the
East–West Programme of the
Economic Social Research Council

London and New York

First published 1996
by Routledge
11 New Fetter Lane, London EC4P 4EE

Simultaneously published in the USA and Canada
by Routledge
29 West 35th Street, New York, NY 10001

© 1996 Geoffrey Pridham and Paul Lewis

Typeset in Times by Florencetype Ltd, Stoodleigh, Devon
Printed and bound in Great Britain by
Clays Ltd, St Ives plc

British Library Cataloguing in Publication Data
A catalogue record for this book is available from the
British Library

Library of Congress Cataloguing in Publication Data
A catalogue record for this book has been requested

ISBN   0–415–11802–6
ISBN   0–415–11803–4 (pbk)

Contents

Illustrations

Contributors

Attila Ágh is the Head of the Political Science Department at the Budapest University of Economics and Director of the Hungarian Centre for Democracy Studies. He edits the *Yearbook of Hungarian Politics* (since 1988) and the *Budapest Papers on Democratic Transition* (since 1991). He has been visiting professor in Dar es Salaam, Delhi, and Vienna Universities. His major interest is comparative politics in the Central and East European democratic transitions, with special reference to parliamentary and party affairs, and linkage politics. He has recently edited *The Emergence of East Central European Parliaments: The First Steps.*

András Bozóki is Associate Professor at the Department of Sociology at the Eotros University Budapest and Lecturer in the Department of Political Science at the Central European University, Budapest. His main research interests are the transition to democracy in comparative perspective, political ideologies and the role of intellectuals in the transition. His main publications (in English) are (co-editor), *Liberty and Socialism* (Sarage, MD: Rowman and Littlefield, 1991); (co-author and co-editor), *Post-Communist Transition: Emerging pluralism in Hungary* (London-New York: Printer Publishers, St. Martin's Press 1992); (editor) *Democratic Legitimacy in Post-Communist Societies* (Budapest-Tubingen: T-TWINS Publishers, 1994). He has also written and edited books in Hungarian.

Maurizio Cotta is currently Professor of Political Science in the University of Siena. He was previously Visiting Professor at the University of Texas (1989–90) and at the European University Institute of Fiesole (1992–3). He has co-edited (with Liebert), *Parliament and Democratic Consolidation* (1990) and has contributed to: J. Higley and R. Gunther (eds), *Elites and Democratic Consolidation in Latin America and Southern Europe* (Cambridge: CUP, 1992); T. Vanhanen and G. Pridham (eds), *Transitions to Democracy in Eastern Europe* (London: Routledge, 1994); and G. Copeland and S. Patterson (eds), *The Institutionalisation of New Parliaments* (Ann Arbor: University of Michigan Press, 1994). He is presently working on a research project on relations between governments and parties and another on long-term transitions of European party systems.

Tom Gallagher is Reader in Peace Studies at Bradford University. He has published widely on the territorial dimensions of regime change in eastern and southern Europe. As well as a recent work in journal form on the Italian Northern League, a book entitled *Romania: Nationalism Confronts Democracy* (Edinburgh University Press) will appear in 1995.

Paul Heywood is Senior Lecturer in Politics at the University of Glasgow. He has published widely on modern Spain, and is the author of *Marxism and the Failure of Organised Socialism in Spain, 1879–1936* (1990) and *Spain's Next Five Years: A Political Risk Analysis* (1991). He has recently co-edited *West European Communist Parties After the Revolutions of 1989* (1994) and is currently completing a study of the Spanish political system, to be published by Macmillan.

Georgi Karasimeonov is in the Department of Political Science at Sofia University. He was Visiting Professor at Ohio State University (1987–8). His main publications are *The Social Democratic Parties: Political Role and Social Influence* (Sofia University Press, 1986); *Parties and Politics in the United States* (Sofia: Christo Botev Press, 1990); *Political Parties, General Theory* (Sofia University Press, 1993); 'Differentiation Postponed: Party pluralism in Bulgaria', in G. Wightman (ed.), *Party Formation in East Central Europe* (Elgar, 1994). His current interests are political parties in post-communist societies, regime change in east-central Europe, and political institutions.

Paul Lewis is Senior Lecturer in Government at the Open University, where he is concerned with comparative politics, European studies and international relations. Current research interests include processes of political change in post-communist societies and party development in east-central Europe (a project to which this volume is designed to make a major comparative contribution). Recent publications include *Political Authority and Party Secretaries in Poland* (Cambridge University Press, 1989), (ed.) *Democracy and Civil Society in Eastern Europe* (Macmillan, 1992), and *Central Europe Since 1945* (Longman, 1994).

Bill Lomax is Lecturer in Sociology, School of Social Studies, University of Nottingham. He has published widely on the Hungarian revolution of 1956, including *Hungary 1956* (1976) on opposition and dissent under the Kadar regime, and on the transition to democratic politics since 1989. He is a member of the ESRC research project on Regime Change in Eastern Europe, and is currently preparing a study of political change in Hungary since 1985.

Oreste Massari is Researcher at the University of Rome and teaches political science at the University of Urbino. He is author of numerous articles on Italian and European politics. Recent main publications include *Rappresentare e Govenare, I sistemi elettorali delle maggiori democrazie* *occidentali* (co-editor with Gianfranco Pasquino, 1994), and *Modello Westminster e Labour Party* (1994)

Geoffrey Pridham is Professor of European Politics and Director of the Centre for Mediterranean Studies at the University of Bristol. He has published books on Germany, Italy, the European Community, Southern Europe and Eastern Europe. They include: *The New Mediterranean Democracies: regime transition in Spain, Greece, and Portugal* (ed.) (Frank Cass, 1984); *Political Parties and Coalitional Behaviour in Italy* (Routledge, 1988); *Securing Democracy: political parties and democratic consolidation in Southern Europe* (editor, Routledge, 1990); (ed.) *Encouraging Democracy: the international context of regime transition in Southern Europe* (Leicester University Press, 1991); (co-editor), *Democratisation in Eastern Europe: domestic and international perspectives* (Routledge, 1994). He is editing *Transitions to Democracy*, a reader of comparative articles on regime change in Southern Europe, Eastern Europe and Latin America.

Michalis Spourdalakis teaches political sociology in the Department of Political Science and Public Administration at the University of Athens. He is the author of *The Rise of the Greek Socialist Party* (Routledge, 1988) and *On the Theory and the Study of Political Parties* (in Greek and English), (Lynne Rienner, forthcoming). His current research and teaching interests include trade unions, state theory, socialist parties and politics as well as the regional articulation of collective consumption structures.

Gábor Tóka is Lecturer in the Department of Political Science, Central European University, Budapest. His research interests are party systems and electoral behaviour. His most important publications in English are 'The Impact of the Religion Issue on Electoral Preferences in Hungary, 1990–91', in Klaus G. Troitzsch (ed.), *Wahlen in Zeiten des Umbruchs* (Frankfurt: Peter Lang Verlag, 1993); 'Changing Dimensions of Party Competition: Hungary 1990–1991', in Gerd Meyer (ed.), *The Political Cultures of Eastern Central Europe in Transition* (Tubingen and Basel: Francke Verlag, 1993); and 'Being Represented – Being Satisfied? Political Support in East Central Europe' in Hans-Dieter Klingemann and Dieter Fuchs (eds), *Citizens and the State* (forthcoming); vol. 1 of Max Kaase and Kenneth Newton (eds), *Beliefs in Government* (Oxford: OUP, forthcoming).

Michael Waller taught in the Government Department of Manchester University before being appointed Professor of Politics and Director of European Studies at Keele University. His chief publications include *The Language of Communism* (1972), *West European Communist Parties: Decline or Adaptation?* (ed. with Meindert Fennema, 1988), *The End of the Communist Power Monopoly* (1993), *Social Democracy in a Post-*

communist Europe (ed. with Bruno Coppieters and Kris Deschouwer, 1993) and *Parties, Trade Unions and Society in East Central Europe* (ed. with Martin Myant, 1994). He is co-editor of *The Journal of Communist Studies and Transition Politics* and of *Environmental Politics*.

Włodzimierz Wesołowski is the Head of the Section on Structures of Power and Professor of Sociology, the Polish Academy of Sciences, Warsaw. He has published *Classes, Strata and Power* (Routledge 1978), *Social Mobility and Social Structure* (with B. Mach, Routledge 1986) and co-edited *Poczatki parlamentarmej elity. Posłowie 'kontraktowego Sejmu'* (Beginnings of the Parliamentary Elite. Deputies of the 'Contract Parliament', with J. Wasilewski, IFiS Publishers, Warsaw 1992, in Polish).

Preface

This book is one of the outcomes of the project, 'Regime Change in East-Central Europe: Political Parties and the Transition to Democratic Politics', funded for four years under the East–West Programme of the Economic and Social Research Council (ESRC). Members of the research project team, coordinated by Michael Waller (Keele University), also include Paul Lewis (The Open University), Bill Lomax (Nottingham University), Geoffrey Pridham (Bristol University) and Gordon Wightman (Liverpool University).

This work is concerned with Poland, the Czech Republic, Slovakia, Hungary and Bulgaria, but it has been very much conceived within the spirit of the comparative study of political parties and party systems. It is also being conducted within the broad framework of regime transition to democracy. In this respect, it was decided to give special attention to comparisons between the ongoing transitions in east-central Europe and the earlier democratisations in Southern Europe. For this reason, the Centre for Mediterranean Studies (CMS) at Bristol University was involved given its record for research projects and publications on the transition to and consolidation of new democracies in Southern Europe.

The CMS organised an international conference at Bristol in September 1993 on 'The Emergence of New Party Systems and Transitions to Democracy: inter-regional comparisons between Eastern and Southern Europe'. It brought together some thirty colleagues from twelve countries, especially those who had collaborated with the project in their own countries. The papers from this conference were subsequently thoroughly revised or rewritten and form the contents of this book.

As explained in our Introduction, there is a strong emphasis here on comparative approaches to new party systems; and we have opted for certain thematic concerns. We therefore include four comparative chapters dealing with these themes; while the national case-studies from Southern and Eastern Europe are written, as it were, in comparative perspective.

We wish to thank Anne Jewell for help with organising the 1993 conference and for helping with the final preparation of the book.

Geoffrey Pridham, Bristol

Paul Lewis, Milton Keynes
October 1994

Introduction
Stabilising fragile democracies and party system development

Geoffrey Pridham and Paul Lewis

FRAGILE DEMOCRACIES AND THE PROBLEMS OF REGIME CHANGE

New democracies are by definition 'fragile democracies' in the sense that at first they are not formally constituted, elite loyalties are almost certainly not yet confirmed and may well be questioned, while the various political, societal and possibly economic instabilities inherent in the transition process may seem daunting. The political cultures of the countries in question do not necessarily provide a reasonable basis for system support. Initial transition may be an occasion for euphoria, but the overall process is usually the source of considerable disorientation at elite and mass levels.

Freshly launched democracies usually have the likely advantage that the previous authoritarian (or even totalitarian) regime is discredited. But even without any immediate or direct threat from anti-democratic forces which may have some link with that predecessor regime, the kind of problems that often face new democracies may make them vulnerable to collapse or at least involve a lengthy and complicated process of transition with uncertain prospects for their consolidation. New democracies, untried and lacking experience, and possibly also democratic traditions, may become burdened with overwhelming overload of both a governmental and systemic kind. At this stage, indeed, there is a close identification of systemic with governmental fortunes and performance; whereas, in established democracies, a distinction here is usually evident as a result of acquired legitimacy.

The history of different continents is marked by many failures as well as notable successes in democratisation. Some democracies have managed the transition but failed to consolidate. Direct threats to new democracies, notably from the military or authoritarian movements, have then been made. In interwar Europe there were some renowned failures, but the tendency has been for democracies to establish themselves, especially from the defeat of Fascism onwards. But that does not of course in any way guarantee that further cases of democratisation are on the road to success, even accepting the present European international environment as one conducive to democratic institutions and democratic values. This very fragility of new democracies thus cautions against the kind of triumphalist views about democracy that surfaced in some circles after the regime changes in eastern Europe. What happened in 1989 was only the beginning of a long and complicated process. Within little more than a year, it was noted that 'the East Europeans are discovering that there is a large, dangerous chasm between grabbing freedom and establishing democracy; there is no natural progression'.[1]

It is worth clarifying that 'democratisation' as a term describes the overall process of regime change from start to completion, i.e. from the end of the previous authoritarian regime to the stabilisation and rooting of new democracies. It therefore embraces both broad processes of what are conventionally referred to in the comparative literature as 'transition' to a liberal or constitutional democracy and its subsequent 'consolidation'. The outcome is a system that should meet certain basic procedural requirements, such as a commitment to regular elections and institutional mechanisms that provide checks on executive power, as well as the guarantee of human rights and emergence of a political culture that is clearly supportive of democratic political life. The principal objective of consolidation is for the risks and uncertainties typical of transition to be gradually reduced to a point where failure in democratisation becomes highly improbable. Presumably, at some moment when consolidation is well advanced, new democracies cease to be called 'new' and are regarded as established. On average, this is likely to take between a dozen and twenty years.

The nature of demands made by regime change alter during the course of democratisation. By 'democratic transition', we refer to a stage that is obviously decisive. It commences when a previous totalitarian or authoritarian system begins to collapse or disintegrate leading to a situation when, with a new constitution in place, the democratic structures begin to become routinised and the political elites adjust their behaviour to liberal democratic practices. Transition tasks involve, above all, negotiating the constitutional settlement and the rules of procedure for political competition, but also dismantling authoritarian agencies and abolishing laws unsuitable for democratic politics. By comparison, 'democratic consolidation' is usually a lengthier stage, but also one with wider and possibly deeper effects. In general, it involves the full rooting of the new democracy, the internalisation of its rules and procedures and the dissemination of democratic values.

Comparative literature on transitions to democracy has often identified successive phases of this process. Thus Rustow saw three principal ones identified as preparatory, decision and habituation. These involved respectively a struggle by rival groups which sort out their conflicts through accommodation; a decision to accept diversity and to institutionalise democratic procedures; and a phase when political elites and the public begin to operationalise democratic methods and become used (or reconciled) to them.[2] With democratic consolidation, it is possible to speak of two broad dimensions and different levels of that process. A distinction may be made between 'negative consolidation' and 'positive consolidation'. The former refers to the solution of any remaining problems from the transition process and, in particular, to the effective removal of the prospects for system alternatives to liberal democracy; and, the latter to longer-term changes linked to Rustow's 'habituation'.

Further variation on the theme of democratisation usually relates to levels, paths and the scope of the process, and not least outcomes. As to levels, Morlino has elaborated as follows: democratic structures and procedures which adapt and develop decisional practices; relationships between the structures, in particular over conflict management; the development of parties and the party system (organisational strengthening, identity formation, and establishing the conventions of political competition); interest structures (with similar features); relationships between intermediation structures and civil society; and, relationships between intermediation structures and the regime.[3] In considering such levels, transition is usually a more restricted process involving above all elites, especially political ones. On the other hand, consolidation is a much more expansive process with a range of different actors.

Of course, such a broad distinction may be somewhat modified by the path or style of transition as well as its scope. The first has often featured different transitions as broadly revolutionary or evolutionary with clearly varying implications for the course if not the speed of the process. Some studies of democratisation have been more specific about the path of regime change. Thus, Stepan identified eight different versions such as internal restoration after external reconquest, internal reformulation (role of resistance), externally monitored installation (foreign occupation), redemocratisation initiated from within the authoritarian regime (whether by civilian or military groups), society-led regime termination, party pact, organised violent revolt or revolutionary war.[4] Obviously, the style of transition has implications for its scope which is often, broadly, related to whether it is more 'top-down' or 'bottom-up'. Such distinctions provide a useful comparative context for particular cases of democratisation.

Furthermore, it is important not to forget that the kinds of liberal democracies that emerge from that process may also vary in structural, institutional and cultural senses. Lijphart and others, for instance, have argued that the democratic regimes of Italy, Spain, Portugal and Greece are neither sufficiently similar to each other nor sufficiently different from other democratic regimes to fit a distinctive model of democracy.[5] That is, albeit parliamentary, these four systems demonstrated variations of a structural, institutional and political kind. They were examined according to two dimensions – executives-parties and federal-unitary – of the contrast between majoritarian and consensus types of democracy.[6]

Range of inst. options in limited in liberal Democracies.

Q How established is Democracy here.

Of course, institutional differences are most of all highlighted by (semi-) presidential and parliamentary forms of government. From another angle, differences between liberal democracies may well be greater but also more subtle when it comes to national history and political culture, given that the range of institutional options is limited. Rather in parallel, a basic division has sometimes been made between what is called 'procedural democracy' (satisfying certain formal requirements such as free elections) and a more ample or qualitative version sometimes called 'substantive democracy'.

Theoretical approaches to regime change have generally tended to group around two schools of thinking, known as the functionalist and the genetic or as, respectively, macro- and micro-oriented. The former, concerned with long-term developments of a socio-economic kind, has given paramount attention to structural or environmental determinants of political system change. It has inclined to the view that regime changes are predetermined by conditions like economic development or cultural patterns or simply modernisation. On the other hand, the genetic school has given priority to conjunctural factors and strategic choice – and more clearly political determinants. It has preferred to emphasise the importance of political choice and strategy by actors during the actual transition process.[7]

The essential difference between these two general approaches is one of basic outlook. While functionalist views have been criticised for being too deterministic, genetic interpretations have dwelt on the uncertainties of transition and the scope for fateful and perhaps mistaken decisions. There is, nevertheless, more compatibility between these two approaches, when applied to empirical research, than is commonly recognised. For functionalists focus in effect on a different time scale than geneticists, namely on longer-term processes prior to the occurrence of transition and often also those which follow its achievement. It can, therefore, be argued that the two schools are most compatible when looking at the subsequent process of democratic consolidation, which is broadly concerned with inter-actions between politics, society and the economy.

NB

why I am including both

& Am agreed pol.

In the light of recent experience in eastern Europe, theories of regime transition have been criticised for certain shortcomings, in particular their assumption about the predominant importance of (political) elites, their neglect of international factors and also, especially, their neglect of histor-ical explanations.[8] Whatever their merits and limitations, theoretical approaches have nevertheless been enriching in drawing attention to multi-causal explanations of regime change. And it is here that the importance of focusing on party systems and political parties becomes evident. Indeed, they are pertinent to both the genetic and functionalist theories: on the first count they invariably provide the most powerful political actors and are usually seen as strategic vehicles; and, on the second, parties obvi-ously present an important linkage with and channel for the impact of socio-economic determinants on political change.

procedural & substantive Democracy.

① Why my chapter on parties & elections is so important.

DEMOCRATISATION AND PARTY SYSTEM DEVELOPMENT: SOUTHERN EUROPEAN EXPERIENCES

The previous discussion points to many ways in which political parties may play a significant if not central or crucial role in the process of regime change at different levels. They are certainly at the forefront of transition tasks like the management of free elections, drawing up constitutions and government policy-making, not to mention establishing elite loyalties to the new democracy, promoting democratic values through practice or rhetoric and thus contributing to system legitimation. Altogether, they are the political actors which most obviously mediate between the state and its institutions on the one hand and society and the wider environment on the other. Bingham Powell has summarised the conventional view of political parties in comparative literature:

> Scholars and commentators assert that a strong system of political parties is essential for a strong democracy. The party system shapes citizen participation through the electoral process. The stability of political leadership depends on party activities in the electoral and legislative arenas. The dynamics of the party system may either inhibit or exacerbate turmoil and violence. The strategies and commitments of party leaders can be critical for the support of the democratic regime in time of crisis.[9]

What is true of established democracies is also potentially true of new democracies. Or, at least, the ability of parties to perform such varied tasks during democratisation clearly has important implications for the success or not of this process. It is therefore misleading to view political parties as simply one layer of regime change. It goes without saying that there must be a fundamental relationship between the performance and fortunes of new democratic regimes and the performance and fortunes of new party systems. According to Huntington,

> The vacuum of power and authority which exists in so many modernising countries may be filled temporarily by charismatic leadership or by military force. But it can be filled permanently only by political organisation. Either the established elites compete among themselves to organise the masses through the existing system, or dissident elites organise them to overthrow that system. In the modernising world, he who controls the future is who organises its politics.[10]

But political parties are not merely channels for control of power by democratic elites (possibly in the face of challenges from non-democratic groups or elites). They provide, furthermore, a guarantee that power will not necessarily be monopolised as there are competing groups among the democratic elites, and their effectiveness gives weight to constitutional mechanisms of control on executive power. At another level, parties are

Parties

a crucial guarantee of the durability of political pluralism and may there-fore act as a stimulant to the development of a vibrant civil society.

The primacy of political parties and party systems in regime change has been qualified or challenged in some quarters. Thus Mair has argued that newly emerging party systems are likely to differ from established party systems in a number of important ways.[11] Hypothetically, their electorates are essentially unstable, lacking as they do the habits of political support and identification drawn from previous experience, and in this sense they are particularly 'open', though this depends on how far cleavage struc-tures provide a basis for party appeals. Parties are often weakly grounded in civil society at this stage and political competition is unusually intense due to the very uncertainty of political loyalties at the outset of transi-tion and since the political prizes are great. Moreover, the weakness of party identities and of organisational loyalties means that political elites may behave differently, all the more since the rules of the political game are in flux.[12] As Mair concludes, new party systems may settle down in which case it is largely a matter of time and experience. At the same time, it should not be forgotten that inheritances from the authoritarian period or earlier are important, such as whether civil society has been able to develop and in particular whether given countries have some form of democratic traditions embedded in folk memory. Much also depends on the dynamics of transition itself and how they begin to condition the prospects for democratic consolidation.

A different criticism of the centrality of parties has come from those who argue they play an increasingly less dominant role in western democ-racies.[13] In a recent essay on democratic consolidation, Schmitter has questioned this centrality:

> Either it ignores the very substantial changes that have taken place in the nature and role of parties in well-established Western democracies or it anachronistically presumes that parties in today's neodemocracies will have to go through all the stages and perform all the functions of their predecessors. Today's citizens – even in polities that have long suffered under authoritarian rule – have quite different organisational skills, are less likely to identify so closely with partisan symbols or ideologies, and defend a much more variegated set of interests. Moreover, the new regimes are emerging in an international environ-ment virtually saturated with different models of successful collective action. All this may not preclude a hegemonic role for parties in the representation of social groups, but it does suggest that they will be facing more competition from interest associations and social move-ments than their predecessors and that we should revise our thinking about democratisation accordingly.[14]

Schmitter's criticism raises some pertinent questions about the role of parties and, indeed, about the very conception of the modern political party. Is their diminished importance a matter of historical change (as he says), or is it in fact more situational depending on the transition case being examined? On the first count, we are clearly into a discussion about 'waves' or cycles of democratisation. For instance, the role of the media is much more in evidence in the southern European transitions of the 1970s onwards and particularly in the eastern European ones of late than it ever was in the postwar democratisations that occurred in western Europe after the Second World War. And, there is an obvious link here with the prominence of political personalities in the 'wave' of transitions of the past two decades. How much the media provide an alternative to party organisation and membership is a problem that deserves special attention in the study of democratisation.

But there is also evidence that the pre-eminence of parties owes much to the way democratisation develops and in particular whether other actors are discredited or not by the previous authoritarian experience. Thus, political parties came to dominate the postwar Italian transition partly because they were in wartime able to mobilise through the Resistance movement before Fascism collapsed and also, as Pasquino says, since other actors were disqualified:

> The demise of Fascism in Italy left the monarchy totally discredited, the armed forces divided, the business community with tarnished prestige and much fear, the bureaucracy weak and corrupted, and representative and governmental institutions outdated, belonging to a past which could not be revived.[15]

As Oreste Massari shows in his contribution to this book, this collective dominance by parties became the salient feature of the Italian republic and provided it with impressive stability but also, at the same time, the seeds of its own eventual degeneration. Somewhat by contrast, the success of the Spanish transition owed much to the consensual behaviour of the main parties during the constituent phase, but also to other actors like the King or Suarez who had no or a weak party affiliation. As Bar explains, this limited role of the parties was 'partly due to the historic conditions under which the transition to democracy took place in Spain, a transition in which a whole set of different forces converged as active elements'.[16] Decisive among these conditions was the fact that the Franco regime was not overthrown but rather gradually dismantled, so that the military (a key support factor for Franco) was not discredited and operated as a veto group during the transition stage.

The centrality of parties may well be variable in a sequential way, if we agree with Pasquino's dictum that 'not all the processes of transition have been party dominated; but all processes of democratic consolidation have indeed been party dominated'.[17] As Paul Heywood concludes in this volume, political parties came to play the central role in the practice of democratic politics in Spain after the transition. Pasquino was generalising about southern Europe as a whole where special features of some transitions accounted for this difference between transition and consolidation. In Portugal, for instance, the role of the radical military in the 1974 revolution and beyond, including formulating the constitution, allowed influential scope for military personnel in government until constitutional reform in 1982 effectively secured parliamentary government along familiar West European lines. In Greece, Karamanlis in particular but also parties in general played a more dominant part in the transition; however, the reduction of presidential powers in 1986 strengthened parliamentary government and prime-ministerial power.

This bias towards the parliamentary rather than presidential model of government in southern Europe clearly had implications for the scope of parties, since the latter institutionalises a certain degree of personal-political power somewhat independently from the parties. One may generally add that the varied and wider systemic tasks of democratic consolidation are much more attuned to the role of parties than of other types of actor. And in southern Europe this was made much more possible because of the relatively long traditions of party or ideological tendencies. The success of so many 'historical parties' with democratisation in the region attests to this factor. This was especially true of postwar Italy in the case of nearly all parties, but it also applied to parties on the Left in the Iberian states and in Greece. In eastern Europe, on the other hand, 'historical parties' have not been very successful, as just one sign that party system development there has been more difficult to instigate following long non-democratic rule. More striking, on the other hand, has been the resurgence of new social democratic parties with roots in the former communist system.

Democratisation is a complex process, and clearly generalisations are sometimes difficult in the face of significant cross-national variation, both between concurrent examples in one region but also especially across time between regime changes in different regions. What can be said, however, is that political parties while not always the dominant or central actors in (early) democratisation nevertheless play a crucial part in keeping the process on track and in contributing towards its success. Analysing the role of parties and the emerging shape and quality of a party system thus provides important and potentially long-term evidence about how new democracies are functioning and beginning to root themselves.

With this in mind, this study has selected four principal and significant focal points for assessing the fortunes of emerging party systems. We explain briefly the reasons for this choice in the light of the foregoing discussion.

'Coping with the past' in terms of party identities and inheritances is an important dimension of the historical approach to democratisation – which, as noted earlier, has been neglected in the comparative literature.

Generally, it highlights continuities – underlying or visible ones – that remain despite political system change. This thought was present in Linz's distinction between cultural and organisational continuity in party development, a distinction that has a particular applicability to regime change, for while ideological traditions may persist under authoritarian rule adverse circumstances tend to impinge more on the state of rival political organisations.[18] The length of dictatorial rule is a factor of quite some influence concerning the prospects of easy or difficult party system emergence, with long-lasting highly oppressive regimes most likely to uproot competitive party organisational life. In southern Europe, there was a vast difference betwen the Estado Novo which lasted almost half a century in Portugal and the seven years of the military junta in Greece. In Portugal, the depoliticising effects of the dictatorship clearly created difficulties for party mobilisation after 1974;[19] whereas the parties emerged much more readily in Greece that same year.

Reactions to the authoritarian/totalitarian experience also have a formative influence on party development. Thus, parties of either the Left or the Right have identity problems relating to the ideological leanings of the previous regime. These may be relatively short-lived, as parties of the centre-Right found after the left-wing Portuguese revolution of 1974. Or, sometimes, a tradition can be established such as that of anti-Fascism in republican Italy, although this was complicated by the almost simultaneous impact of the Cold War and its persistent effects on the postwar politics of that country. A strong party tradition is clearly a resource of some weight at the start of democratisation, although its advantages are not always unambiguous if historical controversy has any impact. Conversely, new parties have to construct their identities afresh but they are, at the same time, largely free from problems of the past.

Much of course depends on the course and dynamics of transition itself, and it is here that the role of the new democratic political elites can be so decisive. We are concerned with how and whence such elites emerge, whether from within the previous regime or in opposition to it. As Pasquino has shown for the southern European cases, the origins of such elites varied cross-nationally particularly when referring to pre-authoritarian democratic elites for their survival is a matter of both time and circumstance (such as success of authoritarian rulers in erasing them).[20] There is also the problem of whether political elites are able to adapt from their previous patterns of political activity (within authoritarian regime or clandestine) to the different and more varied challenges of democratic political life. Much comparative literature on regime change has stressed the importance of elite settlements or political pacts in the transition process as likely to facilitate democratic consolidation.[21] In general terms, their role in democratisation is neatly summarised by Gunther, Sani and Shabad in reference to the case of post-Franco Spain:

Electoral and party financing laws were the product of conscious deliberations and negotiations among party leaders. Elites were the driving force behind the creation or expansion of party organisational infrastructures. Their electoral strategies determined the ideological stance and overall image they would present to the voters. ... as founders of a new political regime they also greatly affected the nature of the transition, and in doing so they influenced the nature of public opinion itself. Finally, in the absence of long-standing partisan attachments, and in the age of television, party leaders themselves served as significant objects of popular identification and electoral support.[22]

Third, the evolving state of inter-party relationships owe much to the conduct of (rival) political elites and also is a crucial test of political pluralism being managed. A concrete expression of such relationships is the nature of party alliances and coalitions. The strains of transition politics are enormous with system-building the overarching requirement at the same time as government responsibilities make their own heavy demands. On systemic grounds, there is some argument for founding or grand coalitions to cope with these transitional pressures and bridge the first vulnerable years of the fragile new system. The practice of cross-party consensus in Spain in the later 1970s was an informal version of this.[23] Formulating a constitution is usually the most obvious occasion for such co-operation. But, at the same time, the practice of 'normal' democratic politics means recognising the legitimacy of party motivation and interest. And the need for this becomes compelling with the struggle by competing parties for political space. Our concern is over how far the resolution of such conflicting pressures and the management of both collaboration and competition between parties act as a clarifying force for the newly emerging party system.

Finally, the relationship of parties with society is the ultimate test of how democratic consolidation is beginning to develop. Initially, there may be problems here as, conceivably, most parties (other than those well-organised in clandestinity) will initially suffer from the lack of articulated links with society. Furthermore, the demands of system-building may result in party leaders neglecting this aspect of party activity. Clearly, party system development is likely in any case to be more slow-moving at this level, but eventually some stability or continuity of support should be evident, no doubt influenced to a significant degree by its relation to cleavages. Our interest here is whether parties begin to achieve some success in acting as agents of social integration or division, and how they relate to socio-economic interests in particular. Ultimately, the question has also to be answered as to whether they help to promote the legitimacy of the new democratic system.

PARTY SYSTEM DEVELOPMENT IN EASTERN EUROPE: AN OVERVIEW

Of the four focal points for analysis identified in the previous section that of 'coping with the past' has been the most prominent in eastern Europe, not least because there has been so much of the authoritarian past to cope with. Unlike many of the developments seen in southern Europe, recent processes of democratisation in eastern Europe have followed a lengthy period of authoritarian or even totalitarian rule that lasted at least forty years – which followed on almost directly from the years of Nazi dictatorship and, in some cases before that, extensive experience of more traditional forms of authoritarian rule. Only in prewar Czechoslovakia could a relatively robust variant of parliamentary government be seen; elsewhere early hopes of democracy and constitutional order harboured at the close of the First World War received little satisfaction and democratic practices put down weak roots. This stands in considerable contrast to the brief seven-year *caesura* in Greek parliamentary practice – and even to the longer experience of Francoist Spain, where opposition parties maintained a significant existence in emigré form and elements of political pluralism were able to regain some strength. Only in pre-1974 Portugal did the long-lasting dictatorship have serious eradicating effects on political pluralism. East European dictatorship, on the other hand, was both lengthy and far-reaching; it is also important to recognise that the subsequent onset of political democratisation in the region accompanied equally radical processes of economic transformation and energetic attempts to establish the foundations of market capitalism. These factors have exerted a considerable influence on the process of party development in eastern Europe and on the solidity of the social foundations for democratic structures that exist in the region.

Potentially democratic parties in any meaningful form were, then, largely absent from eastern Europe as the structures of communist rule rapidly began to crumble and then came crashing down throughout the region in the second half of 1989. Even less, then, was it possible to talk of anything resembling an emerging pluralist party system. Non-communist parties were, of course, not wholly absent. The Confederation of Independent Poland, for example, had been founded by dissident activist Leszek Moczulski in 1979 and survived to gain significant parliamentary representation in the elections both of 1991 and 1993. A small group had also constituted the Democratic Opposition in Hungary since the 1970s and, in 1988, this took on a more organised form as the Alliance of Free Democrats. A Hungarian Democratic Forum had also been founded during the previous year. In Czechoslovakia, on the other hand, the totalitarian process of 'normalisation' had been highly efficient in forestalling the emergence of organised political opposition and Charter 77, for example (which included a number of prominent post-communist politicians), remained very much a select group of intellectuals separate from a repressed and politically quiescent society. Conditions for the development of opposition parties had been equally unfavourable in Bulgaria and Romania.

At the end of the communist period, then, democratic political parties in eastern Europe existed either in a rather embryonic form or were totally absent. When communist rule ended, the interests of diverse groups and of society as a whole were represented rather by broadly based, loosely organised and ideologically diffuse social movements. This was most obviously the case in Poland, where the traditions of the Solidarity movement (originally laid down in 1980 and 1981) were taken up and amplified with decisive effect. In the absence of any organised political alternative to communist rule Civic Forum and the Public Against Violence, too, suddenly came to prominence in Czechoslovakia and dominated the political space without any significant competition during the early post-communist period. The situation was somewhat different in Hungary, where differences between the Free Democrats and the Democratic Forum represented some form of pluralism and articulated institutionally a form of organised political differentiation. Nevertheless the Forum was also a vehicle of popular (and, to some extent, populist) expression not so different from the Polish and Czechoslovak models. An analogous United Democratic Front emerged in Bulgaria by knitting together the diverse strands of political opposition, but it was considerably weaker than the movements which occupied centre stage in the northern countries. Ceausescu's harsher role in Romania had been even less propitious for the development either of political parties or the social movements that tended to substitute for them in the other east European countries. Much of the subsequent history of party development in post-communist eastern Europe and the gradual emergence of new party systems have been concerned with the disintegration of these movements and attempts to recast their constituent elements in a new organisational form. The question of precisely what a political party is and what it actually does (or should) do has, therefore, been posed quite sharply in eastern Europe.[24]

The crucial test of party strength and a prime determinent of the form taken by new party systems have been the series of elections held throughout eastern Europe.[25] In general terms the elections held after the period of unqualified communist dominance often first endorsed the primacy and central political role of national social movements and only later provided conditions for the emergence and development of properly constituted political parties. Despite the relatively short time that has elapsed since the end of communism in 1989, the form of democratically organised parliamentary elections in eastern Europe (to the extent that we include here the watershed Polish election of June 1989) and their political outcomes have been quite diverse. The first major election in this sense to be held in eastern Europe was the carefully prepared ballot organised in communist-controlled Poland in June 1989 which nevertheless, after lengthy negotiations, reserved a significant place for non-communist forces to compete with representatives of the political establishment. Solidarity-sponsored candidates won all of the seats in the main legislative chamber open to competition (35 per cent of the total) and 99 of the 100 seats in the new Senate. This should, nevertheless, have been sufficient to guarantee the continuity of communist rule but it proved not to be the case as representatives of the formerly submissive satellite parties saw a chance to flex their political muscles and moved to ally themselves with Solidarity forces. In September 1989, then, Tadeusz Mazowiecki emerged as the first non-communist prime minister eastern Europe had seen since the 1940s. The balance of parliamentary forces was clearly important in securing this outcome, but equally significant were the growing signs of fundamental change in the nature of east European-Soviet relations. Developments in Hungary were also rapid and the Hungarian Socialist Workers' Party was the first communist ruling establishment in eastern Europe to go into voluntary liquidation. Hungary was, too, one of the first to hold fully competitive elections and after a final ballot in April 1990 Democratic Forum was able to form a centre-right government with the support of the Independent Smallholders' Party and the even smaller Christian Democrats.

Political change in Poland, meanwhile, continued to be overseen until the free elections of October 1991 by the communist-designed 'contract parliament', although the former ruling party itself ceased to exist in January 1990 and parliamentary forces grouped and regrouped themselves in a confusing array of different clubs and proto-parties. Competitive elections were also held in Czechoslovakia in June 1990 and, in a reflection of the tendency already seen in Poland, Civic Forum and Public Against Violence were swept to power and gained a clear majority in both houses of the Federal Assembly. The pattern of developments in Romania was rather different and considerable ambiguity still exists about the nature of the forces that took the crucial decisions. Just before the capture and execution of the Ceausescus a National Salvation Front was formed by the army and an opposition composed of groups mostly drawn from different generations of the old communist elite. After a few weeks had elapsed the NSF stated that it would not dissolve itself (as originally announced) but would contest the anticipated elections as a political party. When held in May 1990 the NSF won a decisive victory in both houses of the New Assembly. The ability of former communists to perpetuate their ruling position under new political conditions was even more clearly demonstrated in Bulgaria where, having ditched Zhivkov and his immediate entourage, they reconstituted themselves as the Bulgarian Socialist Party and proceeded to win a majority in elections held during June 1990.

If these were the founding elections of the new east European democracies, the nature of their outcomes were in some ways rather different and their implications for the emergence of new party systems quite ambiguous. While Solidarity had gained a clear moral and political victory, for over two years the Polish parliament operated within the structure of a compromise struck between communist and opposition forces whose basis soon lost its original validity. A variety of political groups then emerged in parliament whose relationship with broader social forces was tenuous to say the least. It was only in 1991 that these parliamentary groups were put to a decisive electoral test and the contours of a new, and by no means fully formed, party system began to emerge. In a fashion similar to the progressive dissolution of the Solidarity movement, the broad-based, organisationally diffuse movements of Civic Forum and Public Against Violence in Czechoslovakia soon began to lose their unified character and split into a range of smaller, more diverse parties. Without either the unifying structures of communist rule or the shared idealistic optimism of the immediate post-communist period, the considerable cultural and economic differences between Slovakia and the Czech lands soon fed into the rapidly changing pattern of the federal republic's political life. The second general election held, as planned, in 1992 two years after the first gave expression to these differences in terms of party representation and political style, leading directly and rapidly to the abolition of the federation at the end of the year.

Although, too, the main features of the Hungarian government formed after the elections of 1990 survived intact throughout the full four-year life of the parliament, the clear divisions and straightforward organisation of the original post-communist party system gradually eroded, party divisions and political divisions becoming increasingly complex in ways by no means advantageous for the effective conduct of parliamentary life and government business. By October 1993, the six parties originally represented in the Hungarian parliament elected in 1990 had split and transmuted into 17 different groupings. Before second elections held in October 1991, too, the Bulgarian UDF split, although its main component went on this time to win slightly more parliamentary seats than the BSP and then to act as the major force in a new governing coalition. But this grouping also failed to survive beyond the end of 1992 and further UDF splits occurred, with some former adherents moving to support the BSP in another coalition. In Romania, on the other hand, the original National Salvation Front remained in power in one guise or another (called, from July 1993, the Party of Social Democracy of Romania) and the main opposition alliance, the Democratic Convention of Romania, languished as a loose and weakly organised grouping subject to considerable internal division.

While, then, the dominance of the social movement as the typical political form of the early post-communist period soon disappeared it was by no means the case that a reasonable diversity of identifiable political parties with some capacity for medium-term survival was developing to take their place. But the development of a range of such political organisations was clearly necessary if anything that deserved the name of a party *system* was to be identified in the aspiring democracies of post-communist eastern Europe.[26] It was hardly surprising in this context, too, that the electorates of Poland and Hungary, in 1993 and 1994 respectively, showed considerable willingness to lend their support to political organisations that had grown directly out of the political establishment of the now defunct communist system. However 'post-communist' their representatives might appear or claim to be, they could still appeal to the more attractive ideals of the former period and play on the virtues of continuity and stability in a situation of rapid social change which by no means spelt improvement in living conditions or enhanced prospects for even the majority of the population. It also remained the case that the post-communist formations retained more of a stable, mass membership than newer groupings, had a more developed national organisation and retained much of the political experience and certain skills necessary for operating effectively within any political framework.

Indeed, while the initial phase of post-1989 political life in eastern Europe could, at least in the northern tier, be characterized by the weak development of a party system but one where there was no significant communist or post-communist presence, the picture looks somewhat different five years on. After the early instabilities of post-communist rule, it is now clear that forces associated with the former political establishment have returned to act as one pillar of the new party systems (in the Balkans their presence was a significant one from the outset). It is on the right wing and in relation to liberal forces that the pattern is unclear and less stable (with the significant exception of the Czech Republic, where Vaclav Klaus's Civic Democratic Party retains a dominant influence and it is the opposition and left wing that appears disunited and largely lacking in political influence). It is a pattern that raises a number of major questions, particularly in relation to the prospects of further democratic development. The question of the democratic credentials of the post-communist parties only five years after the demise of the authoritarian order from which they derived must remain an open one, while the disarray of right and liberal forces directs attention to the nature and strength of any civil society in eastern Europe – both in relation to the late communist period, which saw the emergence in many countries of an anti-communist opposition, and to the subsequent years during which post-communist developments seem to have provided only moderately favourable conditions for effective new party development.

INTER-REGIONAL COMPARISONS: DEMOCRATISATION AND THE EMERGENCE OF NEW PARTY SYSTEMS IN SOUTHERN AND EASTERN EUROPE

It is hardly surprising, therefore, that problems associated with 'coping with the past' have emerged as some of the most intractable in post-communist eastern Europe. The sheer length of the communist period, the depth of its social penetration and the scant experience of democratic practices before the communist takeover have all contributed to the problems encountered in pressing ahead with the democratisation process and consolidating the achievements already made. The relevant past in eastern Europe is not, however, restricted to the heritage of the former communist period. While the impact of social cleavages on the formation of party systems in western Europe was closely linked with consequences of industrialisation and a particular trajectory of socio-economic development, in the east issues surrounding the consolidation of the state and establishment of the bases of political legitimacy also exerted a very strong influence. Only a little more than two years after the end of communism the existence of the Czechoslovak state was terminated, while similar tensions made their presence in considerably more violent form in other post-communist countries whose study does not form part of this volume. The establishment of a stable democratic order and the development of party systems is that more difficult in countries where the nature of the basic territorial unit remains a matter of conflict or dispute, as different visions of national destiny intertwine with the articulation of different sectional interests. But, understandably, it has been the consequences of communist rule that have weighed most heavily on political life and the gradual emergence of new party systems. The freely-won electoral victory of post-communist forces in Lithuania, Poland and Hungary (as well as in some areas of the former East Germany) cast a surprising light on the political preferences of post-communist populations and the strength of particular strands of the communist legacy. Equally, the problems encountered by right-wing forces in forming effective political groups and articulating their interests within the developing democratic systems testify to the difficulties experienced by alternative political associations in formulating new strategies and policies to cope with contemporary demands and creating new political organisations to help satisfy them. Elements of continuity, particularly in Italy, Greece and Spain, were considerably stronger and certainly helped to establish components of a new party system and consolidate democratic practices in the post-authoritarian systems.

The issue in eastern Europe has been further complicated by the problems encountered in defining new party identities, and that particular process is analysed in this volume by Michael Waller in his study of party inheritances and party identities. While critical for effective political action, the question of party identity is a complex one which requires a fine judgement to be made on whether identities are just modified and subject to normal processes of evolution or become so transformed that a new kind of party has come into being. At issue here are commitments to ideology and the formulation of policy, persistence of structure and particular forms of organisation and not least, continuity of leadership and party membership in terms of the actual people concerned. The survival and recent resurgence of left-wing forces in the region so soon after the end of communism makes such judgements particularly sensitive and critical ones. The increasingly influential post-communist parties are formally social democratic in character and in principle are fully committed to the procedures of liberal democracy. They tend, further, to be strong supporters of economic reform and consolidation of the market economy. There can, however, be little doubt that much of their electoral success has derived from a backlash against the social impact of the post-communist changes and a certain nostalgia for the stability of the former system, although the newly born social democrats devote considerable energy to emphasising their departure from the policies and practices of the former regime. Equally, the length of time that has elapsed since the pre-communist period has made any notion of continuity on the other side of the political spectrum very difficult to maintain. Right-wing parties have thus borne little resemblance to southern European counterparts, while few parallels can be drawn in the area of policy in terms of conservative orientations and the defence of established capitalist interests. Reconciliation of these conflicting tendencies and the emergence of a more coherent political identity will clearly take some time and will have to proceed considerably further before stable party systems can be fully acknowledged.

The formation and performance of new elites has, understandably, also been critically affected by inheritances from the former political system. 'New' elites have often, by no means always to the satisfaction of the post-communist public, looked surprisingly like the 'old' elites. Most obviously, the new post-communist leaders generally have easily identifiable origins in the institutions of the former communist system. This is clearly the case in Romania, but it is also relevant to other countries in eastern Europe. Even new elites deriving from associations of a more clearly anti-communist nature, like those of the former Mazowiecki government in Poland, included former communist party members (even though of some time ago) or others of a clearly identifiable socialist nature. Regardless of their origins and political outlook, however, new elites of all persuasions have tended to look rather similar to those of former communist regimes in that they have tended to remain distant from the constituencies they claim to represent and have, in most cases, found it difficult to forge close relations with social forces and discrete groups. The political class has remained remote from much of the population and has often led a relatively closed life within the new post-communist

Formation of New Political elites [handwritten]

parliaments or shown considerable interest in colonising the state administration. In this their position bears similarities not just to the leadership of the former system but also to the ruling class of the pre-communist system – and particularly to the dominance within it of an intelligentsia which played a major political role in an area where capitalism had weak roots and the influence of the domestic bourgeoisie was relatively weak. In this sense, again, the formation of new political elites in the post-communist countries has been more problematic than in southern Europe not least, once more, because of the protracted and far-reaching nature of totalitarian rule. *legacy at Com? what Pts have not ben* [handwritten]

Analysis of the contemporary continuities in eastern Europe with the communist period in this respect form a major part of the study by Attila Ágh contained in this volume. Five kinds of political actor are identified in the new, transitional elite, several of whom have roots in the old order. In this area Ágh distinguishes what he terms politicians of morals (those with roots in the former opposition), politicians of historical vision (who made their presence felt on the political scene just before the transfer of power but who also, because of their grasp of the historical nature of that turning-point, served to link post-communism with the period preceding communist rule), politicians by chance (a relatively large group of individuals who became prominent largely because of the inherent confusion of the situation), the old nomenklatura (active politicians of the communist period who moved into alternative political circles), and the beginnings of a new professional political elite (some, though not all whom, may have emerged from positions held under the former regime). Nevertheless political parties, Ágh maintains, were (as in southern Europe) central actors in the pre-transition crisis and have continued to be so during the period of democratic transition. Their relative weakness, however, has also been responsible for an overparliamentarisation of political life and its particisation – parties having succeeded in excluding other actors from the political sphere and concentrating on their own ideological and political struggles. On the basis of this analysis, Ágh draws major parallels between contemporary eastern Europe and the experiences of southern Europe, and particularly with those of Italy (to which his idea of particisation already makes strong reference) and the model of the 'Italian Road', which he sees east European countries taking with their particular blend of privatisation and pluralism. This refers to the development of a fragmented party system and a deeply embedded network of what he terms 'clientura'. It is a line of analysis whose implications are neither particularly positive for eastern Europe nor complimentary to the democratic achievements of Italy or southern Europe in general. It nevertheless opens up a useful comparative and historical perspective on the ambiguous nature of the democratic transition in eastern Europe.

An equally problematic dimension of political change in eastern Europe has been the formation of party alliances and viable government

dissolved [handwritten margin]
what remains of the [handwritten margin]
Social grups. [handwritten margin]
Lobbyests [handwritten margin]

Party systems & parties obstructing the cause of Dem and proper Redist of power during the period of consolidh

coalitions. In some cases (Poland, Slovakia and Bulgaria, for example) processes of coalition formation have produced considerable problems for government formation and the conduct of effective state business. The early stages of alliance formation in the transition, or even pre-transition phase (Hungary and Poland), were easier to organise and more effective in securing a commonly desired result – the radical transformation of the established communist system. It was only at this stage that eastern Europe saw anything like the cross-party consensus that emerged in Spain during the late 1970s. Subsequent alliances have been more difficult to arrange and generally less successful in their outcome. Broader problems of party formation and overall party development have meshed in with this process and further obstructed the progress of post-communist democratisation. Coalition formation and the maintenance of effective alliances have been imperilled by personal ambitions, individual likes and dislikes, and sharp clashes of temperament. The fragmentation of political forces and the rapid formation and dissolution of parties have only added to the confusion. Successive elections and the institution of new electoral mechanisms have made further inputs to this situation – in one case, like Czechoslovakia, leading to the swift dismemberment of the existing state and in another, like Poland, leading to the near-total exclusion of all right-wing forces from parliament and subsequent moves to forge effective political and electoral alliances across a range of disparate goups and fragmented political forces – although the emergence of a relatively stable party system lies some way in the future (if, indeed, one comes into being at all). It is clear that party alliances and inter-party relationships in general need to be assessed within the broad question of political space and structuring new party systems; and this Maurizio Cotta does in his analysis.

Many of these problems of post-communist democratisation and party-system development may be directly linked with the more general issues surrounding the relations of new parties with the societies in which they are situated. Clearly articulated links between new parties, on the one hand, and society and particular classes and groups, on the other, are generally lacking and processes of representation are subject to considerable confusion. This is hardly surprising when the social formation and much of the economic order is itself subject to rapid change and a fundamental overhaul. There is also little likelihood that the new east European parties will act as central agencies of socialisation, education and integration during a period of rapid change and potentially revolutionary upheaval as did the newly established parties of western Europe and the United States during the middle and latter half of the nineteenth century. Such parties are unlikely to be seen again and Schmitter (note 14) is clearly right to identify a changing role for parties in established democracies and to note that post-communist societies will not follow the path of institutional evolution previously seen in the West. There are clear

NB

comparative → "Catch all" parties becoming imp here

signs of a significant gulf persisting in eastern Europe between the political class and the rest of the population that makes the task of parties that much more important but also considerably more difficult to perform. The low turnout seen in a number of east European elections (down to 34 per cent in the local Polish elections of June 1994) has been but one sign of this but, as always, sweeping generalisations are best avoided in such matters. Turnout in Czech elections has been high, for example, and the pattern in Western democracies has also been generally downward. There are, then, signs not just of some major differences between eastern and southern Europe but also important contrasts within eastern Europe itself.

Voters behaviour

This is, indeed, one of the conclusions drawn by Gábor Tóka from his well-documented analysis of the relations that have developed between the new parties of eastern Europe and their post-communist electorate. Czech and Slovak voters seem to face a significantly clearer and more meaningful electoral choice than their neighbours in Hungary or Poland. But even in the case of the latter countries, he argues, the lack of structure in party systems and apparent confusion of party politics should not be over-emphasised or too easily assumed. The novelty of the east European party systems does not in itself seem to have a particularly strong influence on electoral activities in that area. Voters seem able to choose when presented with clear alternatives, and their behaviour is not that different from their equivalents in Western countries. This conclusion is reached on the basis of analysis of substantial empirical material gathered to produce answers to three deceptively simple questions: are government and opposition parties identifiable as such?; does the electorate perceive some policy differences between them?; and does a party exist that electors accept as representing them adequately? Differences within eastern Europe are not insignificant, and Poles in particular have found it difficult to distinguish between government and opposition parties. While, too, Czech and Slovak parties tend to have constituencies as ideologically homogeneous as British parties used to have, those in Hungary and Poland were rather more differentiated. It is, indeed, an early stage within the post-communist democratisation process at which to essay any general conclusion, but it is at least clear that the diverse forms of comparative analysis contained in this book will make an important contribution to our understanding of the party systems that have emerged or are emerging in eastern Europe and the resemblances they show to the characteristics of democratic transition in southern Europe and to the procedures of more established democracies.

NOTES

1. *The Times*, 19 January 1991.
2. D. Rustow, 'Transitions to democracy: towards a dynamic model', *Comparative Politics*, April 1970.
3. L. Morlino, 'Consolidamento democratico: definizione e modelli' *Rivista Italiana di Scienza Politica*, August 1986, pp. 203, 205.
4. A. Stepan, 'Paths toward redemocratisation: theoretical and comparative considerations', in G. O'Donnell, P. Schmitter and L. Whitehead (eds), *Transitions from Authoritarian Rule: prospects for democracy*, John Hopkins University Press, Baltimore, 1986, Pt III, pp. 64–84.
5. A. Lijphart et al., 'A Mediterranean model of democracy ?' *West European Politics*, January 1988.
6. Ibid.
7. G. Pridham (ed.), *The New Mediterranean Democracies: regime transition in Spain, Greece and Portugal*, Frank Cass, London, 1984, ch. 1 for a summary of these different approaches.
8. G. Pridham and T. Vanhanen (eds), *Democratisation in Eastern Europe*, Routledge, London, 1994, introduction, pp. 3–4; P. G. Lewis, 'Democracy and its Future in Eastern Europe', in D. Held (ed.), *Prospects for Democracy*, Polity Press, Cambridge, 1993, pp. 298–300; also, D. McSweeney and C. Tempest, 'The political science of democratic transition', *Political Studies*, September 1993.
9. G. Bingham Powell, *Contemporary Democracies: participation, stability and violence*, Harvard University Press, Cambridge, 1982, p. 7.
10. S. Huntington, *Political Order in Changing Societies*, Yale University, New Haven, 1968, p. 461.
11. P. Mair, 'How, and why, newly-emerging party systems may differ from established party systems', paper to conference on The Emergence of New Party Systems, Centre for Mediterranean Studies, Bristol University, September 1993.
12. Ibid.
13. Alan Ware, *Citizens, Parties and the State*, Polity Press, Cambridge, 1987, pp. 218–19.
14. P. Schmitter, 'The consolidation of democracy and representation of social groups' *American Behavioural Scientist*, 1991, pp. 426–7.
15. G. Pasquino, 'Party elites and democratic consolidation: cross-national comparison of Southern European experience', in G. Pridham (ed.), *Securing Democracy: political parties and democratic consolidation in Southern Europe*, Routledge, London, 1990, p. 53.
16. A. Bar, 'The emerging Spanish party system: is there a model?', *West European Politics*, October 1984, p. 134.
17. Pasquino, op. cit., p. 52.
18. See J. Linz, 'Il sistema partitico spagnolo', *Rivista Italiana di Scienza Politica*, no. 3, 1978.
19. See K. Gladdish, 'Portugal: an open verdict', in Pridham, *Securing Democracy*.
20. Pasquino, op. cit., pp. 44–8.
21. See J. Higley and R. Gunther (eds), *Elites and Democratic Consolidation in Latin America and Southern Europe*, Cambridge University Press, 1992.
23. R. Gunther, G. Sani and G. Shabad, *Spain after Franco: the making of a competitive party system*, University of California Press, 1986, p. 395.
24. P. G. Lewis, 'Civil society and the development of political parties in east-central Europe', *Journal of Communist Studies*, December 1993.

25. The main features are outlined in R. East, *Revolutions in Eastern Europe*, London: Pinter (1992).
26. See S. Berglund and J. A. Dellenbrant, *The New Democracies in Eastern Europe: Party Systems and Political Cleavages*, Aldershot: Edward Elgar (1991).

1 Party inheritances and party identities

Michael Waller

Political parties are organisations with considerable durability. Like boats that must stay afloat whilst having planks added or replaced, they maintain themselves in being by adjusting to changing circumstances, at the risk otherwise of perishing. If they do adapt, a part of their identity is modified. Yet that identity is a composite thing; a marked shift in party doctrine can be carried through by virtue of the party's organisational strength, whilst changes of name and leadership can cloak a continuity based on the link between a party's traditional support and doctrinal consistency.

In the transition from Communism in Poland, the Czech Republic, Slovakia, Hungary and Bulgaria, which are the countries treated in this chapter, the circumstances of flux obtaining since 1989 have served as the midwife of a number of new political parties. Less obvious has been the element of continuity. But such continuity as the region has witnessed has involved an extremely strenuous adaptation on the part of existing parties. In these circumstances party identities have been strained to the utmost. Old parties have had to seek for new strategies and images, whilst the newer creations have had to mark out their niche within a political space that has necessarily been very mobile.

A useful distinction has been made between an identity that a political party has acquired through its historical experiences on the one hand and, on the other, what it stands for in competition for support within a party system at any given time. It is a distinction, in Sartori's words, between an 'historically-derived identity' and 'contemporary political appeals'.[1] There is on the one hand an internal identity, built up of the traditions, discourse and folkways of an organisation, through which its members recognise each other and confirm their common purpose and collective being. On the other hand there is an externally derived identity based not on commonality but on difference, on what enables the world to see the party as distinct from others.

The difference between an internally and an externally derived identity is crucial for any analysis of party life.[2] For example, it forces the analyst to separate activists from voters. The voters can affect the fortunes of a party without any concern whatsoever for its history or the nature of its bonds of solidarity. They identify the party in relation to others on the basis of its appeals; they do not thereby have to identify *with* the party. Come the next election their support can be bestowed elsewhere. For the membership, however, and perhaps above all for the party's leadership, internal identification *with* the party is crucial. A party can survive a series of electoral disasters if its members 'close ranks'.

For an analysis of east-central Europe since 1989 this distinction might appear problematic. On the one hand the dual disruptions in the party systems of the region occasioned first by the imposition of the communist power monopoly and then by its implosion suggest that the search for historically-derived identities will not be easy, and is likely to show that history has dealt a very uneven hand to the various parties of the region. On the other, it has taken time for settled constituencies to form and for stable programmes to emerge, of a kind that could present clear party profiles to voters, who are in any case unaccustomed to electoral competition. That said, the distinction does in fact have a great value for an analysis of the development of the new political systems of the region, despite all the fluidity of present circumstances and the ruptures with the past, which in any case were rarely as complete as they appeared at the time.

The questions to which answers must be found in a study of party identities in east-central Europe since 1989 are, first, what constitutes identity in the case of political parties and who confers it. A second question concerns the historical factors that have contributed to the shaping of the identity of today's parties in east-central Europe. Thirdly, to what extent do today's parties carry a demonstrable continuity from yesterday's parties? Finally, how are today's parties setting out to acquire a contemporary identity, in the sense of marking themselves off from other parties in the newly opened competitive arena?

The last of these questions will not be treated here, partly because party competition on the basis of contemporary appeals is dealt with comprehensively in Gábor Tóka's chapter below, but partly also because the historical inheritances at work in the process of party formation in east-central Europe both merit and can support a separate treatment.

First the question of what constitutes party identity is addressed. The associated question of who confers identity has been for practical purposes answered by the distinction that is being made between historically derived identity and that based on contemporary appeals. That is, it is in one respect internally generated and must be a prime concern of the party managers, who will use all the arsenal at their disposal to maintain the internal unity of the organisation against rivals and enemies; whilst, when the party is operating in a competitive environment, another aspect of its identity is conferred by the appeals it is making for support in the wider electorate. The second section of this chapter will focus on the historical factors that have contributed to present identities. The third part will deal with continuity and change – the extent to which existing parties have changed, and the extent to which the newer parties are really new. To put it figuratively, the second section seeks to distinguish old wine from new, the third looks at old and new bottles.

I COMPONENTS OF AN HISTORICALLY-DERIVED IDENTITY

Any listing of the components of party identity at the most general comparative level must include both ideological and organisational elements. These, moreover, will have been shaped not only by the party's history within its own society and party system, but in international frameworks which can at times have a significant impact.

First, in the ideological field, programmatic statements and traditional doctrinal positions clearly merit pride of place. Not only are they particularly visible, but they must indeed be made visible by the party leadership, both in soliciting support from voters and in maintaining the solidarity of the membership. Changes in a party's programmes are the landmarks of its history, and those programmes will often contain phrases that retain immense symbolic value for that membership, even after their literal contemporary meaning has become obscure. Indeed, the more an historically-derived identity is being fostered at the expense of one based on present appeals, the more important in the party's life become the doctrinal symbols.[3] This has been amply illustrated in the case of the western European communist parties, whose attachment to the dictatorship of the proletariat as a programmatic goal served a predominantly organisational function until it became dysfunctional as those parties embraced the logic of electoral competition in their Eurocommunist phase.[4]

A less visible element of a party's ideology, but central to its identity, is its folklore.[5] This comprises the collective memory of significant battles fought and corners turned, the party's pantheon and also its demonology – not only the record of its leaders' qualities and contributions, but also that of the perfidy of the party's external foes and internal cowards who have flinched and traitors who have sneered. Associated with this, and constituting an important part of the cement that holds a party together, acting as the standard to which the faithful will rally, is the paraphernalia of banners, logos, songs and anthems, and (particularly significant in the Bulgarian case) an assigned colour.

Second, the organisational aspects of party identity are crucial at the level of the party's membership. There can be no identity without structure, and the history of very many parties has revealed how structure, and an attachment to it that has at times become ideological, can enable a party to survive when it is under pressure, either through an enforced adaptation to changed circumstances or through stressful leadership changes, or both. What is involved is the structure of responsible positions within the party, together with the rules that regulate the relations between offices and power-holders, that lay down the rights and duties of members, set disciplinary arrangements and fix the powers of local branches. Once again folkways are important beyond these formalised arrangements, the way in which a party conducts its business often being a matter of tradition. And folkways, of course, can survive even when the party is brought to change its formal rules in order to adapt to changing circumstances.

It should not be forgotten that organisational continuity is frequently a matter of flesh and blood people. If a party should be brought to change its programme and statutes, and yet the old leadership remain in place, the presence of the familiar personalities must render vulnerable any conclusion that the party has undergone a categorical organisational change. It should further be noted that longevity, and simply time, are central factors. Longevity is important because it allows traditions to be built up and to acquire value. Time is needed for contemporary appeals to crystallise into an ideology, for a folklore to be generated, and for a structure to be built up. Those parties in eastern Europe that are new on the political scene have the task of creating an identity that they do not inherit. But on the one hand the time required for myths to form and for ideological positions to emerge can be foreshortened at times of rapid change and, on the other, the past is always present to some extent on the stage of today. It is available as a source on which a new party can draw in its attempts to build an identity.

Finally, both the ideological and the organisational aspects of the identity of many parties have been affected by their international links. The extent to which this is the case in east-central Europe varies quite remarkably, with most agrarian and nationalist parties forming one rather diffuse pole of a continuum, and the parties stemming from the Comintern, the internal international linkages of which were unusually strong, standing as an extreme case at the other pole. In between fall the member parties of various internationals – socialist, liberal, or Christian democratic, for example. Through their role in accrediting parties as *bona fide* members of their club, these internationals have exercised a strong influence in fixing party identities.

II THE LEGACY OF THE PAST

These components of party identity, however, are empty boxes that must be given content in the case of individual parties. In this section the factors that have determined that content are addressed. Given the range of national cultures and the depth of the history involved, the account is unavoidably selective. Necessarily, more contemporary and contingent factors will not be given the prominence that they would merit in a fuller account, perhaps particularly the role of personality and the individual basis of party formation and identity, which were particularly strong, for example, on the Polish right.

State, nation and social cleavages

Social cleavages have been assigned a particular prominence in the discussion on the determinants of party identity and competition. Largely due to the seminal work by Lipset and Rokkan, but developed later by the post-materialist thesis of Inglehart and others, this analysis, it will be recalled, locates the origin of the various families of parties in European party systems in a series of historical crises, passing from struggles concerned with the consolidation of the state and the legitimacy of the political order, through the upheavals of the industrial revolution, to the postwar salience of quality of life issues.[6]

Whilst the societies covered in this chapter all shared in the general European development of mass political parties from the end of the nineteenth century, in their case this process took place contemporaneously with struggles over the establishment and consolidation of the state and over questions of legitimacy – for instance the creation of the dual monarchy in 1867 and the revolutionary events in Hungary that led up to it, and the emergence of Bulgaria from Turkish domination at the close of the 1870s. Indeed it was not until some half a century later that a Czechoslovak state was created, and a Polish state was re-created which was to undergo further territorial redefinition and was to suffer crises over the political order that was to obtain within that state.

It is not surprising therefore that problems of the definition of the political unit and of inclusion in the political order have been at least as prominent in the region as tensions deriving from industrialisation; and if western Europeans have had difficulty in locating a right and a left in today's eastern Europe, the problem is not entirely one of a transition from communist authoritarianism to a political and economic market. The landmark year of 1848 and the subsequent 'compromise' in Hungary, the trauma in the same country caused by the Trianon treaty of 1920, the numerous crises over the status or very existence of the Polish state, Bulgaria's ambiguity over alliances in both world wars, the uneasy cohabitation of Czechs and Slovaks and the lingering attachment in the latter to the Slovak state during the Second World War, the authoritarian coups between the wars in the first three countries mentioned – all these have left strong residues in the attitudes and traditions that still mark the politics of today, and have a clear relevance to party identities. Uncertainty about the parameters of the political unit, and about the rules governing inclusion and participation, associated in all cases except the Czech lands with a degree of economic and social development that lagged behind that of the leading nations of western Europe has meant that what parties stand for has concerned much more one or another view of the nation's destiny than a sectional interest.

Religious cleavages have, in turn, been strongly affected by this same factor, the strength of the Catholic Church in Poland being closely connected with the struggle of Poles to maintain a communal identity as long as the question of Polish statehood remained unresolved or unconfirmed, and the monasteries of Bulgaria having served a predominantly political role in the nineteenth century as symbols of the assertion of Bulgarian independence against the Turks in the temporal stand against the Greeks in the ecclesiastical realms.[7]

Historical cleavages relating to the nation's history and destiny as a factor determining party identities have not affected only the longer-established parties. Quite the contrary. The newest of parties in eastern Europe will link what they stand for to one or other position in struggles of the past, and to a claimed entitlement to speak for a national destiny, especially at a conjuncture when the structure of sectional interests is in disarray.

A divided left

On the left of the political spectrum, residues of this nationalism associated with emancipation and the defence of independent statehood were overlaid, from 1920 onwards, by the universal division of the left in Europe into socialist and communist strands as a direct repercussion of the Russian revolution. But in east-central Europe, with the very important exception of Czechoslovakia, this split was taking place in socialist parties whose social base at the time reflected the weakness of industry in relation to agriculture in those countries. Poland, Hungary (which included Slovakia until the Treaty of Trianon) and Bulgaria were all agrarian nations, and agrarian parties played as prominent a role in them as did socialist parties with a worker base. Indeed, having won 31 per cent of the vote in the 1919 election against 18.2 per cent for their Communist rivals, the Bulgarian Agrarian National Union under Stamboliiski went to the country in the following year, confirming its position and governing Bulgaria from 1920 to 1923.[8] It was the agrarians in Bulgaria, as in Hungary and Poland, who were best capable of mobilising the masses in favour of political change, and indeed it is estimated that 96 per cent of the Communist vote in 1920 came from the peasantry and the middle class.[9] The agrarian, or peasant, parties of Bulgaria, Poland and Hungary were to live on, and in the first two cases were even to enjoy a degree of organisational continuity during the communist years.

To that extent the party structure of east-central Europe reflected stages of economic development and industrialisation. With the clear exception of the Czech lands, socialist parties had a narrower social base than in the more industrialised societies of western Europe. That said, in all the countries covered here worker-based socialist parties were in existence at the time of the Russian revolution, Rosa Luxemburg in Poland (or that part of Poland that was at the time included in the Russian empire) playing a key role in setting the parameters of the debate that led to the 1920 split in the European left. After the split the communist parties – at that time all officially sections of the Communist International – were weak in relation to their socialist rivals in both Poland and Hungary, but stronger in terms of that relationship in Bulgaria. In all three of these countries the left as a whole was subjected to political disabilities of varying severity during these years. In Czechoslovakia both communists and social democrats had a strong presence in the party system; indeed, the two strongest communist parties outside the Soviet Union in the interwar years were the French and the Czechoslovak parties.

In view of arguments to be presented below it should be noted that both the Hungarian and the Polish communist parties were abolished in 1936 and 1938 (owing partly to Soviet diplomatic interests, but also to their own weakness), being revived after and during the Second World War respectively. They also passed through a number of changes of title – although such changes can often be more a sign of adaptation than of weakness, on which more will be said below.[10]

It should not be forgotten that after the split in 1920 the Communist International was there to adjudge which parties of the left was acceptable as communist and which not. Even when the Comintern was abolished in 1943 the Soviet Union remained to fulfil that role, until it in turn passed away. From that point on there could only be doubt about what Communism constituted in contemporary terms. But by that time the communist parties had changed their names and looked to the Socialist International for a new accreditation on a new basis. Events after 1989 were soon to show that the old rivalry between social democracy and Communism in Europe was ending in the social-democratisation of the formerly communist parties.[11]

The heritage of Communism

One of the key features of Communism as a system of rule was the characteristic way in which the ruling parties exercised their monopoly of power. It involved an intolerance of autonomous political organisation, but the creation and promotion of a massive network of party-sponsored organisations through which the party set out to dominate strategic sections of society.

A number of aspects of this structure of rule were to influence the transition from Communism, both postively, in providing growth points from which, to the party's discomfort, change was to come, and negatively in imposing impediments to the development of the democratic behaviour and attitudes.

For the first, the mass organisations that the party set up – such as the trade unions or a single national youth organisation – could operate as 'transmission belts' conveying the preferences of the centre to the grass roots of society as long as the party was able to ensure that the belts ran only in that direction. In the case of the trade unions it succeeded in all cases until the end, but both the youth organisations and the party-sponsored peace councils were to play a significant role as the party's monopoly of power became vulnerable during the 1980s.[12] Moreover, in Poland, Czechoslovakia and Bulgaria the ruling party had maintained in existence other parties which it subordinated to itself and whose role was, in fact, assimilated to that of the mass organisations. These 'bloc' parties had the resources, once the communist monopoly fell, to secure a niche for themselves early on in the process of party formation after 1989.

As for the impediments to the development of democracy bequeathed by communist rule, pride of place must be given to the relative success of the communist parties in instilling a sense of the priority of communal over sectional values, the effects of which were aggravated by the simple lack of experience in conducting political relations in a competitive environment. This affected the communist parties themselves as well, of course, though they at least had had some experience of politics in the more general sense. The communist parties were also to some extent victims of their own propaganda. Being accustomed to presenting themselves as guardians of the social interest, they were as well prepared to champion nationalist causes as they were ill prepared to pose as the champions of the oppressed. Experienced in one kind of politics, they still had to learn another. And one of the legacies of Communism was that many who did not wish to learn new ways of doing things were well entrenched in administrative – or economic – positions which were relatively untouched by the competitive arrangements that now affected more public life.

If in terms of the political system the communist heritage was relatively uniform, in the economic realm it was much more diverse. In Poland, for example, private ownership in agriculture, which had in any case been relatively little affected by an earlier policy of collectivisation, was given freer rein in 1956, this being but one of the factors that contributed to the relative gradualness of the transition from Communism in that country. Reform of the system of central command planning also, taken further in Hungary from 1968 than elsewhere in the Soviet bloc, and leading to the development and expansion of small business concerns, had a similar effect in that country. At the other extreme, the linking of economic reform with calls for political change in Czechoslovakia in that same year of 1968 led to retrenchment and to a severe police oppression that was to last until 1989. In fact the years 1956 and 1968 were symbolic moments of crisis in those three countries, the crises affecting the internal life of the ruling parties themselves. To those symbolic years were to be added 1970, 1976 and 1980–1 in Poland as a new working class in gestation, itself the product of the modernising policies of the ruling party, flexed its muscles in confrontations with the party.[13]

Such was the legacy of Communism in terms of the structure of the communist political system and of the economic policies that the ruling parties adopted. A second legacy was in a sense a mirror image of the first. In setting up a certain form of rule, the communist parties thereby shaped the nature of dissent to that rule, and from that dissent were to come many of the political parties, trade unions and movements of the transition. From about the time of the signing of the Helsinki Accords in 1975 new patterns of dissent emerged in east-central Europe which were able to gain a purchase in the hostile environment of communist rule. This evolution of dissent was to feed the formation of new political parties after the watershed of 1989. The historical roots of the latter are to that extent shallow. They embody what will be termed in the discussion of the final part of this chapter the liberation myth. They merit a preliminary word at this point.

First, movements of dissent focusing not only on human rights but also on issues of peace and the protection of the environment developed with particular strength from around 1975 in the GDR, Poland, Czechoslovakia, Hungary and – beyond the countries covered in this study – Slovenia. They did not develop until very late in Bulgaria, even though Bulgaria did not suffer from the extravagant dictatorship that afflicted its Balkan neighbour Romania.

Second, the concern of these dissenting movements with quality of life issues such as peace and the protection of the environment raises the question whether there were New Left influences at work, or whether these movements represented the arrival of post-materialism in the east of Europe, or both. For the first, New Left ideas were taken up and propagated by individual dissenters in the GDR, Poland, Hungary and to a lesser extent in Czechoslovakia, a prominent example being the open letter addressed to the ruling party in Poland by Jacek Kuroń and Karol Modzelewski in early 1965.[14] There is a strong continuity from that letter, through the formation of the Committee for the Defence of the Workers (the KOR) in 1976, and on into the admittedly uneasy relationship between KOR and Solidarity.

The argument that the surge of dissent from the late 1970s represents the arrival of post-materialism in east-central Europe, on the other hand, is difficult to sustain. There were in the circumstances of those years good strategic reasons for Charter 77 in Czechoslovakia to append the issues of peace and protection of the environment to their preferred cause of human rights.[15] The environmental movements which peaked in those years collapsed after 1989 as the dissenters became ministers in the new

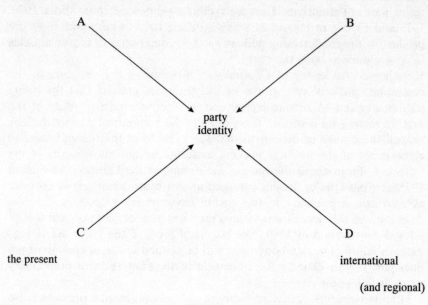

Figure 1.1 Factors influencing party identity in east-central European countries

governments and as the green parties met catastrophic defeat in the early elections everywhere except in the deviant case of Bulgaria. Nor was there much sign of the feminism which has been one of the chief manifestations of post-materialism in western Europe. As for the decline of the working class acclaimed by André Gorz and others in western Europe, if the KOR was tinged with post-materialism, the same can hardly be said for the worker-based Solidarity.

The heritage of the communist period, therefore, was mixed, in that it contained not only a strong residue of the pattern of politics shared by all the bloc countries, but also growth points for differentiated futures. Moreover, not only was that differentiation to bear the marks of each country's individual experience of Communism, but it was often to reflect deeper historical factors that divided a Balkan from a central European past and, in the detail of the thing, each country from the others.

The treatment offered here of party identities has focused exclusively on historically derived identity at the expense of an identity provided by contemporary appeals, which will be treated elsewhere in these pages. That other aspect of party identity can, however, usefully be brought back in conclusion, to provide one reference point in a diagram illustrating the various factors that have influenced party identities in east-central Europe (Figure 1.1 above).

In turning now to historical inheritances in the party systems of eastern Europe, two general considerations must be borne in mind. The first is that the countries of eastern Europe have been diverging markedly since the fall of communist power in ways that concern party identities and party competition, and generalisation is becoming increasingly difficult. At the same time such divergences are the fuel of comparative politics. I would like to offer a comparativist's apology for any errors concerning individual countries or parties that may be encountered below. As Hans Daalder put it in a similar statement: 'It is up to those who really know the individual political systems concerned to test, prove or more likely to disprove, my generalisations.'[16]

Second, whilst the process of party formation in the countries covered here has been subject to this differentiation, the experience of them all differs vastly from that of most of the territories of the former Soviet Union, where the process has moved far more slowly. Whatever difficulties Poland, the Czech Republic, Slovakia, Hungary and Bulgaria are encountering in re-establishing a parliamentary life, and however divergent now is their experience of party formation, geo-politics and continuities from a not too distant pre-communist past have benefited them – assuming, that is, that becoming more like Western Europe is to be considered a benefit.

III CHANGE AND CONTINUITY

Partly because of the abruptness of the withdrawal of Soviet support for the Eastern Europe regimes and partly also because of the very inflexibility of the communist power monopoly, which meant that it would break under pressure rather than bend, the change of regime in Eastern Europe appeared to many at the time more as a rupture that as the culmination of changes over time. But whilst the abruptness of the actual fall of the regimes had important consequences, an overemphasis on it can be very misleading.

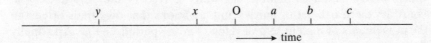

y   The communist parties come to power
x   The signing of the Helsinki Accords, which was a major turning point in the evolution of the dissenting movements that were to inherit power
O   1989 – the fall of the communist regimes in the region
a   Completion of legislation guaranteeing freedom of association and establishing an electoral procedure
b   The first election
c   The second election

Figure 1.2 The chief phases of the process of political change in eastern European countries

The chief phases of the process of change can be presented in a simple diagram. Though simple, Figure 1.2 marks the cardinal points in the creation or re-creation of party identities in eastern Europe.

The critical moment of 1989 was preceded by a period when challenges to the regimes, connected with an important turn in the Soviet Union's policies, were able to obtain a foothold.[17] This period, $x \rightarrow$ O on the diagram, can be dated from the signing of the Helsinki Accords in 1975.[18] It was followed by a period (O $\rightarrow a$) during which the first legal and administrative implications of the change of regime were confronted, including the passing of laws guaranteeing freedom of association and of the press, and also electoral laws (point a). The diagram serves, in passing, to show that the discussion about democratisation is distinct from that about party identities, if for no other reason than that some of the parties with the strongest identities were the least democratic. The process of democratisation, whatever harbingers of change economic reform in the period $y \rightarrow$ O or the fitful birth of political initiatives between x and O presaged, could not take place until point O had been reached, whilst party competition proper could not get under way until point a had been reached. As Sartori points out, competition involves not only a market 'but rules to govern it'.[19] For a comprehensive account of party identities, however, the full range of the diagram is needed.

The continuities, the breaks in continuity, and the new creations of the transition can all be mapped with reference to this simple diagram. It serves also as a basis for a categorisation of the political parties that emerged to compose the party systems after 1989. First, the communist parties have existed throughout the whole span of the diagram, but with breaks in their continuity that clearly call for analytical attention. Secondly, the 'bloc' parties which the communist parties subordinated to themselves during the period $y \rightarrow$ O have likewise existed across the whole span, but their role in the communist period obviously marks them off from the communist parties. A third category is composed of the 'historical' parties which were banned at point y but were revived in the period O $\rightarrow a$. Fourthly, there is a set of parties and coalitions that owe their origins to the movements of dissent that developed in the period $x \rightarrow$ O. And finally there are the parties that arose in response to the new opportunities for autonomous organisation after point O. These categories may fruitfully be examined in turn.

It will be recalled that both the Polish and Hungarian parties ceased to exist in the late 1930s, to be re-created respectively during and at the close of the Second World War. At that point the Polish party changed its name, but it was to change it again, this time with the Hungarian party, when the forced merger took place between the communist and socialist or social-democratic parties at the onset of the cold war.

The Hungarian Socialist Workers' Party dissolved itself in October 1989, the bulk of its members going on to constitute the new Hungarian Socialist

Party. In January 1990 the Polish United Workers' Party accomplished the same feat, this leading to the creation of Social Democracy of the Polish Republic, and of a smaller formation, the Polish Social-Democratic Union. The Bulgarian Communist Party, for its part, never dissolved itself, but at the end of that same month of January 1990 changed its name on the basis of a party referendum, becoming the Bulgarian Socialist Party. It had in fact maintained an unbroken organisational continuity from its origin in the Bulgarian Social-Democratic Party created in 1883, though it had already passed through one name change when it became the Bulgarian Communist Party in the aftermath of the Russian revolution. A further name-change took place when the Slovak arm of the Czechoslovak Communist Party became the Party of the Democratic Left before the June 1990 elections in Czechoslovakia. Only the Communist Party of Bohemia and Moravia was to retain the discredited term 'communist' in its title.

It is doubtful if any family of political parties has been faced with so acute a problem of identity as the erstwhile ruling communist parties of eastern Europe after the turning-point of 1989–91 which saw not only the collapse of communist rule, but also the demise of the CPSU and the Soviet Union themselves, which in turn had served as the essential point of reference for communist parties round the world. Given these circumstances, and given the change not only of their names but also of the goals and alliances that they now espoused, could they reasonably be deemed to be the same parties as they had been?

In one sense that question is hardly worth asking. For the orthodox who refused to follow the new line, the change of name and direction spelled the end of the party they had known; conversely the new-named party's enemies had everything to gain from claiming that this was still the same party. It is none the less worth drawing up the balance between rupture and continuity, since what was involved was really an extreme case of the tensions to which any political party is exposed at one point or another in its life.

First, a factor counting strongly on the side of rupture with the past was the undeniable fact that one of the primary planks in the ideology of these parties had been removed. Moreover, that ideology had been forged over the years in contradistinction to the positions of social democracy. With the international structure of Communism gone and with the Soviet Union itself having followed the Comintern into history, the post-communist parties were extremely vulnerable. It was difficult to know what Communism might mean without the CPSU and without a Soviet Union. The fact that the post-communist parties so often set out to re-define themselves as social democratic can only be seen as a major rupture in their ideological continuity.

A second factor suggests a reservation in the direction of continuity. Despite all the strictures concerning party unity enjoined by the 'Leninist principle of democratic centralism', these parties were all to a greater or lesser extent factionalised. That is, the adoption of a new line was in no case a simple conversion on the part of the party leadership as a whole; it represented often the victory of one faction within that leadership. Even the Czech party, which was the most resistant to hoisting visible signals of change, carried within itself the residues of past struggles associated, for example, with the Prague Spring. This was perhaps most clearly the case in the Polish party, as was revealed at the PZPR's crucial Central Committee meeting as 1988 turned into 1989.

But the strongest case for continuity is based on organisation, on continuity of leadership roles and of property. Indeed, the aim of the proponents of a name-change was often quite simply to save 'the shop', in terms of the party's assets. Those assets were only partially physical. To have a headquarters in a locality, with its communications equipment and its human networks stood for something more than just the cash value of buildings. This was to become strikingly clear even in the first elections, when the discredited post-communist parties pulled in a respectable vote across the region – one on which they were able to build spectacularly in the elections in Poland and Hungary in 1993 and 1994.

A somewhat analogous balance between rupture and continuity can be discerned in the case of the second category of political parties of the transition. In Poland, in the then Czechoslovakia and in Bulgaria the ruling party had, in consolidating its power, subordinated to itself in a People's, Patriotic or Fatherland Front a series of other parties which it saw as 'progressive'. The political role of these 'bloc' parties was assimilated to that of the mass organisations through which the communist power monopoly encadred and controlled strategic social groups. But they maintained a separate organisational existence, with a structure of their own, often considerable property and premises, and a press. As Paul Lewis points out in the Polish case, 'the allied parties ... played a significant part in the collapse of communist rule and the unravelling of the 1989 agreement that had originally appeared to guarantee its continuation'.[20] The organisational resources of which they disposed was to stand them in good stead once their communist sponsors had fallen from power.

These parties had a lesser problem of identity than the post-communist parties. First, they often spoke for a clear sectional constituency, as was the case particularly with the Polish United Peasant Party; and secondly, they could with reason claim to be resurrecting an identity which their subordination to the communists had suppressed.

A somewhat separate case of continuity, but overlapping with that of the bloc parties, is presented by the third category of parties of the transition – the parties that had existed before the communist period, but were banned during it and were revived after 1989. The exceptional nature of communist authoritarianism meant not only that there could be no organisational continuity in most cases but that the social base of these parties was usually severely disrupted, first through radical changes in property relations and secondly through urbanisation and the other social changes that the communist regimes, particularly in the Polish and Bulgarian cases (though not, at the other extreme, in the economically developed Czech lands) had effected.

The same question must be asked in relation to the revived parties as was asked in the case of the communists. In what sense are these the same parties that they were? In their case, the discontinuity was, of course, substantial. The consideration that must count most in their case is the fact that, precisely because of the circumstances of the communist period, new elites and individual competitors for positions of power had to seek a means of mobilising support, and a pre-communist existence offered an available option in this regard. A little over forty years is not too long for collective memories to persist, or for a politician to raise aloft a name associated with the past to establish himself or herself. The leader of the Nikola Petkov wing of the Bulgarian Agrarian National union's leader from 1992, Anastasya Mozer, benefited in this way from the memory of her father-in-law, 'Gemeto' Dimitrov.[21] In these cases future viability is a question that remains to be resolved in the context of current competitive appeals. The revival parties are in fact the only parties in all five countries to have retained the names that they bore before the transition. They had need of them, whilst expediency required that all the others slough off a previous title.

Each of the parties just named has, at the time of writing, contrived to remain viable as independent organisations – as have the social-democratic parties of Bulgaria and the Czech Republic, which constitute a special, and complex, case of revival. Other revivals have had to seek salvation through mergers of various kinds. The old Polish Socialist Party maintains a precarious presence by fielding electoral candidates on the tickets of other socialist formations. The Czech Agrarian Party (a revival) merged with the 'bloc' Socialist Party and the electorally unsuccessful new Green Party to form the Liberal Democratic Union late in 1991. The case of the Czech Agrarians is an interesting one both from the point of view of continuity and of identity. The revival involved a name-change, and whilst changes of title are not conclusive evidence of a changed identity, the policy of the party underwent an equally remarkable sea-change. From having defended independent farmers against nationalisation in the earlier period, they now take the part of co-operatives faced with privatisation. This has not prevented a Czech analyst from regarding today's component of the Liberal Democratic Union as a continuation of the earlier party, in an article establishing that the vote for the Liberal Democratic Union in the 1992 election reproduced to a remarkable extent the distribution of votes characteristic for the Agrarians before the Second World War.[22]

The organisational factor, then, was sufficiently strong to give the communist and 'bloc' parties continuity into the post-communist period, whilst the earlier existence of a party in the pre-communist period could serve as one available resource for mobilisation, once the electoral process was reopened. In the case of a fourth category of parties organisational continuity could obviously play only a minimal role. This was the category of the parties that stemmed from the movements of dissent during Communism's final years – the period $x \rightarrow O$ on Figure 1.2. In their case, current competitive appeals have counted far more than inheritances from the past. Yet history can move at different rhythms, and in the period from 1975 (the signing of the Helsinki Accords) to the holding of the first free elections a highly condensed process of aggregation of political preferences took place, yielding a correspondingly rich repertoire of elements that contributed to the identity of those parties that were to be most successful in the transition. A decade and a half was long enough, and its events dramatic enough, for the creation of a myth, widely shared across the region, that was to provide a common, if foreshortened, heritage for a whole range of parties in the re-established assemblies.

So varied is the cultural background of the societies involved, and so different was the manner of Communism's fall, that to generalise about that myth is difficult. Its clearest feature was a rejection of the communist past, associated with a differentiated element of anti-Russian sentiment, strongest in Poland and Hungary, weakest in Bulgaria. Put in the simplest terms, it was a myth of liberation which, in its most extreme manifestations (for example the Orange Alternative and Wolę Być in Poland) developed into libertarianism, giving the process the atmosphere of a western European 1968 which was largely deceptive.[23] As a founding myth of many of Eastern Europe's political parties it was problematic. On the one hand, given the geopolitics of the region, the myth's anti-Communism complemented its rejection of the past with an inferred, if not explicit, vision of a society reformed on Western lines. But also, the nature of the struggle against Communism imparted to the myth an endorsement of a certain style of political action and a certain sense of social purpose that were incompatible ultimately with electoral politics in a competitive arena. This became explicit when the movements of the period $y \rightarrow O$ confronted the prospect of organising to contest the first competitive elections, the sharpest contradictions emerging in the Czech Civic Forum and the GDR's Neues Forum.

The liberation myth therefore came to unite in a common purpose a community of people whose policy preferences would turn out to be at variance with one another when forward-looking strategies replaced the attitude to be taken to Communism as the determinant of party identity after 1989. At that point differing national cultures and historical experiences led to differing outcomes. In Czechoslovakia, Civic Forum's anguished debate of late 1990 as to whether or not to enter the arena of competitive party politics was resolved in favour of the latter option, after which the movement split into two factions. Of these, the movement-oriented Civic Movement atrophied remarkably soon, with the Klaus faction embracing with alacrity the comportment appropriate to electoral politics as the Civic Democratic Party. But the Civic Forum was to contribute also to the re-creation of a viable social-democratic party, formed partly from within the Forum (Battěk's Association for Social Democracy) and partly from a revived Czechoslovak Social-Democratic Party itself.[24] In Poland no fewer than nine parties which won parliamentary representation in October 1991 could appeal to the Solidarity myth and drew a part of their identity from that. Yet already by then a rift had opened up among the parties owing their origins to Solidarity between, on the one hand, those formations that adopted a strategy of seeking a government role and embraced a party competitive mode and, on the other, those that combined a retention of the movement spirit with a necessarily paradoxical detachment from party competition (for example, the Solidarity Trade Union and Labour Solidarity in its early phase). By the time of Solidarity's fifth congress in 1993, Wałęsa himself had bidden farewell to that organisation; but it was Zbigniew Bujak who, although leader of one of the smallest formations to enter the Sejm in October 1991, summed up the former position with a phrase that encapsulates the eclipse of the liberation myth (although it was produced with that aim): 'Sorry about Solidarity!'

The Hungarian case was complex. Here no single consolidated liberation movement developed to contest the communist regime, and three embryo political parties spoke for the opposition in the 'triangular' talks of 1989. This meant, however, simply that three formations played their part in the creation of the liberation myth – the Hungarian Democratic Forum, the Alliance of Free Democrats and the Alliance of Young Democrats. On the other hand, the chief mobilising issue in the period preceding 1989 – the proposed construction of a system of dams on the Danube at Gabčikovo in Slovakia and Nagymáros in Hungary – generated its own interestingly complex aggregating movement, at the centre of which was the Danube Circle. Protest over the dams epitomised the liberation myth in two ways. First, it rallied support for the cause of environmental protection which, with peace and human rights, was one of the universalising issues around which the dissenting movements mobilised in that period. But the scheme also evoked a good deal of national feeling, given the historical meaning that that particular area of the Danube carried in the national consciousness. The fact that the general movement of dissent was compartmentalised in this way in Hungary, and the fact that after 1989 the Danube Circle, together with the whole environmental issue, had difficulty in maintaining any salience in the political life of the country, is a good illustration of the composite, contradictory and ultimately provisional nature of the liberation myth.

As for the Democratic Forum, the Alliance of Free Democrats and the Association of Young Democrats, it has often been pointed out that despite their separate existence these early-formed parties did not represent distinct policy options, but were rather personally connected clubs of intellectuals, each containing differing strands of opinion which to a considerable extent overlapped with each other.[25] This is supported by the way in which each of these parties later developed factional disputes. Despite this view, the three formations at their birth had rather distinct identities, which were indeed to a considerable extent imparted by the individuals involved and by the nature of each 'clan'. The Hungarian Democratic Forum was close to reformists in the ruling party, and Imre Pozsgay, a prominent leader of the Hungarian Socialist Workers' Party, took part in its early deliberations. The Alliance of Free Democrats was associated in the public mind with political traditions established by the urban intelligentsia, particularly that of Budapest, including its historically strong Jewish element. The Alliance of Young Democrats' requirement that members be under the age of 35 was in itself sufficient to give the party a particular identity, involving a rejection of the communist past, carried further to an independence also of earlier Hungarian traditions. This prepared the way for the party to take on a role as spokesman for the new entrepreneurial interest.

In the Bulgarian case – in so many ways the most interesting – the anti-Communist movement, forming relatively late, has been held broadly in its original form by the continuing strength of the former communist party, renamed the Bulgarian Socialist Party.[26] The Union of Democratic Forces grouped together at the end of 1989 a number of movements and parties that included revivals – such as the Social-Democratic Party, the Democratic Party and the Radical Democratic Party – and a series of new foundations, in the creation of which the personal factor was in most cases strong, but mobilising often around the symbols and issues of the contestatory period, foreshortened as it was in the Bulgarian case. Such was the case with the Clubs for Glasnost and Democracy, Ekoglasnost, the Green Party and the Committee for Religious Rights, Freedom of Conscience, and Spiritual Values.

In sum, a substantial number of the parties that emerged as electorally significant in the early phase of the transition in Eastern Europe could claim organisational continuity with the past. A pre-communist existence has also been available as a mobilisation resource, in circumstances where the personal element in party formation has been pronounced. The international factor was also important in promoting a party identity based both on contemporary links and an historical tradition. Finally, the preparatory phase of the transition created a powerful myth of liberation – but it was not one that could in the long term provide differentiated identities for the new parties that came into being after 1989.

NOTES

1 Giovanni Sartori, *Parties and Party Systems: A Framework for Analysis* (Cambridge: Cambridge University Press, 1976), p. 171; see also Peter Mair, 'Continuity, Change and Vulnerability of Party', in Gordon Smith and Peter Mair (eds), *Understanding Party System Change in Western Europe* (London: Frank Cass), p. 170.

2 In the rather less recent history of the western reaches of Europe, this tension has lain at the heart of the catch-all phenomenon, or rather of the predicament of a party that has until a certain point prized its identity in terms of loyalty and internal solidarity, and is now drawn to lay greater emphasis on that aspect of its identity that is based on appeals to a marginal voter, whose loyalty to the party will be, by definition, minimal. This shift – the example of the SPD at its congress in Bad Godesberg in 1959 is the most frequently cited example – is often seen as a shift of identity. What the party stands for in terms of its policies has changed, and this may affect the organisational norms that have sustained an earlier emphasis on unity and solidarity. Is it, then, still the same party? Those who leave it in disgust will claim that it is not; for them the historical chain, essential to their commitment to the party, has been broken. For those who remain, and surely for most external commentators, the party has adapted to changed circumstances and is still the party. To use an image that will be evoked below, 'the shop' in most of such cases survives, and indeed the change of strategy has been made expressly to preserve the shop. Thus whilst it is possible to view such shifts of strategy – in both eastern and western Europe – as changes in a party's identity, they can perhaps more fruitfully be seen as shifts in the party's approach to its identity, from an investment in an historically-derived identity to an attention to contemporary political appeals. The *locus* for the catch-all argument is Otto Kircheimer, 'The Transformation of the Western European Party Systems', in Joseph LaPalombara and Myron Weiner, *Political Parties and Political Development* (Princeton: Princeton University Press, 1966); see also Angelo Panebianco, *Political Parties: organisation and power* (Cambridge: Cambridge University Press, 1988) Ch. 13.

3 And the party's discourse itself. See D. Labbé, 'Le discours communiste', *Revue Française de Science Politique*, vol. 30, no. 1 (1980).

4 For one treatment among many, see Ronald Tiersky, *Ordinary Stalinism: Democratic Centralism and the Question of Communist Political Development*, George Allen and Unwin, 1985, pp. 33 and 54.

5 The standard term for this aspect of party identity is 'mythos'. 'Folkways' has been preferred here to prevent confusion, since the term 'myth' will be used below to refer to the entire set of beliefs that a party holds about its goals, its social role and the justification for its collective action.

6 S.M. Lipset and S. Rokkan, 'Cleavage structures, party systems and voter alignments: an introduction', in S.M. Lipset and S. Rokkan (eds), *Party Systems and Voter Alignments: Cross-National Perspectives* (New York: Free Press, 1967); Ronald Inglehart, *The Silent Revolution: changing values and political styles among western publics* (Princeton: Princeton University Press, 1977); Grew, Raymond, *Crises of Development in Europe and the United States*, Princeton: Princeton University Press, 1978.

7 It has been pointed out, for example, that in Bulgaria the struggle for emancipation from Turkish rule in the second half of the nineteenth century pitched the 'young' against the 'old' among the Bulgarian political class, restricted as it was at that time. The 'young' were radical in opposing the *status quo* and in bearing the standard of national liberation. The 'old', many of whom had

been educated abroad, urged moderation and accommodation to towards the Turks. The latter were 'cosmopolitans, open to Europe and to "tested" foreign models'. These opposed strands of political thinking were to become, respectively, the left and the right of the Bulgarian political scene after the liberation in 1878. Commenting on this, Antoni Todorov sees the consequent failure of Bulgaria to develop a traditional conservative right as a 'typical Bulgarian peculiarity' (Politicheski kulturi v moderna Balgariya, *Politicheski izsledvaniya*, 3, 1993). Whilst it would be unwise to question, in today's circumstances of increasing diversity, any suggestion of national idiosyncrasy, the difficulties of the right in other countries of the region since 1989 can with reason be attributed to somewhat similar factors concerned with national emancipation and the consolidation of an independent statehood.

8   R.J. Crampton, *Eastern Europe in the Twentieth Century*, London: Routledge, 1994.

9   L.A.D. Dellin, 'The Communist Party of Bulgaria', in Stephen Fischer-Galati, *The Communist Parties of Eastern Europe*, New York: Columbia University Press, 1979, p. 50.

10 A useful introduction to the history of the communist parties of the region is Stephen Fischer Galati, *The Communist Parties of Eastern Europe* (New York: Columbia University Press, 1979).

11 Heinz Timmermann, 'A dilemma for the Socialist International: the communist parties' successors in east-central Europe', in Michael Waller, Bruno Coppieters and Kris Deschouwer, *Social Democracy in a Post-Communist Europe* (London: Frank Cass, 1994).

12 Michael Waller, 'Groups, interests and political aggregation in East Central Europe', in Ronald J. Hill, *Beyond Stalinism: communist political evolution* (Frank Cass, 1992).

13 See David Lane and George Kolankiewicz, *Social Groups in Polish Society* (London: Macmillan, 1973).

14 An English text is given in Jacek Kuroń and Karol Modzelewski, *Open Letter to the Party* (International Socialism, no date). Another celebrated example of this particular influence at work was Miklos Haraszti, *A Worker in a Worker's State* (Harmondsworth: Penguin, 1977).

15 Michael Waller, *Peace, Power and Protest in the Gorbachev Era* (London: Centre for Security and Conflict Studies, 1988).

16 Hans Daalder, 'Party elites and political development in Western Europe', in Joseph LaPalombara and Myron Weiner, *Political Parties and Political Development* (Princeton: Princeton University Press, 1969 (first published 1966), p. 44.

17 For an account of this period see Karen Dawisha, *Eastern Europe, Gorbachev and Reform* (Cambridge: Cambridge University Press, 1988).

18 This period $x \rightarrow$ O corresponds to Rustow's 'preparation phase' in his analysis of processes of transition 'Transition to Democracy: Towards a Dynamic Model', *Comparative Politics*, vol. 2, no. 2 (1970).

19 Giovanni Sartori, 'European political parties: the case of polarised pluralism', in Joseph LaPalombara and Myron Weiner, *Political Parties and Political Development* (Princeton: Princeton University Press, 1969), p. 158.

20 Paul G. Lewis, 'Poland's New Parties in the Post-Communist System', paper presented at the ECPR Joint Sessions, Limerick, 1992, p. 1. The largest of the mass organisations in each country in the communist period – the consolidated trade union body – have likewise constituted an element of continuity from the communist past. Only in Poland have they participated directly in parliamentary life, with the OPZZ forming part of an electoral coalition with the former communist party; but they now represent across the region a major

political force of which the political parties must take account.

21 The Bulgarian Agrarian National Union split at the time of the accession to power of the Communist Party, one wing remaining in Bulgaria as a bloc party, the other, associated with the name of Nikola Petkov (whom the incoming Communist leadership hanged), going into exile.

22 Tomáš Kostelecký, 'Parliamentary elections in 1990 and 1992 in the Czech Republic: changing voting patterns of changing political parties', paper presented to the conference on Party Formation in east-central Europe, Prague, 1992.

23 Vladimir Tismaneanu, *In Search of Civil Society: Independent Peace Movements in the Soviet Bloc* (London: Routledge, 1990); Michael Waller, 'The break-up of the communist power monopoly in Eastern Europe', in Maurice Wright and Michael Moran, *The Market and the State* (Basingstoke: Macmillan, 1992).

24 The formation of political parties in east-central Europe is covered in the chapters by Georgi Karasimeonov, Paul Lewis, Bill Lomax, Michael Waller and Gordon Wightman in Gordon Wightman (ed.), *Party Formation in East-Central Europe: Post-Communist Politics in Czechoslovakia, Hungary, Poland and Bulgaria* (Edward Elgar, 1995).

25 David Stark, '"Path dependence" and privatisation strategy in East-Central Europe', *East European Politics and Society, vol. 6, no. 1 (1992)*; see also György Márkus, 'Parties, camps and cleavages in Hungary', in Michael Waller, Bruno Coppieters and Kris Deschouwer, *Social Democracy in a Post-Communist Europe* (Frank Cass, 1994).

26 Georgi Karasimeonov, 'Bulgaria: a case of deferred differentiation', in Gordon Wightman (ed.), *Party Formation in East-Central Europe*, 1995.

2 From nomenclatura to clientura

The emergence of new political elites in east-central Europe

Attila Ágh

THE POWER TRANSITION AND THE HETEROGENEITY OF ELITES

All elites are very complex social groups, composed of representatives of economic, political, social and cultural-ideological powers. Political elites, usually, are 'functionally distinct elites'; namely, 'those who make or influence state decisions are members of the political elite'.[1] However, in Central Europe this functional differentiation has never reached the classical Weberian distinction among elites, because the state has remained powerful in the economy and vice versa. This fusion of functionally different elites can be observed in the case of other elites as well. Thus, Central European elites have always been very heterogeneous along these lines, even in the age of state socialism. In that period the party state tried to homogenise the power elite in the spirit of the unity of powers against the separation of powers. This traditional Central European heterogeneity – involving mutual animosity as well as some large overlap among the different elites – increased considerably in the period of pre-transition crisis. This can be described as the rise of potential or actual counter-elites, with their competitive infighting and their common struggle against the state socialist regimes.

The transition of power between ruling elites in 1989–90 was seen by many as an absolute turning point in systemic change and was advertised by the new ruling elite as the 'end' of the process, in which there was an almost total change in the top political elite. It is true that this power transition led to significant changes; but it was not an absolute turning point in systemic change, since continuity prevailed in many ways. This could be seen mainly in its institutional and cultural – although not in personal – dimensions. First, the previous elites have not lost their power and influence completely, even in the east-central European (ECE) countries, for only the old party elite has been excluded from power and the other, governmental and economic-management elites have partly survived. Paradoxically not only the survivors of the old elite, but first of all the new politicians represent the strongest continuity in their mentality and patterns of behaviour preserving the model of state socialism. Such continuity is much stronger, however, for party elites and leading politicians in south eastern Europe (SEE), and in the western republics of the former Soviet Union than in ECE. Second, the elite change was neither completely new, nor sudden, since the competitive fight for power between the various counter-elites, at least in Hungary, dates back to the period of pre-transition crisis. Third, political transformation itself cannot be reduced to a change in the elite which holds power. Systemic change has also economic and social dimensions, with their own elite continuities and discontinuities, overlapping at least partly with the political elite.[2]

The periods of pre-transition crisis and democratic transition can be described as those of acute and intensive elite conflict, which can be related to institutional and cultural problems. Systemic change has involved rivalry between different power elites, and this rivalry has been based on their own institutions as power sub-centres and on their different sub-cultures, ideas, programmes and forms of elite behaviour. The elite struggle has involved institutions as well as the skill and adaptability, the values and political discourses of the elite groups. Institutions as power bases obviously matter a lot for the competition between parties, but in ECE the cultural fight between the future party elites has been decisive in the party formation process, and the cultural or ideological fight is still the most important issue for the new parties.[3]

This chapter focuses on the recent situation in the process of democratic transition; it does not discuss the nature of elites in state socialism and the classical theories associated with these. Thus it deals only with the elites of regime transition, first with the political elite, then with the larger elite and relations between its component groups.[4]

There are now two major tendencies evident in the development of elites: the consolidation of the transitional elite in a neo-traditional form; or its transformation into a professional elite through the process of European integration. Basically, the question of alternative elite development is still open. In the long run it is likely that the professionalisation cum Europeanisation alternative will prevail (as the elections in 1993 and 1994 indicate), but what we have seen in the past few years is the dominance of the transitional elite, with a magical transformation from a system based on the nomenclatura into a system based on the clientura.

THE TRANSITIONAL ELITE AS 'ONE' ACTOR

The transitional political elite has some obvious common features: its sudden rise to power and its lack of professionalism. This is true for the whole political elite and not just its dominant part – i.e. not just the ruling or governing elite. Taken together, these political elites appear before society as one elite – i.e. for the non-elite there is *one* actor which monopolises politics and exercises control over all social life. It is only within this monopolised sphere of politics that elite fragmentation and internal rivalry become manifest. In this paper I treat the political elite as one actor, without specifically analysing the elite infights at the government–opposition level or the conflicts in the emerging ECE political party systems. This 'collective' political elite, at the same time, has to be distinguished not only from the other elites 'from outside', but also from the other social and political actors and agents of transition, who have tried to get representation 'from below' in the newly emerging narrow political elite. This fight for inclusion by outsiders or exclusion by insiders has also been one of the characteristic processes of democratic transition – i.e. the problem of a small, exclusive elite versus a big, inclusive elite. The extension of the elite is a complex problem to discuss; it is enough to mention here that the transitional elite is generally opposed to this extension, because it wants to preserve its own exclusivity.[5]

This exclusive political elite is composed of five characteristic 'transitional' types of politician:

1   *Politicians of morals* – that group of politicians which played a role in the opposition and was seriously at variance with the previous regime. Thus they gained moral legitimation in the democratic transition process as public figures. They tended to be the most important actors in the very first period of power transition. Their special style of moralising politics, however, has turned from an asset to a liability, since it has meant the preservation of the closed, secretive, and improvised political style of their earlier oppositional activities. The claim to be a 'revolutionary aristocracy' (a term coined by the Czechs), destined for political leadership 'by birth', has been weakened by their inability to transform themselves into professional politicians. This is because their moral background and principles have not conditioned them for rational compromises in politics. These non-compromising personalities, who have a direct continuity with their 'heroic' past, have been marginalised step by step in political life, including within their own parties.

Some leading figures in this group have also kept their oppositional roles in the new regime (e.g. Adam Michnik), and in such a way they have retained their influence, role and popularity by remaining outside the realms of official power. However, some others – like Václav Havel – have wanted to make a virtue of necessity, by inventing 'post-modern politics' (which in fact involves a role conflict). This post-modern politics, allegedly, is based on moral principles, and stands opposed to routine professional politics, in the spirit of 'new politics'. In fact, it seems to be a combination of two negative features ('revolutionary aristocracy' and non-professionalism), not the two positive features (bridging the gap between the elite and the masses, and effective democratic politics) deemed necessary at the moment. Actually, the politicians of morals can come very close to the 'man in the street' in their everyday behaviour, so they can feel their real problems and share their worries. However, they are very far from them in their mentality, in their moralising intellectual 'aristocratic' approach.[6]

After some years people in Czechoslovakia – and elsewhere in ECE – have experienced the disadvantages of the 'post-modern politics' and this aristocratic approach. It is not by chance that Jan Strásky, the prime minister of the last federal government became increasingly popular in the public eye, since he represented a type of respectable and reliable civil servant, 'a "bureaucrat", as he himself used to say, who the public, suffering fatigue as a result of the great metaphors and political fireworks, considered a calming, stabilising actor after the first years of more or less sparkling representatives from the ranks of dissidents and non-political politicians' – concludes Zdenka Mansfeldová.[7]

2 *Politicians of historical vision* – these are the politicians who arrived on the political scene just before the power transition, without real oppositional legitimacy, but with a determined historical vision of restoring the historical continuity of the nation and re-creating the past in the coming future (like József Antall, late prime minister of Hungary and so many other politicians of the region). They represent, in turn, an indirect continuity – i.e. a continuity with the 'pre-communist' past, because they historicise politics and politicise history. They compromised with the previous regime, and thus they cannot present themselves as politicians of morals (although they claim this title, but without too much credibility). Since gaining power they have made a series of unprincipled compromises among themselves, yet they have not been able and ready to compromise with the other elite groups.

The politicians of morals have maintained the previous political approach, even unwillingly, through their black-and-white, polarising and moralising political style, i.e. by deepfreezing the old political divides. Direct political continuity has been reproduced also by the politicians of historical vision, in a completely different way; namely, by preserving the ideological manner and political style of the state socialist regime. Although they challenge the ideas and values of the previous regime – turning them from 'communism' into 'nationalism' – they also reinforce its continuity. This is because they claim a monopolistic representation of general interests on behalf of the nation, in contrast to the so-called particularistic and short-term interests of civil society. The situation is the same with their arrogant and noncompromising elitist political style. Both types of politicians are, of course, negative products of the previous regime – they oppose it but at the same time they continue it. The differences, however, between the two groups involved here are very important.

The politicians of the historical vision are also notorious in governing positions because of their non-professionalism in politics. At the same time, they dislike the 'man in the street' and tend to disregard his/her everyday problems. They concentrate on mythical 'National History' and consider the hardships of the population as trifles and temporary discomforts that should not demand too much effort. Thus they neglect economic and social crisis management and give preference to the restoration of the façade of nationhood (symbols, decorations etc.) and national identity through culture, the media and social sciences. They hover above social reality and feel deeply offended if the suffering population does not appreciate their historical vision and their efforts to return to the 'History That Never Was'. They feel bitter now but expect their roles to be properly treated in the historical schoolbooks of the future.[8]

The politicians of the historical mission have appeared, in Slovakia as 'rational nationalists' e.g. in the person of Jan Carnogursky, since – as Sona Szomolányi presents him – 'His vision of achieving an independent Slovakia was based on a strategy of small steps within the constitutional and legal boundaries.' There have been, however, a great number of 'irrational nationalists' (in this case, proposing my term) in the ECE countries in Slovakia obviously one can think of Vladimir Meciar and the leaders of the Slovak National Party. The analysis of Szomolányi proves that under these political circumstances the actions of rational nationalists may unleash a political change in which the irrational nationalists prevail, although in ECE only for a transitory period:

> Carnogurky's aim to utilise and even consciously mobilise the nationalist movement in order to achieve his supreme goal – the statehood for the Slovak nation – led him often to overlook some acts of nationalist groupings that already trespassed against the legal norms of the democratic order. It may be argued that he helped to unleash nationalist forces assuming that it was possible to keep them under his control. As soon as he realised that somebody else used the nationalist wave for his own interests, even in his own Christian Democratic Movement, it was too late to cope with it.[9]

3 *Politicians by chance* – that group of politicians (the largest in number) which has come to power only because of the chaos of the circumstances of transition. There has been an 'overpersonalisation' of political life in general, i.e. political personalities have mattered more because of weak institutional development, but it has been demonstrated as a problem above all by the 'small men in politics' in particular. Both of the other groups mentioned above have contributed to the alienation of the population from politics to a great extent; but this very 'transitional' third group has virtually pioneered this alienation process, since their striking political inability has been on display all the time. It is marked by an aggressive exhibitionism and an emphasis on personal career, and these become for them the only real public issues. It is very difficult to illustrate this group by mentioning some of their representatives, because they are characteristic, at most, as 'crying mice', small people trying to catch the public eye

by provoking scandals and making absurd declarations in the spirit of social and national demagogy.

4 *The old nomenclatura* – this has survived to some extent and in different ways in the ECE countries as well. In some countries, like Hungary and Poland, there were counter-elites, half-oppositions and reform-wings in the ruling parties, although in Czechoslovakia none of them could emerge under state socialism. Still the old nomenclatura survived also in Czechoslovakia, in Slovakia (Meciar and many others) more than in the Czech lands; and there has been more reform than continuity in Hungary and Poland in the reform-wings of the former ruling parties. In general, one has to look for the succession *process* and not for successor *parties*, because most active former party members can be found in the new ruling parties everywhere in the region, including the Czech and Slovak Republics, and not in the so called successor parties. These people have turned into devoted Christians from devoted communists overnight and nowadays they are often the best known extremists in the right-wing parties, carrying on the behaviour and political culture of the former authoritarian regimes. Presumably the biggest change of the old nomenclatura happened to the Polish elite in the first period of transition, since there was a counter-elite to take over the elites' roles, but also the new Solidarity elite has quickly lost its popularity. Thus, the least compromised and youngest members of the old elite were able to arrange a comeback in September 1993 with a good chance to develop into a professional elite. As Wojtek Lamentowicz argues, however, there has been a continuity in the 'social centralism' (a term coined by J. Kuroń) which means the 'consultations of very influential people on the grounds of social contacts and multiple-year knowledge'.[10]

5 *An emerging new professional political elite in ECE* – this group is a mixture of new and old, with experts and professionals from the previous regime, and new politicians mainly from the younger generation. The latter are on the way to becoming professionals. This fifth group is still relatively small in ECE and has not yet become the trend-setter in politics. As the existence of democrats is not essentially the precondition but the result of democratic transition, professional politicians, too, do not appear in the first period of transition in large numbers; their emergence is primarily connected with the consolidation period.[11]

ELITE–MASS LINKAGES IN THE PRE-TRANSITION AND TRANSITION PERIODS

The composition of the political elite includes narrow party elites and their expert groups. The emergence of a political elite to some extent has normally been connected with the gradual institutionalisation of parties, or vice versa. Institutionalisation as a legal process of establishing organisations was an easier task than the recruitment and socialisation of the political elite, so it came earlier and proceeded more quickly. However, this big emphasis on the elite recruitment and socialisation may give the false impression that the whole story of systemic change – as 'negotiated transition', or 'pacted revolution' – is only about the elite as an actor. In fact, the elite *and* the masses have played very important roles in the whole process. In addition, these roles have been different in the different countries of central and (south) eastern Europe, and thus without analysing and classifying elite–mass linkages we cannot discuss properly the particular elite developments. This is because they have happened in a political space, articulated by external factors (coming from outside a given country) and mass movements. After the collapse of the state socialist regimes and the capitulation of their political elites, the ECE countries were 'forced to be free' and the new party elites were 'appointed', or at least legitimated by the Western powers through governmental and party contacts.

The suddenly 'appointed' party elites, however, were caught unawares by the quick collapse and the capitulation of the state socialist regimes; consequently, they were not immediately able to govern properly. In the West, on the one hand political elites are organised or articulate representatives of civil society, and on the other hand structured civil society appears in the form of social movements. This approach presupposes, as a result of a long historical process, some kind of social dialogue with 'rational' messages coming from both sides. The masses formulate their demands in a politically articulated way and the elites respond to them by proposing new solutions. This articulated relationship or 'rational' partnership has been historically missing in central and eastern Europe, and when it has emerged in recent times it has been very controversial.

The ECE transitions began earlier than those in SEE, and the (counter-)elite–mass linkages had many more precedents. Also, the democratic political culture had more traditions and institutions upon which to build. The populations were more mobilised and therefore the counter-elites more motivated and influenced by the populations. However, the SEE transformations were started only by the snowball effect of the ECE 1989 revolutions. They were violent, ranging from civil war to regular street riots and mass demonstrations, and were marked by elite–mass antagonism, even in the case of the 'new' oppositional elites. The political struggle in ECE has been articulated into an institutional framework and channelled within alternative party programmes, but in SEE it has remained more or less on the level of the inimical clashes. In ECE the elite-mass linkages have led to a more or less articulated political structure with rather clear elite profiles and roles. Being 'gatekeepers' these respond to the social demands in an 'Eastonian' way – i.e. more or less according to the Western model, albeit in its initial stage. In SEE the elite–mass linkages have not only been inimical and antagonistic, but also disruptive or 'revolutionary'. In other words, communication between elite and mass has too often been through the medium of mutual violence. Neither elite commands nor social demands have been moulded into packages of alternative political programmes.[12]

The level of articulation in the elite–mass linkage lies behind the emergence of a political elite as against mass movements – i.e. their emergence as two 'organised' entities with their own feedbacks. This level differs from country to country in SEE, e.g. with Bulgaria much closer to the ECE type and with Yugoslavia as the extreme case of non-articulated politics.[13] Political analysts have taken it for granted that in ECE the masses or movements did not play any important role in the pre-transition crisis, and 'pacts' have been usually treated as a usurpation of historical decisions by elites. However, the judgement above on 'pacts' reflects only the demobilisation of the masses by the new elites in the second period of the transition and extends it to the first period. There was an important turning point in ECE at the time the former ruling elites relinquished power, especially with respect to patterns of elite–mass linkages. Before the power transfer, however, the masses were mobilised and they were active, optimistic and had high expectations. Yet soon after the takover by the new, transitional elite they became bitter, disillusioned and pessimistic, because this transitional elite then tried to demobilise them and to remove them as influential actors in politics. In other words, all party leaderships as political sub-elites want to demobilise the masses in order to give themselves a free hand. At the same time, each sub-elite has tried to remobilise the masses against other sub-elites.[14]

Up until 1990 elite–mass linkages developed in the most organic way in Poland, and an organic counter-elite grew from out of the large mass movement. Yet even the classic Polish case shows the paradoxical situation of elite–mass linkages in ECE. As Wesołowski puts it,

> It is difficult for the elite to discern exactly what society wants ... society itself finds it difficult to define its interests ... the political elite does not receive from society strong and specific signals about what is expected of it. This gives the political elite considerable freedom to choose the precise path of reform and to determine how the 'general will' ought to be translated into detailed measures. The decisions of the political elite are characterised, then, by a high level of social indeterminism.[15]

This argument clearly describes the situation of the (relatively) non-articulated interests on both sides and explains the reasons for the missing social dialogue during democratic transition. Even so – as we shall see later – the political elite has not made real efforts to start any social dialogue.

In Poland, the post-Solidarity period has led to more and more elite games among the fragmented elite groups and to an increasing alienation of the masses from the new elite. History, to some extent, is repeating itself in Poland. The rump Solidarity, as a mass movement and trade union, has been reorganised; yet this time this has taken place against the post-Solidarity leadership. In fact the latter has split up to form several parties. Thus, the articulation process has begun anew in Poland – the mass movement has been using its all-round traditions of popular struggle, even though it has sometimes demonstrated anomical features as well. The party elites are also hopelessly overfragmented. In the September 1993 elections the post-Solidarity parties and their elites lost ground and the reform-wing of the former ruling elite managed a comeback to some extent. But it is still an open question whether this would lead to a further elite fragmentation or to an elite extension or incorporation.

In Hungary, until the late eighties, popular political mobilisation was less developed and less direct than in Poland. However, the social struggle for individual and/or societal autonomy was more effective for it was based on the widening second economy. The emerging counter-elites had large mass support and direct popular connections. Thus they had many followers and sympathisers for their 'culturally' articulated and politically competitive programmes. The years 1988–9 were full of mass demonstrations, pushing new elites into the foreground and giving them the confidence to make decisions. In this way the mass actions prepared the way for official political events, such as negotiations, pacts, and parliamentary decisions. Thus the new political elite's course was almost entirely pre-determined. The Hungarian case, which demonstrates the most articulated elite and movement structure in the democratic transition process, is at the opposite pole to SEE developments. In SEE spontaneous mass demonstrations were only angry reactions and corrections to previous events in formal or official politics; these involved opposition to the results of elections, or to the formation of governments or constitutions. In Hungary the mass–elite linkages were very delicately elaborated before the former ruling elites relinquished power. However, these articulated relationships were fatally weakened, and then almost completely cut by the new, transitional elite; this situation has produced a myth that the Hungarian population has lost interest in politics.[16]

In Czechoslovakia popular pressure and active resistance existed in a potential form, but in November 1989 it became actual when international circumstances changed drastically. For two weeks or so the well-disciplined masses were the prime-movers behind change, being more conscious and determined than the small revolutionary aristocracy itself. They pushed ahead for fundamental changes until these were fully converted into official politics. Mass action then slowed down and soon disappeared. In ECE, however, mass mobilisation was lowest in Czechoslovakia because of the obvious reasons of (1) the quick changes in a latecomer country, catching up rapidly with the transformations of other countries, (2) the interwar democratic traditions, which led back to 'normal' political participation instead of street politics and (3) the increasing conflict between Czechs and Slovaks; and this opened up new directions for street politics, because the masses had become preoccupied with nationalist, rather than democratic, issues. Political demobilisation and fatigue have also appeared in Czechoslovakia with new elite–mass antagonisms, but they have combined with the process of the 'velvet divorce' – i.e. with a mobilisation for the nationalist agenda, this tendency being more apparent in Slovakia than in the Czech lands.

The contrasts between the smoother ECE elite–mass articulations and the sharper SEE confrontations can be seen clearly, not only in the period of pre-transition crisis but in that of the democratic transition as well (although it is true that some kind of deeper confrontation between the new elite and the demobilised masses is now evident in ECE). In the summer of 1990 the political changes in ECE slowed down and it became apparent that the new power elites had neither the possibility nor the capacity to cope with the economic crises confronting them. Political elites in ECE thus began their de- and/or remobilisation strategies. However, the mass movements started to redefine their goals according to the situation then emerging *before* the political elite-groups. This was because the latter were still preoccupied with their ideological fights. Nevertheless, these new confrontations in ECE have not been similar to those parallel events in the SEE countries, because the new mass movements and rising political mass dissatisfaction in ECE have so far observed the normal channels for articulated political pressure. They have not threatened to create public disorder or pursue campaigns of violence.

It has been often predicted that the populist pressure that also exists in ECE could lead to an eruption of public discontent, and then to the 'breakdown of democracy', in a 'Latin-American' way. If democratic order has been jeopardised in ECE, however, this has been due to the actions of the new elites and not the masses – regardless of how dissatisfied the latter have been with the political changes and with the lack of economic crisis management.[17] There are two kinds of populism: (1) classical populism that arises from below, feeds on economic hardships and operates by means of social demagogy (as in Latin America), (2) and gentry or political populism, which is transmitted to the masses from above, from the dissatisfied strata of the traditional political class (who use political demagogy to bring about a redistribution of power and wealth). This second, 'right-wing' type of populism can at present be witnessed in ECE; however, the first, 'leftist' type of populism has as yet not emerged there as a serious threat to democracy, although it has appeared in the other form of a strange 'elite-populism'. The latter has tended to be very detrimental to the process of democratic transition.

THE POLITICAL BLIND ALLEY OF THE TRANSITIONAL ELITE

In ECE the elites of the political transition have usually been *transitional elites*. There has been a permanent effort on their part to monopolise the power they have recently assumed: by excluding the possibility of a wider political elite; by refusing to form partnerships with other elites; and by denying the need for any type of social pact or social dialogue. This has caused a 'premature senility' as a lack of development of the young democracies as well as an early ossification of their political systems. These efforts at monopolisation were first attempted by the governing or ruling elite, but the new opposition has not been exempt from these problems. Systemic change has to be, at least, a threefold process, involving political, economic and social (as well as cultural, ideological etc.) transformations. In the pre-transition crisis political transformation has an absolute priority. This is so that after the fundamental political changes the new political elite can turn to the management of the socio-economic crisis. What has happened, in fact, is just the contrary: 'selfish' politics has led to the neglect of the social and economic transformation to a great extent, and has focused – even in the period of democratic transition – on a long series of ideological elite infights and media wars.[18]

The new ECE democracies were born as elite democracies because the construction of a new democratic order and its institutions began in the political macro-sphere – i.e. from above. Therefore, unavoidably, political transformation has stopped here and half-democracies have emerged. In these, the formal definition of democracy can actually be met (electoralism as a regular, free process entailing competitive elections in order to change the political elites). Yet full and real democratisation has not yet begun, because there has been no substantial definition of what democracy should be. If this had happened organised interests and big social organisations, as well as civil society associations, would have had a better chance of being organically connected with macro-politics through different levels of interest articulation and mediation. In this elite democracy, however, no other actors have been admitted and the process of elite integration or incorporation has been blocked by those in power. After the power transfer between the old and new elites following the first free – so called 'founding' – elections, the new political elite has tried to deepfreeze inter-elite relations and elite–mass linkages. It is clear, however, that only the permanent process of elite incorporation, as an extension of a multiparty system into a 'multi-actor' system, can produce a successful democratic transition.[19]

The party elites have tried to monopolise politics not because of their strength, but because of their weakness. The (parliamentary) parties, as the chief actors in the process of political transition, have been politically very strong; but socially they have been very weak: almost a case of 'leadership but no followship'. This is not an 'anti-party' approach, but a realistic one, which reveals the paradoxical nature of the formation of the ECE parties as a very difficult institutionalisation process. The ECE parties have very small memberships (around twenty thousand, even in Poland rarely forty thousand), weak national organisations and hardly any party activities at the grassroots level. However they have compensated for this weakness by being over-active in the sphere of macro-politics. I call these phenomena *overparliamentarisation* (parliament has not been only the central site of politics, but almost the only one where parties have been active) and *overparticisation* (parties have excluded other actors from political life and have concentrated only on their ideological and political struggles). These phenomena are the most important features of the new internal contradictions of politics, and they have produced an *eliticisation of democratisation*, or degeneration into elite democracy.[20]

Linz's distinction between cultural and organisational continuity can be very helpful in the analysis of this degeneration of elites. After 1989 the biggest surprise for everybody was the extent to which value and belief systems, the patterns of behaviour and the outdated, anachronistic ideas had survived. They had persisted even during the very long period of state socialism, under authoritarian conditions. The persistent survival of the old values has been even more intensive among the intellectuals who have come to power, i.e. among those of the new political elite. This feature has been much less in evidence among the administrative and technocratic elites and the population in general. The first political elites of the new democracies have been trapped, or taken hostage, by the past. The new rulers have arrived with ideas that are too old and/or too abstract. Their 'deepfrozen' values of the past embody a traditional conservatism made up of dogmatic-moralistic ideas posing as a neophyte liberalism.

The confrontation of outdated values and the new realities has been clear from the very beginning of the power transfer. It has provoked a very painful political learning process for the political elite – a sobering process that has warned many either to give up or change ideas fundamentally. On the other hand, for some governing circles and 'conservative' party elites it has produced a voluntaristic and over-historical attitude of despising the facts or the present reality. This syndrome of provoking reality with wishful thinking has been general in the ECE countries and has caused a confrontation with the interests of all social strata. On behalf of History, this conservative attitude has led to a 'societal war'. Certainly, the traditional conservatives in the ruling elites have no understanding for the European reality of the late twentieth century at all. 'Comprehensive planning' requires a strategy, but it is clear that no ECE parties or elites have any viable strategy and they have been unable to produce a realistic long-term vision or blueprint for the future.[21]

The political elites, as Wesołowski puts it, certainly face a 'gigantic task of initiating and directing transformation of the whole societal system'.[22] This task is gigantic, indeed, since the economic, social and political transformations have been running parallel and it has been very difficult to create a harmony between them. The political elites in ECE have shown themselves to be incapable of doing this important job properly, and there is a huge contradiction between their opportunities and capacities. Both ruling groups (the politicians of morals and those of historical vision) are typically comprised of those intellectuals who have a 'Great Design' for the future, or 'Grand Theories' about world history; but they also demonstrate a neglect for details and feasibility, contempt for the masses and popular perceptions, and at the same time they blame people for the slow pace of transformation.

After the power transfer there was a need to change political identities and personalities in order to bring about a permanent adaptation to the new democratic system. However, most members of the emerging political elites failed even in the first phase of adaptation. Oppositional intellectuals were required to re-define their political identities completely – e.g. trade union leaders were to become ministers of privatisation etc. This was not just because of their own changing roles and duties, but also because of the transformation of the whole system, within which they were to play their new roles. The new politicians were required to place themselves unambiguously within the structure of the democratic polity instead of preserving the old identities and patterns of behaviour. Yet in the event most of the transitional elite have been unable to do so consciously – neither individually, nor collectively as a 'self-definition of elite identities'.

As a result of this weakness and uncertainty, the ECE elites are now unable to meet the normative requirements of comparative politics in order to form 'elite cartels' or to pursue 'pactism' with any degree of 'remarkable skill'. Beyond the problem of the first adaptation 'there is a problem of adapting to democratic life from clandestine politics with its rather different requirements and skills'. The ultimate problem for the political elites has been the need to adapt permanently to the changing circumstances and to maintain openness for 'transactions' and compromises. In the new political elite skills for both permanent adaptation and compromise-making are still missing. They think they are entitled to deal with politics because of their moral legitimation or historical mission. Therefore, in most cases they are simply not ready to adapt or to change. We realise now in ECE that democratic transition is a kind of 'permanent revolution', which needs a second opening or, at least, a series of 'transitions in transition'. However, the new rulers have not realised this and, therefore, they have to face a cruel natural selection process instead of the new 'gigantic tasks'. This is indeed a transitional elite which should soon 'whither away', as was the case in southern Europe, where the overwhelming majority disappeared after eight years, i.e. after the third general elections.[23]

This necrology of the transitional elite leads us to the question: who comes after this?

PRIVATISATION AND PLURALISATION – THE 'ITALIAN ROAD'

The future of the political elite will be decided to a great extent by its interrelationships with the other elites, first of all with the economic and administrative ones. The Iron Triangle of Power, not unknown in the Western policy communities, represents a 'coalition' of the political (party), the administrative elite, and the technocratic groups. Such a coalition of elite groups emerged in ECE countries in the eighties, if not earlier. In fact this Triangle works everywhere in modern politics, usually as a combination of the political elite, the techno-bureaucrats and organised interests. The crucial issue is how they can balance, influence and control each other in the decision-making process. In state socialism the nomenclatura principle was introduced to control the party elite itself from above and, through the party elite, the growing staff of experts and professionals in high positions. The organised interests were not independent power centres, but the differentiation between the more subservient administrative and the more active, initiative technocratic elites was extremely important.

With the erosion of state socialism, technocrats and bureaucrats in Poland and Hungary became less and less dependent on the party elite and two major systems of interest articulation emerged more and more markedly: the apparat-pluralism from above and the state-corporatism from below. In the short period of the political vacuum just before the power transfer parts of the administrative and technocratic elites even became independent power centres on their own. The consolidation of the new political elite, however, resulted in many changes and most of the leading experts – including many of those on the middle-level – were purged. This deep cut in the technocratic and administrative elites has also weakened the new political elite itself, because poverty in skill and expertise is one of the major reasons for the low performance of the new regimes. The experts, who 'compromised themselves' with the previous regimes (in fact, in Hungary and Poland they were mostly ideologically neutral, politically uncommitted persons with professional ambitions) have gone to the private business sector and become successful enterpreneurs. Although some process of rooting out the politically most compromised people was necessary and positive, the suicidal act of a deep cut has been counterproductive. It can be seen as revenge on the part of the new governing elite (with its inferiority complex) and as a 'revolt of deputy bosses' (i.e. a revolt of those less talented and more frustrated experts) who have offered their political loyalties to the new rulers.[24]

The control principle based on nomenclatura has been replaced with that based on the clientura. Both principles are aimed at preserving political loyalty, but through nomenclatura it was secured in a rigid, manifest and administrative way, by the visible hand of the party leadership which distributed both duties and benefits. The clientura way is flexible, hidden and lucrative, and controlled by the invisible hand of the new rulers, therefore neither the decision-making process, nor the mutual benefits can be seen. The clientura principle was also known in state socialist regimes, but it mainly oiled the middle and lower levels of politics and the decision-making process in order to make it work more smoothly. It had, therefore, a secondary function – complementary to the nomenclatura on the highest political level and more prevailing on the middle and lower levels of power, where the shortage economy was more depressing and this situation invited people to exchange goods and services for political loyalty – albeit good enough to keep the patterns of behaviour from the 'pre-communist system' alive. It grew tremendously in the late period of state socialism, coming as a prelude to the brave new world of the present 'state capitalism'. The clientura principle belonged to the good old cherished values of the traditional ruling classes, and it is their ideological descendents who now hold the reins of power in ECE. The new ruling elite has consciously created job insecurity among the elite groups mentioned above, so that they can force them into dependent positions. By declaring unconditional political loyalty, the chief administrators and technocrats might be able to keep their top positions. The socio-political conditions for the clientura formation, or re-formation, are embodied in the following slogan of the new rulers: 'Our communist, in fact, was not a communist'. It involves keeping some of the most compromised experts and firing most people who refused to offer the new elite their personal political loyalties.[25]

The Iron Triangle of Power has been reconstructed as the combination of the new political elite with the new-old technocracy on one side, and the new clientura on the other. The first results of a multinational survey in central and eastern Europe have shown, according to Iván Szelényi, that during systemic change elite circulation prevails over elite reproduction.[26] Both arguments mentioned above, however, refer to a larger elite, and therefore it is high time to calculate the size of the different elites and the extent of their transformation. As a rough estimate, big powers have a top political elite of ten thousand, smaller countries around one thousand, and the medium-sized countries about five thousand or below. However, one also has to take into account the surrounding and parallel elites (economic, social and intellectual, which are probably each about the same size). These might leave or enter the political elite proper, because elite change means not only vertical, but also horizontal mobility.

In Hungary, according to the estimation of M. Bihari, the top political elite may number 1,200 people and the middle level administrative-technocratic elite about 10,000 people – altogether some 11,200 people. 'Between the spring of 1989 and the autumn of 1990 some 80–90 per cent of the Hungarian elite was changed. The transformation concerned at least ten thousand persons, i.e. more than ten thousand new persons entered the Hungarian political leadership by the first half of 1990.' The new governing elite went even further, as Bihari argues, and wanted more radical personnel change. It wanted to take over all positions in society to make a spoils system, but it soon failed in this 'societal war':

> Instead of concentrating on the governmental tasks, it carried on the political programme campaign of the 'change of regime'. It fixed ever newer deadlines and events for the completion of the 'change of regime', and extended its political campaigns to ever newer social subsystems. The obvious failure of the campaign-like re-election of managers of enterprises ... the massive change of hospital directors and heads, the scandals concerning the change of university heads and leading bodies, the political campaigns waged against leaders of the press and editorial offices and the subsequent indignation, clearly showed the mistakes of government policy. With these political 'campaigns' (and its campaign launched earlier against the agricultural cooperatives), the government became entangled in political *trench warfare* with almost the entire society.[27]

The upward mobility of some 10,000 people has created ample opportunities in Hungary for building up a whole world of clientura by organising a dependent administration, with personal-political bondage and manifest loyalty. Those who left, however, have formed the hard core of a new – not political, but politically relevant – counter-elite in the economic and social organisations. This is because – according to Ferenc Gazsó – 71.4 per cent of 'bureaucrats' had convertible skills (professional knowledge and languages), compared with the 28.5 per cent of party apparatchiks.[28] This ex-elite has partly joined forces with those other tens of thousands of mid-level experts threatened with job insecurity through the 'societal war' of radical economic transformation launched by the government. In addition it has countered the government attack with some passive resistance. Society has become polarised again into two camps: into those outsiders who offered their political loyalties and obedience for higher positions and those insiders who tried to protect their – more or less deserved – professional positions.

All these processes, however, have been connected with 'pluralisation', i.e. with the emergence of multiparty politics in its initial stage. At the same time, the other major process, involving privatisation as a re-allocation of state assets, has been closely intertwined with these political processes. I can indicate only briefly the major socio-political types of privatisation in order to show their impact on elite changes. In my view, there have been three major types of macro-level privatisation: (1) the spontaneous (or nomenclatura), (2) the government controlled and (3) the foreign capital led privatisations.

Spontaneous privatisation was characteristic of the last period of the old regime and earliest period of the new one. It might have concerned 5–7 per cent of state assets in Hungary and 15–20 per cent in Poland. It has indeed produced a nomenclatura-bourgeoisie, but its scale has been much less than expected. Rough estimates have been extrapolated on the basis of earlier years, and then overgeneralised into a theory of a 'Grand Coalition' between the former Nomenclatura and the new Grand Bourgeoisie. As we have mentioned, convertible skills, managerial positions, market contacts, and networking with Western firms were much more effective in this conversion process than political elite positions.

The new governments stopped this process using legislation. They have re-nationalised state assets and put them under the control of new government-administered agencies (privatisation ministry in Poland, State Property Agency in Hungary). The privatisation has now slowed down and become over-bureaucratised, but more significantly it has turned out to be the most important vehicle for creating a dependent bourgeoisie. The privatisation tenders have usually been won by those politically loyal to the governing parties, with very favourable credit schemes attached. The new owners have acted as political allies, generously financing the new state-parties' and governing personalities' campaigns and other actions. There have been all the nuances between 'white' corruption (exchange of mutual services without money) and 'black' corruption (transfer of money to private bank accounts), with the dominance of grey-white forms. Corruption has permeated, however, public and political life: e.g. state-owned banks have financed the new government-owned media.

The role of foreign capital has been different in ECE countries, but its role has been by far the biggest in Hungary. Therefore the emergence of a 'comprador' bourgeoisie can also be observed in Hungary in the most marked way. The best and most dynamic part of the Hungarian economy has become, at least partially, foreign-owned. This sector offers the best job opportunities, with good, well-paid and prestigious careers for the most talented, relatively young and most ambitious people. This comprador bourgeoisie has a vested interest in representing and protecting foreign interests, and as a pressure group it has a strong capacity both politically and professionally for interest representation.

All of the three above mentioned socio-economic elite groups have played a big political role in democratic transformation, and their influence has been felt in different ways according to their proportionate size in different ECE countries. The broad advance of privatisation and the emergence of new small enterpreneurs have been more sluggish than claimed by the new governments, even though this new middle class could have served as a wide base for the new democratic society. The formation of new economic elites that have significant political influence has been much quicker; thus we can see two kinds of dissatisfaction. First, there are those who expected the total re-allocation of power and wealth among the ruling parties – they are dissatisfied because they feel that they are the real losers in the societal war. These nationalist-populist, extreme right-wing forces are now pushing for the 'second revolution'. Second, there are those who expected real and genuine marketisation, with enter-preneur-friendly governmental policies and politics-free privatisation (a form of 'privatisation of privatisation'). They have either tried to organise political representation for themselves (involving the further frag-mentation of the party system), or they they have turned against politics by abstaining in the elections and offering passive resistance against governmental actions in particular, and elite actions in general.[29]

This dominant socio-economic and political tendency of elite formation may be called the 'Italian Road'. It comprises a fragmented party system and a broadly extended, deeply embedded system of clientura. The major actors in the clientura are the top political ruling elites and their two part-ners: the politically dependent administration and the economically dependent bourgeoisie. There is also a growing private sector, but the public sector is still overwhelming, and its dominant economic and political role has been re-inforced by the paternalist étatism of the new state-parties. There have also been efforts by the new rulers to centralise and strengthen the administration in their drive for total power. Therefore they have allocated more and more resources from the state budget in order to widen and strengthen the central bureaucracy. This is now the mainstream tendency in the formation of the new ECE political elites – i.e. an unholy alliance and partial fusion of the political elite proper with the dependent administrative elite and the dependent new, half-state, half-private bourgeoisie.

However, the fights taking place around the process of elite formation are still going on. The counter-elites in politics, society and the economy have resisted very actively the 'Italianisation' of ECE politics, by which I mean the tendency of the emerging 'partitocrazia' or 'partilitarian rule' which leads to widespread corruption and secret deals between the polit-ical and business elites. This resistance is likely to increase, even in the short run. The transitional elites of the early democratic transition will certainly disappear, but the 'Italian Road' as a blind alley, leading to state dependent middle classes, is still threatening the ECE countries. We can only hope that our elites will be Westernised and professionalised instead of being 'Southernised' and 'clienturised'.

THEORETICAL CONCLUSIONS

There are two extremes to avoid when describing the ECE political elites: the over-rationalisation of elite behaviour on one side, and its primitivi-sation on the other. It would be completely misleading to describe the ECE political elites as rational actors, who negotiate consciously with regard to 'opening' and power sharing; nor do they have an adequate idea about their own interests, opportunities, bargaining power and room for manoeuvre. They have made big efforts to act rationally, but to a great extent they have been captured by the 'false consciousness' mentioned above, and limited by their inexperience and lack of information. It is due to such factors that the new elites have been confined to 'short-termism'. In other words, they have had to react suddenly to accelerating domestic events and to the overwhelming changes in the international system. Yet at the same time they have also been actors. They have directed changes and made decisions about the fates of their populations. This has been done rather arrogantly and thus the populations have not been treated simply as puppets in the historical show of recent re-democratisation. As usual, ECE elites are in a comparatively in-between situation, being less conscious and articulated than their south European (particularly Spanish) counterparts, but more developed than their SEE counterparts.

In conclusion, we can summarise the negative and positive tendencies of the (party) elites' behaviour, all of which have emerged in recent years:

1   Since parties have played *the* central role in democratic transition, indeed, they have also had the biggest opportunity to abuse the newly gained power. Parties were rather unpopular in the pre-transition crisis, but nowadays parties are even less popular, and so are party elites (although some political leaders may be popular as personalities). People feel that parties have not done a good job in creating democratic institutions, and have not shown any particular ability when passing laws for the new democratic polity. In addition, the gap between party elites and ordinary citizens has been growing. As yet the ECE political elites have no strategy for democratic transition and thus they are unable to adjust to its progress accordingly. If democratic transition is 'the phase of acute uncertainty' – or a period of creative chaos – in which democracy is not the only option, then these are the new political elites who are mostly responsible for it.

2   The major parties were originally 'loyal' to the new democracy, but since the collapse of state socialism some anti-systemic extreme right-wing parties have emerged and also some 'communist' successor parties have consolidated their positions. These manifestly anti-systemic parties have not yet threatened the young democracies as such; but what is much more dangerous is the absence of a sharp demarcation line between the nationalist-populist extreme right-wing and their centre-right allies. When the new, inexperienced actors entered the political stage, all of them were naively pro-Europe and pro-modernisation. Indeed, for a while they acted as agents of political education in democratisation, i.e. in the internalisation of democratic values and behaviour. However, since then there has been a polarisation of party and/or political life. The 'conservative',

traditionalist-nationalist parties and their elites have turned, partially and unofficially, against democratisation. As we saw in the late forties, the same claims have re-appeared in the early nineties for ideological hegemony in the education system. The aim here is to re-traditionalise and re-evangelise the young generation. They have also gained control of the media so that they can manipulate and misinform public opinion. Thus, the political learning process of elites and populations has been going on in parallel with the de-democratisation process, which is itself a re-inforcement of anti-democratic traditions.

3   The party elites have also played a decisive role in drawing up constitutions as basic rules of the new, democratic political game. However, the constitution-making process has not been promoted too well. Except for Hungary in 1989–90, most ECE countries have not yet finished this process. The most they have done is partially develop a Bill of Rights and 'little constitutions'. The transformation of legal systems has been very sluggish and contradictory. These have been devised 'empirically', in a 'trial and error' way, because the constitutional coherence would have needed an elite strategy and legislative agenda – i.e. an elite consensus concerning the major rules and values, and an open bargaining behaviour with all partners. It is these features that have been conspicuously missing. Since the 'negotiated transition' the new elites have not been ready to continue negotiations, to make new political pacts, and even less to make new social pacts. In this transitory situation only transitory laws have been passed by the simple majorities in the parliaments, and 'basic laws' have usually been avoided because of the lack of a wider elite consensus.[30]

4   Parties have not performed too well in the first, 'chaotic' period of democratic transition – neither in government, nor in opposition. Considerable progress has been made, but this has been coupled with low efficiency and many setbacks. The setbacks have been incrementally detrimental in the first couple of formative years of the new democracies. The political elites have been angered and frustrated by their failure to control developments and by their lack of popular support. The populations, in turn, have become increasingly pessimistic and alienated from recent politics, although not yet from the democratic polity and parliamentary democracy. Still, it would be a mistake to assess the first years of democratic transition in ECE in a negative way only, and to state that these countries are doomed to failure in the democratisation process. This is far from being the case, but the pendulum has necessarily gone to the other extreme after the long period of authoritarian rule. The external conditions for democratic transition, such as Western attention and assistance, have been much less favourable than they were in southern Europe. The political learning process has advanced, but it has been slower, more painful and contradictory than we thought it would be.

The pre-transition crisis was very different in the three ECE countries, but the above mentioned problems and the emergence and formation of new, transitional political elites are very similar. Using Huntington's terms, we have seen some kind of a transplacement in Poland, where democratisation resulted largely from joint action by government and opposition groups. In Hungary there has been a transformation, where the elites in power initiated democratisation. In Czechoslovakia there has been a replacement, where opposition groups took the lead in bringing about democracy. These terms express to some extent the divergencies of elite actions in the pre-transition crisis and at the time of the power transfer. Nevertheless, they do not explain the present similarities and dissimilarities. For the recent problems the distinction between the disunified elite and the consensually unified elite is very useful. The former indicates the present situation, in which structural integration and value consensus are minimal; the latter could possibly be the next stage of elite formation, in which elites are relatively inclusive, and there is a positive sum game instead of the recent negative sum game.[31]

In east-central Europe – Absurdistan or Amnesia if you like – we have a bright future, but we also have big problems with a chequered past. It is high time to send the transitional elite back to the past and to elect and educate a new professional political elite. This new elite should develop an articulated relationship with organised interests and civil society at large. The next elections could and should do the first part of this job. Yet how to get rid of the newly emerging clientura is still an open question. The invention of democratic tradition, like democratic transition and consolidation as a whole, is and will be much easier for the masses than for the elites.

NOTES

1. See Włodzimierz Wesołowski, 'The Role of Political Elites in Transition from Communism to Democracy: The Case of Poland', *Sisyphus* (Warsaw) 2(VIII), 1992, pp. 77–8.
2. Ferenc Gazsó, in his paper 'Elitváltás Magyarországon' (Elite change in Hungary), *Társadalmi Szemle* (Budapest), no. 5, 1993, describes these three types of sub-elites of the previous political elite and gives data referring to elite recruitment and elite change. See also Ferenc Gazsó, 'Cadre Bureaucracy and the Intelligentsia', *The Journal of Communist Studies*, vol. 8(3), September 1992.
3. Most authors in ECE suggest that the cultural struggle (Kulturkampf) was the decisive factor in the process of party formation, and it was initiated by the would-be party elites. I have dealt with the cultural struggle of elites in my paper, 'The invention of democratic tradition in Hungary', *Budapest Papers of Democratic Transition*, no. 65, 1993, especially with the return of traditionalist conservatism and nationalism among the ECE ruling elites.
4. The theories of Iván Szelényi (the intelligentsia seizing power or the recent emergence of a comprador bourgeoisie), of Elemér Hankiss (the 'Grand Coalition' of old nomenclatura and new bourgeoisie) and of some other

authors will be discussed here only in their recent context, because the analysis of the previous elites would need a whole paper of its own. This would also be true for the government–opposition dimension or the emerging party systems. Therefore I concentrate in this chapter on the ruling political elite, although the problem is more complex.

5   It is not by chance that in the ECE transition there has been no social pact which could organically incorporate middle level elites into the whole political structure. This would require a simultaneous extension of the political elite to a 'multi-actor' system. Western elites are more tolerant politically than their populations, because of their different socialisation and regular exposure to different views (for more on this see John L. Sullivan and his co-authors, 'Why politicians are more tolerant: selective recruitment and socialisation among political elites in Britain, Israel, New Zealand and the United States', *British Journal of Political Science*, January 1993, pp. 52–3). The new ECE elites, however, are certainly less tolerant politically than their populations.

6   The argument for 'postmodern politics' has appeared most definitely in the writings of Václav Havel. However, without any theoretical criticism, one has to note that the very influencial president of Czechoslovakia has become the weak figurehead of the Czech Republic, symbolising the fate of the politicians of morals in general. See Andrew Nagorski, 'Homecoming At Hradcany', *Newsweek*, 1 February 1993, pp. 24–5: 'his return will be nothing like his triumphant ascension to power after the Velvet Revolution of 1989. Nor will he command the same unquestioned moral authority that he did during his early period in power, when he reigned as a virtual philosopher king.'

7   Zdenka Mansfeldová, 'The Emerging New Czech Political Elite', paper prepared for the 22nd annual joint sessions of the ECPR, 17–22 April 1994, Madrid, p. 16. This paper gives a theoretical overview and data on the new Czech elite.

8   I have analysed the first three years of the Hungarian parliament in this respect, see 'Bumpy Road to Europeanisation: policy effectiveness and agenda concentration in the Hungarian parliament (1990–1993)', in A. Ágh (ed.), *The Emergence of East Central European Parliaments*, Budapest: Hungarian Institute of Democracy Studies, 1994. For details about the change of the parliamentary elite, see Ákos Róna-Tas, 'The Selected and the Elected: The Making of the New Parliamentary Elite in Hungary', *East European Politics and Societies*, vol. 5, no. 3, Fall 1991.

9   Sona Szomolányi, 'Old elites in the new Slovak state and their current transformation', paper prepared for the 22nd annual joint sessions of the ECPR, 17–22 April 1994, Madrid, p. 13. This paper is a general overview of the Slovak elite transformation.

10 Wojtek Lamentowicz, 'New Political Elites in Poland', Warsaw, 1993 (mimeo), p. 15.

11 Tamás Kolosi, the director of TÁRKI (the Hungarian institute collecting international comparative data) has summarised the results of the international elite survey in an interview as follows: there were radical elite changes in Hungary in the eighties several times and the positions of the nomenclatura were shaken. The new elite emerged from three groups, (1) from those elements of the nomenclatura with convertible knowledge and skills, (2) from the successful entrepreneurs of the second economy, (3) from the clientura of the new ruling parties (intellectuals as well as entrepreneurs) (see *Magyar Hirlap*, 26 February 1994). TÁRKI also indicates that more than three quarters of managers of big enterprises have been changed in Hungary in the last

four years (*Népszabadság*, 7 March 1994), 5,500 out of 13,500 army officers have left the Hungarian army (see the interview with the Commander of the Hungarian Army, *Heti Világgazdaság*, 5 March 1994).

12   Philippe C. Schmitter and Terry Karl have described democratic transition according to these two axes: elite–masses (state–society) and pact–violence (intensities–numbers). This also gives a clear typology for ECE and SEE countries. See their paper, 'The Types of Democracy Emerging in Southern and Eastern Europe and South and Central America', in: Peter M.E. Volten (ed.), *Bound to Change: Consolidating Democracy in East Central Europe*, New York–Prague: Institute for East-West Studies, 1992.

13   Dimitrina Petrova gives us a thorough description of the elite changes in Bulgaria, with the previous party elite turning towards social demagogy and populism, and intra-fights in the new political elite between 'light blue' (former opposition as liberals) and 'dark blue' (new anti-liberal nationalists) wings. See her paper presented at a conference in Budapest, September 1992 – 'Bulgária: a "permanens forradalom" két éve' (Bulgaria: two years of the 'permanent revolution'), *Mozgó Világ* (Budapest), no. 2, 1993.

14   Edmund Vnuk-Lipinski has shown the different party strategies as well. He writes that in Poland the centre-left parties want a smooth transition and therefore they have tried to de-mobilise people; in turn, the centre-right parties have pushed for 'radical changes' and made efforts to mobilise people (I discuss this as 'populism from above'). See 'A lengyel átmenet paradoxonai' (The Paradoxes of Polish Transition), *Mozgó Világ* (Budapest), no. 2, 1993.

15   Wesołowski, op. cit. p. 82. He emphasises that 'the level of popular mobilisation, which existed in 1980–1, has never emerged again ... Democracy was won in Poland in 1989 without the required new politicisation and activation of population.' According to Wesołowski, the demobilisation later appeared in two forms: 'The first is recurring and intermittent strike activities that aim at securing jobs ... The second psychological stream is the growing disillusionment of the population at large.' (op. cit., pp. 92–3)

16   See Charles L. Taylor, 'Parties in Search of Cleavage: Elite-mass Linkages in Hungary', *Budapest Papers on Democratic Transition*, no. 16, 1992. In fact, Hungarian people are disappointed in the politics of the governing elite and not in politics in general nor in the democratic order; this is probably true for all ECE countries. See the public opinion data in the paper by László Bruszt and János Simon, 'The Great Transformation in Hungary and Eastern Europe, Theoretical approaches and public opinion about capitalism and democracy', in: György Szoboszlai (ed.), *Flying Blind, Emerging Democracies in East-Central Europe*, Budapest: Hungarian Political Science Association, 1992.

Country	A	B	C
Belarus	60	35	46
Bulgaria	42	55	72
Croatia	13	42	73
Czech lands	28	70	85
Hungary	68	43	72
Poland	42	56	69
Romania	35	68	82
Slovakia	47	57	78
Slovenia	46	77	87
Ukraine	55	25	49

The latest public opinion data above suggests that compared to the performance of the pre-1989 governments (*A*), the populations are mostly disappointed in the performance of the present governments (*B*), although they are optimistic concerning the near future (*C*).

The table shows points on a scale between 0 (worst) and 100 (best) for dissatisfaction–satisfaction. The survey has been made as a 'Democracy Barometer' by the Fessel Institute (Vienna), and was published in Hungary by *Magyar Hirlap* (a Budapest daily) on 7 July 1993.

It is clear that the performance of pre-1989 governments means quite different things for the populations concerned. It is usually a general assessment of the state socialist regime; however, in the case of Croatia 'pre-1989 government' means Yugoslavia (Serbia). For Hungarians 'pre-1989 government' does not necessarily refer to the previous regime in general but its last government. This was popular and relatively successful in managing the economic crisis and privatisation, as well as in overseeing the transition of power smoothly. All in all, in most cases the cumulated data show that the populations think the performance of new elites is very much below expectations.

17 See Ellen Comisso, Steven Dubb and Judy McTigue, 'The Illusion of Populism in Latin America and East-Central Europe', in György Szoboszlai (ed.), *Flying Blind, Emerging Democracies in East-Central Europe*, Budapest: Hungarian Political Science Association, 1992.

18 I summarise here the arguments of my paper, 'The premature senility of young democracies: the Central European experience', *Budapest Papers on Democratic Transition*, no. 67, 1993. In the present chapter I develop further my concept of the party elites.

19 See Maurizio Cotta's historical analysis in his paper, 'Elite unification and democratic consolidation in Italy: An historical overview', *Working Papers of Siena University*, no. 2., 1992.

20 I have described 'overparticisation' and 'overparliamentarisation' in detail in some of my writings; for example, see 'The Hungarian Party System and Party Theory in the Transition of Central Europe', *Journal of Theoretical Politics*, vol. 6, no. 2., 1994, and 'The Parliamentary Way to Democracy: The Case of Hungary', in György Szoboszlai (ed.), *Flying Blind: Emerging Democracies in East-Central Europe*, Budapest: Hungarian Political Science Association, 1992. Wesołowski describes the weakness of parties in a similar way: the parties' national structure ends mostly at the level of 'county leadership'. (op. cit., p. 90)

21 See Geoffrey Pridham, 'Coping with the Past, Confronting the Future: Party Strategies in Democratic Transition', a paper presented at the ECPR Limerick conference, 30 March–4 April 1992, p. 6. We can also make comparisons with ECE using the work of R. Gunther, G. Sani and G. Shabad. In discussing the post-Franco party system they say that 'the behaviour of political elites was by far the most important factor in the emergence of the new party system' in general. However, it would be an exaggeration to state for ECE in particular that 'electoral and party financing laws were the product of conscious deliberations and negotiations among party leaders' etc. See their book, *Spain after Franco: the making of a competitive party system*, 1986, p. 395, quoted from Pridham, op. cit., p. 5.

22 Wesołowski, op. cit., p. 96. See also his analysis about the changing political identities in Poland, op. cit., p. 83. See also Irena Jackiewicz, 'The Roles of Polish Parliamentarians in the Post-Communist Years' and Irena Panków, 'The Polish Diet, Political Identity and Responsibility of the Deputies', in Ágh (ed.), op. cit., 1994.

23   See Pridham, op. cit., pp. 9, 16, 24.
24   There has been a big debate around the 'purges'. For some analysts the deep
     cut was not deep enough. See Rudolf L. Tőkés, 'Hungary's New Political
     Elites: Adaptation and Change, 1989–90', *Problems of Communism*,
     November–December 1990; or in a milder way, in his later paper, 'Democracy
     in Hungary: The First Hundred Days and a Mid-Term Assessment', in Peter
     M. E. Volten (ed.), *Bound to Change, Consolidating Democracy in East-
     Central Europe*, New York and Prague: Institute for East-West Studies, 1992.
     See also Tamas L. Fellegi, 'Regime Transformation and the Mid-Level
     Bureaucratic Forces in Hungary', in the same volume. Tőkés has introduced
     a classification of the old, 'holdover' and new elites.
25   Personal loyalty means a return to personal dependence instead of an admin-
     istrative dependence (the latter disappeared to a great extent in late state
     socialism). Thus the new political systems have produced a series of 'one-man-
     shows' and the new leaders have demanded personal loyalty. As an illustra-
     tion of the changes in late state socialism it should be noted that 83 per cent
     of mayors in the small Hungarian settlements were re-elected in the first free
     elections for local government. This is because they were newcomers to local
     power in the 1980s, they were experts (many with a diploma in legal sciences)
     and the new party candidates were much less liked by the population.
26   In the Hungarian context, Erzsébet Szalai has analysed the emerging tech-
     nocracy and its relationship with the other elite groups; she has been very
     influential with her writings about the old and new 'nasties' who have used
     political power to grow rich as quickly as possible. For Szelényi, see his inter-
     view in *Népszabadság* (a Budapest daily, 26 May 1993), where he also shows
     that the real continuity is cultural: namely, those who took an active part in
     the second economy had come from families with marketing traditions. This
     type of indirect cultural heritage, in my view, also plays a very important role
     in socio-political behaviour and it may be the key for understanding the behav-
     iour of the new political elite.
27   Mihály Bihari, 'Change of Regime and Power in Hungary (1989–90)', in:
     Sándor Kurtán et al. (eds), *The Political Yearbook of Hungary, 1991 (PYH)*,
     Budapest: Hungarian Centre for Democracy Studies (with Economix), p. 36.
     See also Fellegi, op. cit., pp. 124–5 and 143–5. I think that both the figures
     and the elite proportions are similar in ECE, but the personal changes are
     different.
28   Ferenc Gazsó, manuscript, quoted from Fellegi, op. cit., p. 138.
29   I summarise here my recent paper, 'Europeanisation through Privatisation
     and Pluralisation in Hungary', *Journal of Public Policy*, no. 13 (1), 1993.
30   In Hungary, Fidesz (Young Democrats) proposed a 'Moncloa pact' of the six
     parliamentary parties in Spring of 1992, for the purpose of economic and
     social crisis management. However, the ruling coalition refused it by saying
     that it would curtail its responsibilities for governing the country. Incidentally,
     Fidesz – a unique party, until 1994 with a membership aged below 35 – is in
     itself a criticism of the new party elites. It has 'no history' behind it, and its
     central values are those of rationality and expertise. For example see Csilla
     Machos, 'FIDESZ – Der Bund Junger Demokraten, Zum Portraet einer
     Generationspartei', *Südosteuropa* (Munich), vol. 42(1), 1993.
31   See Samuel P. Huntington, *The Third Wave, Democratisation in the Late
     Twentieth Century*, Norman and London: University of Oklahoma Press, 1991,
     p. 114, and Michael Burton, Richard Gunther, and John Higley, 'Introduction:
     elite transformations and democratic regime', in: J. Higley and R. Gunther
     (eds), *Elites and democratic consolidation in Latin America and Southern
     Europe*, Cambridge: CUP, 1992, pp. 10–11.

3 Structuring the new party systems after the dictatorship

Coalitions, alliances, fusions and splits during the transition and post-transition stages[1]

Maurizio Cotta

NEW PARTY SYSTEMS IN NEW DEMOCRACIES

The making of a competitive party system after the breakdown of a non-democratic regime, which by definition had suppressed party pluralism, entails not only the creation (and consolidation) of a greater or smaller number of party units with their specific ideological, programmatic and organisational identities, but also the shaping of 'political space' within which these units will interact. In fact, in a competitive system, even the identities of individual party units cannot be fully determined without locating them in the political space, i.e. in the systemic dimension. The notion of political space applies both to the mass and to the elite dimension of politics.[2] At the mass level it concerns the location of voters and parties with respect to the electoral competition. The (unimodal or polymodal) distribution of voters, the number of dimensions (one or more) required to interpret political space, the (greater or smaller) degree of rigidity of voters and parties in moving their positions within this political space, are some of the crucial questions. At the elite level the specific features of political space are particularly relevant for the process of building coalitions between parties for the making of governments but also affecting parliamentary behaviour. It is not unwarranted therefore to say that the features of political space are at least as important as those of individual party units for understanding the working of the new political systems that have emerged after the failure of authoritarian regimes.

The purpose of this chapter is to discuss the interactions between the building of parties and the shaping of political space during the first steps of the new democracies. The empirical cases will be drawn from the three waves of democratisation that have taken place in Europe since the end of the Second World War.[3]

The starting point for our discussion must be the difference between a consolidated democracy and a new one. In the former the features of political space are to a great extent a given. They change only incrementally and gradually (at least until a serious crisis sets in). This is not the case in a new democracy. Under the non-democratic regimes a meaningful political space did not exist. When the transition brings back pluralism it has therefore to be shaped more or less from scratch (or 'revived' from a previous democratic experience). The consequences are also different. In a consolidated system party units are strongly constrained in their behaviour by the existing structure of political space. At the same time the high degree of structuring of political space plays an important role in enhancing the stability of parties. In a new born democracy, since a stable structure of political space is still lacking, the new party units are much more exposed to the uncertainties and vagaries of an ill defined space, but are also to a much greater extent involved in its definition. This is one among the reasons why politics in new democracies is a rather more risky game than in consolidated polities. It is also a reason why leadership skills (and particularly the ability to choose untested paths) may play a specially important role.[4] Obviously political actors are far from being completely unconstrained in this game. They do not control all the factors at play and their resources are limited. To put it briefly one could say that in a consolidated democracy the configuration of the political space is a constant, while in a new democracy it is a variable.

At the mass level the rate of volatility between elections offers a prima facie indicator of the degree of structuring of political space. In a structured political space volatility should be rather low; the dimension(s) of the political space is (are) well defined; parties have a fairly well established and acknowledged position in the political spectrum and the same is true of a majority of voters. Electoral mobility is therefore limited. In a not yet structured political space these conditions do not apply (or apply only in a limited way); as a consequence electoral volatility should be higher.[5] The data of Table 3.1 indicate that with few exceptions in new democracies the electoral structuring of political space is not immediately achieved.[6] In most of these countries high volatility rates can be measured in one or more of the first elections after the restoration of democracy.

If we move from the mass level to the level of the political actors, party splits, party fusions and coalitions provide interesting insights for our discussion. All these phenomena can be linked to the complicated process of shaping and consolidating the new political space.

The first two phenomena (splits and fusions) are placed on the border between the party unit level and the party system level.[7] In the case of party splits what at one point in time were within-party relations between party factions (party unit level) become later inter-party relations between independent parties (party system level). The opposite is the case for fusions of parties: relations between two or more parties (party system level) are transformed into within-party (party unit level) problems of factional coexistence. In consolidated democracies the border line between the two levels is normally pretty well established. We can fairly easily distinguish between phenomena relating to each of the two levels.

Table 3.1 Total electoral volatility after redemocratisation

Country	Elections		
	Second	Third	Fourth
Austria	12	4	6
France	6	20	20
Germany	21	9	11
Italy	23	14	5
Greece	22	27	6
Portugal	11	10	5
Spain	11	42	12
Czech Rep.	28+		
Slovak Rep.	41+		
Poland	70?	25+	
Bulgaria	20		
Romania	30+		
Hungary	23		

Sources: Bartolini and Mair 1990, Mackie and Rose, relevant issues of *Electoral Studies.*

Notes: The elections considered are for Austria: 1949, 1953, 1956; France: 1946b, 1951, 1956 (I have skipped the first election of 1945 and used as second election the November 1946 election); Germany: 1953, 1957, 1961; Italy: 1948, 1953, 1958; Greece: 1977, 1981, 1985; Portugal: 1976, 1979, 1980; Czech Republic: 1992; Slovakia: 1992; Poland: 1991, 1993; Bulgaria: 1991; Romania: 1992; Hungary: 1994. The measuring of volatility is in some cases debatable due to transformations undergone by parties: in the Polish, Czech, Slovak and Romanian cases the values of volatility given in the table marked + are conservative estimates.

Phenomena that entail the crossing of this line (in one or the other direction) are rather rare. Moving the boundaries between the two levels requires overcoming strongly entrenched interests and generally entails serious risks for the political actors involved. In new unconsolidated party systems such a phenomenon of boundary crossing should be more frequent. The distinction between unit and system levels is less clearly defined. First because the (organisational, ideological) identities of party units are not yet strongly defined; second because the features of political space are still in a state of flux. As a consequence problems internal to parties easily become problems of the party system and vice versa. We should have therefore more cases of within-party conflicts becoming party splits, of coalitions transformed into fusions, and of situations where it is not clear whether a political group is really a party or simply a faction.

A few more words are required about coalitions. There is little need to discuss here the very important role that the study of party coalitions has gained for understanding the working of democratic politics (except of course in the rather rarer cases where a two party system format prevails). Studying what types of coalitions are formed, their size and composition, their duration and how payoffs are distributed among partner parties provides important insights into the features of the political space and the dynamics of political life.[8] In consolidated democracies coalitions are generally rather predictable and limited in number. The main reason is that a stable configuration of political space effectively constrains coalition-making by excluding a good number of the theoretically possible coalitions. The most important factors of change in the shape of coalitions are changes in the electoral weight of parties; such changes however tend to be limited.

Coalitions are therefore a reliable reflection of the most important features of political space: (1) its unidimensional or multidimensional character; (2) its breadth, i.e. the distance between relevant parties located at the extremes of the party system (or to put it in Sartori's words the degree of polarisation);[9] (3) and the location of individual parties within that space and their *Koalitionsfaehigkeit*.

In new party systems coalitions will be less constrained and more volatile because a well-structured political space does not exist yet. We should expect patterns of coalition-making to change more easily as a consequence of the changing conditions of a political space in the making, of the search by parties for more favourable positions for political competition, of the more easy birth and death of party units (also as a consequence of party splits and fusions).

In order to understand the making of the new party systems, it makes sense therefore to study together coalitions, fusions of parties, and party splits. These phenomena are much more related to one another when a party system is in the making than in a more stabilised party system. They offer basic information for our keeping track of the changes going on in the crucial years of new democracies. They provide furthermore the starting point in searching for an answer to the question concerning the factors at play in the shaping of the new party systems (and of new political space) after the non-democratic periods. Legacies of the past (originating both from pre-dictatorship democratic experiences and from the non-democratic period); variable conditions of the transition from the non-democratic regime to democracy; new issues emerging with the normalisation of political life once the transition phase is concluded and the implantation of the democratic regime has succeeded: these three sets of factors and their impact upon the party system can be explored by looking at the above mentioned phenomena.[10]

Comparing cases from central and eastern Europe with those of Western Europe, I will try to evaluate how the formation of the new party systems and changes in the shape of political space have been interconnected in the first years after the fall of the non-democratic regime. Attention will focus on the passage from the transition to the post-transition stage. There are good reasons to expect that during this period the configuration of political space will undergo significant changes (with important consequences for the parties and the party system). The transition period is dominated by the problems of extrication from the previous regime and of creating the bases of support for launching the new democratic regime.

Other problems (of a substantial nature like economic problems) may obviously exist during this phase too, but they will tend to be subordinated to the first ones. In fact if this was not the case the instauration of a democratic regime would be endangered. But once the transition has achieved its goals and the instauration of the new regime has proved successful it is all too natural that other problems and issues will come to the fore. The political environment within which political actors (and in particular parties) operate will tend to be therefore rather different in the two phases.[11] Risks and opportunities, constraints and incentives that enter the political calculus of actors will also be different.

THE STAGE OF TRANSITION POLITICS

Given the special conditions of the transition stage and the fact that this stage coincides with the breaking of the previous power monopoly and with the formative period for the new political movements, there are very good reasons to expect that it will have a significant impact in shaping the new parties (party unit level) and relations among parties (party system level). But this means also that it is highly probable that party formations and/or party coalitions will be born (and enjoy an initial success) that are based at least partly on an inherently transient situation. Opposition to the old regime, the need to overcome obstacles faced by the democratisation process and generally to keep the process on the right track are bound to play a very significant role in promoting and keeping together during this period such parties or movements or coalitions of parties. The role of these political formations during the extremely delicate and dramatic months or years of the transition may be crucial for turning the transition to democracy into a success. But once that goal is reached and new issues arise their cohesion, following and prestige will face a serious challenge and might even evaporate very quickly. What previously were factors of strength may turn very quickly into weaknesses.

Grand coalitions of all (or most of) the parties that opposed the previous regime are one of the typical products of transitions. Processes of re-democratisation after the Second World War provide some relevant examples of these 'transition-coalitions'. With the sole exception of Western Germany anti-fascist grand coalitions dominated the transition stage in postwar Europe.[12]

Italy is a very clear case in point. After the internal crisis of the fascist regime of July 1943 leading to the dismissal of Mussolini and the first liberalisation of political life, the rebirth of parties soon followed and with it a grand coalition of all anti-fascist parties was quickly agreed.[13] The main factors driving the parties (the Communist party, the Socialist party, the left liberals of the Action Party, the Christian democrats, the right-wing Liberals) together in spite of their ideological differences were on one side the need to fight against the German occupation and the fascist regime restored by it (the so called Repubblica Sociale Italiana), on the other side the determination to push the monarchy from liberalisation to democratisation and to gain a greater control over the transition process. The grand coalition was also made possible by the fact that none of the parties foresaw as yet the chance of playing a dominant role in the transition; and each party because of the peculiar political, military and territorial situation of Italy controlled some important resources that the other parties did not have. The communists and the left liberals had their strength in the resistance movement in northern Italy, the Christian Democrats could rely on Church support with all it meant in terms of international legitimation and popular following, the Socialist party could boast its tradition as the oldest and strongest mass party, and the right-wing liberals had good relations with the monarchy and economic elites. Moreover each of the parties had some special relation at the international level with the members of the anti-Nazi alliance (e.g. the Communist Party with the Soviet Union, the Socialist Party through the Labour Party with the British government).

A coalition appeared therefore both a feasible and a rational solution for most of the actors. Its basic rules were equal representation of all parties and unanimity in decisions. Different views on a number of questions (in particular on the problem of keeping or abolishing the monarchy and on economic programmes) were temporarily shelved for the sake of unity. But the lack of more substantial political homogeneity within this coalition became a growing problem with the advance of the transition and the more the agenda inevitably shifted from the problem of opposing the old regime and German occupation to the substantial policies of the new democratic regime. Centrifugal forces began to surface in the coalition. The first step (1946) in this direction was the exit of the right (the Liberals). But not much later (1947) a further shift of the main cleavage line separated the Communist and Socialist left from Christian Democracy destroying thus what was left of the anti-fascist coalition. The coalitions that followed after 1947 were consistently based on post-transition alignments.

The French case has some similarities with the Italian case. Here also it began under the sign of the anti-fascist grand coalition. Under the leadership of the resistance hero de Gaulle, the three main parties (Communists, Socialists, and Catholics of the MRP) plus other minor groups built the first governments. The first coalitions were thus the continuation of the alliances grown during the resistance against German occupation. But constitutional issues soon proved much more divisive for these coalitions than in the Italian case. This was partly to do with the important role of a non-party actor (General de Gaulle) having rather personal and obstinate constitutional views of his own, but also with the provision that constitutional drafts should be subjected to a referendum thus encouraging parties to act more uncompromisingly in the Constituent

Assembly (waiting for revenge in the popular arena). The coalition lost its first element at the beginning of 1946 with the departure of de Gaulle.[14] The further split, this time between Communists and the other partners of the coalition occurred in 1947 over matters of internal and external policies (wage policy and Indochina). This split, balanced by the inclusion of the rightist parties, until then kept somewhat at the margins because of their collaboration with the Vichy regime, effectively sealed the end of the anti-fascist coalitions and opened the phase of post-transition coalitions.

The Austrian case, although initially similar, is the least homogeneous of the three. It is true that even here the first period saw a coalition of all parties qualifying for political activity under occupation conditions. Socialists, Catholics and Communists joined forces on a more or less equal footing in the first provisional government under Renner. This coalition survived the first free elections (November 1945), and a three party cabinet under the Catholic prime minister Figl governed for the next two years until November 1947 when, similarly to France and Italy, the Austrian Communist Party (which was in any case a much smaller party than the PCI or the PCF) was left out. The Austrian peculiarity is that the grand coalition of the two major parties, SPO and OVP, did not dissolve soon but lasted until 1966 (when it gave way to seventeen years of one party governments). Austria is the only case where a large coalition originating in the transition years (or at least a great part of it) survived for a rather long period after redemocratisation was accomplished.

That the Austrian grand coalition at least at its start was a solution encouraged by the conditions of transition to democracy is rather clear. The choice of this type of coalition, even when other solutions like a single party government (as was the case after the elections of 1945) or other coalition types (for instance a smaller coalition with the Liberals after 1949) might have been theoretically possible, can be seen as an answer to three specific problems of the Austrian transition from authoritarian rule to democracy. The first is the need to have an authoritative government able to face military occupation and to win back as soon as possible national sovereignty. The second is the need to overcome in the new democracy the hostility between the two main political camps that had destroyed the first republic.[15] To this should be added the political exclusion of the third political force, the Liberal Party, tainted by its collusion with the Nazi regime and its pan-German nationalism which appeared hardly compatible with the principle of Austrian autonomy.[16]

The duration of the grand coalition beyond the transition period suggests that some of the factors responsible for its creation were not just temporary and linked with the transition but long term components of the Austrian political system. The high degree of continuity in Austrian political life during this century is probably a key to understanding this peculiarity. The ability of the two main parties of the first republic to survive as the dominant actors of the second republic faced them with a serious dilemma: either to follow a competitive course and run the risk of reviving the old hostility that had torn asunder the first republic or to reduce competition drastically by way of a stable agreement and thus avoid the risk of an experience which had proved seriously damaging for both sides. Negative memories of the past helped to tilt the balance in the direction of co-operation. But the Austrian problem could not be reduced to a problem of the transition phase: in fact it had to do not only with the instauration of democracy but with the more lasting problem of ensuring its consolidation. The strategy of co-operation between the two main parties could be seen as an answer to the possible resurgence of dangerous tensions.[17] To this should be added that the limited *Koalitionsfaehigkeit* of the Liberal Party was also a factor with lasting effects.

If we move from the level of relations among parties (as is the case with coalitions) to the level of party formations we can find other phenomena that are strongly linked to the peculiar conditions of the transition. It is not uncommon that parties or political movements defining themselves mainly in terms of an opposition to the old regime or conceived as an instrument for solving the special problems of the transition to democracy play a central role during that period very much like some of the coalitions discussed above.

Different as they may be the stories of Solidarność in Poland, of the Civic Forum (OF) and Public Against Violence (VPN) in Czechoslovakia and in some sense also of the UCD in Spain, provide some interesting examples of these kinds of phenomena. Similar to the 'transition coalitions' of Italy and France, these parties or movements after playing a crucial role in the transition faced a major crisis when the transition came to an end. The UCD virtually disappeared leaving behind a few small splinter parties unable to play a significant role in the political game. Solidarność exploded into many groups and parties with very distinctive political and ideological profiles. Civic Forum and its Slovak counterpart Public Against Violence faced serious splits; the first survived deeply transformed and the other practically disappeared from the political scene. As we will see some striking parallels can be found with the three cases discussed above.

The Polish and Czechoslovak cases, more than the Spanish one, show some interesting similarities with the French and the Italian case. Opposition against the old regime is in these cases the dominant and rallying theme of the transition. But in the two Central European cases, differently from Italy and France, this need fostered the birth of one large political movement (Solidarność in Poland and OF/VPN in Czechoslovakia) rather than of a grand coalition of democratic parties. The main reason for this difference lay probably in the extreme weakness, as a result of forty years of communist rule, of a party tradition from which to revive old parties.[18] The party components for building an anti-regime coalition were lacking. The first step is rather a 'non party' mobilisation of public opinion in opposition to the communist regime. The composite ('coalitional') nature of the two opposition movements was however clear from the beginning. Their success derived indeed from their ability to bring together different streams of opposition to the communist regime that had previously been divided. This is particularly clear with the Solidarność movement. Its great success in the early 1980s, which was the basis for its future role at the end of the decade, originated precisely from its ability to overcome former divisions between catholic and secular, working class and intellectual, nationalist and liberal oppositions to the communist regime. Civic Forum's story is shorter than that of Solidarność but even in this movement one can easily detect a 'coalition' of different streams unified by opposition to the regime in power.

Both movements played a central role in pushing the communist regime on the road to democratisation and to its final defeat; they won the first free or semi-free (this was the case of the Polish elections of 1989) elections thus gaining the leadership of the first democratic governments. But victory very soon turned into the beginning of their decline. Leadership rivalries, ideological differences soon started to undermine the unity of the two movements. Solidarność, after having undergone a first major split already at the presidential elections in 1990, had by the time of the second parliamentary elections and the first ones to be fully competitive (1991) broken down into several groupings. Six or seven of these survived as significant players until the elections of September 1993. Their individual political identities and relations among them were now defined predominantly by the new issues of the post transition stage. Obviously some of the problems linked to the legacies of the old regime (economic reform, privatisations, lustration laws) had considerable weight in this phase. This fact coupled with the existence of 'successor-parties' (notably the Democratic Left Alliance and the Peasant Party) produced in the new party system a dividing line, with 'post-Solidarność' opposing 'post-communist' parties. This line crosscut other cleavage lines and to some extent constrained coalition-making between 1991 and 1993. However attempts to bridge that division in order to build majorities able to face other issues soon took place. The 'less dangerous' of the two post-communist parties, the Polish Peasant Party (PSL), became an increasingly more acceptable player. At one point for instance it came to the help of the Olszewski government in rebutting a censure motion in the Sejm and later it lent its leader Pawlak for a presidential attempt to build a more friendly cabinet after the fall of Olszewski. But even the Democratic Left Alliance from time to time, during the Bielecki and Suchocka governments, provided the parliamentary support to sustain the majority on some legislative issues. With the elections of 1993 it has become clear that the cleavage line opposing 'post-Solidarność' and 'post-communist' parties may still play a significant role in defining electoral alignments and coalition agreements. But it has acquired a rather different meaning than the confrontation between Solidarność and the communist regime of just a few years ago. What is at stake now are substantial policies and the societal interests affected by them rather than the regime question. The times of the anti-regime coalition and of the unbridgeable gap between 'them' and 'us' are out.

The Czechoslovak case (which in 1992 became the Czech and Slovak cases) shows a somewhat different type of transformation. Both national wings of the opposition front (Civic Forum and Citizens against Violence) a little after having won power thanks to their identity as anti-regime movements underwent a major split out of which emerged the leading parties of the two new states : the Civic Democratic Party of V. Klaus in the Czech republic and the HZDS of Meciar in the Slovak republic. Even if the two new parties were in some way (the CDP of Klaus more than the HZDS of Meciar) born from the opposition fronts, both meant a clear step away from transition issues into the new post-transition problems. The Civic Democratic Party of Klaus derived its identity mainly from choices concerning the economic strategy. The HZDS on its side had as its central point the (then) dominant question of Slovak independence. Other splinter parties derived from the two fronts were left with little weight in the Czech and Slovak party systems.

Rather similarly to the Italian and French case we have seen in the two Central European countries the crucial role and then the rapid decline of political formations (be they coalitions or movements) based on the fight against the non-democratic regime. In Poland, in a striking similarity with France, the crisis of the transition formation was accelerated by the role of a charismatic leader (Wałęsa as de Gaulle) who, after the restoration of democracy, could not find a satisfactory place in that formation and in the new regime. The main difference compared to the two western European countries lay in the strong comeback of the successor parties which by now (and with the exception of the Czech republic) seems a common feature of post-communist political systems.[19] This has produced an apparent continuity between transition and post-transition: the two sides of the political game seem indeed to be the same. But the continuity is only apparent because the environment and the focus of political competition have deeply changed. It is not a case that now it has become much more difficult to bring together the former components of the anti-communist movement.

The Spanish case deserves special attention among the cases of western Europe due to the extraordinary political cycle of the UCD. Interestingly enough the Spanish transition, in spite of its important consensual aspects,[20] was not engineered through a fully fledged coalition of democratic parties. The UCD, thanks to the crucial role of its leader Suarez in the transition process and to the great electoral success at the first free elections of 1977, was able to play almost alone the governmental game. Given the credit acquired by this party for the smooth transition to democracy, its disastrous defeat at the 1982 elections and its subsequent end as a significant party may appear difficult to explain unless we take into account on one side the special features of this party [21] and on the other the transformations of the political space. More specifically it must be remembered, first, that this party started as an electoral confederation of many parties (or proto-parties) with different ideological identities. Second, the factor that buttressed the unity of these different forces was essentially linked with the problems of transition. It was the need to build a coalition at the centre bringing together the moderate opposition to the past regime with liberalising sectors of the Francoist elite in order to offset the risk of renovating the confrontation between a conservative right and a radical left that had doomed Spanish democracy in the past.[22] It is not unwarranted to say that the UCD embodied within one party the need of a broad coalition that is so common during regime transitions. But it was not so much a coalition against the past regime, but in some sense a coalition bridging old and new, bringing together the moderates of the two camps (and therefore separating them from the extremes of each of the two sides).

The reasons for this special type of coalition had to do with the special features of Spanish history. If Francoism had meant the victory of one of the two camps of the civil war, democracy could not be based on the victory after forty years of the other half of Spain, it had to be founded upon an agreement between the two sides (the agreement that had failed in the thirties). In the first steps of the transition, when it was not yet clear whether the hardliners of the old regime and the more uncompromising forces of the opposition were amenable to play co-operatively the game of redemocratisation, a coalition at the centre of the political spectrum was probably perceived by many political leaders of different colours as the most responsible and potentially successful path to be pursued. Some degree of similarity could be found with the Austrian situation. In both cases the confrontation between the two political camps of the left and the right had degenerated into a civil war (albeit much more dramatic in Spain than in Austria) followed by the victory of one of the camps which had then betrayed democracy. The overcoming of the past had to be based on the bridging of that gap. In a country like Austria, where the political expressions of the two camps (i.e. the Socialist and the Catholic party) had been able, thanks to their tradition of organisational strength, to survive more or less unscathed the authoritarian period, a grand coalition of the two was the most obvious solution. In Spain the much weaker party tradition, especially at the centre and right of the political spectrum, compounded with the much longer democratic interruption made a solution similar to the Austrian one less easy to realise. The creation of a party at the centre of the political spectrum was an easier 'functional alternative' for the solution of the crucial transition problem. But the persistence of the party itself (not just of a coalitional agreement) was bound to be at risk if the conditions that had promoted its formation were to change. Very soon indeed the defeat of the Francoist hardliners and the moderate course adopted by the left created a situation where the risk of a repetition of an all out confrontation between left and right became unrealistic. The reasons behind the UCD became therefore much less compelling and centrifugal forces (organisational tensions, personal rivalries between leaders and ideological differences between clerical and secular groups, between former Francoists and their opponents) could gain the upper hand.[23]

The common feature of the three countries is that the main party actors of the transition have disappeared or transformed themselves into substantially different parties. Not a minor role in this process was played by the fact that all these parties or movements were in some sense heterogeneous 'federations' housing under the same roof quite different ideological streams (and leaders), united mainly by the need to fight against the previous regime (Solidarność and OF/VPN) or to engineer a peaceful transition (UCD). When confronted with the new issues arising after the accomplishment of the transition, internal ideological differences (and personal rivalries between leaders) could not be overcome anymore and unity gave way to division. Along with the crisis of these parties also the structure of the party system underwent a deep reshaping.

Among central and eastern European countries two cases – Bulgaria and Romania – stand out as peculiar when compared to the ones already mentioned. In both cases broad alliances of parties opposed to the old regime were formed during the transition process. This took place at an earlier stage in Bulgaria, where the Union of Democratic Forces conglomerated from the beginning a number of different parties and movements in challenging the refurbished Communist Party (the Bulgarian Socialist Party) which proved able to keep a significant popular following. In Romania the Democratic Convention of Romania was formed only after the first election which saw a débâcle of the anti-communist parties and the victory of the ambiguous National Salvation Front of Iliescu. What makes these cases different, at least in the first phase, from the previous ones is the ability of a party more or less openly linked to the past regime to survive as one of the dominant actors through the transition from the communist regime

In Bulgaria we have the rather unique situation of the ruling party of the old regime being able to survive with little more than a change of name as a major political force for the first two rounds of democratic elections.[24] It is not a case that the anti-communist coalition as well lasted for a relatively longer period than in other eastern European countries. The Romanian situation is a bit more unclear. The first point is that the NSF was a much more ambiguous political creature than the Bulgarian Socialist

Party. In evaluating this party one must take into account its role both as a crucial actor in the destruction of Ceausescu's regime and as an instrument of continuity for part of the old political establishment. The fact that an 'anti-old regime front' did not develop from the beginning may in fact derive from this ambiguity. Only later, when continuity with the past became more evident in the NSF, could an anti-coalition (the Democratic Convention of Romania) be formed. Interestingly enough this ambiguity affected also one of the old opposition parties (the National Liberal Party) leading it to join for some time both the NSF based Stoloyan government and the opposition front.

The confrontation between old regime and opposition forces is thus perpetuated in these countries well into the first years of competitive politics. The reason for this peculiar pattern lay essentially in the substantial continuity in the transition between the old and the new regime. Rather than discussing here the reasons for this continuity (the greater degrees of consent these non-democratic regimes enjoyed compared to those of other countries, the greater weakness of opposition movements?), it is relevant to raise the question whether this pattern may continue into the future. This question goes hand in hand with the next: compared with the other post-communist countries of east-central Europe, are Bulgaria and Romania to be considered cases of delayed development (because they did not break so thoroughly the political linkages with the past regime) or on the contrary as anticipating a common trend (the comeback of refurbished communist parties)? The crucial point if we want to find an answer to these questions is whether the regime cleavage remains the dominant feature of the political space or whether its place is taken by other dimensions. As we will see below there are some signs that behind the outward continuity of the anti-politics a new political space is taking shape.

At the end of this analysis we are left with three exceptions: Germany, Greece and Hungary. In these countries the transition period *per se* appears to have had a much smaller impact in the shaping of the party system. Neither grand coalitions nor political movements or parties specifically geared to facing the problems of extrication from the previous regime seem to have played a major role.

The German case is emblematic. After the breakdown of the Nazi regime political life in Western Germany followed the path of open competition between the CDU/CSU with its allied parties on one side and the SPD on the other.[25] A coalition of all parties opposed to the non-democratic regime was never attempted at the national level.[26] The main political cleavage thus divided the democratic forces. And this structuring of political space lasted in a rather stable fashion into the future.

In a very different historical context the Greek case followed a not too dissimilar path (at least from our point of view). Open competition among parties rather than large coalitions prevailed. The political leader of the democratic Right (Karamanlis) together with his party (New Democracy) took from the beginning full control of the government and of the democratisation process.[27] The choice to avoid a coalition with the left-wing opposition to the dictatorship and to base the first governments on a democratically reconstructed right was probably dictated among other reasons by the need to prevent the resurgence of a non-democratic right which might have found it easier to capitalise on old fears and denounce a coalition 'dominated by the left'. Whatever the motives of Karamanlis's strategy, developments of the following years have shown how effective this course was for the consolidation of the party system beyond the transition stage. Contrary to the case of Suarez's UCD, Karamanlis's New Democracy was able to survive the 'passage to normality' and repeated electoral defeats and to regain power after some years in opposition. In this case very much as in Germany the early shaping of the party system proved to be also the foundation for its long term structure.

In post-communist Europe the Hungarian case seems at first a near replica of this pattern. Contrary to most other cases of central and eastern Europe a united front of oppositions hardly played a role in the transition to democracy. In fact the two main opposition groups parted ways at a very early stage, at the time of one of the first institutional decisions of the transition (the one concerning the type of election for the head of state).[28] And in the first free elections the competition between different anti-communist political formations, the Hungarian Democratic Forum with its allies on one side, the Alliance of Free Democrats and Alliance of Young Democrats on the other, almost overshadowed the other more obvious axis of competition between post-communists and anti-communists.

I have omitted so far the Portuguese case because of the difficulty in locating it among the other cases. Here the unifying effect of the revolutionary euphoria was soon blocked by the dramatic conflicts among the forces opposed to the old regime over the control and goals of the transition process. The initial success of the Portuguese Socialist Party may have been due largely to its ability to appear, a bit like the UCD in Spain, as a middle of the road solution between the two extremes of the conflict. And its substantial decline in the following elections might be interpreted as a consequence of the declining importance of the original conflict among parties. One could say then that the PSP was at the centre of the first structuring of the party system linked to the special conditions of the Portuguese transition. The road from this initial stage to a new structuring proved to be rather long and complicated, partly because the conflict over institutional solutions (concerning mainly the problem of the powers of the head of state) was divisive and partly because the consolidation of a large centre-right party took some time.

From our brief discussion of the cases we have seen that the appearance of broad coalitions or of large movements (mostly formed as a

Table 3.2 Country groupings according to initial pattern of political life

Dominance of anti-old regime political formations		Political formation bridging old division	
Coalition	Party	Coalition	Party
France	Czechoslovakia	Austria	Spain
Italy	Poland		
Balance between old regime and anti-old regime political formations		Competition between democratic parties	
Bulgaria		Germany	
Romania (?)		Greece	
		Portugal	
		Hungary	

conglomerate of different groups) that derive their political identity from the special needs of the transition to democracy is a rather common phenomenon (see Table 3.2 above). These 'transition oriented' political formations (be they coalitions of parties or individual parties or movements) are typically the result of a common struggle against the past regime and are a response to the goals and challenges that are peculiar to transition. Particularly relevant are their efforts: (1) to push the old regime in the direction of (full) democratisation (Poland, Czechoslovakia, Bulgaria); (2) to wrestle the control of the transition process away from other actors internal and/or external (Italy, Austria, Romania); (3) to overcome the unfavourable legacies of extreme rivalries of previous democratic experiences (Spain, Austria); (4) to integrate and find a balance between different streams of opposition (France, Italy, Poland).

Transition politics more easily takes the form of a large coalition of parties when parties with distinctive identities and organisations are able to re-establish themselves as soon as the crisis of the non-democratic regime starts. This is easier when previous democratic traditions have been stronger.[29] When such conditions do not apply broad opposition fronts (like Solidarność and Civic Forum) are more likely to appear. An intermediate situation is that of parties resulting from the fusion of other parties (UCD in Spain) or of electoral alliances within which parties maintain to some extent their identity but lose to a great extent their freedom of action (like UDF in Bulgaria).

Since these coalitions, fronts, and alliances of parties are a response to similar challenges they should face similar crises when such challenges are overcome. This means that coalitions will dissolve and their member parties will follow different political paths (possibly joining different coalitions). In the case of opposition movements, of conglomerated parties or of alliances of parties the need to redefine their political identity is likely to produce splits or even complete breakdown. The consequence is that the more the transition process with its special problems and challenges affected the initial landscape of the party system the more substantial will probably be its restructuring after the first years.

As we have seen there are also some important exceptions to these phenomena. In a few countries (like Germany, Greece, Hungary) the transition to democracy produced much less 'transition politics'. Neither grand coalitions nor ad hoc movements developed. Two factors in particular were at play here: (1) for internal or external reasons the transition to democracy and the achievement of its goals seemed more assured and less dependent on a special effort of the parties;[30] (2) one political group foresaw the possibility of leading the game on its own without the need to ask for the support of others; and the risk of seriously antagonising the other actors appeared reduced.

STRUCTURING THE POLITICAL SPACE AFTER THE TRANSITION STAGE

When the challenges of the transition phase have become less important what directions will the development of the party system take and what factors will affect it? The cases of western Europe provide obviously longer time spans for evaluating the post-transition phase and attempting to answer these questions. In eastern Europe on the contrary we can assess at this moment only the first steps of the new phase. Any judgement will necessarily be more tentative.

By and large the lesson to be derived from the more prolonged experiences of western European countries is that a mixture of long-term political cleavages and of new issues and problems channels the political developments after the end of transition. Return to 'normal life', after the special problems of the transition have been solved or have in any case lost some of their intensity, means in most cases that some 'permanent' (or at least 'durable') socio-political issues and cleavages (e.g. centre–periphery tensions or workers–owners conflicts) regain the foreground that they had lost in the turmoil of the regime transformation. Indeed it was often these issues, not satisfactorily dealt with by the first democracy, that had provided the ground for the rise of the non-democratic regime and that in most cases had been left unsolved by the latter (contributing in the end to its fall). The new democracy soon finds that it has to face them and that it can find here a basis for structuring its new party system. At the same time there are good chances that new issues arising from the specific conditions (internal or external) of the period when democratisation takes place will have to be faced. A changed international context or serious internal problems arising from the need of economic reconstruction or economic reform, or from the definition and implementation of the new constitutional system appear in many cases on the political agenda.

Table 3.3 Main variations at the party unit or party system level before or at the moment of elections

Country	Elections			
	Second	*Third*	*Fourth*	*Fifth*
Austria	limited coalition change persistent coalition pattern			
France	major coalition change	new medium party	new medium party	→
Italy	major party split major coalition change	persistent coalition pattern		→
Germany	progressive absorption of smaller parties persistent coalition pattern			→
Spain	decline to irrelevance of medium party transformation of a medium into a major party	breakdown of major party alternation in government		
Greece	uncertainty in coalition patterns		alternation in government	→
Portugal	split of major party rise of new major party			
Czech Republic	collapse of major party rise of new major party	new coalition		
Slovak Republic	disintegration of major party party fragmentation – uncertain coalitions	comeback of post-communist parties		
Poland	new coalition pattern			
Bulgaria	split of transition party alliance of opposition parties			
Romania	split in governing parties alternation in government comeback of post-communist party			
Hungary				

The rise of new parties or at least significant variations in the electoral following of the existing ones, changes in ideological and programmatic self-definition, splits or fusions of parties, or new coalition patterns are phenomena that often accompany the passage to the new phase. They are the answers to the new political agenda and the indicators of the changing political space. We should not however expect in all cases the restructuring of the party system to be equally significant. Where the need for the party system to adapt to the specific problems of the transition had been less pronounced we should expect also that the differences between the two phases will be less strong (Table 3.3 above).

Whatever the degree of change between the two periods the next points that have to be considered are: (1) what factors contribute to defining the structure of the political space and of the party system in the post-transition stage; (2) to what extent and with what speed the new structure becomes consolidated.

Starting with the cases of Western Europe it is quickly apparent that they show significant variation both from the point of view of the degree of change between the two phases and of the degree and speed of consolidation of the party system.

Of the countries where the transition stage had strongly affected the shape of the party system Italy showed rather soon most of the signs of a significant post-transition restructuring of the political space. The first challenge to the political configuration based on the anti-fascist coalition came from the birth of new parties. These parties (Front of Common Man and Monarchist Party) appeared on the right side of the political spectrum and were not directly linked to the past non-democratic regime; but their political identity was clearly defined in opposition to the anti-fascist alliance. The exit of the Liberal party from the grand coalition and its move to the right was another significant (and connected) step. The two things together left the main non-leftist party of the anti-fascist coalition, the Christian Democrats, unprotected from open competition on its right flank. On this internal situation, that became more relevant as soon as the government confronted the problems of economic reconstruction, was soon superimposed the great international cleavage of the postwar years that cut right down the middle of the anti-fascist coalition. This cleavage produced not only a split in the coalition, but also in one of its most important members – the Socialist Party. The international alignment (with all its political, economic, social and cultural implications) became also a crucial element in the political identity of the Christian Democratic party and its dominance counteracted previous challenges from the right. Out of these new conditions a dominant coalition pattern emerged based on the double exclusion of the left parties linked to the 'wrong' side of the international alignments (PCI and for the first years PSI), and on the right of the parties critical of the original constitutional settlement (Monarchists and Neo-Fascists).

We find then most of the indicators of a restructuring of the political space: new parties, a major split, the redefinition of political identities, changes in coalitional alignments. The result was to be a new and very stable structuring of the party system: coalitional alignments and opposition lines were extremely rigid for the next decades. But the effects were also very important at the party unit level. Particularly relevant was the process of consolidation of the DC as the leading national party which took place during these years;[31] and on the opposite side the downgrading of the Socialist party to the rank of a relatively small (and fragile) party.[32]

It is interesting to compare the Italian case with the French one because of some significant similarities but also some important differences. In France too the international issue put an end in 1947 to the anti-fascist coalition. In this case however the communism/anti-communism cleavage was not enough to produce a strong structuring of the party system. The Gaullist challenge on the right (centred upon the choice of constitutional arrangements with particular regard to the legitimation of executive power), which began to develop even earlier than the international conflict, prevented the consolidation of a strong centre-right party comparable to the Italian DC. Clear evidence of the weak structuring of the party system comes from the appearance of flash parties (the Gaullists in 1951 and the Poujadists in 1956) and from the level of electoral volatility which remained very high (and among the highest in western Europe) throughout the fifties (see Table 3.1). Coalition patterns were determined first of all by the permanent exclusion of the Communist party and then by the more traditional cleavage lines of French society (socio-economic left/right, secular/clerical) which divided what was left of the political spectrum. Institutional conflicts and later decolonisation issues added new complications to this political landscape. The fragmentation of the party system and the need to incorporate in the coalitions, in order to reach a parliamentary majority, parties divided by some of the traditional cleavage lines contributed a great deal to governmental instability.[33] Only after 1958 with the Fifth Republic (and the solution of the institutional and colonial conflicts) did a second restructuring produce a more stable party system structure.

The Austrian case, as we have mentioned before, followed a rather peculiar path. The grand coalition of the two largest parties, a typical solution of transition years, far from being removed in the following years remained in place as a durable feature of the party system. It lasted in fact until 1966 and after a period of one party governments and a short experiment of small coalition it was revived in 1987.[34] The explanation for the extraordinary prolongation of the grand coalition derived only partly from the format of the party system. It is true that only rarely was one of the two big parties able to attain the absolute majority in parliament. But to this must be added that possible solutions like minority governments or smaller coalitions of one of the two big parties with the third smaller one were generally discarded and an alliance of the two big ones preferred. The reasons for this choice require a further explanation: interestingly enough they did not seem to have lost completely their strength with the transition stage. The original need to coalesce in order to preserve the democratic state against dangerous partisan rivalries has increasingly transformed, in a country with a weak national identity like Austria, into a strong association of the two largest parties with stateness itself. Although not absolutely compulsory, an alliance of Catholics and Socialists has come to be perceived as the most 'natural' option for handling the political problems of the country.

In the two cases of Germany and Greece the features of the party system had been affected much less by the need to reach special 'transitional arrangements'. As expected also the signs of a restructuring of political space were much less apparent. What aspects then have determined the main lines of the party system? In the German case competition between SPD and CDU/CSU provided the dominant feature of the political system more or less from the beginning. The complete defeat of the non-democratic regime added to the strong control gained by the occupying powers and the delayed instauration of the new democratic regime created a situation where the need for coalitions of all democratic forces was much less compelling than in other countries and on the contrary the risks for the parties of going alone were not substantial. Moreover the choice of a competitive path suited better the two major parties in their attempt to forestall the birth and strengthening of competing parties to their left (for the SPD) and right (for the CDU). This problem was less acute for the SPD since the international cleavage that had divided Germany in two pieces made a possible challenge from the Communist party much less dangerous than in the past. But it was much more significant for the Christian Democratic party. It must be remembered that the CDU itself was in some sense the result of a coalition of political forces bridging the old confessional divisions and also those between right and centre. To this should be added the fact that several other parties appeared at the beginning of Bonn's history on the centre-right vying for a similar electorate. The choice of a coalition with the other parties of the centre-right area, rather than with the left proved with the passing of time rather successful in defusing their competitive potential. With the exception of the FDP the other parties were progressively absorbed by the CDU or lost their electoral following. The left–right dimension became thus the main factor structuring the German party system.

In Greece the success of Karamanlis' strategy and of Papandreou's response was shown by the disappearance of the Centre Union and by the weakness of the extreme right. The return to power of New Democracy after the three elections of 1989/1990 further underlined that the party system remained more or less on the lines of its early structuring. The traditional left–right antagonism has been channelled in a quasi-two party system which has been freed, as a consequence of past events, of the threats of anti-democratic actors (like the military and the crown).

In the Spanish case the passage from the transition to the post-transition stage coincided with the breakdown of UCD, the disappearance of a centre party and the new left/right, PSOE/AP dualism. The breakdown of UCD was linked to a restructuring of political space that produced a moderate competition between left and right after the ghosts of the civil war had been tamed during the smooth transition process. The success itself of the transition left little space for a centrist conglomerate of parties like the UCD. The factors that had brought and kept together the different groups in that party weakened once the danger of a radicalised conflict between left and right was overcome. The collapse of the UCD coincided with (and explains/is explained by) the great electoral successes of the moderate left (PSOE) and of the right (AP). In the case of the latter electoral success was accompanied for some time by serious problems concerning the political identity of the party (and its transformation from that of a purely rightist party into that of a more acceptable centre-right one). This problem affected for some years the ability of AP to win a majority and gain access to government.

After the downfall of the UCD the Spanish party system acquired from the traditional (long-term) centre/periphery cleavage a special character. This cleavage seriously weakens the electoral following of the (central-istic) right in the autonomist regions of the country and inhibits a coalition of this political force with the regional parties. This situation gave to the moderate Socialist party the chance to become a predominant party (or else to build coalitions with regional parties). Summing up, the main features of political space in Spain were determined by the effective solu-tion of the transition problems and of the legacies of a stormy past, by some long-term factors (the regional cleavage), and by a rather normal left–right alignment now freed from the weights of the past.

For most east European countries it is still too early to judge the struc-ture of political space and of the party system. We can observe just the first steps beyond the transitional period.

In Poland the post-transition phase developed through the 'explosion' of Solidarność, the hyper-fragmentation of the party system and then the great comeback of the 'post-communist' parties in the 1993 elections. The years between the elections of 1991 and 1993 witnessed rather diffi-cult coalition-making processes. A combination of factors were at work. As a legacy of the transition, the exclusion from cabinet coalitions (but not necessarily from occasional parliamentary majorities) of the post-communist parties (SLD and PSL) still held. But the common origins in Solidarność of most of the other parties had lost much of their strength and could not provide a strong and durable basis for coalitions. The political landscape was defined less by opposition to the old regime than by the institutional conflict between (most) parties and the president and by three other cleavage lines, one related to the economic dimension (state intervention versus market-oriented reform) and the other two to the cultural dimension (cosmopolitanism versus nationalism, secularism versus clericalism).[35] Coalitions formed after the 1991 elections have incorporated these features in different ways. After the Olszewki government based on a coalition leaning toward the clerical, nationalist (and anti-presidential) pole, the next coalition supporting the Suchocka government was based on a compromise bridging the cultural cleavages lines (cosmopolitan/national; secular/religious), on a less conflictual attitude toward the president of the republic and on support for continuing the economic reform. The fact that the last coalition has reassembled most of the parties originating in the Solidarność movement does not mean that the politics of the transition period have returned.

This coalition has shown rather clearly that the common ground of the anti-communist tradition could not hold a coalition together for very long. In less than a year dissension over economic problems (public sector wages, privatisation, agricultural subsidies) has demonstrated that the old links deriving from opposition to communism were not enough to hold together the successor parties of Solidarność. The decline of the Suchocka government and then its crisis have also produced renewed tension between presidentialism and parliamentarianism. The decision of Wałęsa to create his own party (with the ominous acronym of BBWR)[36] suggests that the institutional cleavage might prove somewhat like that in the Fourth French Republic a recurrent factor affecting political alignments and coalitions and making the stabilisation of the Polish party system more problematic, not to mention the legitimacy problems it may involve for the democratic regime itself.[37] The great electoral success of the post-communist parties (SLD and PSL) and the débâcle of most post-Solidarność parties in the 1993 elections (magnified by the new electoral system) have transformed again and simplified the political landscape. A clear message of these results is that the political delegitimation of the communist regime no longer entails the delegitimation of the successor parties which on the contrary can profit from discontent produced by the 'economic' transition (privatisations, etc.). Paradoxically enough, it is precisely the fact that the political transition is finished that enables the economic transition (with all its problems) to become the main battle-ground for the parties. When the other cleavages lose ground in the face of the dominant economic preoccupations, the post-communist parties can present themselves as representing the very diffuse interests endangered by a deep and fast economic transition. On the other hand, the reform front remains divided by the cultural and institutional cleavages and cannot build for the time being a unified alternative.

Compared to Poland, the Czech case seems to have been following an easier developmental track. The passage to the post-transition phase was even clearer. The rapid breakdown of the anti-communist movement has left in the Czech part of the old Czechoslovakia a more simple political space than in the neighbouring country. The lack, or the limited importance, of the institutional problem of the presidency (due to the weaker personal role of Havel compared to Wałęsa, and to the clearer constitutional choices),[38] and the weakness (for the time being at least) of the cultural cleavages[39] have contributed to produce a lower degree of fragmentation among the successor parties derived from the dissolution of the anti-communist movement. The economic left–right alignment has emerged as the dominant one and one party, the Civic Democratic Party of Klaus has clearly identified with the market-oriented economic reform line and has been able to inherit a large part of the following of Civic Forum. The Klaus government finds its support in a centre-right coalition (which includes two small Christian Democratic parties) and is faced by a divided left made up of the Communist party on one side and of the recently born 'Realistic Bloc' (an alliance between Social Democrats, the Liberal Social Union and other minor groups) on the other side. The situation that has emerged is almost the opposite of the Polish one: a united and strong (economic) reform front in the Czech Republic, a divided one in Poland; a weak state interventionist camp in Prague, a strong one in Warsaw. The importance of the economic reforms for defining political alignments is the same, but the winning side is the opposite. The different results seem due to the weaker impact of the other lines of conflict on the reform side. The question that remains to be answered in the Czech Republic is whether the alliance of the parties of the non-communist left and the governmental alliance will remain coalitions of distinctive parties or else give way to fusions or the absorption of the member parties into larger units.

In the Slovak Republic the definition of political space seems much less stabilised. After the transition 'out of communism' the country has undergone also the transition 'out of Czechoslovakia' which has produced a new structuring of the party system. The sudden shift of political attention from the exit out of communism to the national problem has quickly destroyed the anti-communist movement (VPN), seriously damaged the Christian Democratic party and favoured the spectacular growth of the new nationalist movement (the HZDS of Meciar). Other parties like the Party of the Democratic Left and more understandably the Slovak National Party and the Hungarian minority coalition have not been significantly affected by the change in the political agenda. The main alignments in the political system have been determined by the national issue. Christian Democrats and the party of the Hungarian minority which were less favourable or opposed to the secession have joined in an opposition front. The Party of the Democratic Left after the initial support of Meciar has also moved towards the opposition. On the other side the Slovak National Party has followed a more uncertain course. After supporting the government it has joined for a short period the opposition and then has moved again in the direction of the government.

Once the main goal of the nationalist movement has been reached dissension has soon emerged in the HZDS and a number of splits have taken place. In the end the opposition parties, from the Democratic Left, to the Christian Democrats, to the splinters born from the nationalist parties have been able to join forces and bring down Meciar's government. This very heterogeneous coalition means however that the nationalist/anti-nationalist conflict remains for the time being the dominant dimension of the party system. Only the winning side has changed. Minority and border problems with Hungary, and now with the Czech Republic, until solved in a satisfactory way, keep that issue alive and could easily produce another reversal in the balance of the two political sides.[40]

Hungary seemed to have entered much earlier into a post-transition political stage than the other cases of eastern Europe, in fact more or less from the beginning of its democratisation process. The governing coalition formed after the first free election was indeed based more upon a cleavage line dividing the anti-communist parties, than upon the opposition to the old regime. To a great extent it was a revival of traditional cleavages in Hungarian society, with Christian and nationalist values against more liberal and secular positions, plus the centre–periphery antagonism between the provinces and Budapest, which provided the basis for a division between the governing coalition of the Hungarian Democratic Forum, the Smallholders Party and the Christian Democrats on one side and the liberal parties on the other.[41] The last years of the Antall and then Boross governments and the elections of 1994 have indicated that even in Hungary the political landscape is far from stabilised. The governing coalition and its leading party have had to face internal tensions and their location in the political space has gone through a process of at least partial redefinition. Clashes over land restitution have led the leadership of the Smallholders party to leave the coalition (February 1992), and this produced a split in this parliamentary party when 35 out of 45 deputies remained faithful to the government. In the HDF the nationalist wing became increasingly suspicious of a move toward the centre of the political space by the party and cabinet leadership and of a possible co-operation of the cabinet with one of the two liberal parties (the Alliance of Young Democrats). In the end the leader of this wing, Czurka, left the party to create the new nationalist Justice Party. The possibility of a tripolar party system with at the centre the liberal parties and perhaps part of the HDF, a post-communist pole on the left and a nationalist one on the right seemed for some time the most likely result. But with the elections of 1994 a situation rather similar to that of Poland has developed: the divisions of the non-communist camp and the costs of the economic transition have favoured the success of the post-communist party, which has become the largest party and is faced by a fairly strong liberal party (AFD) and by a fragmented centre-right area with four smaller parties (AYD, HDF, Christian Democrats and Smallholders).

The Bulgarian and Romanian cases are still rather difficult to interpret. On one side there is the survival in these two countries of very significant political forces with important linkages with the past regime. This raises some special problems. We can ask even whether a transition to democracy has really been achieved. If the answer is negative, the system of political forces is bound to undergo significant changes in the next years. If the answer is positive should we conclude also that the post-communist parties (BSP in Bulgaria and DNSF in Romania) have succeeded in redefining their political identity as democratic parties representing current political interests and are not just the instrument for attempting to save the past ? In this case what will be the political identity of the conglomerated parties which were united by opposition to the old regime? There are in fact some signs that behind the outward continuity of the anti-politics a new political space is taking shape. In Romania the National Salvation Front underwent a split in March 1992. After some time each of the two branches started looking for alliance opportunities in the camp of the new parties. The DNSF of Iliescu has established an increasingly strong alliance with extreme right nationalist parties (like the Greater Romania Party and the Party of Romanian National Unity) which gave their support to the Vacaroiu government (November 1992 onwards). And in July 1993 it has changed its name to that of Party of Social Democracy of Romania. On the other side the NSF of former prime minister Petre Roman agreed first to a fusion with a small Democratic Party (changing its name into Democratic Party-NSF) and has recently established a closer relationship with the main opposition alliance (the Democratic Convention of Romania). The political landscape is thus taking a shape that even if still conditioned by the survival of elements of continuity with the past incorporates already new facets. The new alignments and coalitions seem partly dictated by legacy problems (speed of decommunistisation, privatisation) but also by post-transition cleavages like the ethnic and nationalist one.

Also in Bulgaria features of post-transition politics seems to be emerging. Contrary to Romania the opposition front (UDF) was able to win governmental power sooner (and to place one of its men in the position of head of state) from the former communists. The Dimitrov government (November 1991–October 1992) consisting of UDF politicians and enjoying the support of the Turkish minority party (MRF) embodied more or less the model of the grand coalition of the anti-old regime parties. But the unity of this grand coalition began rather quickly to weaken. Some parties like the Petkov-Agrarian Party and the Social Democratic Party had left the UDF already before the elections of 1991. But more serious conflicts developed during the Dimitrov government pitting president Zhelev against the UDF leadership and producing splits that eventually brought down the first opposition government. The new technocratic Berov government (from December 1992 onwards) has enjoyed the support of an unexpected coalition of the Bulgarian Socialist Party, the Turkish MRF and splits from the UDF (the New Union for Democracy). A mixture of personal rivalries and of more substantial differences concerning economic, taxation and church policies seems responsible for this reshaping of the political space. Particularly astonishing is the co-operation between the Turkish party and the BSP given the strongly nationalist stance opposed to autonomy for ethnic minorities taken by the latter party in the electoral campaign. The explanation for the MRF's behaviour could be its interest in acquiring a pivotal position between the two main political forces in order to protect more effectively its own clientele.[42]

CONCLUSIONS

As expected the analysis of the empirical cases has shown rather clearly that the first years after the return to democracy offer a great variety of forms of transformation both at the party unit and at the party system level (Table 3.3). The birth of new parties, splits and fusions of already existing ones, the redefinition of the original identities, changes in coalition patterns are fairly common events. The frequency of these events shows very clearly that the political space is undergoing significant transformation in the passage from the transition to the post-transition stage (Table 3.4). The following points summarise the results:

1   The first structuring of the party system in new democracies is in most cases strongly influenced by the special problems that have to be faced in the transition period. The need to join forces for displacing the old regime, creating a sufficient base of support for the new one and dispelling the ghosts of past democratic failures tend to favour the birth of specific political formations and/or of special relations among parties (coalitions in particular). Front-like parties or movements uniting very diverse ideological streams and large coalitions are a typical response to these situations.

2   There are however a few notable exceptions where the specific impact of the transitional period is less pronounced and the structuring of the party system is from the beginning determined by other factors. The explanation has probably to do with the fact that in these cases the transition from the non-democratic to the democratic regime did not constitute a special problem for parties (either because it was strongly controlled from outside, or else because it was easily and quickly solved). The relevant empirical cases are Germany, Greece and at least partially Hungary.

3   The first structuring favoured by the special needs of the transition is by its own nature temporary. With the solution of the specific problems of the transition, the aspects of the party system (coalition

Table 3.4 Transformation/continuity of political space between transition and post-transition phases

Country	Time ————————————————————————————>

Austria
  Grand coalition
    Persistence of grand coalition
France
  Anti-fascist grand coalition
    Gaullist contestation
    Electoral volatility
      Anti-communist coalitions
Italy
  Anti-fascist grand coalition
    Party splits – electoral volatility
      Anti-communist coalitions
Germany
  Centre-right coalitions
    Consolidation of left–right competition
Greece
  Left–right competition
    Alternating parties in government
Spain
  Transition conglomerate party
    Dissolution of party
      Left–right competition (and regional cleavage)
Poland
  Anti-communist front
    Dissolution of front
      Party fragmentation. Multiple dimensions
        Resurgence of post-Communism
Czechoslovakia
  Anti-communist front
    Crisis of front
    Redefinition of party identities
  Czech Republic
    Left–right competition
  Slovak Republic
    Nationalist/non-nationalist alignment
Bulgaria
  Communism/anti-Communism cleavage
  Anti-communist coalition
    New alignments?
Romania
  Anti-Ceausescu front
    Split of front
      Anti-communist coalition?
Hungary
  Centre-right coalition
  Liberal/national populist cleavage
    Resurgence of post-Communism

alignments or specific party formations) that had been fostered by the need to face them increasingly lose their compelling nature and come more easily under attack. The political space widens and gains new dimensions. Relatively high levels of electoral volatility will appear; the search for new alignments becomes a central preoccupation. This is a propitious moment for the birth of new parties, the insurgence of splits in the old ones and also for the crisis of existing coalitions.

4   The new structuring of the party system that develops after the transition stage reflects the combined effects of the legacies of the past (previous democratic experiences, long term socio-political cleavages, legacies of the non-democratic regime) and of the new key issues and durable conflicts that are dominant at the time when democratisation takes place.

5   Interesting similarities can be found between countries belonging to the three waves of democratisation we have examined. Central and eastern European cases show however some peculiar features. The limited weight of old democratic parties makes the structuring of the party system more difficult from the start and throughout the two phases. The enormous problems of the economic (and societal) transition from a state to a market economy encourage a resurgence of parties linked to the past non-democratic regime that has no parallel in the western cases.

6   Where a fairly long period of observation is available, that is to say for the countries of the first wave and to a lesser extent for those of the second wave, the structuring of the party system, once having overcome the passage from transition to post-transition, has been fairly rapid and with long-term effects. Where this did not happen (as in the French Fourth Republic) the instability had very much to do with an original dissension concerning the legitimacy of democratic institutions. The existence of a similar problem in one of the east-central European countries we have examined (Poland) and in other ones that we have not discussed (like Russia for instance) suggests that interesting parallels between the two parts of Europe can be drawn also on this point.

NOTES

1   The first draft of this paper with the title 'The new party systems after the dictatorship: coalitions, alliances, fusions and party splits during the transition and post-transition stages', was presented at the conference 'The emergence of new party systems and transitions to democracy: inter-regional comparisons between eastern and southern Europe' organised by the Centre for Mediterranean Studies, University of Bristol, 17–19 September 1993. For the analysis of political developments in east-central Europe I have made large use of the Research Reports of Radio Free Europe and Radio Liberty.

2 The concept of 'political space' as an instrument for understanding the working of party systems has been widely discussed starting from Downs (*An Economic Theory of Democracy*, New York, Harper, 1957) to Sartori (*Parties and Party Systems*, Cambridge, CUP, 1976) to more recently Budge and Keman (*Parties and Democracy: Coalition Formation and Government Functioning in Twenty States*, Oxford, OUP, 1990).

3 The first wave coincides with the end of World War II (and affects Austria, France, Germany and Italy plus, but for a very short period, most central and eastern European countries); the second wave is a purely southern European one (Greece, Portugal and Spain in the 1970s); the third one in the late 1980s concerns the countries of the former Eastern bloc.

4 The role of elites in the consolidation of new democracies is at the centre of M. Burton, R. Gunther and G. Higley, 'Elite transformations and democratic regimes', in the book by John Higley and Richard Gunther (eds) *Elites and democratic consolidation in Latin America and Southern Europe*, Cambridge, CUP, 1992.

5 For a more in-depth discussion of the relationship between electoral volatility, party structuring and democratic consolidation see L. Morlino, 'Parties and democratic consolidation in Southern Europe', in R. Gunther, N. Diamandouros and H. J. Puhle (eds) *The Politics of democratic consolidation in Southern Europe*, Baltimore, The Johns Hopkins University Press, 1995.

6 In order to have a comparative yardstick one should remember that Bartolini and Mair (*Identity, competition and electoral availability. The stabilisation of European electorates 1885–1995*, Cambridge, Cambridge University Press, 1990, pp. 68 ff. and 98–9) calculated an average total volatility of 8.6 per cent over 303 European elections (covering the years 1885–1985) and a somewhat higher average of around 10 per cent for the 1940s.

7 The distinction between the two levels is well clarified in G. Sartori, *Parties and Party Systems*.

8 The bibliography on this subject is vast; the recent books by Budge and Keman (*Parties and Democracy*), and Laver and Shofield (*Multiparty Government*, OUP, Oxford 1990) provide an interesting discussion of some of the main themes.

9 Sartori, *Parties and Party Systems*.

10 I have discussed these themes at greater length in *New party systems after the dictatorship: Dimensions of analysis. The East European cases in a comparative perspective*. Working Paper no. 9, Università di Siena, 1993 and in the chapter 'Building new party systems after the dictatorship. East European cases in a comparative perspective', in T. Vanhanen and G. Pridham (eds) *Democratisation in Eastern Europe*, London, Routledge 1994.

11 An interesting similarity can be found between the points developed here and the assumptions specified by Budge and Keman in their theory of democratic party government. They order 'preferences' of parties and state that 'the chief preference of all democratic parties is to counter threats to the democratic system' while 'socialist-bourgeois differences' and 'group-related preferences' come only after (*Parties and Democracy*, pp. 32 ff.); in a similar way I assume here that preoccupations with the building of democracy prevail until this goal is reached.

12 I will discuss here only the cases of Italy, France and Austria and not the cases of central Europe where the special conditions of Soviet occupation left much less freedom of choice to the political actors and quickly determined the end of democratisation.

13   The first agreement among parties was reached in 1943. For a discussion of this transition stage see Gianfranco Pasquino, 'The Demise of the First Fascist Regime and Italy's transition to Democracy: 1943–1948', in G. O' Donnell, Ph. C. Schmitter and L. Whitehead (eds), *Transitions from Authoritarian Rule: Southern Europe*, Baltimore, The Johns Hopkins University Press, 1986.

14   Philip Williams, *Politics in Postwar France: Parties and the Constitution in the Fourth Republic*, London, Longmans 1958, pp. 14 ff.

15   For a discussion of the linkage between past hostility and later co-operation between the parties Adam Wandruska, 'Oesterreichs politische Struktur. Die Entwicklung der Parteien und politische Bewegungen', in H. Benedikt (ed.), *Geschichte der Republik Oesterreichs*, Wien, 1954; Frederick C. Engelmann, 'Austria: Pooling the Opposition' in R. Dahl (ed.), *Political Oppositions in Western Democracies*, New Haven, Yale University Press 1966, and William T. Bluhm, *Building an Austrian Nation: The Political Integration of a Western Nation*, New Haven, Yale University Press, 1973 offer a good starting point.

16   One should remember the peculiar feature of Austrian nationalism which during the interwar period had proposed the Anschluss with Germany in the name of the common German tradition.

17   In the First Republic a short term co-operation of Catholics and Socialists had soon given way to an increasingly sharp confrontation (on this Wandruska, *Oesterreichs politische Struktur*).

18   Cotta, 'Building new party systems', 1994.

19   The reason has probably to be found in the deep social and economic transformation produced by these regimes thanks also to the destruction of the private economy.

20   This point is discussed in detail by Richard Gunther, 'Spain: the very model of the modern elite settlement', in John Higley and Richard Gunther (eds), *Elites and democratic consolidation in Latin America and Southern Europe*, Cambridge, CUP, 1992.

21   Carlos Huneeus, *La Uniòn de Centro Democràtico y la transiciòn a la democracia en España*, Madrid, Centro de Investigaciones Sociologicas, 1985, chs 4 and 5.

22   Richard Gunther, Giacomo Sani and Goldie Shabad, *Spain after Franco: The making of a competitive party system*, Berkeley, University of California Press, 1988, pp. 92 ff.

23   Huneeus, *La Uniòn de Centro Democràtico*, chs 7 and 8.

24   Bogdan Szajkowski, 'Bulgaria', in B. Szajkowski (ed.), *New Political Parties of Eastern Europe and the Soviet Union*, Harlow, Longman, 1991.

25   See on this point Geoffrey Pridham, *Christian Democracy in Western Germany: The CDU/CSU in Government and Opposition*, London 1977, and Gordon Smith, *Democracy in Western Germany: Parties and politics in the Federal republic*, London, 1986.

26   It must be said however that in the Länder, on the contrary, there were often between 1946 and 1948 governments based on broad coalitions (Hans Georg Ruhl ed., *Neubeginn und Restauration*, Muenchen, DTV, 1982, pp. 497–500).

27   Nikiforos Diamandouros, 'Regime Change and the Prospects for Democracy in Greece: 1974–1983', in G. O' Donnell, Ph. C. Schmitter and L. Whitehead (eds) *Transitions from Authoritarian Rule: Southern Europe*, Baltimore, The Johns Hopkins University Press, 1986.

28   Attila Ágh, *The Parliamentary Way to Democracy: the Case of Hungary*, Budapest Papers on Democratic Transition no. 2, Budapest University of Economics, Budapest 1992

29   Cotta, *New party systems after the dictatorship*, 1993, and 'Building new party systems', 1994.

30 In Germany because it was in the hands of the occupying powers; in Hungary because it was fairly easily conceded by the ruling party; in Greece because the military were looking desperately for a way out of their political involvement.

31 How this could take place is discussed at length in Morlino (ed.), *Costruire la democrazia: Gruppi e partiti in Italia*, Bologna, Il Mulino, 1991.

32 Today after the crisis of communism as an international factor we understand better to what extent the Italian party system has hinged on the problem of a big opposition party deprived because of its international allegiances of coalition and governing potential. This feature of the political game defined for forty years the main frame within which other cleavage lines were constrained.

33 Williams, *Politics in Postwar France*.

34 Peter Gehrlich and Wolfgang Mueller (eds), *Zwischen Koalition und Konkurrenz: Oesterreichs Parteien seit 1945*, Wien, Braumueller, 1983.

35 Stanisław Gebethner, *Political parties in Poland after the semi-free elections of 1989*, mimeo, 1993.

36 The acronym is the same of the movement (the Non-partisan Block for Co-operation with the Government) created by Piłsudski in 1927 as the instrument of electoral legitimation of his authoritarian rule (Joseph Rothschild, *East Central Europe between the Two World Wars*, Seattle, University of Washington Press, 1990, pp. 59 ff.).

37 The potential conflicts between democratic stabilisation and presidential arrangements are explicitly discussed by Juan J. Linz, 'Presidential or Parliamentary Democracy: does it Make a Difference?', in J. Linz and A. Valenzuela (eds), *The Failure of Presidential Democracy: Comparative Perspectives*, Baltimore, The Johns Hopkins University Press, 1994.

38 It is not the case that in Czechoslovakia the constitution-making process reaches its conclusion earlier and more easily than in Poland and the issue quickly disappears from the political scene.

39 There is no real equivalent to the Polish cleavage between nationalist and cosmopolitan orientations, and due to the much greater weakness of the Church the secular/clerical cleavage is also much less relevant.

40 This is indeed what took place in the autumn of 1994.

41 Andras Korosenyi, 'Stable or fragile Democracy? – Party System in Hungary', *Government and Opposition*, vol. 28 no. 1 (1993), pp. 87–104.

42 Georg Karasimeonov, 'Sea Changes in the Bulgarian Party System', *The Journal of Communist Studies*, vol. 9, 1993.

4 Parties and electoral choices in east-central Europe

Gábor Tóka

INTRODUCTION

In this chapter the performances of four east-central European party systems are compared with regard to the 'meaningfulness of electoral choice' that they offer to the voters. This is attempted by analysing several survey-based indicators of patterns in east-central European electoral behaviour. The aim is not so much the testing of well-established hypotheses about the circumstances facilitating the rapid structuration and consolidation of party space in newly established democracies – which do not abound – but description and inductive speculation about possible explanations. In view of the number of indicators that are utilised and the number of parties operating in the four countries, most of the statistical evidence that will be referred to cannot possibly be reproduced here: interested readers can, however, find them in the original conference paper version of this chapter.[1] Since the compilation of that body of evidence quite a number of the parties mentioned in this chapter have experienced mergers, splits, or major changes in their electoral strength. The reason why only occasional reference will be made to these developments is that those patterns of electoral behaviour that are discussed here seem to prevail in more recent survey data too.

THE PROBLEM

Linking the characteristics of party systems to democratic legitimacy has a considerable tradition in the political science literature. Therefore, it suffices here to make only a brief reference to that component of the argument which is relevant for assessing the data presented in this paper. Since (1) representative democracies claim legitimacy partly on the ground of adequately transforming popular preferences into changes (and persistence) in government composition and public policies; and (2) the main democratic channels of political representation are the political parties, it may become a serious delegitimating factor if the party system fails to provide either meaningful, relatively attractive and electable alternatives, or a sufficient degree of government stability (the latter being a prerequisite to establish a visible link between voters' decisions and policy outcomes). This state of affairs is believed to lead some citizens either to vote for extremist parties – cf. Werner Kaltefleiter[2] about the supposed effect of the CDU/CSU-SPD grand coalition on the upsurge of the neo-Nazi vote in the late sixties in the Federal Republic – or to turn their back on institutionalised democratic processes altogether: see e.g. Tamás Kolosi et al.'s hypothesis[3] about the causes of the low turnout in the 1990 Hungarian, and *ceteris paribus* in the 1990 and 1991 Polish elections.

To be sure, the party system may be a merely residual factor in the equation. The recent east-central European data suggest that the citizens of Poland, the Czech and Slovak Republics, and Hungary were markedly more dissatisfied with the functioning of their democracies in the early nineties than the citizens of any EC-country – save Italy – used to be throughout the 1970s and the 1980s. But the correlational analysis of the evidence suggests that the differences in political satisfaction levels between individuals, countries, and various points are most likely explained by the evaluation of economic conditions and prospects, and hardly by political factors.[4]

Nevertheless, some indirect empirical support is available at least for the hypothesis about the delegitimating potential of an electorate's lack of opportunity to vote a party out of office. Throughout the 1970s and 1980s, Italians were reported to be more dissatisfied with the functioning of democracy than the citizens of any other EC-country;[5] by 1991, at least, the Japanese rate of satisfaction with the political system was just as inferior to comparable figures from other Western democracies as the alarmingly low Italian levels.[6] Some Swiss findings also give support to the above-mentioned hypothesis.[7] Finally, Frederick D. Weil's cross-national analysis of time-series data from the larger Western countries seems to confirm that mass support for the democratic regime has much less to do with changes in macro-economic conditions than with the capacity of the party system to 'present voters with clear alternatives, each capable of rotating into office, and none likely to destroy democracy. And governing coalitions should be stable and reflect voters' choices as directly as possible.'[8] Thus, it seems justified to assume that different patterns of party competition may affect the quality and popular acceptance of the democratic regime.

It is therefore taken for granted in the following discussion, and not solely on the ground of relatively plausible argument, that the growth of democratic legitimacy in eastern Europe is partly a function of whether the party system provides a meaningful choice between the incumbents and at least one electable alternative. Furthermore, all this is assumed to mean the following requirements:

1   government and opposition parties should be identifiable as such;
2   the electors must perceive some policy differences between them;
3   the parties must be willing and able to implement the policies associated with them by the voters; and
4   large sections of the electorate must not be deprived from the gratifying feeling that ...
    a)   there is at least one party which represents them adequately and that party is electable within the given international and domestic environment. An electable party is defined here by being pro-system and sufficiently endowed with the virtues of statesmanship and competence;
    b)   those parties to which they would prefer any other alternative have no reasonable chance to become the major government party.

The operationalisation of these criteria is, of course, dependent not only on the chosen theoretical focus, but also on the nature of the available data. Therefore, the details are saved for the discussion of the analysis. I reckon that conditions 1 to 4b are never fully satisfied in the real world: rather, they denote the endpoint of a scale along which we can legitimately rate the existing democracies. Between the two fictitious endpoints I leave a great deal of uncertainty as I cannot propose anything about how these criteria should be weighted in order to arrive at a sensible combined scale of the 'meaningfulness of electoral choice'. Finally, note that the relevance of these criteria for the evaluation of east European party systems can be justified even if they would happen to have no effect on legitimacy at all. For they denote conditions which can be valued on their own right; thus, they can help us to distinguish between more and less attractive party systems.

In the following discussion, the performance of the four east-central European countries are assessed only in regards to criteria 1, 2 and one aspect of 4a. The data come from comparative mass surveys administered to random samples of the adult populations of the four east-central European countries between October 1991 and December 1993. Though a party system's and an electorate's capacity to prevent those parties from winning substantial electoral support which advocate mutually exclusive, strongly controversial or simply untenable goals should, I think, be a key concern in evaluating various patterns of electoral competition, the limitations of the available data prevent any survey-based assessment of the performance of the systems concerning criteria 3 and 4b.

ARE THE EAST-CENTRAL EUROPEAN PARTIES ATTRACTIVE TO ANYONE?

The question posed in the subtitle goes into the heart of criterion 4a, but it is impossible to answer without saying something about the 'relative to what' problem. What we can consider is as follows.

Table 4.1 Representation of the public's views by political parties and non-party groups

Responses for the question: 'Now I would like to ask you to tell me how much each of the following organisations expresses or opposes your views and interests. ... If you think that an organisation expresses your views and interests very well, then give a score of 1; if you think that the organisation is strongly (sharply, completely) opposed to your views and interests, then give a score of 7; if you think that the organisation expresses your views and interests in some respects, but it is opposed to them in some other important respects, then give a score of 4 and so on.'

Party/Group	Ratings on the original 1–7 scale			
	Poland	Czech R.	Slovakia	Hungary
Average rating of the 8 main parties	4.5	4.5	4.4	4.5
Average rating of the most liked party	2.3	1.8	1.6	2.2
The rating of interest organisations:				
(Old) trade unions*	4.7	4.4	4.1	5.1
(New) unions	4.3	–	–	5.5
Catholic Church	4.0	4.6	4.3	4.8
Entrepreneurs' organisations	4.9	4.0	4.7	4.9
Agricultural producers' organisations	4.2	3.8	3.7	5.1
Environmentalist groups	2.7	2.8	2.8	4.0

Percentage of respondents who gave better rating to selected organisations than to any major party (percentage giving equal rating to ... and to the most preferred party is shown in parentheses):

	Poland	Czech R.	Slovakia	Hungary
Old unions*	4 (16)	3 (9)	3 (17)	4 (12)
New unions	9 (15)	–	–	2 (10)
Catholic Church	12 (20)	4 (13)	5 (19)	7 (15)
Entrepreneurs' organisations	5 (12)	4 (15)	2 (11)	4 (15)
Farmers' organisations	9 (18)	5 (16)	4 (24)	4 (12)
Environmentalist groups	26 (31)	13 (32)	10 (32)	11 (22)

Percentage of respondents who gave better rating to at least one interest organisation than to any major party (percentage giving equal rating to any interest organisation and to the most preferred party shown in parentheses):

	Poland	Czech R.	Slovakia	Hungary
	31 (37)	17 (41)	14 (46)	18 (30)

Source: Central European University (1992). *The Development of Party Systems and Electoral Alignments in East-Central Europe.* Machine-readable data files. Budapest: Department of Political Science, Central European University.

Note: * Old unions mean OPZZ in Poland, and MSZOSZ in Hungary. These unions are aligned with the 'post-communist' SdRP and MSZP, respectively. New unions mean NSZZ 'Solidarność' in Poland and Liga in Hungary. In the Czech and Slovak Republics the respondents were asked about trade unions in general.

Political parties are the principal actors in parliamentary democracies anyway. One reason suggested by some opinion polls for the legitimacy problems of the new democracies was exactly the contradiction between this objective characteristic of the political system on the one hand, and the new political parties' supposedly limited capacity to make themselves recognised by the public as the most important channel for articulating the public's political interests and views (see e.g. Attila Ágh on the contradiction between the 'overparticisation' of the east European democracies and the supposedly weak performance of the new parties in interest articulation and aggregation).[9] It was also often suggested that interest organisations could be more readily recognised by large parts of the public as their effective political representative, and therefore a strong reliance on corporatist decision-making processes might increase popular support for the new regimes. One assumption of this argument is clearly contradicted by the data presented on Table 4.1 above.

The respondents in the CEU (1992) surveys were asked to rate various organisations (including the eight – in Hungary, six – most important parties operating in their country) on a seven-point scale according to 'how well they represent their views and interests'. It seems to be true at first sight, that east-central Europeans tend to rate 'political parties' (in plural) rather unfavourably. The average score of all parties was surprisingly similar (around 4.5, that is, unfavourable rather than neutral) in all four countries, and almost all non-party organisations were rated more favourably than that everywhere except in Hungary. This, however, is probably not a legitimate comparison. What a well-functioning representative democracy presumes is certainly not that citizens trust every single party, but rather that almost everybody finds at least one which they recognise as a good representative of their interests and views. Therefore it is more important to look at the best rating each individual gave to any one of the main parties. By September 1992, the country means of this indicator were considerably more favourable in both parts of Czechoslovakia than in Poland and Hungary, but they were around 2 in all four nations: a quite favourable rating both in absolute terms (indicating that the average citizen found at least one party which almost always 'expressed his views and interests well') and relative to the rating given to non-party organisations.

Indeed, in all four countries it was only a small minority (between 10 and 26 per cent) of the respondents who gave a more favourable rating to *any* of the non-party organisations than to their most preferred party (see Table 4.1 for details). Even this minority was provided mostly by the sympathisers of the hardly institutionalised environmentalist groups (on strikingly similar West German results with, in fact, a slightly less favourable rating of political parties see Bernhard Wessels[10]). Thus, the overwhelming majority of citizens tend to find their best political representative in a political party, rather than in other organisations. On this score the east-central European parties seem to live up to their privileged role in the political system. If there is a deep problem with political representation in east-central Europe, then it must have at least as much to do with the interest organisations as with the political parties. Corporatist arrangements may be good for a number of things, but the evidence on their capacity to make east-central Europeans feel better represented seems missing. Though Polish parties may do a little less well than others, the cross-national differences are negligible on this score once we discount the debatable case of environmentalist groups (which are hardly visible on the Polish political scene).

THE IDENTIFIABILITY OF GOVERNMENT AND OPPOSITION

The moral of criterion 1 is that for party attachments to have any political meaning, we must surely expect the voters to be aware of whether they will contribute to the survival or to the downfall of a government, if they vote for Party A instead of Party B. In September–October 1992 our respondents were asked to name the government and opposition parties of their country. Table 4.2 shows the percentages of Poles, Czechs, etc. who mentioned the parties in question as a government or as an opposition party (insignificant parties and parties without parliamentary representation are not shown). For various reasons the Hungarian FKGP and the parliamentary club of the Polish NSZZ 'Solidarność' trade union could, at that time, be just as legitimately called government parties as opposition; therefore they will be ignored below. Apparently, small parties rarely came into the mind of the respondents when they answered this question; and Slovaks apparently saw an incumbent in all parties that tended to vote with the government at that time irrespectively of whether they participated in the government or not. Apart from these technicalities which we just need to keep in mind during the analysis, the first thing to strike the eye is how few Poles identified ZChN and UD as government parties. (See section at the end of this chapter for Acronyms used throughout the chapter.) The relative novelty of the government cannot explain this finding. The Suchocka government was exactly as old at the time of this survey as the Czech Klaus and the Slovak Meciar governments. Since minor government parties (e.g. PL or KLD in Poland, ODA and KDU-CSL in the Czech Republic, and KDNP in Hungary) were certainly less often identified as government parties than the major coalition partners, it makes sense to argue that the peculiarity of the Polish case is due to a certain consequence of high party fragmentation. For in the 1991–3 Sejm it was indeed impossible to create any government in which *the* major partner would have been promptly identifiable, since no party gained more than 14 per cent of the mandates and seven got from 7.5 to 12.3 per cent of the 1991 votes. Furthermore, with minority

Table 4.2 Voters' ability to identify government and opposition parties by name

'Which parties do you think the government (opposition) parties are?'
Percentage distribution of answers by parties, Fall 1992.

Poland					NSZZ				
	KPN	PSL	SdRP	PL	'S'	ZChN	UD	PC	KLD
Government	6	8	2	6	9	40	55	9	25
Opposition	37	12	39	1	2	0	1	24	1

Government parties at the time of the survey: UD; ZChN; KLD; PL (plus several smaller parties not shown on the table).
Ambiguous relation to the government: NSZZ 'Solidarność'.

Czech Republic	KSCM	CSSD	LSU	HSD-SMS	SPR-RSC	KDU-CSL	ODA	ODS
Government	3	5	4	2	2	45	62	92
Opposition	75	44	31	11	51	2	0	0

Government parties at the time of the survey: ODS-KDS; ODA; KDU-CSL.

Slovakia	MKM-EG-M	KDH	SNS	HZDS	SDL
Government	1	4	62	94	58
Opposition	47	78	2	0	7

Government party at the time of the survey: HZDS
Legislative support for the government: SNS, SDL.

Hungary	KDNP	MSZP	MDF	SZDSZ	FKGP	FIDESZ
Government	55	6	79	13	57	11
Opposition	5	58	1	54	10	61

Government parties at the time of the survey: MDF; KDNP.
Note: FKGP officially left the government coalition in March 1992 but three-fourths of its legislators (who were then expelled from FKGP) remained on the government benches and founded an independent caucus claiming the FKGP banner.

Source: Central European University, *Development of Party Systems* (1992).

Note: Table entries are column percentages. Percentages do not sum up to 100 because the frequency of respondents not naming the party in question as either a government or an opposition party, or naming it as both is not displayed.

governments becoming the normal practice, no party could make such a big impression on public policies in Poland as ODS and HZDS had in the last days of Czechoslovakia.

That it is indeed voters' ability to realise the potential or real impact of a particular party on policies which gives us the clue to understand the figures displayed on the table is supported by several facts. The Slovak

National Party (SNS), despite being a minor party, saw its policy on the greatest issue of Slovak politics (the future of Czechoslovakia) eventually adopted and implemented by the major government party: hence Slovaks' marked propensity to discover its presence in government (despite the fact that it was not a government party proper at that time). In Poland, the proportion naming UD as government party went down from 55 per cent in early October 1992 to 49 per cent in the January 1993 CEU survey, whereas the proportion naming ZChN as a government party increased by four per cent at the same time (data not shown). An ad hoc, but over-whelmingly plausible explanation of this would be that in August and September 1992, the main issue was the Suchocka government's handling of some large strikes, and commentators agreed that the tough policy of the government reflected Democratic Union's commitment to balancing the budget, and not the ZChN views. Then in early January came the new abortion law which was arguably ZChN's major policy success and UD's loss of face.

Additional evidence is provided by Hungary. In numerical terms, this country had a less fragmented party system and a much older configura-tion of government and opposition in 1992 than the Czech Republic and Slovakia. Neither am I aware of any marked difference between the three countries which would suggest that majoritarian as against consensual drives are less prevalent in the Hungarian institutional arrangements and policy style than in those of the former Czechoslovakia. Still, signif-icantly fewer Hungarians recognised MDF as a government party than did Slovaks and Czechs with HZDS and ODS. Furthermore, Czechs and Slovaks were more likely than Hungarians to identify correctly the main opposition parties – KSCM (i.e. the Left Block), KDH, and SZDSZ, respectively. Moreover, Table 4.2 also shows that Hungarians were the most likely of all to give clearly incorrect answers. This result again has an easy ad hoc explanation in the fact that Czechs and Slovaks saw more marked and consistent ideological differences between government and opposition parties than Hungarians did.[11] Thus, the moral of the Hungarian data can be summarised as follows: a moderate legislative fragmentation and a majoritarian drive in policy-making does not auto-matically increase the electoral accountability of government. If clearly defined policy differences between government and opposition are in dearth, the government parties may remain unaccountable also for their overall performance, since many voters will not be aware who the incum-bents are.

But it also appears that a majoritarian style of policy making may have payoffs to offer the voters, as I will later argue, particularly for lower-class voters. This gain may probably be realised without being inevitably forced to put up with a high degree of ideological polarisation:[12] parties simply need to be distinctive. The sort of data discussed above surely cannot tell us to what extent Poland enjoyed the benefits of consensual policy-making in 1992–3, and to what extent it was ruled by unaccount-able civil servants. But it does suggest that in addition to making an end to a constitutional deadlock, Slovakia and the Czech lands surely enjoyed a supposed advantage of majoritarian democracy: whoever planned to vote for or against the government (had there been an election there at that time) certainly knew which parties were to be praised or blamed for the government's record and how far this should go.

This was less so in Hungary and much less so in Poland. Note that the percentages of respondents correctly identifying the main government party in each of the four countries show a remarkable similarity to what we know about differences between the four countries in terms of electoral turnout in general elections. To check whether we can possibly speak about a causal relationship here, some regression analyses were carried out (data not shown). The dependent variable was intention to vote if there were a general election next weekend (responses coded on a four point scale ranging from 'surely wouldn't' to 'surely would go out to vote'). The predictor variables were respondents' self-reported interest in politics; his/her ability to identify the government parties (which was measured by subtracting the number of incorrect from the number of correct answers given by the respondent on the question about the partisan composition of government); and social status (a composite index which summed up the information about respondents' education and occupation). With the exception of Poland, social status had no direct effect on the intention to vote once political interest and knowledge about government parties were controlled for. The invariably significant zero-order correlation between voting intention and status (which we can observe in each country) was mostly or entirely the result of the latter's effect on interest and knowledge. Thus, the fact that the status–participation correlation was substantially stronger in Hungary and Poland than in Slovakia and the Czech Republic found its explanation partly in the weakness of the correlation between status and knowledge in the last two countries (i.e. weak compared to the strength of the same correla-tion in Poland and Hungary).

Cross-sectional survey data alone will never be able to tell us whether these cross-national differences have something to do with the whole polit-ical system's capacity to let the voters know which one is the main government party. But this brief detour suggests that probably not only the differential dissemination of this basic information, but also the differ-ences in electoral turnout and the degree of social inequalities prevailing in political participation and knowledge are influenced by the govern-ment's electoral accountability. As long as the 'one person – one vote' principle is to be upheld, this proposition enhances the score achieved by the party systems of the former Czechoslovakia and underwrites the rela-tively bad score given to the Hungarian and particularly the Polish patterns of party competition.

SOCIAL GROUPS AND ELECTORAL ALIGNMENTS

The widespread view is that

> in Poland and Czechoslovakia ... the new parties are just emerging from the unspecified opposition movements. The analysis of the Hungarian party system may offer a short explanation for the genetic defects of the democracy in Poland and Czechoslovakia as well. The common weaknesses of parties are the missing links to the social actors, i.e. [they stem] from the lack of dialogue between the social and political actors which would be the case in a developed liberal constitutional state ... The parties are still 'hovering' over the social and economic realities, they are not yet articulated according to relevant programmes and value systems, which is the major reason for the missing party identities and party identifications.[13]

Moreover, there are at least three rather deterministic arguments which suggest that the new east European democracies cannot help providing a less meaningful electoral choice than consolidated democracies do, and the parties of the region are mere puppets of forces beyond their control. The first argument says that because of the burden of debt service, the dependence on foreign trade, and the disastrous legacy of state socialism, the economic policy options of east European governments are extremely limited: on matters of economic policy, responsible parties cannot offer a real choice.[14] Let me just briefly indicate why I find this argument not entirely convincing. A high foreign debt not only rules out certain policy options, but also creates real dilemmas: e.g. it does make a difference whether a government party intends to be a good debtor or asks for a moratorium. Dependence on foreign trade is simply not a regional but a small-country phenomenon: it is extremely difficult to tell whether, for instance, the Dutch or the Polish government is more constrained in its policies by world recession, changes in foreign-exchange rates, and the like. Finally, though I myself do believe that the legacy of state socialism makes the economic policy options of east European governments skewed in one direction (and in this sense no 'left wing alternative' is viable), I know of no evidence which would suggest that mine is a majority opinion among east European voters. Therefore, I see no insurmountable obstacle for political parties to try proving the opposite (cf. the evidence presented in Tóka ('Parties and Political Choices') about the fairly crystallised left-wing ideological profile of Slovak government parties in late 1992). In other words, even if there is no alternative, parties may still behave as if they were one. Even more importantly, the whole argument about the legacy of communism can be turned upside down. One can easily argue that because of the depth of the economic crisis and the vast concentration of economic power in the hands of the state, a one point change in the government parties' location on a left–right scale makes tremendously more difference in eastern Europe than in the consolidated market economies.

The second deterministic argument says that even if some parties have a fairly distinctive and comprehensive political profile, the voters of the new democracies are doomed to remain largely unaware of that for quite a long time. First, learning takes a long time (i.e. in this case much more than just a couple of months or years; for some evidence apparently supporting this point in regard to Germany see Hans-Dieter Klingemann and Martin P. Wattenberg[15]). Second, since at least at the very beginning of post-communist transition most voters certainly lack any habitual party attachment, the electoral market is extremely competitive and volatility is high.[16] Therefore, the incentives to create more and more new parties abound,[17] and by being expected to learn a little bit about a vast number of new parties, voters may remain fairly ignorant about all.

Furthermore, the third argument adds that even the existing differences between the individual parties are likely to be obscure. Given the relatively unstructured character of post-communist societies and the weak development of the civil sphere, the process of interest articulation is anything but smooth, and hence parties are doomed to be relatively ineffective in interest aggregation.[18]

I have only two objections against the last two arguments. First, they stop short of asking the really crucial question: what sort of factors – other than heritage – can accelerate the structuration of the party system in the new democracies? Second, there are points where the available empirical evidence seems to contradict them. Let me start demonstrating this second point by an intuitively appealing method of measuring whether parties provide for a meaningful choice: namely by looking at the social composition of their constituencies. Unfortunately, mass surveys alone cannot provide a judgement on whether a very close or increasing correlation between social background and party choice is an indicator of democracy's health or – as Seymour M. Lipset insists[19] – of the preponderance of sectionalist appeals, extreme polarisation, and a crisis of democracy. But the kind of systematic data from which we know that the US Republicans keep on nominating Black candidates, whereas the Bolsheviks did not try to attract *kulak* voters in the 1918 elections to the Constituent Assembly is absent in the case of the new east European parties. What we can try to assess is whether the correlations between social background and party preferences in east-central Europe are entirely due to the presence of some parties that have no visible policy commitments outside a narrowly defined issue domain and no voting support outside a correspondingly isolated section of the electorate. Such parties may be available for offering their legislative support for policies which would otherwise never obtain majority support in exchange for such concessions that are also disagreeable to solid majorities. Thus we have four questions to be answered:

1 Do the differences in the social basis (however little these differences may be) of the various parties correspond in some meaningful way to the general understanding we have about the profile of these parties?
2 How strong are the correlations between social background and party preference?
3 Do these correlations get stronger as the party systems become more mature?
4 To what extent are these correlations due to the presence of a few unambiguously sectional parties?

The statistical evidence on these scores was presented in Tóka.[20] The short answers are, respectively, 'yes', 'just about as strong as in the Western democracies', 'they are stable or decreasing over time', and 'not exclusively'. There were not many surprises in the details. In the 1992/1993 CEU surveys, only one of the MKM-E-MLS supporters in Slovakia failed to declare a Hungarian ethnicity, and the HSD-SMS supporters in the Czech Republic were equally exclusively found only among Moravian residents. With the exception of Slovakia, peasants tend to vote either for peasant parties (PSL, PL, 'Solidarność' RI, etc. in Poland, the Czech Agrarian Party incorporated in LSU, and FKGP in Hungary) or for Christian parties; the latter are supported by frequent church-goers, who, in turn, are over-represented among farmers and the elderly. The existence of these relatively minor parties accounts for quite a good deal of the correlation between party choice on the one hand, and ethnicity, religiosity and place of residence on the other. The Christian parties of the region have virtually no (i.e. invariably between 0 and 1 per cent) electoral support among those who never attend church, and only the Czech People's Party (KDU-CSL) would barely pass the electoral threshold if it had as much electoral support in the total population as among those who attend church only irregularly (i.e. only a few times a year or less frequently). In Poland, Slovakia and Hungary only about 3 per cent of these voters support the Christian parties (the Hungarian MDF and FKGP are not counted here as Christian parties because they have a much more complex appeal and far more electoral support among irregular church-goers and the non-religious than the cited clerical parties).

In this period KDU-CSL attracted some 30 to 40 per cent of devout Czechs, KDNP some 20 of the Hungarian, and KDH and SKDH together about 35 per cent of Slovakian regular church-goers. In Poland the electorate of the Christian parties (ZChN, SLChD, PChD, ChD) was somewhat less skewed towards a narrow sectional base, but this difference may simply be due to the fact that our church-attendance variable may be unable to discriminate the truly devout part of the population in a country where about 70 per cent of the electorate are monthly church-goers. Thus, the east-central European Christian parties appear to have had a usually more sectional base than their sister parties in most of continental Europe.

Is this sectionalism also visible in their popular perception? As shown by Tóka ('Parties and Political choices') by Fall 1992, all four of the main Christian parties were believed by the public to be committed to both market-oriented reforms and to the welfare state, but – precisely reflecting the known differences between the policies of these parties – Slovaks felt KDH to be more committed to the first, whereas Hungarians saw KDNP laying more emphasis on left-wing economic goals. Czechs and Poles found ZChN and KDU-CSL relatively centrist in this respect. But the fact of the matter is that in each country only a relatively small section of the public attributed any distinctive views to these parties on socio-economic issues and they were overwhelmingly associated with goals in the moral domain (moral renewal, increasing church influence, banning abortion). Thus, the limited electoral base and strength of these parties indeed reflects a relatively sectional appeal.

The picture about the agrarian parties shows much more cross-national variation and somewhat fewer signs of an exclusively sectional appeal. In Slovakia, no significant peasant party came into being and HZDS appears to have (or at least, to have had) a large majority in the farming population. In the Czech Republic, the smallish agrarian party became incorporated into LSU (i.e. into a permanent coalition with the Greens and the Socialist Party). The Small-Holders Party (FKGP) plays a controversial role in Hungarian politics, but with its complex appeal to anti-communist, nationalist, Christian, and to generally pro-market, but in particular agrarian-protectionist sentiments, it can in no way be described as a truly sectional party.

In Poland, the agrarian population is larger, and not only small-scale farming, but also the separate political representation of agrarian interests maintained a continuity throughout the communist period. Moreover, the farming population suffered an exceptionally large (supposedly about 50 per cent) decline of real income in the first years of transition. Therefore it is hardly surprising that the Polish peasant parties have a more sectional appeal than their Czech and Hungarian counterparts. However, a move away from an intransigent sectionalist politics seems already visible. The party fragmentation of the agrarian scene dramatically decreased after the 1991 election, with PSL destined to emerge as the unitary representative of agrarian interests after the 1993 election. PSL thus gained more space to compromise on questions of agrarian policy. Getting rid of its former 'blockflute', or satellite party, image[21] PSL also increased its legitimacy and *Koalitionsfähigkeit* (cf. the designation of party leader Pawlak for premier in June 1992 by President Wałęsa).

By and large, electoral support for these three agrarian parties (PSL, LSU and FKGP) in the non-farming population was pretty much above the 50 per cent of their national total, and even in larger cities (i.e. more than 100,000 inhabitants) they attracted around 2–3 per cent of the party preferences. Even so, their electoral support seems to be more heavily concentrated in the rural areas than that of the Scandinavian agrarian parties.

The point to be emphasised at this stage is that their existence cannot explain everything from the correlations between social background and voting patterns in east-central Europe. Parties with a clear-cut appeal to the pride and pains of the working class (i.e. NSZZ 'Solidarność' and KPN in Poland, and to some extent HZDS in Slovakia) consistently had a predominantly working-class electorate. Parties contesting the pro-market field – UD, KLD, PC, ODS, ODA, OH, SKD (i.e. the ex-ODU), and MDF – drew a disproportionately large group of their supporters from among white-collar workers and large-town residents. This, however, was not necessarily the case with the Hungarian liberal parties. The reasons for their deviation in terms of their class base were discussed in Tóka, 'Parties and Political Choices'. Here it is enough to take a note of the fact that by Fall 1992 they were the only significant pro-market parties in the region who had not yet been involved in any government.

Another factor which frequently produces correlations between the social background of voters and their party preferences in east-central Europe is age. Young people rarely vote either for the post-communist or for the Christian parties; rather, they prefer the secular anti-statist parties (KLD in Poland, OH, ODA, ODS in Bohemia, FIDESZ and SZDSZ in Hungary) or parties known for their troublesome nationalist radicalism (the Polish KPN, the Czech SPR-RSC, and the Slovak SNS). Most probably the latter parties do better among lower-class people at least partly because of their relatively low social acceptability in the eyes of the more educated voters (as was noted above, this may be only a part of the story in the case of KPN which also has an explicit appeal to industrial workers).

Therefore, there is little in the direction of the links between social groups and parties that would appear chaotic or abnormal. To be sure, there is at least one peculiar phenomenon in these relationships, the 'negative class voting' which often occurs in the case of the ideologically left-wing parties of eastern Europe. Up to 1994, in all four east-central European countries save the Czech Republic, where the white-collar vote became almost monopolised by the direct successors of Civic Forum (ODS, ODA, OH), both post-communist and social democratic (i.e. CSSD in Bohemia and SDSS in Slovakia) parties had more support among white-collar workers than in any other occupational group. The parallel to the East German case is obvious (on the former DDR, see Dalton, 1992[22]). But the puzzle is real only in the case of the Czech and Slovak social democrats. At this point, it is enough to note that the social composition of the post-communist vote reflects hardly more than the social composition of the ruling parties in the last forty years. After controlling for former party membership in a multivariate design, not a single socio-demographic variable appeared to have a consistent impact on post-communist party preference in any of the four countries (data not shown). Table 4.3 shows the relationship between former Communist party membership (as reported by the respondents in the interviews) and current post-communist party preference in five successive comparative surveys.

Again, the important thing to note is the initial existence and then the move away from an at least partly sectional electoral base. At the beginning of our period (in 1991–2) these parties had a more or less similar level of support in each of the four countries,[23] and drew fifty per cent or more of their supporters from among former party members. When some of these parties started to gain more support, their percentage gains tended to be even bigger among former party members than in the total population (see the Polish, Slovak, and the Hungarian figures in Table 4.3). Nevertheless, as a by-product of these electoral gains, the portion and the relative over-representation of former party members in their electorate decreased in each of the three countries where these parties increased their electoral strength. By early 1994, only the Czech post-communists (themselves going through a split of the original party into three successor organisations and heavily losing votes to the social democrats) had such a sectional base as before. On the other extreme, a May 1994 exit poll suggested that among 18–40 year old voters the Hungarian Socialists already had more support in the industrial working class than in any other occupational categories. Thus, the puzzle of negative class voting may already wither away, and it had never been more than apparent concerning the post-communist parties.

But even if the links between specific parties and groups look quite ordinary and meaningful, the strength of these links may still be abnormally weak. In other words, a randomly selected voter's party preference may be virtually unpredictable from his occupation, religiosity, etc. Whether this is so in east-central Europe we can check by comparing the strength of association between selected variables and party choice in our four countries to the ones found in established democracies. Among the many alternative measures of association the uncertainty coefficient was preferred here. Though it is less widely known and has fairly low numerical values even in the case of relatively strong relationships (as e.g. the one between church attendance and party choice in Italy), it provides reasonably comparable results across different predictor variables and across countries with widely different levels of party fragmentation. Table 4.4 reports our data about the strength of association between occupation, urban vs rural residence, education, age and religiosity in eight western democracies and East Germany in 1990, and in Poland, the Czech and Slovak republics and Hungary in the 1991–3 period.

The lesson is fairly unambiguous: the age of the party system is totally unrelated to the social distinctiveness of the various parties' electorates.

Table 4.3 Former Communist Party (CP) membership and voting support for SLD, KSCM, SDL and MSZP in five successive surveys

Country	Oct. 1991	Oct. 1992	Jan. 1993	Aug. 1993	May 1994
Poland					
Former CP members as percentage	14	11	13	13	15
of total among SLD-supporters	50	32	40	35	26
Percentage of former CP members					
supporting SLD	26	23	21	42	33
SLD-supporters as percentage of total	7	8	7	16	19
Czech Republic					
Former CP members as percentage	22	19	20	23	24
of total among KSCM-supporters	65	57	60	64	70
Percentage of former CP members					
supporting KSCM	13	36	34	24	24
KSCM-supporters as percentage of total	4	12	12	9	8
Slovakia					
Former CP members as percentage	17	16	16	19	21
of total among SDL-supporters	66	38	36	36	38
Percentage of former CP members					
supporting SDL	22	45	59	58	39
SDL-supporters as percentage of total	6	18	25	31	21
Hungary					
Former CP members as percentage	15	16	13	18	17
of total among MSZP-supporters	55	39	36	33	28
Percentage of former CP members					
supporting MSZP	30	34	40	62	57
MSZP-supporters as percentage of total	8	14	14	34	35

Source: Central European University, *Development of Party Systems* (1992, 1993, 1994) Dohnalik, Jacek, Jan Hartl, Krzysztof Jasiewicz, Radoslaw Markowski, Peter Mateju, Lubos Rezler, Gábor Tóka, and Milan Tucek, 1991. *Dismantling of the Social Safety Net and Its Political Consequences in East-Central: An International Comparative Study Initiated and Sponsored by the Institute of East-West Studies, N.Y.–Prague.* Machine-readable data file. Distributors IEWS, New York and TARKI, Budapest.

Note: All table entries were calculated by cross-tabulating the answers for the questions about respondents' former CP membership and voting intention 'if there were an election next weekend'. All respondents who failed to name a party on this latter question were excluded from the calculation of the reported percentages. In the 1994 Czech data, supporters of KSCM are merged with SLB- and SDL (two recent splinter parties) supporters

Whichever social background variable we look at, its correlation with party choice tends to show as much variation and a similar average among Western countries as in east-central Europe. If we concentrate only on the most widely discussed issue, we can indeed see that the coefficient for class voting is much higher in Britain than in east-central Europe. But the rest of the continental sample does not really differ from Poland, the

Table 4.4 Strength of association between party preference and various social background variables in east-central Europe in 1991–3 and various other party systems in 1990 (uncertainty coefficients, with party preference as dependent)

PREDICTOR VARIABLE

Country	White collar		Worker		Farmer	
	uc		uc		uc	
Poland	.04	s	.01	s	.04	s
Czech Rep.	.01	s	.01	so	.02	s
Slovakia	.01	s	.01	so	.01	so
Hungary	.01	s	.00	ns	.01	s
Australia	.00	s	.01	s	–	na
USA	.01	s	.01	ns	.00	ns
Ireland	.00	ns	.01	ns	.01	s
North.Ireland	.01	s	.01	ns	–	na
Great Britain	.04	s	.04	s	–	na
Norway	.01	s	.01	s	.03	s
West Germany	.00	ns	.01	s	.01	s
East Germany	.01	s	.01	s	.00	ns
Italy	.00	ns	.01	s	–	na

PREDICTOR VARIABLE

Country	Size of community		Education		Age		Church attendance	
	uc		uc		uc		uc	
Poland	.07	s	.06	s	.02	s	.03	s
Czech Rep.	.02	s	.02	s	.03	s	.06	s
Slovakia	.02	s	.03	s	.03	s	.08	s
Hungary	.02	s	.03	s	.07	s	.05	s
Australia	.03	s	.01	s	.01	s	.01	s
USA	.02	s	.02	s	.01	s	.01	ns
Ireland	.03	s	.03	s	.01	s	.01	s
North.Ireland	–	na	.03	s	.02	s	.02	s
Great Britain	–	na	.02	s	.01	s	.02	s
Norway	.01	s	.02	s	.02	s	.08	s
West Germany	.02	s	.05	s	.06	s	.05	s
East Germany	.02	s	.04	s	.01	s	.02	s
Italy	.02	s	.03	s	.02	s	.05	s

ns: not significant
so: significant at the 0.05 level in at least one of the three data sets
s: significant on the 0.05 level in each data set
na: data not available

Source: compiled from Dohnalik et al., *Dismantling of the Safety Net*; Central European University, *Development of Party Systems* data files (1992, 1993); *ISSP 1990: The Role of Government*. Machine-readable data file. Distributor: Zentralarchive, Köln. For the east-central European countries, the average of the three separate surveys is reported

Czech Republic and Slovakia (Hungary looks rather like the US and Ireland on this count). The closeness to the continental pattern is also underlined by the similarly strong effect of church attendance on party choice in West Germany, Italy, the Czech Republic, Slovakia and Hungary. Though the peculiarities of individual countries are readily visible in the results – note the uniquely strong effect of farming occupation and place of residence on party preferences in Poland, and the strong effect of age in West Germany and Hungary – there are no signs of systematic differences between the eastern and western democracies in this sample.

DO ELECTORAL CHOICES LACK POLITICAL CONTENT?

A frequent assertion is that even if east European voters have something in their mind about the individual parties, it is most likely to be a black-and-white evaluation based on misperceptions, hasty generalisations, the attributes of the party leaders and a host of other things which have little to do with party policies and ideologies. The problem with most earlier

---

Notes to Table 4.4:

1 Coding of the predictor variables:
   White collar: 1=non-manual employees; 0=all else
   Worker: 1=non-agricultural employees doing manual work; 0=all else
   Farmer: 1=farmers and agricultural workers; 0=all else
   Size of community: 1=rural residence; 2=small town resident; 3=big city residents
   Education: 1=low; 2=elementary; 3=secondary; 4: college or university
   Age: 1=18–29; 2=30–44; 3=45–60 years old; 4=61 years old and older
   Frequency of church attendance: 1=every month; 2=less often; 3=never

2 Respondents who had no party preference and supporters of smaller parties were excluded from the analysis. The party preference variable was normally derived from answers for the question 'If there is a parliamentary election next Sunday, which party would you vote for?', except in the US, Britain, West Germany and Northern Ireland, where party identification was asked; and in Italy and East Germany, where vote in the last election was asked. The answers were recoded into the following categories:

   Poland: peasant parties (PSL, PL, Solidarność RI, Samoobrona); Christian parties (ZChN, PChP, SLChD); PC or RdR; NSZZ 'Solidarność'; liberal parties (KLD, UPR); UD; KPN; SdRP (or SLD)
   Czech Republic: KSCM; CSSD; LSU and CSS; HSD-SMS; Agriculture Party; Greens; SPR-RSC; OH; ODA; ODS-KDS; KDU-CSL
   Slovakia: KDH; ODU or VPN or SKD; DS; MKM-E-MLS; SKDH; SNS; Greens; HZDS; SDSS; SDL
   Hungary: MDF, SZDSZ, FKGP, MSZP, FIDESZ, KDNP
   Australia: Liberal; Labour; Country; Australian Democrats
   USA: Democrat; Republican
   Ireland: Fianna Fail; Fine Gael; Labour P. or Workers' Party; Progressive Democrats
   Northern Ireland: Conservative; Labour P. or Workers' Party; SDP or Alliance (Mainland) or Alliance (NI); DUP; OUP; SDLP
   Great Britain: Conservatives; Labour; Liberal Democrats
   Norway: Labour or Red Electoral Alliance; Progress P.; Conservatives; Christian Democrats; Centre P.; Socialist P
   West Germany: CDU/CSU; SPD; FDP; Greens
   East Germany: CDU/CSU; SPD; FDP; Greens or Bundnis; PDS
   Italy: MSI; DC; PLI; PRI or PSDI or PR; PSI; Liste Verde; PCI; Leghe

studies on this question is that they compared their findings (or simply preconceptions) about the east European voters only to normative ideals about the well-informed citizen. To avoid this mistake in Tóka[24] we reported some Polish, Czech, Slovak and Hungarian findings from the Fall 1992 CEU-survey which were presented in a format comparable to the 1972 and 1987 German, and 1952 and 1980 American figures reported by Klingemann and Wattenberg.[25] In all these six countries, representative (i.e. random) samples of the electorate were asked to say what they liked and what they disliked about each of the most important parties operating in their country. The answers were then recorded and later aggregated into broad categories in order to assess how much political content the responses had and how sophisticated it was. In terms of the percentage of respondents who had nothing to say about the various parties, the Czech and Slovak figures came quite close to the 1972 German and 1952 American results, and – especially if we consider the much greater number of parties which the Czech and Slovak voters were expected to be aware of – were usually much smaller than the respective percentages in the US in 1980. The respective Polish and Hungarian percentages were on this score closer to (but still lower than) the 1980 US results, which means that they were more discouraging than either the 1952 American, or the 1972 and 1980 German results. In respect to black-and-white thinking all four east-central European electorates were somewhere between Americans and Germans: the Germans are much less, the Americans are much more likely than them to have either only positive or only negative things to say about the individual parties.

Thus, the most immediate message of the data confirms what political science and journalism taught about the pre-1980 decay of the American party system. The point to be stressed in the present context is that the mere age of the party system again fails to have much predictive power in matters of electoral politics. Again, the results have a similar message as in the case of the identifiability of government parties. In one way or another, parties need to generate intense feelings about themselves in order to make the voters aware of their existence, and Czech and Slovak parties may do this better than Hungarian and Polish ones. There is, though, a difference between the frequency of likes and dislikes about SPD and CDU/CSU on the one hand, and the former Czechoslovak parties on the other, and it may well be that the differential fragmentation of these party systems is responsible for that.

Concerning the content of the answers, the default expectation that we can draw from the deterministic theories cited in the introduction is that east Europeans are much less likely to mention ideologies, supposed party linkages to social groups or concrete policies than Germans and Americans when they explain what they like or dislike about the parties. East Europeans may also be expected to refer to the personalities of party leaders more frequently. By and large, these expectations were partly met.

In Germany and the US, the main right-wing parties were a little more often evaluated in terms of their links to social groups than the main government parties of east-central Europe in 1992. All east-central European post-communist parties were much less frequently liked, but usually more often disliked for their association with certain social groups (i.e. the former nomenclatura and the like) than the American Democrats or the German SPD. Only the east European Christian and nationalist parties were at least as frequently liked or disliked because of their ideologies as the German and American parties. The east-central European secular liberal and left-wing parties were indeed less frequently judged on the base of their ideologies than American and German parties.

A more complicated picture emerged in the case of domestic policy references. Probably surprisingly in 1992, but less so in light of their later electoral performance, the post-communist parties were, in all eastern countries, about as often associated with attractive domestic policies (almost exclusively in the socio-economic domain) as US Democrats in 1980 and the SPD in 1972. There was no systematic difference between the two western countries on the one hand, and the two parts of Czechoslovakia on the other in the likelihood to which non-communist parties were liked for their domestic policies. In this respect, Poland and Hungary clearly lagged behind again. The most likely reason for these cross-national differences was twofold. First, only those east European parties which have already been involved as senior partners in government coalitions were about as much disliked for their domestic policies as the major German and American parties. (But the latter were probably more frequently *liked* for the same reason than UD, ZChN, ODS, KDH, HZDS, and MDF.[26]) Second, in the new democracies the parties associated with highly controversial policies (that is, the three Christian parties mentioned above, the Hungarian Small-Holders associated with land restitution, and the Czech ODS with its radically Thatcherite economic policy rhetoric) appear to have had a much clearer profile in terms of domestic policies than the rest. This suggests that the development of clear party profiles may have a price. Namely, the factors which can probably most easily accelerate this process are frequent alterations of government and opposition on the one hand, and parties' advocation of such public policies which are highly unpopular for many on the other. Of course, while the rapid development of clear party profiles may indeed be advantageous for the consolidation of competitive party politics, both of these factors may alienate some from democratic politics.

ARE PARTY CHOICES UNRELATED TO POLITICAL ATTITUDES?

Thus, east-central European voters have almost as clear and sophisticated images of some (rather Czech than Hungarian or Polish, rather clerical-nationalist or post-communist than liberal and social democrat, and rather government than opposition) parties as Americans and Germans do. Considering that the east-central European voter is expected to be aware of a much greater number of parties beyond his own, this is no small achievement. But this, however, does not really answer the question whether the east-central European public's party images are based on misperceptions more often than those of the electorates in consolidated democracies. If the cause of misperception is only the sheer novelty of the parties, then we should expect one voter to err in one direction in his/her judgement of a party, and another in the opposite one.[27] In this case, the only politically relevant consequence of misperceptions is that a relatively large number of voters will vote for a different party than they 'should' on the base of their own policy attitudes. Whether the proportion of such voters is bigger in new than in consolidated democracies we can determine by comparing countries in terms of the overall correlation between respondents' party preferences and issue attitudes. This, in other words, means that we compare the countries in terms of the ideological homogeneity of the constituencies of the various parties.

The comparison between the four east-central European countries is methodologically straightforward, as the Fall 1992 CEU survey contained some twenty identically-phrased attitude questions in each country, and a few country-specific items on the dismantling of the Czechoslovak federation as well. The comparison with Western countries is somewhat cumbersome, partly because there are obviously large differences between the various countries in the content of the relevant issues. The closest possible landmark that I could utilise was provided by a British study,[28] which tried to predict party preferences from answers to a large number of attitude questions supposedly covering virtually all major issue domains of British politics. Although the items that I used were different in their content, and smaller in number than the ones utilised by the British study, I assume that they covered most of the relevant issue domains of east-central European politics. The methodology of the analysis was identical. Briefly, a discriminant analysis provided an optimal weighting of the answers for various attitude questions in order to predict the respondents' party preference. The overall correlation between the weighted sum of attitude positions and party preferences can be conceived as a measure of the overall congruence between policy views and party preference in the various countries.

In Britain, almost all issues pitted Labour-voters against Tories, and liberal supporters were normally in the middle. Therefore almost all issues were incorporated into one ideological superdimension (corresponding to the British understanding of the left–right divide). In contrast, in the east-central European multiparty systems about three different ideological dimensions were found to discriminate between various party blocks (i.e. one between religious and secular parties, another one between pro-market vs social-protectionist parties, and sometimes a third one which had a country-specific content). The overall canonical correlations between the three most important issue dimensions and party preference were 0.74, 0.46 and 0.35 in the Czech Republic; 0.64, 0.58 and 0.46 in Slovakia; 0.49, 0.47 and 0.38 in Poland; and 0.51, 0.37 and 0.29 in Hungary. The first issue dimension had around 0.75 correlation with party preference in Britain at the time of several successive general elections in the seventies and early eighties.[29]

By now, the lesson should have become very obvious: the Czech, and probably also the Slovak parties tend to have constituencies as ideologically homogeneous as British parties used to have, but Poland and even more so Hungary differ quite a bit from Britain in this respect. Thus, the results suggest that the sheer novelty of parties does not necessarily increase the random error component of party images to such heights that would be unprecedented in ideologically disciplined, not very fragmented, and relatively old party systems. A good deal of issue- or ideology-based voting may easily occur in new democracies, which again suggests that it is probably less the capacity of the student, but rather the content of the lesson that determines the speed of advance.

CONCLUSIONS

One of the main thrusts of the argument in this paper was that the novelty of the party systems may not count for too much in matters of electoral politics. If voters are presented clear alternatives they will react accordingly, no matter how recent the advent of democracy was in their country. The first thing to add to this now is that this is only half-true. Even in the most recent elections of the region, total electoral volatility (i.e. the percentage of vote that 'changed hands' compared to the previous election) was almost 34 in Poland in September 1993, and a little more than 28 in Hungary in May 1994. These figures, of course, are almost three times bigger than the west European average between 1885 and 1985.[30] The novelty of the party system obviously counts in many, but as we argued above, not in all respects. There are emerging stable elements in electoral behaviour in east-central Europe, and these were the focus of our analysis.

We saw that for east-central Europeans it is rather one of the significant parties than an interest organisation that they see as the best representative of their interests. We also saw that in at least one or probably two of the four east-central European countries, namely the Czech Republic and Slovakia, voters tend to face just as 'meaningful' an electoral choice – along any criteria of meaningfulness that we utilised – as the citizens of more mature democracies. Why these two countries differ in this respect from Poland and Hungary is difficult to tell partly because the number of possible explanations may easily exceed the number of cases at hand. Differences in pre-1948 democratic development, differential levels of socio-economic development, the more revolutionary scenario of democratic transition, which – unlike Poland and Hungary – freed the post-communist left from any visible responsibility for the introduction of market-oriented reforms (and could thus help the development of greater policy polarisation in the socio-economic domain) may all have played their role.

Considering this, it looks less promising to speculate about the causes of between-country differences than to collect some of the propositions that the analysis concerning individual parties have generated. As we saw, more or less sectionalist parties may eventually find their place in the broader ideological configuration of the emerging party systems, and yet make substantial contributions to the meaningfulness of electoral choice by providing for clearly visible and – even for the most uninformed voter – easily conceivable links between parties and broader social groups. Frequent changes in the government may probably undermine the very basis of governments' electoral accountability. But frequent changes of government can apparently help voters to develop a more realistic understanding of what the different parties can deliver: a knowledge that does not appear to abound in the region (cf. our above remarks about HZDS and the Hungarian liberals). A majoritarian drive in policy-making may also have desirable by-products. As we saw, one can make an intuitively convincing case for the considerable effect of party policies on the sheer identifiability of the incumbents. This, in turn, may have some noteworthy implications about the merits and vices of majoritarian systems. The capacity of the political system to inform the voters about the most trivial facts of politics, and the voters' ability to absorb this information are quite arguably related to the extent to which social inequalities prevail in political participation in east-central Europe. The same can be said about the advocacy of controversial policy positions and a relatively high ideological polarisation between parties: the more a country has of these, the more knowledgeable and equal the electors can be.

Maybe these propositions do not fit well into the recommendations of the consolidation literature. But that does not make any of them invalid either. Maybe there is a real trade-off between the rapid and smooth consolidation of new institutional arrangements and the degree of electoral accountability that can develop within that framework. The first may require consensus and compromise even beyond the constitutional domain, but the second requires doctrine and conflict in whichever domain they may be found.

NOTES

1 See Tóka, Gábor, 1993. 'Parties and Electoral Choices in East-Central Europe'. Paper prepared for presentation at a Conference of the ESRC East–

West Programme at the Centre for Mediterranean Studies, University of Bristol, 17–19 September 1993.

2 'A Legitimacy Crisis of the German Party System?', in: *Western European Party Systems: Trends and Prospects*, ed. Peter H. Merkl, New York: The Free Press (1980), pp. 597–608.

3 'The Making of Political Fields in Post-Communist Transition dynamics of class and parties in Hungarian Politics, 1989–90' in *Post-Communist Transition – Emerging Pluralism in Hungary*, eds András Bozóki, András Körösányi, and George Schöpflin, London: Frances Pinter (1992).

4 Tóka, Gábor, forthcoming. 'Being Represented – Being Satisfied? Political Support in East-Central Europe', in *Citizens and the State*, eds Hans-Dieter Klingemann and Dieter Fuchs, Oxford: OUP.

5 Fuchs, Dieter, Giovanna Guidorossi, and Palle Svensson, forthcoming. 'Support for the Democratic System' in *Citizens and the State*, eds Hans-Dieter Klingemann and Dieter Fuchs, Oxford: OUP.

6 See data reported in Duane F. Alwin, 1992. *The International Social Justice Survey*, Codebook, Ann Arbor, Michigan.

7 See Glass, Harold A., 1978. 'Consensus and Opposition in Switzerland: A Neglected Consideration', *Comparative Politics* 10, pp. 361–73.

8 'The Sources and Structure of Democratic Legitimation in Western Democracies: A Consolidated Model Tested with Time-Series Data in Six Countries since World War II', *American Sociological Review*, 54 (1989), pp. 682–706.

9 'The "Comparative Revolution" and the Transition in Central and Eastern Europe', *Journal of Theoretical Politics* 5 (1993), pp. 231–52.

10 *Bürger und Organisationen – Ost- und Westdeutschland: vereint und doch verschieden?* Working paper, Berlin: Wissenschaftszentrum (1992).

11 See Tóka, 'Parties and Electoral Choices'.

12 True, inasmuch as a bipolarisation of the party system tends to make electoral decisions mostly a matter of voting for or against the incumbents, a majoritarian tendency in policy making may provide some marginal advantages for relatively extreme opposition parties over those who are less readily identified either as opposition or government parties: Poles were more likely to realise that SdRP and KPN were in opposition than to discover that PC and UP were there too, and for Czechs opposition was more likely to mean the communists (LB) or the xenophobe Republicans (SPR-RSC) than the social democrats (CSSD). But this is probably not necessarily so. The average Hungarian thinks that the liberal parties (SZDSZ, FIDESZ), though offering a distinctive package, are ideologically somewhere between the government parties and the socialists: MSZP (see Tóka, 'Parties and Electoral Choices'). But as Table 4.2 shows, this did not prevent Hungarians from naming the liberals as opposition almost as often as the Socialists. Thus, the quite possible short-term disadvantage of the more centrist parties may evaporate eventually.

13 Ágh, 'Comparative Revolution', pp. 242–3.

14 See Béla Greskovits, *Dominant Economy, Subordinated Politics: the Absence of Economic Populism in the Transition of East-Central Europe*, Working paper Series no. 1. Budapest: Dept. of Political Sciences, Central European University.

15 'Decaying Versus Developing Party Systems: A Comparison of Party Images in the United States and West Germany', *British Journal of Political Science* 22 (1992), pp. 131–49.

16 Mair, Peter, 1991, '(Electoral) Markets and (Stable) States', in *Markets Against the State*, eds Michael Moran and Maurice Wright, London: Macmillan.

17   Kopecky, Petr, 1993, 'Fragmentation of Party Systems in Central Europe', Paper prepared for delivery at the seminar 'Disillusionment with Democracy' organised by the Secretariat General of the Council of Europe, Colchester, 8–10 July 1993.
18   Waller, Michael, 1991, 'Groups, Interests and Political Aggregation in East-Central Europe', *Journal of Communist Studies*, 7, pp. 128–47.
19   *Political Man: The Social Bases of Politics*, New York: Doubleday (1960).
20   'Parties and Electoral Choices'.
21   In the forty-odd years preceding 1989, ZSL (the predecessor of PSL) was a permanent 'coalition partner' of the Polish United Workers' Party.
22   Dalton, R.J., 1992, 'Two German Electorates?' in *Developments in German Politics*, eds G. Smith, W. Paterson, P. Merkl and S. Padgett, London: Macmillan.
23   Judging from the discrepancies between pre-election forecasts and true election results, it is likely that in 1990–2 40 per cent or so of the Polish, Slovak and Hungarian, and even more of the Czech post-communist party supporters concealed their preferences in polls. This response bias was, however, gradually disappearing in the later Polish and Hungarian, but most likely also from the Czech and Slovak surveys. Therefore, the true increase in post-communist party support in Slovakia, Poland and Hungary is shown in slightly exaggerated fashion by Table 4.3.
24   'Parties and Electoral Choices'.
25   'Decaying Versus Developing Party Systems'.
26   Though the data does not answer this question, I would give better odds to economic than to political explanations of this.
27   Having only mass survey data at hand, we cannot analyse the question of such systematic misperceptions, when there is a consensus in the public about the policy positions of a certain party, but the content of that consensus systematically differs from the 'true' policy positions of the party.
28   Himmelweit, Hilde T., Patrick Humphreys, and Marianne Jaeger, 1984, *How Voters Decide: A model of vote choice based on a special longitudinal study extending over fifteen years and the British election surveys of 1970–1983*, Philadelphia: Open University Press.
29   Himmelweit, et al., *How Voters Decide*.
30   See Stefano Bartolini and Peter Mair, 1990. *Identity, Competition, and Electoral Availability: the Stabilisation of the European Electorates 1885–1985*, Cambridge: CUP.

ACRONYMS USED IN THIS CHAPTER

Poland

KPN:	Confederation for Independent Poland
PSL:	Polish Peasant Party
SdRP:	Social Democracy of Polish Republic (SLD when in coalition with the OPZZ trade union federation)
UP:	Union of Labour
PL:	People's Agreement (Post-Solidarity peasant party)
NSZZ 'S':	Solidarność trade union
ZChN:	Christian-National Union
UD:	Democratic Union
PC:	Centre Agreement
RdR:	Movement for the Republic

KLD: Liberal Democratic Congress
UPR: Union of Real Politics

Czech Republic

KSCM: Communist Party of Bohemia and Moravia (LB if in coalition
                 with some other left wing groups)
CSSD: Czechoslovak Social Democratic Party
LSU: Liberal Social Union (permanent coalition of the Agrarian Party,
                 the Socialist Party, and the Green Party)
HSD-SMS: Movement for Moravia and Silesia, etc.
SPR-RSC: Republican Party, etc.
OH: Civic Movement
CSL: Czech People's Party (KDU-CSL if in coalition with the Christian
                 Democratic Union)
ODA: Civic Democratic Alliance
ODS: Civic Democratic Party

Slovakia

SDL: Party of the Democratic Left
SDSS: Slovak Social Democratic Party
HZDS: Movement for a Democratic Slovakia
SNS: Slovak National Party
KDH: Christian Democratic Movement
MKM-E-MLS: Coalition of Hungarian Christian-oriented parties
DS: Democratic Party
SKD: Conservative Democratic Party (previously ODU, ex-VPN)

Hungary

KDNP: Christian Democratic People's Party
MSZP: Hungarian Socialist Party
MDF: Hungarian Democratic Forum
FKGP: Independent Small-Holders Party
SZDSZ: Alliance of Free Democrats
FIDESZ: Federation of Young Democrats

5 Italy's postwar transition in contemporary perspective

Oreste Massari

INTRODUCTION

The democratic political system in Italy, which was formed during the post-fascist transition phase between 1943 and 1948, began to come to an end in 1989 with the fall of the Berlin Wall. The state of crisis and dismemberment in which it finds itself accelerated during 1992–3 to such an extent that the model of democracy which was constructed in the transitional period between 1943 and 1948 is now clearly devoid of life, and rejected by the public.

In the last few years, therefore, Italy has been going through a second democratic transition in a manner which is still fluid and confused and is certainly proving disruptive. This time, however, the passage is not from an authoritarian regime to a democratic one (as was the case with the Resistance between 1943 and 1945), but a transition in the form of democracy. The collapse in the institutions and the party system of what we may already term the 'First Republic' requires a critical reappraisal, in the light of contemporary developments, not so much of the limitations of the postwar transition itself, as of the limitations of the model of democracy which emerged from it.

Furthermore, the crisis of the present regime in Italy confirms something which has been a constant factor in its history since unification: that political change and the replacement of the ruling class do not take place along the classic democratic lines of alternation within the institutional continuity of the political system, but either through the practice of so-called *trasformismo* (typical of the parliamentary regime of the last decades of the nineteenth century), or through the change of the political system itself.[1] While the postwar political system certainly kept Italy in a state of peace under democratic rule, and enabled it to achieve considerable success, most especially of an economic nature, it also laid the foundations for a model of democracy which has not stood up to the challenges which became pressing, both from within the country and from outside it, in the period between 1989 and the present. Above all, it has not withstood the terrible degeneration which, from the time of their origins, has affected the governmental parties in particular but also the entire traditional system, and subsequently dragged the political institutions of the First Republic into crisis.

In assessing Italy's transition to democracy from a contemporary standpoint, it is important to introduce a specific point of distinction. The study of Italian democracy cannot be reduced to comparing it with the modes of transition in the southern European countries (Greece, Spain and Portugal), but must also be extended to comparisons with the more developed Western democratic systems (the USA, Great Britain, Germany, France). This requirement is well understood by Pasquino when he notes: 'Italy partakes of Northern Europe and of Southern Europe in its geography, in its socioeconomic structure, in its political dynamic. Even the transition process to a democratic regime provides an instance of the difficulty of locating the Italian case among other Southern European cases.'[2]

In fact, the dynamic which brought Fascism to power in Italy is similar to the general phenomenon of the crisis in the liberal state, which also brought Nazism to power in Germany. Here too there is something in common with northern Europe. How profound these common problems are can be seen from the European integration of the Italian economy which has been pursued since the 1950s. The break-up itself of the party system in the 1990s, with the rise of a regional party such as the Lega Nord, openly secessionist in character, shows that the long-dormant North–South (or centre–periphery) division in the country can be explained by the dynamics of both Mediterranean Europe (an amoral devotion to family interests, the personal patronage system, lack of civicness and a sense of the state) and of northern Europe (manufacturing in the North, values of market efficiency, private enterprise, demand for efficiency in public services).[3]

But alongside the distinction between northern and southern Europe, we need to consider another distinction/set of commonalities relevant to the development of the Italian political system: the division between Western and Eastern Europe. However paradoxical this may seem, this division can be perceived in Italy not only in the presence of a very strong Communist Party linked to the international policy of the Soviet Union, at least up to the beginning of the 1980s, but it can also be noted in other factors. The state interventionism due to the enormous increase in the public sector of the economy pursued as much by the Christian Democrats as by the left, together with the predominant role of the political party as the maximum representative and decision-making institution, and as the point of reference for public confidence, were such as to make the Italian political system resemble that under Fascism but also the communist regimes of the East. Before the 1994 general election, the exceptionally large Italian political class was universally described and perceived by scholars and by public opinion as a *nomenklatura* with a power, a status and life style unequalled in any other Western democracy, and as showing marked similarities to that prevailing in the communist regimes of the East.

In any case, the political regime which emerged from the postwar transition, at the end of its parabola, bears the worst traits of both southern and Eastern Europe. This is not to ignore the undoubted successes attained by this regime in the economic, social and political fields. Democratisation certainly succeeded in preventing the destruction of the constitutional framework in the toughest period of the East–West struggle; the constitution of 1948 was, in its first section of basic principles, extremely advanced, in finding a place for all political forces, restraining traumatic and violent changes, and giving Italian democracy some distinctly innovative characteristics. Democratic and electoral participation became firmly rooted. The economic growth of the country was considerable, to the extent that Italy became fourth or fifth among the industrialised countries. This experiment in democratisation, however historically successful, has, in the long term, shown inherent weaknesses which have led first to the degeneration of the party and institutional system, and subsequently to the actual collapse of the model of democracy itself – even though in an absolutely unprecedented and peaceful way – in the early 1990s. The fact is that even though the democratisation/transition may have succeeded, the pattern of institutions and democracy itself has not proved so successful over time. It lasted only as long as the international conditions – the polarisation between the USA and USSR in other words – which permitted the party system to maintain its stability. In some important ways the acceptance of the institutional structure and the party system was conditioned by international circumstances. When these ceased to exist, the Italian people were no longer prepared to put up with the degeneration of democratic government in Italy.

THE TRANSITION FROM THE FASCIST REGIME TO DEMOCRACY

As is well known, the salient characteristic of the process of transition to a republican democratic regime is the leading role assumed by the mass political parties. In contrast to other cases of transition, the military played a negligible role. If many different anti- or post-fascist forces operated between 1943 and 1945, such as the monarchy, the Allies, the Church, exponents of the old governing liberal pre-fascist forces; after 1946, when the monarchy was removed from the scene with the referendum of 2 June and the influence of the allies was exercised through the Italian parties – these anti-fascist parties clearly took the political initiative, unlike in postwar Germany where democracy and the Constitution were imported from outside. The political initiative rooted in and deriving legitimacy from that vast armed and political movement called the Resistance was taken over by the parties. The Resistance had opposed the Nazi occupation in Central and Northern Italy after 8 September 1943 (date of the armistice) and ended in 1945 with popular insurrections in the principal northern cities. Even though the popular base of the Resistance was fairly spontaneous, for the twenty months it lasted, fed as it was by the extremely severe conditions of the war and the German occupation in the North of the country, there is no doubt that the anti-fascist and anti-Nazi struggle was directed by the political parties.[4] If then we look at the protagonists (the parties) and the process (the Resistance as an armed, mass struggle for liberation within the context of the Second World War) not only does the particularity of the Italian transition compared with other transitions from authoritarianism to democracy emerge – making comparison difficult with peacetime cases – but also the particular characteristics of the Italian political democratic regime for the next fifty years. The model of democracy which became consolidated and, that is to say, was closely bound up with the form the transition process took contained the seeds of its own eventual destruction.

Even if the Resistance cannot be reduced to a secondary or minor episode of the Second World War, one must not, on the other hand, overrate its importance in relation to the division of the world into spheres of influence among the Western powers and the USSR (the Yalta Conference in 1945), the presence of the Allied army in Italy and the prevalence of conservative forces in the South. The interplay of international and military forces not only prevented the Resistance from breaking out into a revolution, as happened in Greece and Yugoslavia, but also influenced it as a grass-roots reform movement. This influence had an effect on the unity of the internal anti-fascist coalition itself. The anti-fascist parties maintained their unity until 1947. This made it possible to deal with the main institutional decisions to be taken by the new democratic state in a united manner: the referendum of 2 June 1946, which sanctioned the transition from the monarchy to the Republic, and the approval of a Constitution, through a Constituent Assembly, which was extremely advanced in its principles and programmes. The new democratic state therefore was based on anti-Fascism and the components of the anti-fascist parties that favoured the Resistance, among which was the PCI itself, which had been the main actor in the Resistance.

But anti-fascist unity, valid on the level of the State and its Constitution, did not stand up to the test of government and the new international conditions that came into being at the beginning of the Cold War. In the spring of 1947, the government coalition, to which Communists and Socialists belonged, split apart bringing about that ideological break between communism and anti-Communism which was to last at least to 1989 and which would replace the Fascism–anti-Fascism conflict. The consequences of this new rupture were to be immense for the new political system and explain many of the problems and subsequent degeneration of Italian democracy. If the anti-Fascism of the Resistance created the new Republic and the new Constitution, it turned out eventually to be fragile in legitimating all the political forces. The Communists had participated fully in the creation of a Constitution, but this was not to be the case at the government level. Bound as they were to the USSR, they formed an anti-system opposition for many years and therefore could not constitute an alternative political force for government. To rise to the communist challenge, the conservative forces, especially the DC, interpreted their role as a sort of civilising mission, identifying the State with the government itself, thereby thwarting the development of mechanisms and procedures of a genuine democracy. This rupture between Communists and anti-Communists led to a paradoxical situation: the forces opposing the system invoked the defence of the Constitution as a weapon against the government majority, and the latter chose not to carry out all the terms of the Constitution in order to fight the opposition or meet its challenge, since they saw it as a 'Trojan horse' on behalf of communist penetration. Thus, the Constitution became a weapon used by partisan interests instead of the expression of the moral unity of a people translated into supreme juridical principles. Italian democracy did not have a universally accepted set of values and norms as its basis. The Resistance was not sufficient to provide these, since it had taken place only in one part of the country (the Centre and the North), with the conservative South not involved in the anti-fascist struggle of 1943–5. Furthermore, it was split internally by the opposition between Communists and anti-Communists.

As a result, the public did not show loyalty to national institutions as such, because of the split among the anti-fascist forces, but rather to political parties only.[5] Thus, a historical trait of the Italian public ethic came to be perpetuated, according to which the political party (and before that the family, the clan, etc.) came before the State, which was viewed as a distant entity and was not impartial. The complete legitimacy of each of the forces vying for the chance to govern, which is the universal assumption on which democracy is based, never existed.

The transition in Italy is therefore not to be understood as a merely linear passage from Fascism to democracy, but also as an internal split within its democracy involving a double confrontation: that of Fascism and anti-Fascism which kept the MSI out of the democratic structure until 1994, and that of Communism and anti-Communism which has always prevented the PCI from being counted among the governing forces.

THE PARTIES AND THE INSTITUTIONS

In the Constituent Assembly it was the organised political parties which devised the permanent rules of the game – the Constitution and the electoral system. They were also to define the content of the game itself (the material Constitution). Furthermore it was the political parties which provided the main, if not the only, participants in the consolidation of postwar Italian democracy. The result of this was a totally party-oriented political system. To have any access to the decision-making process, all interest groups, the various forms of association, even movements had to deal with the parties. These were the veritable 'gate-keepers' of the decision-making system. They were the mediators and had the final say not only in the political sphere but also in the functional one. The pluralism that came hand in hand with the democratic regime in Italy was first and foremost a pluralism of parties.[6] In order to understand the peculiarities of the Italian political system, we must therefore concentrate our attention on the central role of the parties. The notion of democracy shared by the mass anti-fascist parties (the Catholics, Socialists and Communists) is that of a democracy organised along party lines. The mass party, in the definition of both the Communist Togliatti and the Catholic Costantino Mortati (one of the leading fathers of the Constitution), is 'the society which forms itself into the State'. Fascism had put itself forward as an 'ethical State'. Its fall, dragging the monarchy and all the other State institutions down with it, had left a void which was filled only by what was defined as the 'ethical party'. As Lepre put it, 'the end of the ethical State left a void which was in part filled by attributing to certain parties, the PCI especially, but also the DC, the ethical significance which the state possessed for Fascism'.[7]

For the Communists the party was the expression of absolute values, to which fidelity and loyalty were owed above everything else. From this came the so-called 'double-think' for a long phase in the relations of the PCI with democracy; on the one hand loyalty was affirmed to the democratic Constitution (to the drawing up of which, moreover, the Communists had made their contribution) while, on the other hand, the acceptance of 'bourgeois democracy' was considered only transitory, since the ultimate aim, or the absolute ideal, was still a socialist society on the Soviet pattern.[8]

But for the most committed theorists of Christian Democracy, the party was also understood to be an 'ethical party', in that it provided the incarnation of a project which reached beyond the political sphere into the moral one. For them, especially those gathered around Giuseppe Dossetti, the DC should have been an instrument for asserting Catholic Christian ideals in society. In this case too, the ethical concept of the party involved a totalising vision of social relationships. Communists and Christian Democrats attributed all the positive values to their respective parties, while all the negative values were ascribed to the adversary. In any case, the construction of democracy in Italy was entrusted to the two principal parties whose sources of legitimacy were outside the Italian state (the USSR for the PCI and the Vatican, followed by the USA, for the DC).

Furthermore, in the absence of an alternative in power and in the context of the Cold War, the DC grew to become the natural government party from the mid-1950s. In a certain sense, it was condemned to govern, even when the international conditions dictated by the Cold War ceased to exist. All future coalitions came to be centred around the DC. Thanks to cross-party agreement on an extended form of State capitalism, the DC became more and more a regime party, with enormous power provided by the direct control over numerous State-owned bodies (among which were industrial and financial giants such as ENI, IRI). Out of this developed the phenomenon known as the 'occupation' and dividing up of the State by the governing parties.[9] The power of the government and of those governing was thus enormous, all the more so in the absence of a challenge from the opposition and it was made legitimate because of the communist menace.

In elections against the PCI, the DC always resorted to the patronage system to create support among the voters (in the South of the country), taking advantage of the enormous power of the government and administrative bodies. Public works were granted and administrative jobs given out, along with favourable laws, and personal recommendations in order to obtain votes. For the same purpose – from the 1950s onward – compromises were reached with criminal forces such as the Mafia, the 'Ndrangheta and the Camorra, all located in the South and all wielding power over their territories.

We cannot fully understand the connotations of the present Italian system if we do not keep in mind these historical roots. From the very beginning of the new regime, the relationship between state institutions and political parties was heavily weighted in favour of the latter. Here one of the key elements in the history of united Italy emerges: it has been a succession of political regimes, none of which has ever achieved a balance between the State and the parties. To a liberal regime based on oligarchies of leading figures without any reference to mass parties, there succeeded a state without parties, but with a single political organisation (Fascism). This was followed by a democratic system of parties potentially without a State (the Republic).

In contrast to the so-called Anglo-Saxon democracies, the Italian mass parties did not grow up alongside the liberal democratic institutions of the country. This could not help having enormous consequences for the behaviour of the parties and the type of institutions which grew up in Italy. It is usual to categorise the Italian republican regime as a case of party government, but it is a type of party government which is very distinctive, and, we should add, antithetical to the type of party government prevalent for instance in Britain.[10] In the latter, the party is the main channel of representation and of decision, but within a self-limitation of its own role according to the obligations and rules of 'responsible government'. It is no accident that the focus of power in the British parties is in the parliamentary party, because it is in the elected representatives themselves that a relationship of political responsibility to a committed programme (the manifesto) in relation to the electors is to be found.[11]

The focus of power in the Italian mass parties is on the other hand in their extra-parliamentary structures, and this fact, as Ostrogorski understood clearly, was bound to deprive the representative institutions of much of their significance. We may clarify this notion by pointing to the practice of coalition government in Italy. After the unique experience of De Gasperi, who was both leader of the party and leader of the governing coalition (1948–53), and with the exception of Craxi and De Mita, the head of the government has always been a figure dependent on the party secretary.

As a result of this it is clear that the separation of the de facto power from the power deriving from the institutional role has placed the government at the mercy of the parties. This explains a paradox of Italy's coalition governments: a very low rate of duration has always gone alongside a very high stability in the actual personnel of the governments. The actual life of postwar administrations has been approximately nine months. What I am seeking to underscore, then, is that in contrast with almost all Western democracies, the Italian parties have not been restricted by any institutional limits and have not been subjected to any kind of 'regulation' either constitutional or legislative. They have more and more become 'actors without a director'.[12]

THE MODEL OF DEMOCRACY OF THE FIRST REPUBLIC

As far as the form of government was concerned, the option was for the classical form of parliamentarism: i.e. a form of 'weak' government which favoured the centrality of the legislative assembly over the executive (part two of the Constitution). The subsequent choice, (introduced by ordinary legislation), of a pure system of proportional representation for the two houses of parliament could only reinforce the role of the parties and ideological identity between them and the institutions of government. The electoral system for the Chamber of Deputies was founded on voting by list, and on the preferential vote being accorded to individuals (with up to four personal preferences allowed). This was to work in favour of the influence of internal factions, especially in the case of the governing parties, and the Christian Democrats in particular. The influence was based on personal and dependency links between candidates and voters, and on the so-called exchange vote. It is no accident that preference votes were used above all in the South in favour of the governmental parties (and again, the DC in particular).[13]

The mixture of parliamentarianism and proportionalism, as has been noted, was to produce structural weaknesses in the institutions of government and central control and domination of the parties over the process of decision-making.[14] Thanks to the system of proportional representation and the supremacy of the legislative over the executive branch, the parties were furthermore able to dominate the decision-making mechanisms in civil society. But the actual system of proportional representation did not encourage coherent party programmes (with the exception of the PCI, with its Leninist structure and ideological nature), since the governmental parties were destined to be parties in the sense of an amalgamation of currents and factions.[15] A central role was played by the parties, then, in the institutions, but without any central role for a party programme responsible to the electorate.

In the historiographic and political science debate, the question is often asked as to whether or not it would have been possible to make different choices as to institutions. Indeed, there was no lack of proposals for strengthening the executive branch, both under a presidential system and a neo-parliamentary one, reorganising the traditional system of parliament (as was the case with the Constitution of Federal Germany in the same period, and would happen in the 1970s with the transitions in power in Portugal and Spain). Greater differentiation between the two Houses of Parliament was proposed as well as a federal structure of the State granting self-government to the regions, legislative regulation of the parties (which were officially recognised in Art. 49 of the Constitution), and an electoral system which would have distinguished more between the two branches of Parliament. It must be borne in mind however that the choices made by the Constituent Assembly were carried out in a climate of unity and collaboration among all the anti-fascist political parties during 1946–8, whereby international or ideological influences were not yet determining factors. Since in the period before 1948, no party was sure of its future support from the voters, the basic choice of institutions and regulations involved a system of reciprocal guarantees, a sort of system of checks and balances. Thus, the executive branch was not strengthened both out of fear of the 'tyrant' (the fascist experience was a negative influence here), and to avoid the future majority having too strong an instrument of power over the opposition. The proportional electoral system had no selective correction (in Western Germany the clause excluding parties obtaining under 5 per cent of the vote was approved), causing in the long run that fragmentation and extreme multi-party political representation that was so strongly to influence the political system of the 1970s and 1980s.[16] The fact that problems of this kind were already felt from the beginning of the new regime is demonstrated by the government majority's action in 1953 to modify the electoral law in the direction of a majority system (the proposal, referred to as the 'fraudulent law', subsequently defeated by the opposition in the 1953 election, provided for a considerable bonus to the majority).

Since a move in the direction of genuine competition in Italian democracy was excluded for all these institutional and political reasons, the system acquired a form of association between the majority and the Communist opposition.[17] Beneath the ideological confrontation between pro-Western and pro-Communist forces, a sort of under-the-table agreement operated between government and opposition forces. Even in the years of the sharpest ideological conflicts there was agreement on many policies of public interest between the DC and the PCI in the back-rooms of parliamentary committees. As the pioneering studies by Sartori and Cazzola, of legislative activity in Parliament have shown,[18] underneath the ideological conflict the DC and the PCI had a tacit agreement on much legislation and many of the policy choices (such as early elections, major reforms, such as the institution of the Regions in 1970). While the two major parties remained divided on foreign policy, domestic policy remained the result of agreements, negotiations, mediation and deals between them, and this gradually involved all the parties and social forces.[19]

Various factors accounted for this situation. In the first place, the under-lying solidarity of the anti-fascist parties during the Resistance was still important. Second, the DC and the PCI, albeit divided on ideology, agreed in their conception of the role of the mass party in society. Third, propor-tionalism in the electoral system and 'guaranteeism' in parliamentary assemblies led not to the politics of competition, but to a consensual type of politics. This collaboration, finally, was also a way of containing the ideological rupture between the main political parties. The governing forces made some concessions – to the opposition, that is, in the policy-making process in order to avoid a form of political exclusion that might have been ruinous for Italian democracy. Given the nature of the political forces, the problem of Italian democracy became not that of competition over government programmes, but rather the gradual integration of the forces of opposition into the area of government in accordance with a model of democracy by mutual consent.[20] The government coalitions tended to pursue this goal from the end of the fifties onwards: first, the PSI incorporated in the centre-left coalition, then with the governments of national solidarity (1976–9) when the PCI became part of the parlia-mentary majority (not of the government).[21]

This process of integration or model of democracy by mutual consent suited the PCI very well, since it accorded with party strategy. The goal was not to present an opposition to the government in line with a democ-racy of alternation in power. This would have implied its transformation into a social democratic party. Its goal was to keep its ideological iden-tity intact while co-operating with the DC, according to this model of democracy by mutual consent, which had been tried out during the Resistance. The pursuit of this form of inter-party association and the absence of alternation in the Italian system, related to the PCI and East–West bipolarism, had great negative consequences, giving Italian democracy the characteristics of a regime without any political responsi-bility and deprived of those checks inherent in genuine political competition. Only the election of 18 April 1948 was genuinely competi-tive, but this was fought out on the basis of an East–West conflict. After that, the proportional electoral system and the impossibility for the PCI to present itself as a government party prevented genuinely competitive elections from taking place and ruled out a relationship of responsibility between voters and government leaders. Thus, Italian democracy was born out of a certain necessity and remained incomplete. The future degeneration of the system grew out of this fact of history: the irresponsibility of the government parties and that of the Communist opposition. Government irresponsibility in particular allowed the abnormal growth of a system of corruption thanks to the impunity of the ruling class.[22] If that was the outcome, perhaps necessary, of the impossibility of an alternation, and the ideological split in the country, the practice of hidden or under-the-table collaboration only contributed to the general irresponsibility of the political class in the democratic system in the long run.

All these institutional, historical and political factors taken together have meant that the Italian system has not been able to develop a definitive model of democracy throughout its republican history, that is a stable order accompanied by institutional rules and forms of behaviour. In fact, looked at retrospectively, Italy has never been either a full democracy based on the rule of a parliamentary majority or a completely 'consociative' democracy. It only created a negative regime, a 'partitocracy' which has no precedent among Western democracies. This is why Italy has had to face a political transformation in its traditional form of government, put off for too long a time and now essential to Italian society.

THE CRISIS IN THE REGIME SINCE 1989

Various factors and events contributed to the crisis of the regime between 1989 and 1993 and led to a delicate transition phase to what many now call the Second Republic (an allusion to the constitutional change in France in 1958).[23] Some of these factors are international, others domestic, but all are closely interrelated.

The end of Communism in 1989 not only led to the transformation of the PCI into the PDS (Democratic Party of the Left) – which eliminated the major obstacle to alternation in government as well as the primary cause of the blocking of democracy – but it also allowed Italian domestic policy to free itself from the bonds of international bipolarism and from the necessity of opposing the strongest communist party in the West. As long as Communism existed, many of the government parties obtained, so to speak, obligatory votes. The DC above all reaped the benefits of the anti-communist vote. But once this international and domestic factor was eliminated the position of the DC and its very unity as a Catholic party was compromised. The electorate felt freer to vote as it wished. In a situation in which it found itself face to face with the failure of government policies as well as that of the State itself, the electorate began to act. The April 1992 general election and the victory of the Northern

League sanctioned the beginning of the end of the traditional government coalitions that had been centred on the DC. The League was the new movement that, more than any other, challenged the entire, traditional Italian party system starting from the grass roots.[24]

It is no accident that support for the League is concentrated in the Northern regions, that is, in the richest and most productive parts of the country. Its growth – demonstrated by its capture of the Milan city government in the local elections of June 1993, held for the first time under the new rules of the direct election of the mayor – came about under the banner of protest against the 'thieving government' of Rome, against the inefficiency of the public administration, against the parasitism of the South, but above all, as a separatist movement from the rest of the country. The League has put forth the idea of a Federal Italy many times (where the term 'Federal' means division, not unity as at the European level). The country would be divided into three Republics (the North, the Centre, and the South). The proposal of the League, aside from the fact that it has been temporarily shelved, seemed to call into question national unity for the first time, an indication of how precarious national identity itself has become since the national political system became discredited.

Another international factor has been the pressure exerted on Italy by European integration. The objectives of this process of integration, including all of the provisions of the Maastricht Treaty, have been in distinct contrast to the characteristics and functioning of the political and institutional system in Italy. Between 1989 and 1993, the system greatly degenerated in all spheres of public life, including that of the economy, the legal order and public morality. The main features of this degeneration can be summarised as follows:

- abnormal growth of criminal powers; control on the part of Mafia-style organisations over about a third of the national territory (Sicily, Calabria, Campania, Puglia); the influence and participation of all the hidden powers in local and national politics (not just criminal powers, but also secret Masonic lodges, elements of the secret services); in these respects, the Italian State no longer possessed the classic monopoly of force and law over the entire national territory;
- mass illegality throughout the nation in all public and private areas for the purpose of conducting financial transactions or performing services;
- party control over all economic and institutional activities connected with public power (hence the derogatory label 'partitocracy' given to the Italian system);
- as a result, there was no free market, but rather an illegal economy in collusion with public power;
- an enormous increase in the national debt, due both to policies of assistance in a system of patronage aimed at buying votes, and to the

irresponsibility of the ruling class, as well as the effects of the political corruption unmasked by the 'Bribesville' scandal (the bribes to obtain public works contracts were charged to the public treasury); and
– the inefficient state of the bureaucracy in public services and in the public administration.

No comment is needed on how incompatible all this was with European integration. It seems clear that the basic lines of Italian economic and social policy stray considerably from the rigid criteria of convergence for monetary union set at Maastricht. This is due not only to government policy and its inability to cope with the economic situation, but also to facts relating to the basic structure of Italian society. It is quite true that since the postwar reconstruction period, Christian Democratic governments have constantly striven to find a place for the Italian system of production on foreign markets, European ones in particular, and to pursue stability in exchange rates over the long term in accordance with this goal. But this opening up to free trade quickly came into conflict with the domestic social and political equilibrium on which the Italian system had been based from the end of the war to the present. To meet the internal Communist challenge, and to face the demands of a society fragmented and divided from within between an advanced North and a backward South, the ruling class had to pursue a social policy aimed at obtaining consensus, thereby adding to social expenditures involving a strong component of public assistance, a constant policy of inflationary development, an increasing national debt, and the systematic devaluation of the lira. It also had to foster a patronage system in the State administration and collusion with criminal powers (especially in the South). All this was to be uncovered by the 'Bribesville' judicial enquiries of 1992–3. In the final analysis, Europe has been a major factor in exerting pressure for domestic political change. In the face of the requirements for European integration, more and more politicians, entrepreneurs, and public opinion has been convinced of the necessity of changing the domestic political system.

The 'Mani Pulite' (Clean Hands) Judicial Investigation into political corruption, which began in Milan on 17 February 1992 and spread rapidly to very many other Italian cities (Rome, Palermo, Naples, Venice, Reggio Calabria, Bari, Turin, Genoa and others) has definitively compromised the old political system.[25] The investigation has uncovered how the political system really operated in the 1980s. It is not a matter of individual episodes of political corruption – however serious these might have been – endemic to all democracies to greater or lesser degrees, but of a real, institutionalised system of corruption, in which almost the whole of the political class and the governing parties took part, as well as some portions of the Communist opposition, the principal private corporations (such as Fiat, Montedison, Olivetti) and public bodies (such as IRI, ENI), high officials in the civil service, judges, journalists, and a wide range of professionals (accountants, lawyers, architects). In short, the brutal truth is that political corruption was the rule in the functioning of the system, not the exception. From the accusations which have been made by the judges, a whole governing class has been placed under accusation: prime ministers, ministers, secretaries of the governing coalition parties, and many of their families – all accused of embezzlement, corruption, misappropriation and even collusion with the criminal organisations of the Mafia and Camorra. The effects of these accusations on the voters have been devastating. All the old parties involved have either been totally wiped out (the PSI) or greatly reduced in size (such as the DC, forced, in fact, to change its name to 'Partito Popolare' – Popular Party).

Finally, another factor for change has been the movement in favour of a referendum on behalf of electoral and institutional reform. In the face of the stubborn resistance on the part of government parties and all conservatives in favour of present institutions, clinging tenaciously to the proportional system – (these are present in all the parties, including the PCI/PDS and the left) – a reform movement crossing party lines formed at the end of the 1980s. It was composed above all of Catholic, lay and PDS representatives, who intended to use popular referendums as a weapon. The first notable success took place on 9 June 1991 with popular approval of a referendum proposal on a minor question (the reduction of multiple preferences to a single one).[26] The governmental establishment had underestimated and snubbed the initiative (Craxi had suggested that voters go to the beach rather than the polls). The response of the voters constituted a repudiation of the ruling class and an indication of the public will to change the electoral system from proportional to majority. Eight more referendums took place on 18 April 1993 (one calling for the end of the proportional system for the election of the second Chamber, the Senate, another the abolition of public financing of parties, and others the end of central State control in various areas). These obtained great public support. In this instance, the will of the people was unequivocal: a majority electoral system was being called for, along with the end of partitocracy, the end of a political ruling class which had been delegitimated in the eyes of the public. Following the success of the referendum of 18 April 1993, the Ciampi Government (the first in Italian history to be led by someone outside of Parliament, as if to symbolise the exceptional situation in which Italian parliamentary life found itself) obtained approval of an electoral law for the Chamber of Deputies and the Senate on 4 August 1993. It provided for 75 per cent of the seats in both houses to be elected on a majority basis (single-member constituencies elected in a single balloting session) and 25 per cent of the seats under the proportional system (party lists remained for the Chamber of Deputies, with the election of the candidates with the most votes in the single-member constituencies for the Senate).[27] Even if

the new electoral system is the result of a compromise between the requirements imposed by the referendums and the old political ruling class,
and is a defective and muddled system, it concludes what has been called
a veritable 'constitutional revolution', allowing the early election of
26–27 March 1994 to bring about a real upheaval in the political history
of Republican Italy.[28]

CONCLUSION: THE MARCH 1994 ELECTION AND THE NEW ITALIAN SITUATION

What we have defined as a second transition between 1989 and 1994 had
a political outcome in the 1994 election which cannot be classified as a
normal political event. This election was the dividing line between what
was the postwar Republic and the newly emerging political system.
The outcome may not have pleased everyone, just as it displeased the
international community, since a government coalition was formed that
included a component related to Fascism (Alleanza Nazionale – the
National Alliance – a derivation of the MSI), but which calls itself post-
fascist. However, on the basis of just a few developments, it is clear that
the traditional institutional and political panorama has changed considerably.

For one thing, the party system of the First Republic has totally
collapsed. The DC, the party that dominated all the postwar coalitions
obtained only 16 per cent of the vote, after changing its name to the
Popular Party and after splitting several times. The PSI of Craxi has practically disappeared. All the small centre parties have disappeared or have
been drastically reduced in size (Liberals, Republicans and Social
Democrats). Among the old parties, only the ex-Communist PDS, with
20 per cent of the vote has held out. A brand new party has risen out of
the ruins of the old party system: Forza Italia under Berlusconi. By means
of a facelift and a new name, Alleanza Nazionale, based on the MSI,
obtained 13 per cent. One effect of the new electoral system is to make
the competition genuinely bipolar, even though there are three competing
coalitions. The Centre won 16 per cent, and has gained representation in
Parliament thanks to candidates elected on a proportional basis; the right-
wing coalition, Freedom Alliance, made up of Forza Italia, Alleanza
Nazionale and the Lega Nord obtained 43 per cent with a clear majority
in the Chamber of Deputies (no majority in the Senate); while the left
coalition, the Progressives, won 34 per cent. The latter were soundly
defeated despite all the predictions in their favour. For the first time in
its Republican history, Italy has a government on the right, which includes
the post-fascists. For the first time since 1948, there has been real competition for government on the basis of alternative programmes (free-trade
vs governmentalism, and new vs old). The coalition of the right has
succeeded in being recognised as a new alternative for government, in the

name of free trade, opposed to the left which has appeared to protect the old political order. However the impact of this latest election may be judged, there is no doubt that the model of democracy arising out of the transition of 1943–8 is now completely out-of-date. In a confused and even worrying manner, Italy is carrying out a second transition towards new institutions and a new party system.

In retrospect, and in light of the events of the past few years, the first Italian transition to democracy was a fragile one, the result of a constitutional and political compromise, which contained the seeds of a second transition. This did not bring about a cumulative development in democracy, but rather an eventual crisis in the regime. The anti-fascist foundation of the first Republic, which had always excluded the MSI, not only from the government, but also from associated areas, has finally crumbled. Anti-Fascism is no longer an agreed-upon system of values, not because Italy has become fascist, but because most of the voters consider the Fascism issue a thing of the past.

The protagonists of the change taking place are completely new and unknown as a political class. Where the political parties of the first transition had the situation fully in hand, now those carrying out the changes come from mainstream society, social movements, sectors of the State and new political formations (none of which dares to call itself a 'party').

From the above, we can outline some tentative conclusions about the degree to which the Italian situation can be viewed in comparative perspective. As already mentioned at the beginning, it seems difficult to fit the transition to democracy in Italy of 1943–8 into the framework of that of later transitions in Europe. It belonged to an international and domestic setting created by the Second World War and the experience of Fascism as a phenomenon of the same type as German Nazism. The institutional forms of democracy coming out of this transition, characterised by the dominance of the political parties, turned out to be precarious, even if they kept Italy going for fifty years. But it was international bipolarity that congealed the domestic alternatives, buttressing defective institutions and leading to a political system which degenerated into a partitocracy. Thus, there were certain similarities with the nomenklaturas of single-party Communist countries – swollen numbers, a lack of turnover, absence of checks and political irresponsibility, a privileged status, and the life style of a political caste.[29] These two political ruling classes had one thing in common above and beyond the difference in political system and institutions, their intimately oligarchic nature.

The inadequacy of the first transition, given the institutions and the nature of the parties, also explains the inevitability of the crisis after 1989, when international conditions and the growth of Italian society no longer sustained this domestic congealment (in other words, the domination of the DC or the centre) and that particular party system. But the second transition, presently under way, taking place in any case within a democracy, differs from those that took place in the other Mediterranean European countries (Spain, Greece and, we may also include Portugal). It originates in the very international upheaval of 1989. But comparison with the transitions in Eastern European countries stops here. If, on the other hand, we wish to examine situations which are more closely comparable, we should look at the system change in France from the 4th to the 5th Republic. In France, too, in 1958, as in Italy – under the pressure of traumatic events, such as Algeria for the former and 'Bribesville' for the latter – what was called into question was old-style parliamentarianism and the old political class that had prospered under such a system. The comparison is appropriate, for the problems of Italy between 1989 and 1994 have concerned the institutional forms of democracy and the need to redesign the State.[30] But this is a theme which goes beyond the set of problems related to the transition of backward countries and embraces that of the great Western democracies.

NOTES

1   Massimo L. Salvadori writes: '. . . all of Italian history since 1861 has been dominated by an anomaly that corresponds to nothing in the history of the other states of Western Europe. The anomaly is as follows: the succession of three regimes so very different and even diametrically opposed to one another, liberal, fascist and Republican-democratic has left behind one unchanging factor: a relationship between the governing core and that of the opposition such that the former has never been sent to the opposition and the latter to the government. The effect, certainly not a side effect, has been that the State has superimposed itself and crushed the government, thus, the governing forces have ended up taking the form of a 'State' and the opposition – that of an anti-State. The lack of alternation in government within each of the three regimes that have succeeded one another has characterised our entire history', M. L. Salvadori, *Storia d'Italia e crisi di regime*, Bologna, Il Mulino 1994, p. 20.

2   G. Pasquino, 'The Demise of the First Fascist Regime and Italy's Transition to Democracy: 1943–1948', in G. O'Donnell, P. C. Schmitter and L. Whitehead (eds), *Transitions from Authoritarian Rule: Prospects for Democracy*, Baltimore and London, The Johns Hopkins University Press 1986, p. 68.

3   P. Ginsborg, *Storia d'Italia dal dopoguerra ad oggi: Società e politica 1943–1988*, Torino, Einaudi 1989.

4   R. Battaglia, *Storia della Resistenza italiana*, Torino, Einaudi 1953; G. Quazza, *La Resistenza italiana: Appunti e documenti*, Torino, Einaudi 1953; C. Pavone, *Una Guerra civile. Saggio storico sulla moralità della Resistenza*, Torino, Bollati Boringhieri 1991.

5   P. Scoppola, *La Repubblica dei partiti: Profilo storico della democrazia in Italia (1945–1990)*, Bologna, Il Mulino 1991; G. A. Almond and S. Verba, *The Civic Culture: Political Attitudes and Democracy in Five Nations*, Princeton University Press, Princeton 1963; R. D. Putnam, *La tradizione civica nelle regioni italiane*, Milano, Mondadori 1993.

6   L. Morlino, (ed.), *Costruire la democrazia. Gruppi e partiti in Italia*, Bologna, Il Mulino 1993, p. 52.

7   A. Lepre, *Storia della Prima Repubblica. L'Italia dal 1942 al 1992*, Bologna, Il Mulino 1992.

8   M. Flores and N. Gallerano, *Sul PCI: Un'interpretazione storica*, Bologna, Il Mulino 1992.

9   G. Pasquino, *Degenerazione dei partiti e riforme istituzionali*, Bari, Laterza 1982.

10 G. Pasquino, 'Party Government in Italy: Achievements and Prospects', in R. Katz (ed.), *Party Governments: European and American Experiences*, Berlin, De Gruyter 1987, pp. 202–42; S. Vassallo, *Il governo di partito in Italia*, Bologna, Il Mulino, 1994.

11 O. Massari, *Modello Westminster e partito laburista*, Bologna, Il Mulino, 1994.

12 G. Pasquino, 'Regolatori sregolati: partiti e governo dei partiti', in P. Lange and M. Regini (eds), *Stato e regolazione sociale: Nuove prospettive sul caso italiano*, Bologna, Il Mulino 1987, pp. 53–82; G. Pasquino, *Istituzioni, partiti, lobbies*, Roma-Bari, Laterza 1988.

13 M. Calise, *Il sistema DC: Mediazione e conflitto delle campagne democristiane*, Bari, De Donato 1978; R. D'Amico, 'Voto di preferenza, movimento dell'elettorato e modelli di partito. L'andamento delle preferenze delle elezioni politiche italiane', in *Quaderni dell'Osservatorio elettorale*, 18, 1987, pp. 91–147; F. Cazzola (ed.), *Anatonomia del potere DC*, Bari, De Donato 1979; R. Leonardi and D.A. Wertman, D. A., *Italian Christian Democracy: The Politics of Dominance*, Houndmills (Basingstoke) and London, Macmillan Press 1989.

14 G. Di Palma, *Surviving without Governing. Italian Parties in Parliament*, University of California Press, Berkeley 1977; S. Cassese, *Esiste un governo in Italia?*, Roma, Officina Edizioni 1980.

15 G. Sartori (ed.), *Correnti, frazioni e fazioni nei partiti politici italiani*, Bologna, Il Mulino 1973.

16 O. Massari and G. Pasquino (eds), *Rappresentare e governare. I sistemi elettorali nelle maggiori democrazie occidentali*, Bologna, Il Mulino 1993.

17 A. Pizzorno, *Le radici della politica assoluta*, Milano, Feltrinelli 1993.

18 G. Sartori et al., *Il parlamento italiano 1946–1963*, Napoli, Edizioni Scientifiche Italiane 1963; F. Cazzola, *Governo e opposizione nel Parlamento italiano*, Milano, Giuffre, 1974.

19 D. Hine, *Governing Italy: The Politics of Bargained Pluralism*, Oxford, OUP 1993.

20 O. Massari, 'Democrazia dell'alternanza e riforma elettorale', in *Democrazia e Diritto*, 4, 1991, pp. 35–65; G. Pasquino (ed.), *Opposizione, governo ombra, alternativa*, Roma, Bari, Laterza 1990.

21 The experience could have given way to that 'third phase' in Italian democracy, consisting – according to Moro's plan – of preparing the conditions, through a broad coalition government (the historical compromise), for a democracy of alternation, with the complete legitimation of the PCI as a government party. But the plan was cut short by first the kidnapping and then the murder of Aldo Moro in May 1978 at the hands of the Red Brigades. On coalitions in Italy, G. Pridham, *Political Parties and Coalitional Behaviour in Italy*, London and New York, Routledge 1988.

22 Della Porta, *Lo scambio occulto: Casi di corruzione politia in Italia*, Bologna, Il Mulino 1992; F. Cazzola, *L'Italia del pizzo. Fenomenologia della tangente quotidiana*, Torino, Einaudi 1992 and *Della Corruzione: fisiologia e patologia di un sistema politico*, Bologna, Il Mulino 1988.

23 S. Hellman and G. Pasquino (eds), *Politica in Italia. Edizione 1993*, Bologna, Il Mulino 1993. It should be noted that the evaluation of Italian democracy in the 1980s by J. La Palombara was quite positive, J. La Palombara, *Democracy Italian Style*, New Haven and London, Yale University Press 1987.

24 R. Leonardi and M. Kovacs, 'L'irresistibile ascesa della Lega Nord', in Hellman and Pasquino (eds), op. cit., pp. 123–42; R. Mannheimer (ed.), *La Lega Nord*, Milano, Feltrinelli 1991.
25 D. Della Porta, 'La capitale immorale; le tangenti di Milano', in Hellman and Pasquino (eds) op. cit., pp. 219–40.
26 G. Pasquino (ed.), *Votare un solo candidato: Le conseguenze politiche della preferenza unica*, Bologna, Il Mulino 1993.
27 S. Warner and D. Gambetta, *La retorica della riforma: Fine del sistema proporzionale in Italia*, Torino, Einaudi 1994.
28 C. Fusaro, *La rivoluzione costituzionale: Alle origini del regime postpartito-cratico*, Soveria Manelli, Rubettino 1993; M. Calise, *Dopo la partitocrazia: L'Italia tra modelli e realtà*, Torino, Einaudi 1994.
29 A. Mastropaolo, *Il ceto politico. Teoria e pratiche*, Roma, La Nuova Italia Scientifica 1993.
30 K. G. Banting and R. Simeon (eds), *Redesigning the State: The Politics of Constitutional Change in Industrial Nations*, Toronto-Buffalo, University of Toronto Press 1985.

6 The emergence of new party systems and transitions to democracy

Spain in comparative perspective

*Paul Heywood**

INTRODUCTION: PECULIARITIES OF THE SPANISH TRANSITION

Spain's transition to democracy following nearly forty years of dictatorship under General Franco has often been lauded as a model example of how to move from an authoritarian to a liberal, pluralist polity. In addition to the extensive academic debate generated since the late 1970s by the transition in Spain, the recent collapse of Communism in Eastern Europe and the former Soviet Union has resulted in considerable political attention being paid to the 'Spanish model'.[1] Spanish politicians, academics, lawyers and constitutional experts have been much in demand in the former communist bloc, regularly invited to advise and comment upon the formidable political challenges facing the newly democratising countries of east-central Europe.[2]

It is one of the contentions of this chapter, however, that the Spanish model is of only limited relevance to the process of democratisation currently under way in the former communist bloc. Indeed, the Spanish example cannot be seen as prototypical even of the transitions to democracy which took place in southern Europe in the mid-1970s (Greece, Portugal and Spain). Each transition followed a distinctive pattern, with its own specific features and circumstances. To say this is not to adopt an anti-comparativist approach against the search for broad trends or causal sequences; on the contrary, it is clear that long-term patterns of development allowed southern Europe (including Italy) to be considered as a 'distinct and identifiable universe'.[3] A process which could loosely be termed 'modernisation', associated with economic development, occurred throughout southern Europe from the late 1950s and through the 1960s. Its impact was similar in all cases, involving profound changes in social structures: rural exodus, urbanisation, emigration, the influx of tourists, secularisation, the loosening of shackles on intellectual debate and the impact of external influences on latent economic, social, cultural and political conflicts all helped to undermine the dictatorships of southern Europe. Spain's integration into the Western capitalist orbit was a gradual process, beginning with the abandonment of autarky in the late 1950s and continuing throughout the 1960s and early 1970s. The significance of greater harmonisation with the economies of western Europe can hardly be overstressed: it laid the basis for the adoption and acceptance of poly-centric forms of economic and political order, such as markets, social pluralism and public debate. By the time of Franco's death in 1975, there was a widespread belief in Spain that some form of political pluralism was not only desirable, but necessary. In short, the economic growth, social changes and demographic processes of the 1960s are inseparable from the changes within civil society which presaged the emergence of democracy.[4] In the former communist countries, parallel processes did not occur prior to their collapse. Instead, the transition from command to market or free economies has been expected to take place not only coterminously with political transition, but also within an almost impossible timescale. The development required, and which has been demanded as a precon-dition of aid from the Western liberal democracies, took decades or even centuries to achieve in those societies which now seem to imagine that it can be managed in years or even months in Russia and east-central Europe.[5]

The socio-economic 'structural conditions' within which transitions to democracy take place at best set parameters for action rather than deter-mining the precise shape of any given case. The Spanish transition to democracy was marked by a number of features which were *sui generis*. Most important was the remarkable degree of consensus and compromise which characterised Spain's adoption of democracy. Even if the peaceful nature of the transition has been somewhat exaggerated in the literature, there undoubtedly emerged a tacit agreement at all levels of society to engage in a form of 'collective amnesia' in regard to the past. The ex-periences of the Civil War and the Franco dictatorship were neither closely analysed, nor denounced; rather, they were 'forgotten' or at least silenced in a so-called '*pacto del olvido*'. In a sense, a line was drawn and personal involvement in past activities of whatever kind was overlooked. It was this agreement not to rake up the past, not to demand any settling of accounts, which allowed for the extraordinary degree of accommodation which characterised the Spanish transition. The prevailing academic ortho-doxy which has begun to emerge in contemporary Spain is that both the Civil War and the Franco regime were somehow both inevitable and even necessary, thus absolving the need to attribute responsibilities.[6] There has been no equivalent in Spain to the German *Historikerstreit*, still less the opening of Francoist police files to public access as happened with 'Stasi' records in the former German Democratic Republic.

Compromise and accommodation, of course, are necessary features of any stable democratic polity and the Spanish transition in this regard differs in timing and degree rather than kind. Where Spain's experience does manifest a distinctive element is in the remarkable decision by the

Francoist *Cortes* (parliament) to vote itself out of existence in the Political Reform Law of November 1976. This act of political hara-kiri – difficult to explain in terms of any conventional political analysis – can be seen as critical to the subsequent smooth emergence of a functioning democracy.[7] It not only paved the way for general elections in June 1977 to a 'constituent *Cortes*', encharged with the promulgation of a democratic constitution, but also ensured that the initial stages of the transition took place within a legal framework provided by the outgoing state. The process is neatly encapsulated in the term '*ruptura pactada*' (negotiated break). In neither Portugal nor Greece did the existing political authorities voluntarily abandon their claim to power. In a few East European cases, most notably Hungary and Poland, the superficially similar decisions to relinquish political authority were in fact responses to a somewhat different scale of opposition pressure.[8] Moreover, transitions in the former communist regimes were marked by deeper uncertainties than existed in Spain. In eastern Europe, there were fears as to the potential Soviet response; once the Soviet Union had embarked on its own transition, the resistance of 'conservative' forces everywhere threatened in a much more overt way than had been the case in Spain to hinder or even block moves towards democracy.

Ultimately, the actual transition to democracy in Spain was initiated by the actions of key individuals, notably Juan Carlos and his adviser Torcuato Fernández Miranda, as well as Adolfo Suárez. This is not to argue that they were possessed of unique insight which allowed them to orchestrate a process which they knew in advance would result in a functioning democracy; indeed, it could be argued that the choices they made were highly constrained and in many cases responded to considerations of *Realpolitik*.[9] However, the point remains that the transition was immeasurably facilitated by the determination of certain elite actors to embrace pluralist politics, no matter whether this is interpreted as riding with the waves of pressure from below for democracy or trying to hold back the tide of Francoist reaction. The key decisions in regard to Spain's democratic transition were taken during 1976, before the legalisation of political parties (indeed, before the very formation of all but two of the national-level parties which were later to emerge as leading players on the political stage).

It is a second main contention of this chapter that political parties in Spain were as much shaped and influenced by the process of transition – notably in its early stages – as it was shaped and influenced by their actions. In fact, the particular nature of the Spanish transition to democracy had a critical impact on the development of political parties, affecting not only their role but also their structure and functioning. In this respect, at least, there would seem to be some clear parallels with other recently-established democracies: the nature and purpose of party political activity has changed since the age of 'mass parties'. Since the emergence of what has been termed 'mediacracy' (François-Henry de Virieu), in which the mass media play a critical political role, parties have seen their drive for membership subordinated to the search for votes. Whilst this is true to a greater or lesser extent of all industrialised democracies, it is of particular importance in those countries where democratic rules have only recently been established and parties do not have the historical resources of their neighbours in older democracies.

THE BURDEN OF HISTORY: COPING WITH THE FRANCOIST LEGACY

During nearly forty years of dictatorship under General Franco, party political activity in Spain was illegal. Inevitably, the lack of a post-Civil War tradition of electoral competition had a significant impact on the nature of the political parties which emerged in the post-Franco democracy. Even those parties which could claim some form of continuous existence throughout the dark years of dictatorship – the Partido Comunista de España (PCE) and the Partido Socialista Obrero Español (PSOE) – had, effectively, to be re-created under the conditions of democracy.

In broad terms, Spanish political parties are characterised by three distinctive features: low levels of membership reflecting a lack of rootedness in society, a high degree of personalism, and a tendency towards ideological imprecision. To a greater or lesser extent, all of these features (which are currently paralleled in the former communist countries) are related to the legacy of the Franco regime: forty years of dictatorship had inhibited the assumption of individual responsibility, the taking of organisational initiatives, and collective action. In short, there existed neither the tradition nor the experience of associative mechanisms which are central to the functioning of a democratic party system. Not only did democracy have to be established, but the civic culture necessary to sustain it had also to be nurtured.[10]

Political parties thus faced a double challenge in post-Franco Spain: they had both to support the establishment of a democratic culture and to forge their own identities within it. However, there was little time to sink roots in society: parties were legalised just months – or even weeks, in the case of the Communist Party – before the first elections of June 1977. Electoral success inevitably became a more immediate priority than the development of a mass membership. Votes were the first objective; party structures could develop later. Unsurprisingly, there was an explosion of new political parties seeking to capitalise on the new political freedoms: over 300 parties contested the 1977 elections. Most of these 'taxi parties' soon disappeared, leaving just three or four significant national-level parties.[11]

In practice, mass affiliation to the new parties never took place. Compared to a European average figure in the early 1980s of 15 per cent overall membership amongst the population, Spain barely reached 6 per cent.[12] Although falling levels of membership have been a feature of many European democracies, in Spain parties never became mass organisations. For instance, when the Socialist Party took over 10 million votes (48.4 per cent) in the 1982 elections, it had a membership of just 116,514.[13] By the same token, levels of party identification remained low: polls since the return of democracy have consistently indicated that nearly half the electorate claims not to feel close to any party. It has been argued that Spanish parties went from being parties of notables (*partidos de notables*) in the early twentieth century to voters' parties (*partidos de electores*) in the late twentieth century without ever having the opportunity to become mass membership parties (*partidos de masas*).[14] Alternatively, following Lawson, it could be argued that Spanish parties have offered electoral and clientelistic, rather than participatory, linkage to their supporters: party leaders dominate and offer 'favours' in return for votes.[15]

Spanish political parties were legalised in an era of ever-increasing mass media influence. In common with trends throughout industrialised democracies, political leaders were obliged to base their campaigns principally on direct appeals to voters via television, thereby undercutting some of the traditional functions of party organisations.[16] In a televisual age the public image of party leaders assumes an ever greater significance. It is noteworthy that Adolfo Suárez and Felipe González, the two dominant figures in post-Franco politics, were both consummate television performers. Political parties became almost exclusively identified with their leading figures, both in popular perception and media coverage. Indeed, concentration on personalities, rather than issues and party programmes, has remained a marked feature of much political reportage in Spain, a trend which appears to be mirrored in several of the former communist regimes.

The importance accorded party leaders found its reflection in the internal organisation of the major parties. Strictly regulated hierarchical command structures eventually became the norm, with little room for independent initiatives by the, albeit exiguous, rank and file membership.[17] Most Spanish parties conform to Roberto Michels' 'iron law of oligarchy', according to which organisational structures inevitably concentrate power in the hands of a small leading group. Consequently, personal tensions and rivalries abound within all the main parties, although this was especially true of the new parties of the right which were established in the wake of the dictatorship. The founders of the far right-wing Alianza Popular (AP) in 1976, all ex-Francoist dignitaries, were known collectively as the '*siete magníficos*' (magnificent seven); within months, however, deep divisions had become apparent, and by 1979 only Manuel Fraga Iribarne remained of the original seven.[18]

However, perhaps the most significant aspect of party political development during the transition concerns the question of ideological identity.

It is here that the legacy of Francoism may most clearly be seen. Although the prism of a left–right continuum through which political parties have traditionally been analysed in liberal democracies is arguably of declining relevance in what might be termed a 'post-material' world, it remains a useful starting point in regard to the Spanish transition. The Franco dictatorship ensured that the polarisation between victors and vanquished in the Civil War remained a constant of the regime, finding an easy translation into the left being equated with opposition and the right with power. When Franco died, both left and right had high hopes of controlling any post-dictatorial political settlement. In the event, both subsequently engaged in a degree of accommodation which would have appeared unthinkable during the regime's protracted death-throes.

For the left in particular, both historical continuity and opposition to the Franco regime were vital elements of its claim to democratic legitimacy.[19] The PCE had been the main bulwark of opposition to the dictator throughout his rule – a point repeatedly emphasised by both the Franco regime and the Communist leadership. It seemed natural to assume that, in any post-Franco democratic settlement, the PCE could viably seek to play a role analogous to that of the Partito Comunista Italiano (PCI) in postwar Italy. Moreover, in anticipation of such a development, the PCE leadership had stressed its links to an emerging west European communist order which claimed ever greater distance from the CPSU in Moscow. Santiago Carrillo, secretary-general of the PCE since 1960, was a leading proponent of 'Eurocommunism', hosting a summit with colleagues from Italy and France in March 1977. As the June 1977 elections approached, confidence within the PCE was riding high: the party looked first to establish itself as the cornerstone of democracy and then lead a steady advance towards socialism.

The PSOE also harboured ambitions of dominating the politics of the left during any move towards democracy. Although the party's origins dated back to the nineteenth century, the PSOE had only slowly re-emerged from the devastation of defeat in the Civil War. Throughout most of the dictatorship, the Socialists – poorly equipped for the rigours of underground activity – remained marginal to the anti-Franco struggle, drifting ever further into self-absorbed stasis.[20] It was the takeover of the party from the old guard leadership in exile by radical militants from the interior during the early 1970s which proved crucial to its subsequent rise to dominance. Under the influence of Felipe González and Alfonso Guerra, the PSOE emerged to become the key force on the left. The establishment of links between the new Socialist leaders and Christian democrats who had become increasingly disaffected with the Franco regime, such as Joaquín Ruiz Gimánez, proved vital to the PSOE's reconstruction.[21] Such contacts formed the basis of collaboration between the PSOE and various progressive former Francoists in the aftermath of the dictator's death; this collaboration was to prove instrumental in promoting the image of Socialist moderation which was to be so important in the PSOE's eventual electoral success.

Yet, shortly before such success was achieved, the party had in fact shifted sharply to the left. The PSOE's XXVII Congress in December 1976 adopted a radical posture, rejecting 'any accommodation to capitalism or simple reform of the system'. The vision of a classless society, in which the state apparatus would be replaced by self-management, was thus seemingly fixed in the party's long-term horizon. There were two principal reasons for the PSOE adopting such a stance. First, the explicit embrace of Marxism as a feature of the party's identity allowed PSOE leaders to present an image of radical opposition to Francoism which would match that of their rivals in the Communist Party. Compared to the PCE, the PSOE remained a very small organisation, with just 9,141 members at the time of its XXVII Congress (the Communist Party claimed some 200,000 members in 1977). By espousing the doctrine of Marxism, the PSOE sought to negotiate with the PCE on equal terms and to avoid the inferiority complex which might derive from its less visible role in opposing the Franco dictatorship.[22]

Second, Marxism represented almost a badge of identity for the left-wing, anti-Franco opposition: it implied a wholesale rejection not only of the Francoist political system, but also of the capitalist values which underlay it. Moreover, Marxism chimed with the ideological tenor of the time, reflected in the prominence accorded in progressive circles to vogue 'neo-Marxist' thinkers such as Gramsci, Lukács, Althusser, and members of the Frankfurt School. This was a period in which capitalism was held to be on the verge of collapse, whether through legitimation or fiscal crises. The PSOE's adoption of an explicit Marxist self-image was thus seen at the time as neither particularly noteworthy nor surprising. It also helped fix the PSOE as the central focus of the myriad socialist groups and parties which sought to challenge the PCE's anticipated hegemony on the left.

In contrast to the left, the right had no historic parties ready to reclaim their democratic inheritance. Its problems were therefore two-fold. On the one hand, it had to create some form of democratically-oriented political organisation *ab initio*, even though its key protagonists had virtually no experience of democratic functioning. On the other hand, since the Franco regime had protected the right's traditional interests, it had to contend with a widespread rejection of the values it represented amongst the embryonic electorate. Just as in many former communist countries virtue has been defined in terms of a rejection of all ideas associated with the old regimes, so in post-Franco Spain there was a generalised desire to move beyond the narrow values of the dictatorship. Nevertheless, the right remained confident: after all, it had been in the political ascendancy for nearly four decades and perceived little threat from its opponents on the left. In early 1976 Manuel Fraga had told Felipe González that the

Socialists might be legalised in eight years' time, and the Communists never, adding with disdain: 'Remember, I represent power and you're nothing' (*recuerde que yo soy el Poder y Vd. no es nada*).[23]

In the event, of course, the hopes of both left and right were disappointed. Both found themselves obliged to trim their aspirations and engage in a significant trade-off: in a sense, the Francoist political class traded an amnesty over its past in return for easing the re-incorporation of the opposition into political life. The wheels of this implicit, though unstated, deal were oiled by the artifice of Adolfo Suárez, principal architect of the transitional process. The key to understanding Suárez's role in the transition lies in his lack of any obvious ideological conviction. He was a pragmatist *par excellence*. Once selected by King Juan Carlos to oversee the construction of a democratic polity, Suárez set about his task with remarkable dexterity. Suárez's were the critical actions which allowed the transition to proceed: the piloting of the Political Reform Law through the Francoist *Cortes* in late 1976, the legalisation of the Communist Party in April 1977, the calling of general elections for June 1977, the Moncloa Pacts of October 1977. None of these events was dependent upon party political initiatives. Instead, political parties merely responded in accordance with the views of their leaders, with whom Suárez held a series of personal interviews between July and September 1976.[24]

Although not a typically charismatic leader – preferring private wheeling and dealing to populist displays – Suárez can be seen as a classic example of 'swing man'. Parallel figures in the former communist countries arguably include Lech Wałęsa and Václav Havel, though neither had a similar *ancien regime* background. It is Boris Yeltsin whose position is probably most analogous to that of Suárez in that he emerged from the outgoing regime with the responsibility of overseeing its transformation into a democracy (although he had already moved further from the preceding regime than had Suárez on assuming power). Whilst he faces more determined opposition to his reform proposals than did the Spanish premier, Yeltsin has seemed blessed with a similar degree of ideological malleability. This could prove vital for the prospects of negotiations, but Yeltsin's readiness to adopt strong-arm tactics and his determination to retain presidential prerogatives may yet prove a stumbling block to the successful implementation of a democratic constitution. Some may also see a parallel between Suárez and Mikhail Gorbachev, but the Soviet leader was never so obviously committed to democratisation and his actions in any case took place against an entirely different background and on a vastly larger stage. Where a similarity does exist lies in the fact that both men lost control of the reform processes they initiated; as Felipe González commented with prescience during a visit to Moscow in July 1991, rapid processes of political change 'devour their protagonists'.[25]

One result of the Spanish parties' initial tendency to react to events rather than shape them was that major shifts in their identity and nature occurred during the early years of the transition.[26] Again, there would appear to be a certain parallel here with developments in east-central Europe, where ideological identities are not only uncertain, but also unstable. However, in contrast to the current situation in the former communist countries, there was less confusion in Spain as to the poles of reference of ideological identity: 'left' and 'right' retained a clear meaning in Spanish political discourse, even though parties underwent dramatic shifts in their programmatic positions. The left in particular rapidly moved from demanding a *ruptura* to adopting a policy which became known as 'realism'.

In the space of six months between the end of 1976 and early 1977, the PCE shifted from calling for an assault on prisons in order to release their inmates to arguing that street demonstrations were an 'ultra-right provocation', from insulting the monarchy to hurling abuse at anyone who brought a republican flag to party meetings. The determining factor behind these moves was Carrillo's realisation that, without such accommodation, the PCE would never be legalised. Thus, the party's entry to the democratic game was made possible only through the promise of extensive compromise: effectively, the party allowed the terms of its role in the transition to be dictated by former Franco regime apparatchiks such as Suárez. Although it could be argued that the PCE had little option over this, it is equally the case that the consequences for the party were to prove devastating: the sense of betrayal felt by many communist militants led to major internal schisms, mass expulsions, and a haemorrhage of members and support.[27]

For the PSOE, ideological reformulation followed a different logic. The results of the 1977 elections, in which the PSOE won 28.5 per cent of the vote, ended the Socialists' marginal status. Equally, by establishing the party's dominance on the left, they removed a major element of the rationale for its first having embraced Marxism in such an explicit manner at its XXVII Congress. In the aftermath of the 1979 elections, a shift in the PSOE leadership's political line started to become apparent: emphasis was now placed on consolidating the new democratic system and the party's self-definition as Marxist came to be seen as an obstacle to further electoral progress. By the early 1980s the need to defend and deepen Spain's fragile democracy against threats posed by both separatists and the military had become a key feature of PSOE thought. To defend democracy, the Socialists had to win power; to win power, they required sufficient electoral support. It was this simple calculation which lay at the heart of the PSOE's embrace of moderation.

One clear distinction between the Spanish transition and emerging patterns in east-central Europe and the former Soviet Union is that, with the exception of minority movements in the Basque Country, there was unanimity within the political elite over maintaining the territorial integrity of the state – even though there were arguments between centralisers and federalists. The break-up of Spain along ethnically-defined lines was never a realistic possibility, despite the fact that the country has long been marked by acute centre–periphery tensions. The intensity of nationalism which emerged (or re-emerged) after 1989 in former communist regimes such as Yugsolavia and the Soviet Union had no parallel in Spain – although the granting of independence to the Baltic states in 1991 provoked a flurry of demands by Catalan and Basque nationalists for greater 'self-determination'. Crucially, the early stages of the Spanish transition were unencumbered by territorial disputes: all major players were agreed on the physical boundaries of democratic Spain.

The true significance of the 1977 election lay in the electorate's clear transmission of its desire for moderation. The parties whose leaders were most closely associated with the past, the PCE and the AP, fared badly in comparison to the PSOE under the youthful González and the Unión de Centro Democrático (UCD), headed by Adolfo Suárez. In this sense, parties *responded* to the electorate's rejection of maximalist political options – whether of left or right – rather than setting the ideological agenda themselves.[28] Indeed, it could be argued that the UCD, which emerged as the largest formation with 34.6 per cent of the vote, was not in any very meaningful sense a political party at all. Rather, it served primarily as a vehicle through which Suárez could maintain his hold on power. To the extent that it had no clearly identifiable ideological programme, the UCD bears some marked similarities to various of the umbrella formations which have emerged around charismatic individuals in former communist regimes, such as Vladimir Zhirinovsky's Liberal Democratic Party and Grigory Yavlinsky's 'Yabloka' bloc in Russia or Civic Forum in the former Czechoslovakia. Such 'movement parties', which are primarily concerned with the political survival of their leading figures, are inherently unstable.[29]

The UCD was created in early 1977, just months before the June elections. It followed its victory in those elections with another in 1979, only to suffer a dramatic collapse in the general election of 1982, plummeting from 168 seats in the *Cortes* to just twelve. In early 1983 the party was disbanded. The key to this collapse lies in the internal structure of the UCD. In reality, the UCD was less a coherent political party than an electoral coalition.[30] It encompassed divergent interests – most connected in some way with the Franco regime – which sought to retain their privileged status. Five principal groups, each in turn comprised of several others, made up the UCD: conservative Christian democrats, state officials associated with the *Tácito* group (reformists who came to prominence during the latter stages of the Franco regime), social democrats under Francisco Fernández Ordóñez, various liberal parties under Joaquín Garrigues, and former *Movimiento* bureaucrats, such as Adolfo Suárez himself.[31] Once the UCD had achieved its primary purpose of overseeing the creation of a new democratic constitution, it began to break up. With neither unifying ideology nor organisational coherence, the UCD rapidly disintegrated, its symbolic *coup de grâce* delivered by the resignation of Suárez as prime minister in early 1981.

THE DEVELOPMENT OF A DEMOCRATIC POLITICAL STRUCTURE

The UCD's principal contribution to the Spanish transition was the piloting through the *Cortes* of the 1978 Constitution. The composition of the UCD meant that the constitution-making process would be critically influenced by figures formerly associated with Franco's dictatorship, thus allowing political change to be closely controlled within the confines of social and economic continuity. It is this fact, above all others, which distinguishes the Spanish transition from more recent examples of democratic transition in eastern Europe. Moreover, the June 1977 general elections ensured that, although there now was a formalised opposition, all the major political parties operated according to broad agreement over the constitutional issue being given priority on the political agenda. Other issues, in particular the severe economic crisis facing Spain, were pushed onto a back-burner. Work on the new constitution commenced immediately. At the end of July it was agreed to set up within the lower house a constitutional committee (later known as the Committee on Constitutional Matters and Public Liberties), which at the start of the following month elected a 7-member *ponencia* charged with drawing up a draft agreement.[32]

The *ponencia* began negotiations on the basis of two agreements: first, a procedural accord that each member would submit a separate text to each session and one of these would then be chosen as a discussion document during the secret deliberations; second, a more significant general accord over certain minimum points, accepted by all, which would be reflected in the final document. This latter agreement lay behind the much vaunted 'consensus' which marked the discussions, and which came to influence the entire constitutional procedure. However, it should be noted that the composition of the *ponencia* excluded certain interests from direct involvement in the process. In particular, non-parliamentary groups such as trade unions and employers' federations were able to exert influence only through indirect means, a fact which naturally favoured the latter given the make-up of the *ponencia*. Equally, the secret nature of discussions reduced still further the possibility of outside interests playing a role.

Two drafts by the *ponencia* were published on 5 January and 17 April 1978. These were discussed by the Committee of Constitutional Matters and Public Liberties, which issued its favourable judgment on 1 July, and were approved by the Congress of Deputies on 21 July. Thereafter, the new text passed to the Senate's Constitutional Committee, which introduced some modifications before approval was granted on 9 October.

Given the differences in the texts approved by Congress and Senate, a mixed committee of the two houses met to reach a definitive draft version, which was issued on 28 October 1978. The final formal stage in the process was a public referendum, held on 6 December 1978, in which 88 per cent of those who voted granted approval to the constitutional draft. Although it is a commonplace to talk of the consensual nature of Spain's transition to democracy, as reflected in this overwhelming majority vote, it should be noted that the bare figure masks some important points. In particular, nearly 33 per cent of all eligible Spaniards abstained – leaving the overall vote in favour at 59 per cent of the electorate. Of far greater significance was the fact that abstention rates were much higher in some areas than in others – most particularly in the Basque Country, where in some provinces only a minority voted for the Constitution. Overall, 51.1 per cent of Basques abstained and, of those who participated, 23.5 per cent voted negatively.[33]

In spite of the general consensus within the *ponencia*, a number of critical constitutional issues required delicate negotiation. These centred on the nature and form of the new democratic state – whether it should be monarchical or republican, unitary or federal – and its relationship with leading interests amongst the so-called *poderes fácticos*, such as the Catholic Church. Equally, the distribution of power between executive and legislature, as well as between head of state and head of government, were matters of some considerable debate. It has been argued that certain topics, such as the role of the military, were effectively removed from the agenda: they were considered simply too sensitive to be tackled head on in the immediate aftermath of the Franco dictatorship.[34] All of these issues have their roots in the divisions which have characterised Spain's modern history. According to Jordi Sole-Tura, a distinguished academic and politician who was a member of the *ponencia*, it is necessary to understand the nation's history in order to understand the process involved in instituting a new political order after the death of Franco.[35]

In broad terms, divisions polarised around ideological positions. The right – that is, the *aperturista* reformers from within the Franco regime who were genuinely committed to the creation of a democratic constitution – wanted a short constitution specifying a highly centralised monarchy as the form of state, with checks against constitutional amendment in certain sensitive areas. The left – that is, the party political representatives of the anti-Francoist opposition – was in favour of a federal republic, with measures to protect 'progressive' constitutional provisions from amendment. Ultimately, the final document represented an artfully contrived ambiguous compromise, with sufficient concessions to keep all main players supportive and involved.[36] The search for agreement on the broad outlines of the new democratic state was seen as more important than the committed defence of sectional interests. Once the basic shape of the new constitution had been established, then detailed issues relating to the functioning of democracy could be confronted. Only at this stage would political parties begin to assume a critical importance in the transition process.

ELECTORAL DESIGN AND THE EMERGENCE OF A PARTY SYSTEM

If agreement over the formal structure of the state was critical to the successful institutionalisation of democracy, political parties themselves were more directly and immediately affected by the nature of the electoral system. The electoral process is itself a major stimulus for the development of parties and a party system. A country's electoral system influences its party political structure in two obvious and related ways: first, the electoral system has an important bearing on the number of parties able to attain parliamentary representation; second, any electoral system tends to favour the interests of some parties – generally those involved in its elaboration – at the expense of others. In Spain, the current electoral system remains in essence that which was developed for the elections of June 1977, which had the specific purpose of electing a constituent assembly. Thus, many of its features reflect the exigencies of the earliest stages of Spain's transition to democracy.[37]

In return for voting itself out of existence under the terms of the 1976 Political Reform Law, the outgoing Francoist *Cortes* sought a number of concessions from Suárez in regard to the electoral system. There were three principal demands. First, a bicameral system, with the second chamber (the Senate) designed to favour conservative interests through its system of recruitment in order to protect against the lower house (the Congress of Deputies) adopting radical measures during the constituent process. Second, universal suffrage restricted to those over the age of 21 for fear of the impact of more radical younger voters on the political composition of the constituent parliament. Third, a majoritarian ('first-past-the-post') system of voting, which was believed to favour conservative parties. Although the first two demands were granted (the voting age was subsequently lowered to 18 prior to the 1979 elections), on the third it was decided to restrict the majoritarian system to elections for the Senate and adopt proportional representation for the Congress of Deputies.

The proportional system adopted for the 350-seat Congress was based on the d'Hondt model, in common with several European democracies. The system, which protects against strict one-to-one proportionality (especially in cases where electoral districts have fewer than six representatives), tends to favour larger parties at the expense of smaller ones. A 3 per cent threshold requirement, applicable in each constituency rather than nationally, was designed to protect against extremist groups gaining representation. In practice, larger parties have benefited considerably in those provinces with a small number of deputies (that is, fewer than five) and in rural areas. Equally, small parties with highly concentrated support, such as regional ones, tend to be favoured over those whose support is widely dispersed, a trend most notable in Catalonia and the Basque Country.

It is clear, then, that the design of the electoral system can have a profound influence on the shape of party politics. Equally, systems of party financing can have a decisive impact on parties' prospects. In theory, Spanish parties are bound by a series of laws on funding which restrict them to the proceeds of public subsidies, members' dues and strictly limited donations. The state defrays expenses incurred by parties during electoral campaigns according to their results, measured primarily in terms of seats won. Such an *a posteriori* system clearly has an in-built tendency to favour larger parties, as well as those with close relations with the financial world which allows them to seek credit advances. In practice, of course, political parties have systematically by-passed legal restrictions on funding: the major parties, notably the PSOE and the opposition Partido Popular, have increasingly engaged in what has been termed 'parallel financing'. Given that parallel financing involves favours and trade-offs, access to political power – whether at national, regional or local level – is a prerequisite for its successful operation, which again favours larger parties.

Recent revelations of the scale of political corruption in such countries as Italy, Japan and, to a lesser extent, France and Germany highlights the importance of the financial dimension in any study of political parties in new democracies. The emerging democracies of Russia and east-central Europe face a similar conundrum to that which has confronted Spanish parties, related to the fact that the acid test of any representative democracy is electoral consultations, at all levels from national to local. However, with political success ever more dependent on advertising and access to the mass media, parties are faced with the ever greater financial costs imposed by the inexorable logic of the electoral process. In an era of low party memberships, newly created political parties simply cannot rely on membership dues and donations to keep them solvent. In short, most political parties are over-extended and under-resourced, caught in the trap of having to maintain a high profile even between elections but unable to depend on the efforts of volunteer party workers to perform such traditional roles as door-step canvassing or delivering leaflets. The importance of the modern mass media has changed the nature of party political activity.

In Spain, despite the undeniable success of its transition, there exists what amounts to a power vacuum outside the core executive, with parliament in particular seen as an ineffective institution. Some have even detected a risk of the executive seeking to control the opposition rather than parliament controlling the government.[38] Indeed, parliament has effectively ceased to serve as a public forum in which major national problems are debated. The very procedural rules of the *Cortes* drastically reduce the opportunities for public speech available to members other than party spokespersons, reducing the role of ordinary deputies to little more than that of automatons. Negotiations and agreements are usually conducted at elite level, with little reference to the views of deputies or party activists. Moreover, since political careers depend more on party officials (who determine the composition of closed lists at elections) than on voters, political conformism tends to be the norm, thereby further devaluing parliament as a debating chamber. Strict party control over deputies may serve to guarantee a certain political stability, but it under-mines the relationship between citizens and their representatives.[39]

Concern over the efficacy of parliament as an institution is hardly peculiar to Spain, of course. The 'decline of parliament' is an issue in several liberal democracies. In the Spanish case, though, it is certainly paradoxical that the emphasis on moderation and negotiation which marked the democratic transition led to the establishment of a weak parliament. Conscious of the Italian experience in which the institutional framework of redemocratisation (1947/8) sought to establish the ideal of balanced powers between executive and legislature but in fact emas-culated executive authority, a central goal of the constitutional architects in Spain was to invest particular strength in the position of the prime minister. The function of parliament, meanwhile, was envisaged as being to facilitate negotiation between different political groups. The design of parliamentary rules was meant to encourage a 'pactist' style of decision-making, with negotiation between well-matched forces acting as a symbol of tolerance as well as an effective check on a secure executive.[40] In prac-tice, in a classic example of an unintended outcome of political action, the Socialist Party's electoral dominance between 1982 and 1993 allowed it to ignore the search for consensus. From October 1982, parliament followed government in a docile manner, unable to exercise its constitu-tionally-envisaged controls.

In the former communist countries, the risk of creating democratic structures which in practice undermine the efficacy of parties would appear considerable. Not only are parties desperately short of funds, with poorly defined political programmes, there is also a lack of tradition of parliamentary debate throughout much of the region. Where parliamen-tary debate does take place, it often appears futile or irrelevant to the aspirations of ordinary citizens. Just as a certain disillusionment with democracy took hold in Spain after the early excitement of the transition had worn off, so cynicism appears to have taken a remarkably rapid and firm hold in several former communist countries. The perceived weak-nesses of democratic politics, which inevitably introduces institutionalised uncertainty, enhances the appeal of strong leaders promising dynamic action. The battle-lines of political struggle tend to be formed around forceful personalities, who are often nominally the leaders of political parties which in practice are small bands of personal followers. Without the development of firmly rooted political parties and associative organisations to act as a counterweight to forceful leaders, the very lifeblood of democratic debate is threatened.

CONCLUDING REMARKS: POLITICAL PARTIES, CONSOLIDATION AND DEMOCRATIC DECAY

This chapter has argued that political parties, as such, were not central to the early stages of the Spanish transition: the critical decisions and actions which facilitated the emergence of democracy were taken by elite actors whose association with parties, where relevant, was often little more than nominal. This is not to deny the role of certain parties – most notably the PCE and, to a much lesser extent, the PSOE – in helping bring about the conditions under which a transition to democracy appeared ineluctable. The actual process of transition, however, was largely dominated by figures such as Juan Carlos, Torcuato Fernández Miranda, Fernando Abril Martorell, Adolfo Suárez and others who had no party affiliation. Even Santiago Carrillo, whose contribution to the success of the transition must not be underplayed, operated largely independently of his party (and thereby unleashed bitter divisions within it). Instead, parties emerged to play a central role in the *practice* of democratic politics only after the transitional process was under way.[41]

Nevertheless, political parties remain synonymous with liberal democracy. Once a democracy has been established and begins to take root, parties are its most identifiable political actors. They continue to serve – in however flawed a manner – as channels of popular expression, aggregators of interests, implementers of collective goals, and agents of elite recruitment. Most (though not all) of the elite protagonists who were involved in negotiations to establish democracy in Spain went on to become party political figures: parties inevitably became the vehicles through which democratic politics were played out. Indeed, political parties served to ensure that democracy became firmly entrenched in a remarkably short space of time. Just seven years after Franco's death, there took place a smooth transfer of power at national level from the right-leaning UCD to the PSOE, an event which would have seemed inconceivable just a few years earlier. At regional and local level also, parties (in general) manifested a sense of political responsibility which has helped to underpin a widespread belief in democratic values and practices. Perhaps the greatest testimony to the achievement of political parties in Spain is that it is now a commonplace to talk of Spanish democracy as being 'consolidated'.

Party systems – whether predominant, two-party or multi-party, moderate (centripetal) or polarised (centrifugal) – have also naturally been seen as important indicators of democratic stability. Yet, the *way* in which parties operate in a given democracy is dependent on a host of factors, not least the institutional design of the core executive. It has been argued by Linz and others that parliamentary systems are more conducive to successful transition than presidential ones, since they spread the costs and benefits of change more widely.[42] However, a system's formal designation is not necessarily a good indicator of how it operates in practice. As has been argued above, the *nature* of Spain's political parties was crucially affected by the transitional process itself. Rather than open, interactive organisations responsive to their members' concerns and aspirations, Spanish parties developed into oligarchic bodies demanding unquestioning loyalty from their small memberships. One unsurprising result was that many of these parties became weaker, rather than stronger, as the transition progressed. The UCD, as we have seen, was a case apart and collapsed under the weight of its internal divisions. However, other parties – most notably the PCE and the historic Basque Nationalist Party (PNV) – were also subject to acrimonious internal divisions, resignations and expulsions. The early history of the far-right Popular Alliance (AP, later PP) was similarly marked by personal rivalries and tensions.

The one exception to this general pattern was the PSOE. No less oligarchic than any other party, the PSOE nevertheless benefited from a sense of cohesion and direction under a highly charismatic leader.[43] By early 1980, as the UCD began to break up, it had become clear that the PSOE would almost certainly form the next government. The promise of power had an agglutinative impact, serving to mask any internal divisions and to attract new members. Indeed, loyalty was the more easily ensured by the ample opportunities for political rewards afforded by the PSOE's electoral victory of October 1982. It has been estimated that about 50,000 public posts were given to PSOE members between 1982 and 1984, during which time the party's total membership reached only just over 150,000.[44] In addition, the speed with which the PSOE achieved its national preeminence ensured that local and provincial networks were established only after the centre had become firmly entrenched, making it easier for the leadership to impose its decisions and guarantee discipline.[45] Such was the dominance that the PSOE established over political life that some analysts spoke of a blurring of the distinction between government and state: Socialist governments after 1982 were able almost 'to become' the state.[46] Yet, by the early 1990s even the PSOE had fallen victim to bitter internal divisions, precipitated both by corruption scandals and the struggle for the eventual succession to González.

Thus, in spite of the undoubted contribution of political parties to the transition's success, it is also possible to draw the somewhat paradoxical – and more negative – conclusion that the actions of political parties could represent a potential threat to democratic stability in contemporary Spain. Four trends in particular point towards the risk of democratic distortion and the entrenchment of a clientelistic style of politics.[47] First, political parties have tended to become increasingly oligarchic, with a growing divorce between leaders and members and little effort expended on recruitment. Second, the public discourse of major parties often bears little relation to their actual behaviour. Perhaps the most striking example is the mismatch between the social-democratic rhetoric of the PSOE and its actions in power.[48] However, the opposition Partido Popular's recent claims to be a centrist Christian democratic party have also been belied by a close study of its detailed policy proposals. Third, parties have tended to ignore public opinion in their policy formulation, preferring to deal directly with powerful economic interest groups whilst parliamentary debates are reduced to a banal and trivial level. Fourth, and most important, the revelation of widespread influence-peddling (what the French term *pantouflage*) and corruption within the major parties, together with the opacity of their financial arrangements, has engendered deep cynicism over the probity of the political class as a whole.

None of these features should be exaggerated, and nor is it the argument of this chapter that Spanish democracy is in any imminent danger of collapse. Rather, it is contended that, taken together, these developments in party political activity may contribute to an insidious undermining of civil society, replacing trust in democratic procedures with suspicion and doubts. The failure of political parties to sink deep roots in society and act as genuine participatory linkage organisations (as opposed to clientelistic ones) is a major contributory factor to this risk. Of course, democracy can formally continue to function even in a situation of extreme clientelism, as evidenced in Italy. However, in the light of recent corruption scandals involving parties not just in Italy, but throughout the developed world, it would be foolhardy to be overly sanguine about the likely contribution of newly-created and underfunded political parties to democratic consolidation in the former communist countries. Political parties are central to any representative democracy, but they can also serve to undermine the very survival of the open and free discourse and exchange upon which democratic institutions depend.

NOTES

* I am grateful for their comments on earlier drafts to Mary Vincent, Richard Gunther, Matthew Wyman, and Stephen White. The usual disclaimers apply.

1 See, for example, Samuel P Huntington, 'How Countries Democratise', *Political Science Quarterly* 106/4 (1991–2), p. 592. For a guide to the literature on the Spanish transition, see José A Gómez Yáñez, 'Bibliografía sobre la Transición a la Democracia en España', in José Fálix Tezanos, Ramón Cotarelo and András de Blas (eds), *La Transición Democrática Española* (Madrid: Editorial Sistema, 1989), pp. 809–55.
2 In 1990 one Spanish government adviser made the wry observation, 'One of Spain's main exports these days is the know-how of its transition period.'

Quoted in Geoffrey Pridham, 'Comparative Approaches to Democratic Transition: Southern European Experience, System Change in Eastern Europe and
the Role of Political Parties', paper presented to Political Studies Association
conference (Lancaster, 1991).

3   The term is from Salvador Giner, 'Political Economy, Legitimation and the
State in Southern Europe', *The British Journal of Sociology* XXXIII/2 (1982).

4   This is not the place to enter the 'structure–agency' debate which has characterised much writing on transitions to democracy. It is not my belief that
there is any direct causal link which can be read off in a deterministic or
economistic way between levels of development and the emergence of democracy. Nor do I believe that transitions are simply the result of free choices
made by rational actors. It may be more realistic to argue that economic
growth is neither a sufficient nor even a necessary condition, but rather 'facil-
itates' the development of democracy. Political actors rarely confront
situations as genuine choice-makers; usually, their range of options is strictly
bounded by a given 'structural' situation over which they have little control.
To this extent, they operate within a given set of traditions and institutions
which shape their sense of possible alternatives. See Víctor Pérez-Díaz, *The
Return of Civil Society* (Cambridge, Mass.: Harvard University Press, 1993),
p. 28 and Adam Przeworski, 'Some Problems in the Study of Transition to
Democracy', *Working Papers* (Washington DC: Woodrow Wilson Centre,
1979).

5   See Hannan Rose, 'From Command to Free Polities', *Political Quarterly* 64/2
(1993), pp. 156–71, and Misha Glenny, *The Rebirth of History* (2nd edn;
Harmondsworth: Penguin, 1993), ch. 9.

6   Recent examples of what might be termed this revisionist assessment of Franco
include Stanley Payne, *Franco. El Perfíl de la Historia* (Madrid: Espasa Calpe,
1992) and – more surprisingly – Juan Pablo Fusi, 'Para escribir la biografía
de Franco', *Claves de razón práctica* 27 (1992), pp. 8–15, and Santos Juliá,
'Franco: la última diferencia española', *Claves de razón práctica* 27 (1992),
pp. 16–21. Against such approaches, see Elías Díaz, 'La revista *Triunfo*: cultura
y democracia en España', *Sistema* 113 (1993), pp. 111–18 and Paul Preston,
Franco (London: Harper Collins, 1993), especially 'Epilogue: "no enemies
other than the enemies of Spain"', pp. 779–87.

7   See further José Casanova, 'Modernization and Democratization: Reflections
on Spain's Transition to Democracy', *Social Research* 50/4 (1983).

8   This is not to underplay the role of the opposition to Franco, which was
critical in ensuring that his dictatorship could not long survive his death.
However, although the opposition undermined the dictatorship, it was not
able to dictate the terms of the transition, unlike Solidarity in Poland. The
Hungarian case much more closely parallels Spain, with reform-minded
Communists making the calculation that they would most likely stabilise their
hold on power through direct electoral competition. Yet, even in Hungary,
reform Communists were spurred to action only by the uncompromising
confrontational stance of the organised opposition. See László Bruszt and
David Stark, 'Remaking the Political Field in Hungary: From the Politics of
Confrontation to the Politics of Competition', in Ivo Banac (ed.), *Eastern
Europe in Revolution* (Ithaca: Cornell University Press, 1992), p. 20.

9   The role of Juan Carlos as a 'modernising monarch' has been mythologised
in many accounts of the transition, for example, Charles T Powell, *El piloto
del cambio* (Barcelona: Planeta, 1991). Whilst it is easy to build an *ex post
facto* reconstruction of the transition which presents Juan Carlos as the 'motor
of change' (to use José María de Areilza's term), it is more likely that his
decisions were based less on deliberate calculation than on reactions to

ongoing processes which he neither controlled, nor even necessarily understood. The king would have been acutely aware of the fate which befell the Greek monarchy in 1974 (being married to Constantine's sister, Sofia).

10   Pérez-Díaz, *The Return of Civil Society*, p. 40 argues that successful transitions to democracy will come about only if, and only to the extent that, a civil society or something like it either predates the transition or becomes established in the course of it.

11   Such an explosion appears to be a common feature of transitions. In the former communist countries, 'taxi-parties' (so-called because their entire membership would fit into a taxi) are known as sofa-parties. In Spain, by 1987 there still remained over 200 officially registered parties nationally and a further 300 at regional level. See *Anuario El País* (1987), pp. 97–103.

12   Antonio Bar Cendón, '¿Normalidad o excepcionalidad?: para una tipología del sistema de partidos español, 1977–1982', *Sistema* 65 (1985).

13   José Fálix Tezanos, 'El papel social y político del PSOE en la España de los años ochenta. Una década de progreso y democracia', in Alfonso Guerra and José Fálix Tezanos (eds), *La década del cambio* (Madrid: Editorial Sistema, 1992), p. 46.

14   See Jorge de Esteban and Luis López Guerra, *Los partidos políticos en la España actual* (Barcelona: Planeta/Instituto de Estudios Económicos, 1982) and José Amodia, 'Taxonomía e inestabilidad del sistema de partidos en España', *ACIS* 3/1 (1990).

15   Kay Lawson and Peter H Merkl (eds), *When Parties Fail* (Princeton: Princeton University Press, 1988), pp. 13–38.

16   This development arguably reached its apogee with the election of Silvio Berlusconi in the Italian general elections of March 1994.

17   See Jorge de Estaben, *El Estado de la Constitución (Diez años de gobierno del PSOE)* (Madrid: Libertarias/Prodhufi, 1992), pp. 75–8.

18   See Paul Preston, *The Triumph of Democracy in Spain* (London: Methuen, 1986), p. 108 and Esteban and López Guerra, *Los partidos políticos*, pp. 160–71.

19   For a comparative analysis of the role of the PCE and PSOE during the transition, see Paul Heywood, 'Mirror-images: The PCE and the PSOE in the Transition to Democracy in Spain', in *West European Politics* 10/2 (1987), pp. 193–210.

20   Paul Heywood, *Marxism and the Failure of Organised Socialism in Spain, 1879–1936* (Cambridge: CUP, 1990), Helen Graham, *Socialism and War. The Spanish Socialist Party in power and crisis, 1936–1939* (Cambridge: CUP, 1991), and Richard Gillespie, *The Spanish Socialist Party: A History of Factionalism* (Oxford: Clarendon Press, 1989) together cover the PSOE's development from 1879–1982. See also Paul Preston, 'The Decline and Resurgence of the Spanish Socialist Party During the Franco Regime', in *European History Quarterly* 18 (1988).

21   The development of what might be termed an anti-Franco liberal intelligentsia during the 1960s was of inestimable value to Spain's transition, since they went on to become the democratic political elite. Through journals such as *Cuadernos para el Diálogo* and *Triunfo*, they were able to develop a democratic agenda based on direct experience of west European models. In east-central Europe it appears that the urban intelligentsia had a much smaller influence prior to the collapse of the old regimes, in spite of the promotion of Western liberal values by such dissidents as Václav Havel and Adam Michnik. See Glenny, *The Rebirth of History*, p. 19.

22   See Santos Juliá, 'The Ideological Conversion of the Leaders of the PSOE, 1976–1979', in Frances Lannon and Paul Preston (eds), *Elites and Power in*

Twentieth Century Spain. Essays in Honour of Sir Raymond Carr (Oxford: Clarendon Press, 1990). On PCE membership, see Juan Botella, 'Spanish Communism in Crisis. The Communist Party of Spain', in Michael Waller and Meindert Fennema (eds), *Communist Parties in Western Europe. Decline or Adaptation?* (Oxford: Blackwell, 1988), p. 70.

23 Quoted in Preston, *Triumph of Democracy*, p. 87.

24 Gregorio Morán, *El precio de la transición* (Barcelona: Planeta, 1992), p. 189. Suárez met with the Catalan, Christian Democrat and PSOE leaders between July and September 1976, and also made contact with PCE leader Carrillo through an intermediary, urging him not to place obstacles in the way of the transition. See further, Preston, *Triumph of Democracy*, ch. 4.

25 The comment was made at a special course in Moscow on Spain's transition. In contrast to Gorbachev, who effectively lost any real power through the Yanayev coup in August 1991, Suárez resigned *before* the attempted coup of 23 February 1981 came close to wrecking the Spanish transition.

26 Suárez himself, secretary-general of the *Movimiento* at the time of Franco's death, ultimately became disillusioned with the UCD, which he headed between 1977 and 1981; in 1982 he established a new party, the Centro Democrático y Social (CDS). In its first five years of existence, the CDS tried to carve out a distinctive centre-left identity, then allied in municipal elections with the right-wing Popular Alliance against the PSOE, before claiming to stand to the left of the PSOE at the 1987 European elections. Thereafter, in 1990, Suárez entered an informal pact with the Socialists, before abandoning politics altogether two years later.

27 See Gregorio Morán, *Miseria y grandeza del Partido Comunista de España, 1939–1985* (Barcelona: Planeta, 1985), pp. 506–632.

28 As Pérez-Díaz, *Return of Civil Society*, p. 34, has commented, 'at critical turning points in the spring and winter of 1976 and the summer of 1977, it was the public response that proved to be the key factor'. According to survey data, the ideological self-positioning of the Spanish electorate between 1976 and 1990 on a scale of 1 (far left) to 10 (far right) fluctuated between a maximum of 5.5 (1977) and a minimum of 4.5 (1980 and 1983). The period average was 4.8. See Luis Moreno, 'Las fuerzas políticas españolas', in Salvador Giner (ed.), *España. Sociedad y política* (Madrid: Espasa Calpe, 1990), p. 306.

29 See John Lloyd, 'Democracy in Russia', *Political Quarterly* 64(2), p. 154; Stephen White, Matthew Wyman and Olga Kryshtanovkaya, 'Parties and Party Formation in Post-communist Russia', *Political Studies*, 1994 – forthcoming.

30 It should be noted that this view of the UCD has been disputed by some analysts, such as Richard Gunther, who argues that it had established an extensive institutional base prior to its collapse (personal communication, September 1993.)

31 On the UCD, see Carlos Huneeus, *La Unión de Centro Democrático y la transición a la democracia en España* (Madrid: CIS, 1985), Mario Caciagli, 'La parábola de la Unión de Centro Democrático', in Tezanos, Cotarelo and de Blas (eds), *Transición Democrática*, pp. 389–432 and Preston, *Triumph of Democracy*, passim.

32 The *ponencia* comprised 3 UCD members, 1 PSOE, 1 AP, 1 PCE-PSUC, and 1 CiU/Basque-Catalan Minority. No representative of the Basque Nationalist Party, the PNV, was elected. See Gregorio Peces-Barba, *La elaboración de la Constitución de 1978* (Madrid: CEC, 1988), Jordi Solé-Tura, *Los comunistas y la Constitución* (Madrid: Forma, 1978), Miguel Herrero Rodríguez de Miñón, 'La elaboración de la Constitución', *Cuenta y Razón* 41 (1988), pp. 65–75.

33   Robert P Clark, *The Basques: The Franco Years and Beyond* (Nevada: University of Nevada Press, 1979), pp. 361–3.
34   See José María Maravall and Julián Santamaría, 'Transición política y consolidación de la democracia en España', in Tezanos, Cotarelo and de Blas (eds), *Transición Democrática*, pp. 207–8.
35   Jordi Solé-Tura, 'The Significance of Consensus', in María Antonia Turner and Kenneth Maxwell (eds), *The 1978 Spanish Constitution and Spain's Transition to Democracy* (Report of symposium held at the Spanish Institute, New York, 7 June 1988).
36   The 1978 Constitution has become almost a 'sacred text' (Pérez-Díaz) of Spanish democracy, generating a huge outpouring of literature, most of it written from a juridical standpoint. A representative example is the immensely detailed Enrique Alvarez Conde, *El rágimen político español* (4th edn; Madrid: Alianza Editorial, 1990).
37   See Esteban and López Guerra, *Los partidos políticos*, pp. 55–6; Richard Gunther, Giacomo Sani and Goldie Shabad, *Spain After Franco. The Making of a Competitive Party System* (Berkeley: University of California Press, 1986), pp. 45–53.
38   For example, Javier Pradera, 'Obsesiones, arrebatos y sarampiones', *El País*, 2 February 1992.
39   Alvarez Conde, *El régimen político español*, pp. 357–8.
40   See Paul Heywood, 'Governing a New Democracy: the Power of the Prime Minister in Spain', *West European Politics* 14:2 (1991), p. 110.
41   The argument put forward here is thus in line with Gianfranco Pasquino's observation that 'not all the processes of democratic transition have been party dominated; but all processes of democratic consolidation have indeed been party dominated.' See his 'Party elites and democratic consolidation', in Geoffrey Pridham (ed.), *Securing Democracy: political parties and democratic consolidation in southern Europe* (London: Routledge, 1990), p. 52.
42   Juan Linz, 'Transitions to Democracy', in *The Washington Quarterly* (Summer 1990).
43   Richard Gillespie, *The Spanish Socialist Party*, makes much of factionalism in the PSOE, arguing that it has been almost a defining feature of the party's development. In fact, one of the PSOE's great strengths during the transition was that its leadership was able to impose unity and discipline, albeit often by using heavy-handed methods.
44   Víctor Pérez-Díaz, 'Neo-corporatist experiments in a new and precariously stable state', in Ilja Scholten (ed.), *Political Stability and Neo-Corporatism* (London: Sage, 1987).
45   Juliá, 'Ideological Conversion', pp. 280–5.
46   Paul Heywood, 'The Socialist Party in Power, 1982–92: the Price of Progress', *ACIS* 5/2 (1992).
47   See Pérez-Díaz, *Return of Civil Society*, pp. 43–9.
48   On this issue, see Paul Heywood, 'Rethinking socialism in Spain: *Programa 2000* and the social state', *Coexistence* 30 (1993), pp. 167–85.

7 Securing democracy in post-authoritarian Greece

The role of political parties

*Michalis Spourdalakis**

INTRODUCTION

A number of relatively recent developments in advanced, and well established, liberal democracies (e.g. the dominance of the executive over the legislature and the concomitant statist tendencies, new patterns of interest intermediation, the emergence of new institutions of political representation) have cast some serious doubts upon the role of political parties. While this debate continues, and quite often produces a number of analyses of great theoretical insight, the growing literature on transition to and consolidation of democracy in southern Europe seems to converge upon the opposite conclusion: political parties have proven to be key factors in the democratisation process. In this sense any discussion of parties' role in these polities is vital to the understanding of recent developing trends (and shortcomings) in the functioning of these democracies, and may prove didactic in evaluating the democratisation processes well under way in eastern Europe.

The Greek case, as we will see, is particularly instructive regarding this latter point. This chapter attempts a re-evaluation of the democratisation process and the role played by parties in it. It argues that the key factors in the democratic consolidation were both the 'format' and the 'mechanics'[1] of the new post-Junta party system; as well as the system's relation to society and the role of the newly formed democratic institutions, articulated by the leading political elites of the forces who controlled the transition process. However, the chapter concludes that certain characteristics of this otherwise smooth process constituted the germs of the recurrent political oddities of the third Greek Republic and that in fact the analysis of these characteristics can be very beneficial (both methodologically and politically) in approaching issues involved in the democratisation process in post-communist Europe. To put it differently, with the historical luxury of the twenty-year experience of the post-Junta Greek party system, I will try to provoke the owl of Minerva to spread its wings over the logic that prevailed during its foundation and which seems to be responsible for today's trends and dynamics.

ARTICULATING THE STRATEGY OF DEMOCRATISATION

In the summer of 1974, the Colonels' regime collapsed under the weight of internal and external factors.[2] The military coup in 1967 and the dictatorship which followed had caused a major blow to the three pillars of state power – the military, the Crown and the party system, which until the coup, through a number of legitimate and semi-legitimate forms, had comprised the key elements of the Greek system. The army did not manage to establish itself as a legitimate factor within Greek politics and its incompetence was vividly displayed in all fields of public life including the military fortification of the country![3] The controversial role of the Crown towards the dictatorship as well as the usurping of a good part of its civilian (elite) support by the Colonels' regime did not place it in a favourable position. Finally, the fall of the Junta found the party system and the political elites of the country in an only slightly better situation. The pre-1967 political elites, with a few exceptions, had not been mobilised by the Colonels and, given the short duration of the authoritarian regime, were still around. However, their role in the pre-Junta regime (minor partner in the three-way political arrangement) and the 'restrictive parliamentarism'[4] in which they were the key component, did not allow much room for a mere revitalisation of the pre-Junta party system.

What had preceded the *Metapolitefsi*, i.e. both the seven-year dictatorship and the events which led to it, were not particularly conducive to a comprehensive and collective strategy for the democratisation process. The traditionally weak and suppressed civil society appeared, especially after the authoritarian experience, incapable of articulating any strategy for transition 'from below'. The resistance, both within the country and abroad, despite its political glamour had never taken on a mass dimension and its fragmentation was an obstacle to this. Therefore, the weight of the democratisation process had to fall on the shoulders of the dominant and unchallenged charisma of the first post-authoritarian prime-minister, K. Karamanlis. Thus, the transition–consolidation process was to become primarily a 'from above' project, proving once again that when the people are speechless, charisma prevails.

Karamanlis's magnificent performance in the post-1974 period, which resulted in the founding of the Third Greek Republic, was not however accomplished single-handedly. The successful democratisation of the country was also the result of the 'support' he enjoyed or managed to mobilise among the political elites. This 'support' was not always consistent, active or direct but often, and most importantly, tacit and indirect, coming even from some opposition parties namely the Centre Union/ New Forces, at the time the leading opposition party, EDA (United Democratic Left) and the CP (interior) (KKEesoterikou), especially during the first period of the *metapolitefsi*.[5] The consensus Karamanlis enjoyed, however, was not universal. There were voices challenging him which bordered upon 'anti-systemic' rhetoric by some political forces, namely A. Papandreou's newly founded PASOK and the Communist Party of Greece (KKE). These voices, though by no means disloyal to democracy, objected primarily to Karamanlis's dominant role in defining democracy and restricting it to parliamentary and electoral procedures.

In Karamanlis's plan for democratisation, the key role was reserved for political parties. Students of politics have shown repeatedly both in theoretical and empirical studies that political parties are the founding pillar in the functioning of liberal parliamentary democracy. Parties are, after all, unique institutions that can mobilise the citizens; recruit and contribute to the renewal of political personnel; articulate social visions and collective interests at the political level in such a way that provides the people with an object of political identification and affection; and are the sine qua non factor in the organisation of electoral competition through which representatives are elected to parliament. Karamanlis's strategy was not far from this classic perception of the relationship between parties and democracy. In fact, he himself stated, in a fashion appropriate to a political scientist, 'that it is political parties rather than governments to which peoples attach themselves and that a regime's fortune is more affected by the number and behaviour of [its] political parties than by [the rest of] its formal framework'.[6]

If the closing down of parliament is the death certificate of a democratic regime, then parliamentary revival cannot be seen as anything but the hallmark of a well founded democratisation process. Karamanlis seemed to recognise more than anyone else at the time, that an elected parliament would be the cornerstone in the consolidation of democracy. At the same time it seems that he firmly believed that democracy had not been 'functioning smoothly in Greece ... due [to] the fact that the conditions of its existence were missing or could not be created'.[7] To this conservative leader 'these conditions were a moderate political climate, peaceable political mores and institutions adapted to the particular circumstances of [the] country'.[8]

Furthermore, the disintegration of the old hegemonic discourse (nationalism, anti-Communism, politics of exclusion) by the Colonels' regime made the need for reconstruction of a new one particularly pressing. Nationalism with its one-dimensional attachment to US foreign policy had to be redefined and the politics of 'guided democracy' had to be replaced by a strategy capable of guaranteeing a working and prosperous democracy. Thus, the European/EC reorientation of the country's foreign policy was elevated to a major national interest. In Karamanlis's words Greece's EC membership was of prime national interest since it was not only able to guarantee 'our national independence'[9] but also because it would 'render the democratic institutions more secure'.[10]

At the same time, having dealt decidedly with the controversial policies of anti-Communism and the paraconstitution and exclusivist practices of the past, democracy was defined strictly in terms of parliamentary procedures, where the role of the parties was fundamental to democracy but understood as a 'necessary evil'[11] and the role of citizens was confined to that of consensus provider with respect to a predetermined pattern of power distribution and mode of economic development. This newly established hegemonic discourse, in which democracy was seen merely as a process of decision making, contributed greatly to the consolidation of the regime; but in retrospect it had some negative effects on the state–society relationship and the role of the parties in it.[12] Its depoliticising and de-ideologising overtones kept the untamed citizenry in line and protected the infant democracy from possible turbulence, but also laid the foundation for the pragmatic, technical and often economistic framework of political competition and, most importantly, revitalised old practices of clientelism as the prime mode of popular mobilisation and citizens' relation to the state.

At this point one has to say that initially the heavy ideological rhetoric of PASOK and of the communist left stood in opposition to this definition of democracy. However, after 1981, with the country's accession to the EC and Papandreou's rise to power, the Socialists came to terms with the harsh realities of governing the country and soon altered the(ir) political discourse towards more pragmatic and technocratic approaches. The latter was not particularly difficult to accomplish since the ideological rhetoric of the left political forces of the country never went beyond the essentially 'a-political' nature of the alleged 'over-politicisation'[13] that characterises Greek political culture. As for the pathological effects of the resurgence of clientelism, these were also expressed through and promoted by the parties' organisational structure and in their subsequent relation to both the state and society.

This was the logic that prevailed in the political initiatives of the pater patriae of modern Greek democracy, and which marked the dynamics of both the democratisation process and the role of the parties in it. It was a logic imposed by choice (grounded in the conservative orientation of Karamanlis and the leading transition elites) and by necessity (the need for fast and stable transition imposed by the delicate political circumstances). The 1974 'founding elections' set the framework of the developments which followed. The call for early parliamentary elections, only four months after the collapse of the authoritarian regime, resulted in legitimating pluralism, in reducing political uncertainty and in reducing the fragmentation of the political forces since it reduced the number of parties,[14] but it laid the foundation of a peculiar party system, whose 'mechanics' were inspired by a 'winner takes all' logic and a weak parliament.

In fact, to the extent that party systems contribute to the political articulation of state power, the post-authoritarian Greek party system, contributed to the perpetuation of an omnipotent executive, a standard feature of the country since the nineteenth century. Contrary to its European counterparts, where strong party systems had preceded their alleged 'statism', Greece soon displayed signs of an overgrown state, based however, on different presuppositions. It was a strategy which, to be sure, had at its heart political parties, but only as functional instruments for incorporating society into formal democratic procedures. This was vividly shown in the 1975 constitution, which was drafted, debated and finally voted upon by the majority of the leading political parties, as well as in the actual practice of the parliament. Thus, the post-authoritarian party system and the institutions of the political system display both signs of rupture and continuity with the practices of the pre-Junta polity.

This was also a deliberate strategy on the part of Karamanlis and his party. It was a 'two-tiered [strategy i.e. to] establish full political democracy . . . which would be both in tune with the structural changes in Greek society and economy over the preceding quarter century and capable of accommodating new entrants into the political system; [and to] retain control over [both] the timetable' and the changes involved in the democratisation process.[15] This was a process which not only meant the restoration of democracy but also its instauration,[16] the latter, given the democratic distortions of the past, being clearly ascendant.

The restoration–instauration trends which characterised the democratisation process were coupled with the rupture–continuity trend, which characterised post-authoritarian politics, was also graphically reflected in the spirit of the 1975 Constitution and the 'mechanical predispositions' of the party system.

The new Constitution unquestionably narrowed the gap between *'pays legal* and *pays réel'*[17] as it not only did away with the paraconstitutional networks and the practices of political exclusion[18] of the past, but also explicitly referred to the protection and the expansion of civil liberties, which are now better guaranteed. Furthermore, the new constitution recognised a number of social rights in the economic sphere that brought the new Greek polity closer to the constitutional trends of its European counterparts and the principles of the welfare state. On the other hand, however, the new constitution, which was supported by the overwhelming conservative majority of the Karamanlis governing party (73 per cent of the parliamentary seats), included clauses that favoured the executive clearly having the upper hand. This was guaranteed not only by the actual provision regulating the role of the President (though this was never invoked) and the cabinet in the organisation of the state – which led some to term the Greek system as semi-presidential – but also by the provisions which, in line with the country's past, where structures, relations and organisations of civil society are state dependent and regulated.

THE NEW PARTY SYSTEM: RUPTURE AND CONTINUITY

As we have already said, the collapse of the Junta signalled the delegitimation of almost all traditional poles of power of the Greek polity. The pole of power which continued to enjoy some legitimacy and popular acceptance was that of the old parliamentarians, especially those who, in one way or other, had been associated with the resistance against the Junta regime. However, this did not mean that these political elites were capable of resuscitating the old party system. All signs were that any effort in that direction would be like pursuing a mirage and that any partial achievement in that direction would be stillborn.[19] This seemed to be clear to the majority of the political elite, and especially to the most talented among them, K. Karamanlis and A. Papandreou being the prime examples. The new social demands arising from postwar development of the country, which as early as the 1960s pointed to the need for a new form of political representation; the experience of the Junta itself, which had contributed decisively to the bankruptcy of the political discourse of 'guided democracy'; the radicalising impact of the (limited) resistance and the international climate[20] can be listed among the prime factors behind the need to found a new party system.

The early election, however, in combination with the above mentioned traits of the Greek political scene and primarily the filigranic nature of Greek civil society left marks on the new party system. As in the case of the new Constitution the party system appeared at first glance to involve a deep rupture and yet a closer examination could clearly demonstrate significant elements of continuity with the past.

Karamanlis's own party, New Democracy, made this 'agony' for renewal vividly clear even in its name. And in his effort to outline its ideological framework, Karamanlis simultaneously defined the desired political purpose of the new party system itself: 'New Democracy is composed of experienced and healthy, as well as new progressive and radical political forces united in a common goal: to make the name of the party actual reality – to give to the country a new democracy'.[21] Papandreou's newly founded Panhellenic Socialist Movement (PASOK) made similar efforts to promote itself as a completely 'new political movement'.[22]

Therefore, it would have been simplistic if one were to claim that in terms of the left–right axis, ND occupied its right end, as had ERE in the pre-1967 period, and that PASOK occupied the centre, as A. Papandreou's father's Centre Union did in the 1960s. This is not only because of the self-images promoted by ND and PASOK alike, but primarily because both parties were products of and actively expressed a political discourse and approach which had very little in common with the pre-authoritarian period. The collapse of a political system which was based on a political discourse of anti-Communism and engaged in political exclusion, moved the political discourse to the left. The Greek right, previously a major promoter of politics based on these principles, could not continue to do so; and the rapid democratisation process, formalised in the new constitution, pushed PASOK beyond the legalistic demands for democratic reform of the 1960s Centre Union.

Overall however, the post-authoritarian political parties in Greece were made up, at least in retrospect, of two competing trends: one which represented a rupture with the past and expressed its completely new features and the other which displayed strong signs of lack of change. Indeed, all aspects of the party system, which, soon after the first transition period, developed into what was insightfully described as tripolar with bipolar competition,[23] displayed these contradictory trends. Since political parties are anything but static institutions and therefore relate to and affect their environment only within the context of political competition, we will refer primarily to the two major parties (i.e. ND and PASOK), which actually compose the core of party competition on the Greek political scene. And it is they that in effect have determined the party system's impact on the political regime.

To begin with, one has to underline the fact that there was a renewal of the political elites of the parties to a degree almost unprecedented in Greek modern history.[24] However, even in the context of this extensive renewal, signs of continuity were vividly displayed. A case in point is the fact that, even up to the present, there is still a strong element of the old political guard in the top leadership of the two parties, especially among those who were honoured with ministerial portfolios. In other words, while we had a radical renewal of political personnel, as studies of the composition of the parliaments indicate (e.g. 127 out of 220 ND members in the 1974 'founding election' were elected for the first time), the core leadership of both parties (especially in ND) was composed of the old politicians. In PASOK the formation of the party elite was somewhat different as its radical discourse distanced itself from the old political guard and their 'old party' (palaiokommatike) practices in a more explicit fashion than that adopted by ND. Papandreou's party up until 1977, as a result of its general reservations towards parliamentarism, displayed considerable apprehension towards its 'palaiokommatikoi' wing; but after its rise as a leading opposition party (1977) and its anticipated climb to power, it managed to reconcile its old political personnel with the new (radical) one. In this arrangement among the various tendencies of the party, the role of the pre-1967 parliamentarians was particularly strong, as also demonstrated in the post-1981 formation of PASOK cabinets.

But if one can cast some doubt on the parties' contribution to renewing political elites or on the novelty of their ideology; the novelty of their organisation is beyond any doubt. Both ND and PASOK adopted organisational principles which clearly differentiated them from the parties of the past. Greek political parties had (with the exception of the CP and the Communist inspired or patronised parties) followed quite different organisational trends than those in most of western Europe for reasons related to the formation of the modern Greek state, the nature of society, patterns of accumulation and historical experience. Parties were mainly organisational configurations of individual leaders, with highly decentralised structures, where the local notables played key roles in their principal activity, which was managing elections. In spite of isolated declarations of intent to organise on a mass membership basis,[25] the Greek parties were far from being institutionalised. Even after World War II, when they became more centralised and the party leadership was strengthened at the expense of local notables, they did not manage to become institutionalised by opening up to a mass membership. The watershed of the Civil War and the policies of political exclusion which followed, seemed to be a major barrier towards that goal. Mass mobilisation and the overall liberalisation of the 1960s made some intellectual groups within the liberal Centre Union demand that old party practices (palaiokommatike) should be abandoned. But the 1967 coup and the needs of the underground anti-authoritarian resistance cut short any real progress in that direction. However, the fact that it was primarily the 'dissidents' among the party functionaries, who were actually later on in the front line of organising the resistance, while the mainstream of the party system fell into deep hibernation indicated that the organisational structure of post-authoritarian parties was likely to be radically altered.

Thus, one can truly talk of mass parties in Greece only after the demise of the Junta. However, as one might have expected, even then we witness a co-existence of elements of novelty and renewal with the practices of continuity with the past. New Democracy at the outset made it clear that it desired no association with the 'obsolete parties of the past' and certainly that it was not a 'mere continuation of ERE'.[26] Regarding its organisational development ND declared its intention to develop along the lines of a 'party of principle'. Though it was recognised that '(ND) was founded by K. Karamanlis ... it was not a personal party'.[27] It wanted to develop collective procedures and organise on a mass basis. Ironically, contrary to what one may have expected, it was ND – the party of the Greek right – that respected its organisational promises to a large degree and not the socialist PASOK. To this day it has organised numerous party conferences and congresses, expanded its organisational recruitment both regionally and sectorally and managed to change its leadership four times without major internal dissent.

Of course, no one can claim even today, that ND is a typical mass party. Nevertheless, despite the expected democratic shortcomings deriving from the opacity of the Mitsotakis leadership (1984–93), where old organisational practices are still present, we can easily argue that the role of party membership goes beyond the mere legitimising function shaping party strategy. The decisive moves towards the structural modernisation of New Democracy occurred primarily after 1981, when the party of the right found itself outside state power for the first time in decades. In fact its most effective organisational development took place under the leadership of Mitsotakis, who, being an outsider to the party, thought that the strengthening of the party machinery under his strict control would give him an edge over the party's notables, who could challenge his leadership. However, to this day, although ND has come a long way and contributed to the overall modernisation of the Greek party system, it is far from being free either from the extra-constitutional power of its old notables or certainly from practices of clientelism.

PASOK, on the other hand, had less trouble presenting itself as something completely new on the Greek political scene. Being out of power during the transition period and having virtually no pressure from old political notables, PASOK developed quite fast and effectively by promising an organisational structure based on mass membership and democratic participation. In fact its early call for mass 'self-organisation of the people' gave the impression that the party was a popular creation. This idea was soon put to rest in a most dramatic way as its collective bodies and procedures were in effect replaced by Papandreou's charismatic omnipotence. Democratic procedures and mass mobilisation were promoted or allowed only when they were functional to the party's electoralist strategy. Those party members who demanded a form of development closer to the Movement's organisational promises were ousted by Papandreou and his camarilla, proving that the unprecedented participation voiced by PASOK was nothing other than a mere institutionalisation of its leader's charisma. Although PASOK's organisational practices hardly promoted truly alternative forms of participation among the timid civil society, we must nevertheless say in retrospect, that they contributed greatly to the transition–consolidation process. Its innovative organisational approach channelled to a great extent the long-standing (and unpredictable) demands for new (as opposed to pre-Junta) practices of political mobilisation. They helped to legitimate the transition process, while its overtones of organisational continuity with pre-Junta party practices in effect contributed to the consolidation of the newly born democracy.

In brief, the major components of the Greek party system displayed organisational elements that did not resemble the pre-authoritarian parties. However, they were far from being institutional expressions of mass, 'from below', political mobilisation. In fact to the extent to which efforts to that end surfaced, party elites and leadership were hostile and cut them short. At the same time, this should not lead to the conclusion that the major Greek parties are still not institutionalised and that they have no organisational resemblance to their European counterparts. The post-1985 strengthening of ND's party structure as well as the signs of organisational maturity displayed by PASOK especially after its 1991 2nd Congress,[28] are developments which, however, are very little appreciated by political observers of Greek politics, and do not allow us to draw such static and pessimistic conclusions.

PARTIES, STATE AND SOCIETY: A NEW BRAND OF CLIENTELISM

The new party system, however, displayed strong signs of inertia and continuity with the practices of its pre-authoritarian past. This continuity is vividly observed in the parties' relation both to the state, society and the actual functioning of parliament.

Indeed, Greek parties, being victims of their own acceptance of the state's apparent omnipotence, and in view of their hesitation to promote or recognise as political any collective action outside a strictly defined political arena and their guiding 'zero-sum' logic were forced to express their activity through clientelistic practices. But even this clientelism was subject to new, post-authoritarian trends and to the parties' own mass institutionalisation. Thus, the strengthening of the state's executive together with the strengthening of the parties' structures meant that only party infiltration of the state could guarantee the allocation of resources. Since collective interest could not be independently organised by a weak civil society through open competition, party infiltration of the state apparatus meant that party memberships could pursue their fragmented and individual self-interests. The previous personalised clientelism was thus transformed. It went beyond the control of party leadership and became impersonal and institutionalised as it was now articulated by strengthened party machinery. It is now party membership and not the attachment to individual politicians that guarantees the fulfillment of (social but) individualised demands. The ND and PASOK rotation in power further consolidated the democratic system, but also strengthened this new type of clientelism.

In turn this new institutionalised clientelism further weakened the autonomous articulation of demands by civil society, replacing it with a peculiar party omnipotence. Every societal expression was caused or classified by party labels and was immediately either delegitimated or controlled by the parties themselves. To be sure, there is no doubt that this new 'bureaucratic'[29] party-run clientelism had a great integrative effect on society and contributed decisively to the consolidation process. But at the same time it has contributed to both the perpetuation of the anaemic nature of Greek society and to undermining the cornerstone of democratic institutions i.e. the parliament.

Many inspired students have alluded to the consequences which these traits of the party system have had on the parliament of the third Greek republic. The high level of 'partyness', the political polarisation fuelled constantly by the dominant 'zero-sum' logic along with the constitutionally confirmed predominance of the executive powers of the state have resulted in a 'talking' parliament as opposed to a 'working' one.[30] Such a parliament obviously pays lip service to both of its prime functions. Its legislative function is badly performed since legislation never originates there, and this initiative has been left almost exclusively to the government. In fact, on an increasing number of issues, legislative powers are delegated to cabinet ministers (presidential decrees) and even to the other bodies of state administration which are far removed from public accountability.[31] But even when a bill is brought forward for debate, the strict application of party discipline makes it a government bill rather than a parliamentary one. The controlling function of the parliament is performed more efficiently than its legislative one. However, even there the parliament clearly displays a number of shortcomings that derive from the situation within the party system. Parliamentary control of the government is performed in a way that makes it 'unable to allow timely as well as sufficiently documented discussion of crucial contemporary issues'.[32] Usually the various constitutional procedures for the parliamentary control function are the excuse for an overall head-on collision between government and opposition. Deputies rarely debate issues 'on the basis of technical and objective criteria ... [and more often specific issues] are seen as part of globally conflicting socio-economic projects'.[33]

CONCLUSION

In summary, political parties were proved to be vital in the democratisation process in Greece. Although political parties were new formations which were founded in the aftermath of the Junta's fall, both the 'format' and the 'mechanics' of the party system were conducive to the transition–consolidation process. The conditions of the termination of authoritarian rule, the brief period of the transition and the inertia of long-standing political practices and structures of Greek society, however, made the party system (especially its 'mechanics') seesaw between rupture and continuity with its pre-1967 counterpart. Thus, despite the novel character of the party system in all spheres – ideological, organisational, and in terms of political practice and strategy as well as its contribution to renewing political personnel – Greek political parties displayed strong elements of the pre-authoritarian party-political practices. In this sense and to the extent that parties are key partners in the entire political system, the Third Greek republic has not moved away from traditional practices of the past but has been actively reproducing them. The phenomena of intense 'partyness', the practices of (now) institutionalised clientelism, society's incapacity to articulate autonomously its conflicting interests, the actual role of democratic institutions especially the parliament, and the subsequent reproduction of a 'heavy state',[34] all generate practices that are becoming daily obstacles to the further modernisation and renewal of the Greek polity and society. However, in retrospect we have to say that the practices of continuity that marked the democratisation process in post-authoritarian Greece actually proved conducive to it, since they functioned as stabilising factors in the delicate transition–consolidation process.

The generally successful process of democratisation in Greece and the positive role of political parties within it may lead us to a number of theoretical and methodological conclusions.

1 *Political and cultural heritage* plays a key role within every post-authoritarian political configuration and more specifically within the founding and the dynamics of the new party system. In the Greek case, for example, the symbolic impact of parliamentary politics was rather important. Parliament and party politics, despite their short-comings, continued in the pre-1967 period to be associated with the idea of democracy, an idea that even the Colonels' regime did not manage to delegitimate. Even under authoritarian conditions it continued to constitute the collective political vision the society could fall back on. Consequently, one should dig deep into the tradition of individual countries to identify and promote those democratic elements that are entrenched in a country's political culture and therefore are (indigenously) conducive to the project of democrat-isation. Continuity quite often has to do with patterns of political mobilisation, which in turn are related to people's level of polit-ical culture and education, and which cannot be ignored. Traditions of this kind cannot be replaced overnight, without endangering the process of consolidation. To put it differently, the rupture with the past, even in areas where deliberate political will can more easily be imposed, cannot be complete. A stable democratisation process entails the promotion of elements of continuity with some political (democratic) facets of the past.

2 *The ideological framing of party strategies* also plays a key role in the democratisation process. In the founding of the post-authoritarian Greek political parties, the redefinition of national interest functioned as a linchpin for the different political forces and became the congealing factor for the party system. This strategy, despite the systematic undermining of partial (and possibly 'destructive') social interests and its often nationalistic and self-indulgent overtones, created a political discourse, a code of political communication among political parties that secured the consolidation process.

3 The democratisation process, which is accompanied by, if not based on, *the strengthening of the executive with a parallel undermining of the autonomous development of civil society*, has negative effects on the development of the party system. These kinds of strategies in demo-cratising post-authoritarian societies, signs of which we often witness in post-communist societies, have of course short-term benefits, as they

tend to shorten the transition period; but at the same time they force political parties to depend heavily on the state, thus distorting their capacity for social representation and integration.

4   *The performance of the first post-authoritarian government* seems to be of great importance for consolidation. As the performance of the Karamanlis government has shown in the Greek case, the goods-delivering function of the democratically elected government contributes greatly to the legitimation process of the entire party system and the democratic institutions that are involved in it.

5   Finally, while it is obvious that party alliances are conducive to democratic consolidation, at the same time it is wrong to consider *party polarisation* as a necessarily negative development for the democratisation process. In fact quite often political and party polarisation helps decisively in legitimating democratic institutions, not only at the elite but also at the mass level, since they integrate dissent into the system. Party polarisation becomes even more functional to consolidation when accompanied by parties' rotation in power, as the Greek case demonstrates in the 1980s and 1990s.

NOTES

*   I wish to thank Professor N. Diamandouros for his extensive and constructive comments on an earlier version of this article. I have also benefited from comments from the participants in the conference on 'The Emergence of New Party Systems and Transitions to Democracy', organised by the Centre for Mediterranean Studies (Bristol 17–19 September, 1993). Finally, I have to express my gratitude to the editors of the volume for their encouragement and advice; and as always to H. Stefansson for making my English printable.

1   Sartori makes this useful distinction between the number of parties in a party system ('format') and 'mechanics' which refers to the actual workings of that system. In fact the numerical criterion is relevant to understanding how a party system works 'to the extent that it contains mechanical predispositions, that it goes to determine a set of functional properties of the party system first, and of the overall political system as a consequence'. G. Sartori, *Parties and Party System*, Cambridge, CUP, 1976, p. 128.

2   For comprehensive analyses see: N. P. Diamandouros, '1974. Η Μετάβαση από το Αυταρχικό στο Δημοκρατικό Καθεστώς στην Ελλάδα' (1974. The Transition from Authoritarian to Democratic Regime in Greece), *Greek Review of Social Research*, vol. 49. 1983; N. P. Diamandouros, 'Transition to, and Consolidation of Democratic Politics in Greece 1974–1983: A Tentative Assessment', *West European Politics*, vol. 7, no. 2, 1984; N. P. Diamandouros, 'Regime Change and the Prospects for Democracy in Greece: 1974–83', in O' Donnell G., Schmitter C. P. and Whitehead L. (eds), *Transitions from Authoritarian Rule*, Baltimore, The Johns Hopkins University Press, 1986; and S. Verney and T. Couloumbis, 'State-International Systems Interaction and the Greek Transition to Democracy in the mid-1970s' in Pridham, G. (ed.), *Encouraging Democracy: The International Context of Regime Transition in Southern Europe*, Leicester, Leicester University Press, 1991.

3 After the failure of a coup inspired and supported by the Greek Junta against President Archbishop Makarios in Cyprus and the Turkish invasion of the island, Greece was on the brink of war with Turkey.

4 See for example: N. Mouzelis, *Modern Greece: Facets of Underdevelopment*, London, Macmillan, 1978, pp. 115–33 and N. Alivizatos, 'The Emergency Regime and Civil Liberties' in Iatrides J. (ed.), *Greece in the 1940s. A Nation in Crisis*, University Press of New England, 1981, pp. 220–8.

5 See: I. Kaftajoglou, Πολοτικός Λόγος και Ιδεολογία (Political Discourse and Ideology), Athens, Exantas, 1979; and M. Spourdalakis, *The Rise of the Greek Socialist Party*, London, Routledge, 1988, pp. 74–81.

6 Letter to Constantine Tsatsos of 10 May 1966, from Karamanlis personal archives pp. 12064–80 (tentative enumeration); quoted in T. Pappas, unfinished and unpublished Ph.D. thesis on New Democracy.

7 From Karamanlis's proclamation on the foundation of ND, quoted in Clogg, R., *Parties and Elections in Greece. The Search for Legitimacy*, London, C. Hurst & Co., 1987, p. 223.

8 Ibid.

9 The implied national enemy here is no longer the communist threat coming from the North but the actual threat of Turkey which, after its invasion of Cyprus, had started to make territorial and subcontinental claims in the Aegean.

10 Karamanlis speech in Parliament 27 July 1976, quoted in T. Pappas, op. cit.

11 Karamanlis at the Preliminary Congress of ND 2 April 1977, quoted in ibid.

12 This idea about the role of parties was in a way reflected in the 1975 Constitution. In Part III, in the section where it deals with the 'Organisation and Functions of the State' in Article 29 it is stated that: 'Greek citizens possessing the right to vote may freely found and join political parties, the organisation and activities of which must serve the free functioning of the democratic government.'

13 I have argued elsewhere that the intense politicisation displayed by Greek society is essentially a-political since it is not based in any way on collective and articulated competing social interests but rather formed on the basis of sentimental values. It is a type of politicisation that leads to 'zero sum' political practices while it perpetuates the weakness of civil society as well as the dominant role of the state. M. Spourdalakis, 'Ελλάδα 2000: Δρέποντας τους Καρποθς της "Α-πολίτικης Γπερ-πολιτικοποίησης"' (Greece in the Year 2000: Harvesting the Fruits of 'A-political Over-politicisation'), in E. Katsoulis, T. Giannitsis and P. Kazakos, (eds), Η Ελλάδα προς το 2000 (Greece Towards the Year 2000), Athens, Friedrich Ebert Stiftung and Papazisis, 1988, pp. 108–18.

14 G. Pridham, 'Political Parties and Elections in the New Eastern European Democracies: Comparisons with Southern European Experience', Hellenic Foundation for Defence and Foreign Policy, *Year Book 1990. Southern Europe*, Athens, ELIAMEP, 1991, p. 254.

15 N. P. Diamandouros, 'Politics and Constitutionalism in Greece: The 1975 Constitution in Historical Perspective', E. H. Chenabi and A. Stepan (eds), *Politics, Society and Democracy: Comparative Studies. Essays in Honor of Juan J. Linz*, vol. 3, Boulder, Colorado, Westview, (forthcoming).

16 The distinction between restoration and instauration is rather important: The malfunctioning of Greek democracy before the 1967 *coup d'état* meant that the post-Junta regime had to found rather than simply restore democracy in the country. Ibid.

17 Ibid.

18 Although the regime established in the country after the end of the Civil War (1949) functioned under the provision of the overall democratic constitution of 1952 it developed practices whose democratic base was highly questionable. The ideological and political outcome of the historical events of the 1940s within the context of cold-war politics of the 1950s created a regime in the country which only formally/constitutionally could be defined as democratic. That is because the state had developed parallel with the constitution a number of informal practices of discrimination against and exclusion from political rights of a section of the population on the basis of their political beliefs and origins. These exclusion practices were fairly extensive ranging from political detention to governmental denials of essential civil rights.

19 The vanishing of the party Union Centre/New Forces, despite its modernising make up after the 1977 elections is a case in point. On the decline of this party see: T. Veremis, 'The Union of the Democratic Center', in H. R. Penniman, (ed.), *Greece at the Polls*, Washington, American Enterprise Institute, 1981, pp. 84–104.

20 See: S. Verney and T. Couloumbis, op. cit.

21 K. Karamanlis, 28 September 1974 in *Νέες θέσεις. Ανάλυση Ιδεολογικών Αρχών της Ν.Δ.* (New Theses, Analysis of the Ideological Principles of ND), Athens, Edition of the Journal 'Nea Politike', 1976.

22 See 'PASOK's Declaration of 3rd of September', in M. Spourdalakis, *The Rise . . .*, op. cit., pp. 288–96 and pp. 65–70. We will not deal with the 'traditional' (communist) left which were preoccupied with their internal problems and adjustment to the new terms of political competition. In any case the CPs impact has been rather marginal in the 'mechanics' and especially the 'format' of the party system.

23 G. T. Mavrogordatos, 'The Emerging Party System', in R. Clogg, (ed.), *Greece in the 1980s*, London, Macmillan, 1983, p. 82.

24 Only the August and November 1910 general elections, when Venizelos' Liberal Party came to power, which removed the old political elites from parliament can compare to the renewal we witnessed after the first three elections in the post-authoritarian period (1974, 1977, 1981). A.-I.D. Metaxas, Βιοκοινωνική και πολιτισμική χαρτογραφία της Βουλής, 1964–1974–1977' (Bio-social and Cultural Chartography of the Chamber of Deputies, 1964–1974–1977), *Politiki–Political Science Review*, vol. 1, 1981.

25 Here, we are referring primarily to Veniselos' Liberal Party and its promise to become a 'modern mass party', which of course was never realised (see: G. T. Mavrogordatos, *Stillborn Republic: Social Coalitions and Party Strategies in Greece, 1922–1936*, Berkeley and Los Angeles, University of California Press, 1983, pp. 81–7). Mavrogordatos, analysing the political forces of the interwar period characterises the efforts toward the creation of 'parties of principle' as a 'Sisyphean task' for the Greek party system (ibid., p. 64).

26 *Νέες θέσεις . . .*, op. cit., p. 11.

27 Ibid.

28 M. Spourdalakis, 'PASOK in the 1990s: Structure, Ideology, Political Strategy', in J. M. Maravall et al., *Socialist Parties in Europe*, Barcelona, Institut de Ciences Politiques i Socials, 1991.

29 'Bureaucratic clientelism' has been defined as the 'systematic infiltration of the state machine by party devotees and the allocation of favours through it'. Lyrintzis C., 'Political Parties in Post-Junta Greece: A Case of "Bureaucratic Clientelism"?', *West European Politics*, vol. 7, no. 2, 1984, p. 103.

30 N. Alivizatos, 'The Difficulties of "Rationalisation" in a Polarised Political System: the Greek Chamber of Deputies', in U. Liebert and M. Cotta, (eds),

Parliament and Democratic Consolidation in Southern Europe: Greece, Italy, Portugal, Spain and Turkey, London, Pinter Publishers, 1990, p. 144.
31   Ibid.
32   Ibid.
33   Ibid. p. 145.
34   'Heavy state' does not necessarily mean strong state. On the contrary, a strong state is a self limiting state, a state which intervenes in the society primarily through policies and not policing. The former tends to be a rather weak state and this is the main trait of the all interventionist Greek state. For an analysis of the essentially weak state in post-authoritarian Greece see: Sotiropoulos A. D. (1993), 'A Colossus with Feet of Clay: The State in Post-Authoritarian Greece', in Psomiades J. H. and Thomadakis B. S. (eds), Greece, the New Europe, and the Changing International Order, New York: Pella.

REFERENCES

Alivizatos, N. (1981), 'The Emergency Regime and Civil Liberties', in Iatrides J. (ed.), *Greece in the 1940s. A Nation in Crisis*, University Press of New England.

Alivizatos, N. (1990), 'The Difficulties of "Rationalisation" in a Polarised Political System: the Greek Chamber of Deputies' in Liebert U. and Cotta M. (eds), *Parliament and Democratic Consolidation in Southern Europe: Greece, Italy, Portugal, Spain and Turkey*, London: Pinter Publishers.

Clogg, R. (1987), *Parties and Elections in Greece. The Search for Legitimacy*, London: C. Hurst & Co.

Couloumbis, A. T. and Yannis, M. P. (1983), 'The Stability Quotient of Greece's Post-1974 Democratic Institutions', *Journal of Modern Greek Studies*, vol. 1, no. 2., pp. 359–372.

Danopoulos, P. C. (1985), 'From Balconies to Tanks: Post-Junta Civil–Military Relations in Greece', *Journal of Political and Military Sociology*, vol. 13.

Diamandouros, P. N. (1983), '1974. Η Μετάβαση από το Αυταρχικό στο Δημοκρατικό Καθεστώς στην Ελλάδα' (1974. The Transition from Authoritarian to Democratic Regime in Greece), *Greek Review of Social Research*, vol. 49.

Diamandouros, P. N. (1984), 'Transition to, and Consolidation of Democratic Politics in Greece, 1974–1983: A Tentative Assessment', *West European Politics*, vol. 7, no. 2.

Diamandouros, P. N. (1986), 'Regime Change and the Prospects for Democracy in Greece: 1974–83', in O' Donnell G., Schmitter C. P. and Whitehead L. (eds), (1986), *Transitions from Authoritarian Rule*, Baltimore: The Johns Hopkins University Press.

Diamandouros, P. N. (1991), 'PASOK and State-Society Relations in Post-Authoritarian Greece (1974–1988)', in Vryonis S. Jr. (ed.), *Greece on the Road to Democracy: From the Junta to PASOK 1974–1986*, New Rochelle, NY: Aristide Caratzas Publishers.

Diamandouros, P. N. (1993), 'Prospects for Democracy of South-Eastern Europe: Comparative and Theoretical Perspectives', in Stephen Larrabee F. (ed.), *Political Change and Security in South-Eastern Europe: Challenges for the 1990s*, Washington DC.: American University Press.

Diamandouros, P. N. (forthcoming), 'Politics and Constitutionalism in Greece: The 1975 Constitution in Historical Perspective', Chenabi E. H. and Stepan A. (eds.), *Politics, Society and Democracy: Comparative Studies. Essays in Honor of Juan J. Linz*, vol. 3, Boulder, Colorado: Westview.

Duverger, M. (1963), *Political Parties*, New York: John Wiley & Sons Inc.

Duverger, M. (1966), *The Idea of Politics: The Uses of Power in Society*, London: Harper and Row.

Ethier, D. (ed.) (1990), *Democratic Transition and Consolidation in Southern Europe, Latin America and Southeast Asia*, London: The Macmillan Press Limited.

Featherstone, K. and Katsoudas, D. (1985), 'Change and Continuity in Greek Voting Behaviour', *European Journal of Political Research*, vol. 13.

Featherstone, K. (1990), 'Political Parties and Democratic Consolidation in Greece', in Pridham G. (ed.), *Securing Democracy: Political Parties and Democratic Consolidation in Southern Europe*, London: Routledge.

Gillespie, R. (1990), 'The Consolidation of New Democracies', in Urwin D. W. and Paterson E. W. (eds), *Politics in Western Europe Today: Perspectives, Policies and Problems since 1980*, London: Longman.

Giner, S. (1982), 'Political Economy, Legitimation and the State in Southern Europe', *British Journal of Sociology*, vol. 33.

Gladdish, K. (1985), 'From Autocracy to Party Government: Interpreting Regime Changes in Spain and Portugal', *West European Politics*, vol. 8, no. 3.

Kaftajoglou, I. (1979), Πολιτικός Λόγος και Ιδεολογία (Political Discourse and Ideology), Athens: Exantas.

Kohler, B. (1982), *Political Forces in Spain, Greece and Portugal*, London: Butterworth.

Liebert, U. and Cotta, M. (eds), (1990) *Parliament and Democratic Consolidation in Southern Europe: Greece, Italy, Portugal, Spain and Turkey*, London: Pinter Publishers.

Liebert, U. (1990), 'Parliaments in the Consolidation of Democracy: A Comparative Assessment of Southern European Experiences', in Liebert U. and Cotta M. (eds), *Parliament and Democratic Consolidation in Southern Europe: Greece, Italy, Portugal, Spain and Turkey*, London: Pinter Publishers.

Lijphart, A. et al. (1988), 'A Mediterranean Model of Democracy? The Southern European Democracies in Comparative Perspective', *West European Politics*, vol. 11, no. 1.

Limberes, N. (1986), 'The Greek Election of June 1985: A Socialist Entrenchment', *West European Politics*, vol. 9, no. 1.

Linz, J. (1979), 'Europe's Southern Frontier: Evolving Trends Toward What?' *Daedalus*, vol. 108, no. 1.

Lyrintzis, C. (1984), 'Political Parties in Post-Junta Greece: A Case of "Bureaucratic Clientelism"?', *West European Politics*, vol. 7, no. 2.

Manesis, A. (1986) 'Η Εξελιη των Πολιτικών θεσμών στην Ελλάδα: Αναζητώντας μια Δύσκολη Νομιμοποίηση' (The Development of Political Institutions in Greece: In Search of a Difficult Legitimacy), Les Temps Modernes, *Η Ελλάδα σε Εξέλιξη* Athens: Exantas.

Mavrogordatos, T. G. (1983a), 'Rise of the Green Sun: The Greek Election of 1981', London: Centre for Contemporary Greek Studies, Occ. paper no. 1.

Mavrogordatos, T. G. (1983b), 'The Emerging Party System', in Clogg R. (ed.), *Greece in the 1980s*, London: Macmillan.

Mavrogordatos, T. G. (1983c), *Stillborn Republic: Social Coalitions and Party Strategies in Greece, 1922–1936*, Berkeley and Los Angeles: University of California Press.

Metaxas, A.-I.D. (1981), 'Βιοκοινωνική και πολιτισμική χαρτογραφία της Βουλής, 1964–1974–1977' (Bio-social and Cultural Chartography of the Chamber of Deputies, 1964–1974–1977), *Politiki–Political Science Review*, vol. 1.

Mouzelis, N. (1978), *Modern Greece: Facets of Underdevelopment*, London: Macmillan.

184 *Securing democracy in post-authoritarian Greece*

Νέες θέσεις. Ανάλυση Ιδεολογικών Αρχών τηε Ν.Δ. (New Theses, Analysis of the Ideological Principles of ND), Athens, Edition of the Journal 'Nea Politike'.

O' Donnell, G., Schmitter, C. P. and Whitehead, L. (eds), (1986), *Transitions from Authoritarian Rule*, Baltimore: The Johns Hopkins University Press.

Papadopoulos, Y. (1989), 'Parties, the State and Society in Greece: Continuity within Change', *West European Politics*, vol. 12, no. 2.

Pappas, T. (1993). Unfinished and unpublished Ph.D. thesis on New Democracy.

Pasquino, G. (1990), 'Party Elites and Democratic Consolidation: Cross National Comparison of Southern European Experience' in Pridham G. (ed.), *Securing Democracy: Political Parties and Democratic Consolidation in Southern Europe*, London: Routledge.

Penniman, R. H. (ed.) (1981), *Greece at the Polls*, Washington: American Enterprise Institute.

Pollis, A. (1988), 'Introduction. Regime Transformation and Foreign Policy: Spain, Greece and Portugal', *Journal of Modern Greek Studies*, vol. 6.

Poulantzas, N. (1978), *Political Power and Social Classes*, London: Verso.

Pridham, G. (1984), 'Comparative Perspectives on the New Mediterranean Democracies: A Model of Regime Transition?', *West European Politics*, vol. 7, no. 2.

Pridham, G. (1990a), 'Southern European Democracies on the Road to Consolidation: A Comparative Assessment of the Role of Political Parties', in G. Pridham (ed.), *Securing Democracy: Political Parties and Democratic Consolidation in Southern Europe*, London: Routledge.

Pridham, G. (1990b), 'Political Parties, Parliaments and Democratic Consolidation in Southern Europe: Empirical and Theoretical Perspectives', in Liebert U. and Cotta M. (eds), *Parliament and Democratic Consolidation in Southern Europe: Greece, Italy, Portugal, Spain and Turkey*, London: Pinter Publishers.

Pridham, G. (1991), 'Political Parties and Elections in the New Eastern European Democracies: Comparisons with Southern European Experience', Hellenic Foundation for Defence and Foreign Policy, *Year Book 1990. Southern Europe*, Athens: ELIAMEP.

Pridham, G. and Verney S. (1991), 'The Coalitions of 1989–90 in Greece: Inter-Party Relations and Democratic Consolidation', *West European Politics*, vol. 14, no. 4.

Sartori, G. (1976), *Parties and Party System*, Cambridge: CUP.

Sotiropoulos, A. D. (1993), 'A Colossus with Feet of Clay: The State in Post-Authoritarian Greece', in Psomiades J. H. and Thomadakis B. S. (eds.), *Greece, the New Europe, and the Changing International Order*, New York: Pella.

Sotiropoulos, A. D. (1993), 'Κρατική γραφειορατία και λαϊκιστικο κόμμα: περίπτωση του ΠΑΣΟΚ, 1981–1989' (State Bureaucracy and Populist Party: The Case of PASOK, 1981–1989), *Synchrona Themata*, vol. 49.

Spourdalakis, M. (1988a), *The Rise of the Greek Socialist Party*, London: Routledge.

Spourdalakis, M. (1988b), "Ελλάδα 2000: Δρέποντας τους Καρποθς της "Α-πολίτικης Γπερ-πολιτικοποίησης"' (Greece in the Year 2000: Harvesting the Fruits of 'A-political Over-politicisation'), in Katsoulis, E., Giannitsis, T. and Kazakos, P. (eds), *Η Ελλάδα προς το 2000* (Greece Towards the Year 2000), Athens: Friedrich Ebert Stiftung and Papazisis.

Spourdalakis, M. (1990), *Για τη θεωρία και τη Μελέτη των Πολιτικών Κομμάτων* (On the Theory and the Study of Political Parties), Athens: Exantas; forthcoming in English by Lynne Rienner, Westview, Boulder Colorado.

Spourdalakis, M. (1991), 'PASOK in the 1990s: Structure, Ideology, Political Strategy', in Maravall J. M. et. al., *Socialist Parties in Europe*, Barcelona: Institut de Ciences Politiques i Socials.

Veremis, Th. (1981), 'The Union of the Democratic Centre', in Penniman R. H. (ed.), *Greece at the Polls*, Washington: American Enterprise Institute.

Verney, S. and Couloumbis T. (1991), 'State-International Systems Interaction and the Greek Transition to Democracy in the mid-1970s', in Pridham G. (ed.), *Encouraging Democracy: The International Context of Regime Transition in Southern Europe*, Leicester: Leicester University Press.

8 The revenge of history

The Portuguese, Spanish and Hungarian transitions – some comparisons

András Bozóki and Bill Lomax

This chapter focuses upon two aspects of the transition from authoritarian rule to democracy, taking examples from Portugal, Spain and Hungary, with a view to identifying some common characteristics of post-authoritarian political transformations.

While the first section compares the role of reformers in the process of political transformation in Portugal and Hungary, the second examines the fate of the first parties to come to power in the case of Spain and Hungary. The first section looks at the reformers who at first appeared to have failed, only to make a come-back later; the second looks at the first victors of the transition whose success proved short-lived.

Analysis of the role of the reformers directs attention to the similarities in regime legacies that underlay Portuguese and Hungarian developments, and to similarities in elite dynamics at the end of the authoritarian period and during the early phase of democratic transition. The pre-eminence of radical groups soon passed and reformists with strong roots in the former authoritarian regime came once more to the fore. Comparison of the dominant parties during the early transition phase in Spain and Hungary points to the problems of creating parties from the top down and to common factors that destabilise the initial democratic coalitions, thus creating conditions for the emergence of new party associations that characterise the second stage of democratisation.

PORTUGAL 1974 – HUNGARY 1989: THE ROLE OF THE REFORMERS

In 1986 an American scholar, commenting on the outcome of Portugal's 1974 'revolution of carnations', observed: 'Portugal has emerged from its revolutionary experience with institutions more generally democratic than those which were replaced. This tremendous accomplishment separates Portugal from nearly every other revolutionary experience in the modern era.'[1]

Today, the Portuguese experience no longer appears unique, following the 'people's revolutions' of 1989 in eastern Europe that also resulted in the replacement of dictatorships by democratic regimes. The first section of this article compares the Portuguese and Hungarian transitions, with a view to reaching a better understanding of the nature of the changes undertaken and of their most likely final outcome.

At first sight the two experiences could not appear more different. Portugal in 1974–75 was seen by many observers as undergoing a 1917-style revolution, whereas Hungary in 1989 was a revolution against the very spirit and tradition of 1917, a rejection of the entire heritage of marxist socialism.

The Hungarian transition has been described as a 'negotiated revolution' in which mass participation was at a minimum and revolutionary confrontations were studiously avoided. The negotiations took place between elites, and politics was not allowed to fall 'into the street'.[2] In Portugal, on the other hand, popular mobilisation reached unprecedented levels, and almost every stage in the unfolding of events was marked by revolutionary confrontations. 'Popular power' was the order of the day.

Even then, the Portuguese transition to democracy was almost as peaceful as the Hungarian one. There were no armed battles, and only a handful of people died in the course of the political conflicts of 1974–75. The transition may not have been a 'negotiated' one, but it was comparatively bloodless and relatively peaceful.[3]

The liberalisation of the Kádár era, when Hungary was dubbed the 'happiest barracks in the camp' is often held as an explanation for the peacefulness and gradualness of the Hungarian transition. Yet Portugal too had a similar, if shorter, reform era after 1968 when the dictator Salazar's successor Marcello Caetano initiated liberal changes allowing for greater cultural and intellectual freedoms, limited freedoms for trade unions, and encouragement for the more modern sectors of Portuguese and foreign capital. By 1974, the dictatorship was an anachronism, holding back the very social, political and economic forces that made modernisation not only possible, but also necessary for development.

From this perspective, the changes unleashed by the fall of the Portuguese dictatorship can be seen as representing less an effort at revolutionary transcendence of the existing socio-economic system than an attempt to modernise and recuperate that very system. A similar analysis can also be made of the Hungarian experience, where it was equally the inefficiency and malfunctioning of the old system that led to the pressures for change.[4]

Both the Hungarian and the Portuguese experiences effected transformation and modernisation restricted to the level of the political regime and the political elites, while the political forces that would prove finally successful were those that initially sought to bring about not the overthrow, but the reform of the previous system.

The reformers of the Caetano regime

On assuming Salazar's mantle in September 1968, Marcello Caetano initiated a new phase in the history of the dictatorship, represented by the slogan 'renewal in continuity'.

Elections were held in November 1969, in which the democratic and socialist opposition groups had relative freedom to campaign but little chance of winning. The result was an overwhelming victory for the candidates of the National Union, interpreted by Caetano as a triumph for his proposals and a mandate for further progress on the 'road of reform'.

In 1970, Caetano formed a new government bringing in several young technocrats, many of a Catholic background, loyal to his new policies. This was particularly marked in the field of economic policy, where economists critical of the regime's past policies were appointed as state secretaries for Industry, Planning and Trade. At the same time, the promotion of better living standards, social welfare and educational policy was a main theme of the government, as Caetano sought to transform the *Estado Novo* into the *Estado Social*.

Caetano's commitment to reform had encouraged a group of liberal-minded individuals, the most prominent of whom was the Oporto lawyer Francisco Sá Carneiro, to stand in the 1969 elections on the National Union ticket, and some twenty of them were elected to the National Assembly. Besides Sá Carneiro, this 'liberal wing' included the founder of the independent weekly paper *Expresso*, Pinto Balsemão, as well as Miller Guerra, Mota Amaral and Magalhães Mota, most of whom were later to play prominent political roles after the revolution of 25 April 1974. They were also active in SEDES (Social and Economic Development Study Group), an independent pressure group set up in 1970 to promote social and economic change.[5]

Sá Carneiro and the deputies of the 'liberal wing' of the National Assembly initially sought to reform the regime rather than to end it. Technocratic reformers and modernisers, they were liberals in political matters, concerning individual rights and liberties, but not in economic and social ones, where they favoured state intervention and planning and social welfare policies. In many respects they favoured policies that could be considered 'socialist or socialising'. The democratic reforms they advocated were also limited to 'the gradual functioning of institutions'.[6]

At first they believed the Caetano regime was capable of reform, and they did not envisage any political action beyond the perimeters of the regime. Their hopes were soon dashed as Caetano, under pressure from hardliners and the escalating colonial wars in Africa, reverted to more conservative policies and abandoned the earlier promises of reform. As one commentator remarks, 'From late 1971 the process of liberalisation was at a standstill', while even the 'liberal wing' dwindled to six or seven deputies.[7]

The final straw was the decision in 1972 to reappoint the reactionary 78-year old President Tomás for another seven year term. The liberals approached the Governor of Guinea-Bissau, General António Spínola, to stand against Tomás, but Spínola declined, and Tomás won an overwhelming majority in the electoral college. By now, Richard Robinson remarks, 'Caetanist reformism was fatally paralysed'.[8]

Early in 1973, Sá Carneiro and Miller Guerra resigned their seats in the National Assembly, criticising the failure of the government to promote reforms.[9] With the support of SEDES and *Expresso*, they then tried to organise a 'third force' between the National Union and the democratic and socialist opposition, calling for new economic and social policies and a 'new political life'.[10] Once outside the regime, however, the reformers had no political base, and were eclipsed by the more traditional opposition forces that had achieved a united broad-left front at the Congress of the Democratic Opposition in April 1973 in preparation for the elections in October.

The impetus that finally led to the overthrow of the regime came not from the politicians but from the very person whom the 'liberal wing' had looked to as a presidential candidate in 1972, General António Spínola, the former Governor General of Guinea-Bissau. Spínola's book *Portugal and the Future*, published in February 1974, proposed a federal solution to save the Portuguese empire from the onslaught of the independence movements in the African colonies.[11]

Spínola's action encouraged a group of younger officers, increasingly disillusioned with the colonial wars and the regime that continued them, to form the Armed Forces Movement that would lead and direct the coup that finally overthrew the Caetano regime. The motivation of these young captains was to put an end to an increasingly pointless war, and when they launched their uprising on 25 April 1974, far from envisioning a revolution, they called upon Spínola to head the new regime because they felt that he alone could prevent the danger of power 'falling into the street'.[12]

Hungary's reformers

The reformers of the 'liberal wing' of the Portuguese National Assembly before 1974 found their counterparts in Hungary in the 'reform communists' of the Hungarian Socialist Workers' Party (MSzMP) in the late 1980s; technocrats and economic reformers who took over the government to establish its independence from the Communist party, abolishing the leading role of the party and heralding the demise of the one party state.

Just like the Portuguese liberals, the Hungarian reformers wanted reform not revolution, but recognised the only hope for saving the system, and their privileges and powers, was to change the regime. They too hoped to avoid power 'falling into the street' by supporting the presidential ambitions of a respected leader of the old regime, Imre Pozsgay, to ensure stability and continuity in the transition. In the Hungarian case, the 'reformers' were less successful, and Pozsgay failed to make the presidency, due to the more skilful politics of his anti-communist opponents.[13] But Spínola's role in Portugal was also short-lived, and he too was ousted once the popular movement radicalised itself in the months following the coup of 25 April 1974.

In Hungary, reform movements have a longer history than their Portuguese counterparts, going back to the defeated 1956 revolution. The 1980s reformers, however, came from a younger generation that had grown up under the more liberal atmosphere of the Kádár regime, having experienced neither the Stalinist terror nor the revolution of 1956 and ensuing repression. With little ideological commitment, they joined the MSzMP as the only channel for promoting change and pursuing careers.

They were personified by Hungary's last communist prime minister, Miklós Németh, born in 1948 and eight years old in 1956. A lecturer in economics at the Karl Marx University in the 1970s, Németh spent a year as a visiting scholar at Harvard, returning to become an economic functionary of the MSzMP central committee in the 1980s, a central committee secretary in 1987–8, and finally Prime Minister in November 1988. Abandoning the party after the 1990 elections, Németh resigned his seat to become vice-president of the European Bank for Reconstruction and Development.

Németh and his colleagues are remarkably similar to Sá Carneiro and the Portuguese liberals, even though the latter never achieved office under the Caetano regime. Both groups comprised technocratic modernisers rather than ideological politicians; both were *étatiste* and prepared to accept limited forms of democracy. Both criticised the existing political system because of its inefficiency in the modern world. Both were temporarily swept away by the changes they served to inspire.

The Hungarian reformers might have been more successful had the Kádár regime responded more positively to Mikhail Gorbachev's advent to power in the USSR in 1985. Yet whether for fear that Gorbachev would not last and his fall would be followed by a new retrenchment, or that Gorbachev's very success would serve to undermine the system itself, Kádár refused to take any chances and his final years in power were marked by an even greater conservatism and stagnation than in the past. The last years of the regime saw the ascendancy of Károly Grósz who, as prime minister from 1987 to 1988 and party leader from 1988 to 1989, pursued economic reform under hard-line political control.

Grósz's approach served only to radicalise the reformers, who called for more rapid progress. Four of the most outspoken were expelled from the MSzMP in April 1988.[14] The following year saw the rise of a rank-and-file reformist movement calling for changes in the party leadership and the introduction of political democracy. The movement saw its leader as Imre Pozsgay, head of the Patriotic People's Front from 1982 to 1988, who became a Politburo member and Minister of State responsible for political reform in 1988.

Pozsgay was both an ambitious and a cautious politician. In January 1989 he momentarily seized the initiative, declaring 1956 had been not a 'counter-revolution' but a 'popular uprising'. Next, the MSzMP leadership agreed to introduce a multi-party system and to permit the formation of independent platforms within the party. This step enabled the reformers to set up reform circles throughout the country and hold a national 'reform workshop' at Kecskemét in April. Many of the rank-and-file now favoured a complete break with the old party, and went to Kecskemét expecting to take part in the launch of a new one. Pozsgay, however, failed to act, and lost the chance for a clean break with the old regime.[15]

Pozsgay's decision to remain within the MSzMP saw the beginning of a rapid decline in his popularity. The much heralded party congress in October that dissolved and re-formed the party as the Hungarian Socialist Party (MSzP), involved a compromise that satisfied no one and saw the party refusing to abandon its entrenched privileges – its properties, workplace branches and workers' militia. In the public eye, the changes were merely cosmetic.

Pozsgay's ambitions, however, remained, with presidential elections planned for the autumn and parliamentary elections the following spring. The MSzP's opinion poll ratings stood at 30 per cent or over, and party leaders felt that after free elections they would be able to form a coalition government with the opposition Hungarian Democratic Forum whose general secretary, Zoltán Biró, was a close colleague of Pozsgay. They regarded the more radical opposition groups, the Free Democrats and Young Democrats, as students and intellectuals with no substantial constituency.

At this point, the radical opposition forces seized the initiative from the reform communists. The Free Democrats and Young Democrats refused to sign the final agreement of the Trilateral Talks preparing the way for presidential and parliamentary elections, and launched a strident campaign for a referendum over the MSzP's properties, workplace branches and militia, and whether the president should be elected by popular vote as the MSzP wanted, or by the parliament after the elections as they preferred.

The referendum, held shortly after the fall of the Berlin wall and at the height of Czechoslovakia's 'velvet revolution', was won by an overwhelming majority of 95 per cent for the MSzP to abandon its properties, branches and militia, and by the narrowest margin, 50.07 per cent to 49.93 per cent, for the postponement of the presidential elections. The result transformed the Free Democrats and Young Democrats into major political forces, and finally dashed the hopes of Pozsgay and the reform communists.

The eclipse of the reformers

Despite the set-back of the referendum, the Németh government continued in office to become a true government of reformers and technocrats, asserting its independence of party control and acting on criteria of economic rationality and efficiency. In the parliamentary elections of spring 1990, however, the MSzP went down to ignominious defeat, and with it went the hopes and aspirations of the reformers too.

Immediately after the elections, Németh resigned from the MSzP to sit as an independent, and a year later he also resigned from parliament to become vice-president of the European Bank for Reconstruction and Development. From April 1990, Pozsgay served as the MSzP's parliamentary leader, but in November he resigned both from this post and from the party. Though the MSzP had shed its hardliners (who had reconstituted the MSzMP) and abandoned its former practices and privileges to become a fully reformist party with an explicitly social democratic programme, its future prospects looked bleak.

Fifteen years earlier, in Portugal, the fall of the Caetano regime had suggested a new political future for the earlier advocates of reform. With Spínola in the presidency, and a predominantly civilian provisional government formed by the respected conservative Palma Carlos in which two cabinet posts went to members of the former 'liberal wing', Sá Carneiro and Magalhães Mota, leaders of a new Popular Democratic Party (PPD), it looked as though their day had finally arrived.

The 'revolution of carnations', however, swiftly moved to the left and in July prime minister Palma Carlos resigned and Sá Carneiro followed him. In the next three provisional governments, under the premiership of the pro-communist Vasco Gonçalves, the former reformists played only minor roles. Yet in constituent assembly elections in 1975 the PPD, with 26 per cent of the votes, emerged as the second largest party, behind the socialists with 38 per cent but ahead of both the communists and the more conservative Social Democratic Centre.

Emerging as the victors from the elections, the socialists protested against the growing influence of the Communist Party and the military left and boycotted cabinet meetings; finally leaving the government in July, to be followed a week later by the PPD. The ensuing 'hot summer' saw an escalation of conflicts in which the Socialist Party headed the opposition to the Communist Party and the increasingly triumphalist far left.

The onward march of the left was finally halted by the centrist coup of 25 November 1975 in which moderate army officers close to the socialists ousted the far left from key positions in the military and state administration, and restored the authority of the sixth provisional government of Pinheiro de Azevedo that once again included socialist and PPD ministers.

In new national assembly elections in 1976, the Socialists again emerged the victors with 35 per cent of the vote, followed by the PPD with 24 per cent. The Socialist leader Mario Soares had refused a coalition with the communists in 1974–5, and now, though for different reasons, he refused to govern with the PPD, preferring to form a minority administration. With the final consolidation of a democratic regime, the former 'liberals' were once again on the sidelines.

The return of the reformers

The Popular Democratic Party was formed in May 1974 by former 'liberal wing' members Sá Carneiro, Pinto Balsemão and Magalhães Mota. Despite their Catholicism, the PPD leaders resisted the Christian democratic label, declaring theirs to be a social democratic party, advocating 'political, economic, social and cultural democracy'.[16] In November 1974, addressing his party's first national congress, Sá Carneiro declared his commitment 'to construct a true democracy – not only political democracy, but social and economic democracy'.[17] In October 1976 the party renamed itself the Social Democratic Party (PSD).

In the revolutionary atmosphere of Lisbon in 1975, however, the social democracy of Sá Carneiro's party was outflanked on both sides. Its idealism paled before the socialist rhetoric of the far left, while its anti-Communism was eclipsed by the more strident campaign of the Socialists. But the entire political spectrum moved to the right after the coup of 25 November and the 1976 elections, and the PSD moved with it. Sá Carneiro adopted a more conservative stance, waging an aggressive campaign against the nationalisations and land seizures of the revolutionary years, and for a revision of the 1976 constitution that guaranteed them. In new elections in December 1979, his party led a Democratic Alliance formed with the more conservative Centre for Social Democracy and the eco-monarchist Popular Monarchist Party, that fought on a conservative ticket to win 45 per cent of the votes and form the first wholly civilian government since the revolution. The PSD has never looked back. It has never been out of office since.

In 1980 Sá Carneiro again led the Democratic Alliance into an election victory with both an increased share of the popular vote, at 48 per cent, and an increased parliamentary majority. Before the year's end, however, he died in a plane crash, and the leadership of both party and government was taken over by Pinto Balsemão. Balsemão, however, failed to keep the PSD united, and resigned from office in 1983 precipitating fresh elections. The Democratic Alliance fell apart before the elections, and the PSD went into them alone to win 27 per cent of the votes and join a coalition government with the Socialists. In this period the PSD was wracked by internal conflicts, until a new leader emerged in the charismatic style of the party's first one – the former finance minister Anibal Cavaco Silva.

In the general elections of 1985, Cavaco Silva led the party to first place in the polls, with a popular vote of 30 per cent, and formed a minority government until fresh elections in 1987. This time the PSD won 50 per cent of the votes and an overall majority in parliament. Four years later, in 1991, Cavaco Silva again led his party to a similar overall victory. Sixteen years after the revolution that had overthrown the previous regime, the party that originated from the 'liberal wing' of that regime's ruling party had consolidated itself as the dominant political party of the new democratic order.

Hungary is not yet six years from 1989, but there are strong signs that the reformers who first sought to transform the regime from within, who were eclipsed and appeared on the verge of extinction after the 1990 elections, but who are now the dominant force in the Hungarian Socialist Party, are emerging as the most confident political force today. By the end of 1993 the Socialists had moved into first place in the polls, and finally won the elections in May 1994. The MSzP won 33 per cent of the votes in the first round of the elections, and 45 per cent in the second, giving them a landslide victory and an absolute majority (209 seats out of 386) in the new parliament. In July 1994 they formed a coalition government with the second largest party, the Free Democrats.

Paradoxically, the 'final' victors of the transition to democracy in Hungary may not be the champions of human rights and democratic liberties, the dissidents and students who defeated Pozsgay and the socialists in the referendum of November 1989, but the very people who were then trying to cling on to power in the last days of the communist order, the technocratic modernisers and pragmatic reformers of the 'liberal wing' of the Kádár regime.

SPAIN 1977 – HUNGARY 1990: THE FIRST PARTIES TO COME TO POWER

Most of those who study comparative democratic transformations emphasise the existence of certain similarities between the southern European and the east European transitions from dictatorship to democracy. The Iberian changes, and especially the Spanish one, are particularly comparable with the Hungarian case. All three countries had started from an authoritarian regime, which was 'soft-fascist' in the case of Spain and Portugal, or 'soft-communist' in the case of Hungary. The change in Portugal, however, involved a revolution and a radical break with the old regime, whereas in Spain and Hungary the break was not so radical and the transition was a gradual and negotiated one. In this respect, that particularly affects the circumstances in which the first governments are formed, the most relevant comparison is between Hungary and Spain.

If we accept the thesis that a close relationship exists between the nature of the old regime and the type of post-dictatorial political change, we can

also recognise the similar character and method of these democratic transformations.[18] No doubt, there are important differences too, i.e. there was
no equivalent of the Soviet Union in the case of Spain.[19] Still, if there
was a country in the former Soviet bloc which 'followed' the peaceful,
elite-controlled, pact-making, negotiated change of Spain, certainly it was
Hungary.[20] Our goal here is to focus on the emergence and decline of the
first parties to come to power in these countries.

In both Spain and Hungary the first free elections made the hitherto
blurred political fields more or less clear and considerably reduced the
number of competing parties. Spain had more than one hundred and fifty
new political parties in early 1977, and the figure was about ninety in
Hungary in early 1990.[21] As a result of the elections, however, only six
parties were elected both to the Spanish and the Hungarian parliament.
In both countries a competitive parliamentary system has evolved with a
stable governing majority and a strong opposition. A right-of-centre
government came into power under the leadership of Adolfo Suárez and
József Antall respectively in both Spain and Hungary. The strongest
parties have not had a clear political image in either country; rather they
constitute a coalition of different trends. The Spanish Union of Democratic
Centre (UCD) headed by Suárez was the union of a number of smaller
parties including the liberal, Christian democrat, monarchist, 'independent' and even the social democrat trends. The Hungarian Democratic
Forum (MDF) headed by Antall included three ideological trends: the
national liberal, the national populist and the Christian democrat. In Spain
the deep political differences between the right of centre and the left of
centre have not allowed for a grand coalition, and this has been the case
in Hungary too. Despite the differences in the party formation and the
composition of these centre right parties, it is likely that they had a similar
role in the post-authoritarian history of Spain and Hungary.

Adolfo Suárez and the Democratic Centre Union

After the fall of the Franco regime, the greatest difficulty for the Spanish
centre-right forces was to create a broad, post-Franco political coalition
which could embrace the former reformers and moderate opposition of
the authoritarian regime. Credibility became the most important issue for
them, since they were fragmented and badly compromised by the old
regime. Their task was to establish themselves as solid, acceptable parties,
avoiding mass-mobilisation strategy, on the basis of those people who had
wanted moderate step-by-step transformation instead of a radical break.

First, the proto-parties in common ideological families crystallised them-
selves into a political party: the liberals merged into the Liberal Alliance
(AL), the social democrats formed the Social Democratic Federation
(FSD), and finally the Christian democrats founded the Christian
Democratic Party (PDC). The second step of coalescence was the merging

of different ideological families. In December 1976 social and Christian democrats, liberals and others formed the Popular Party (PP), which was the first precedent of collaboration of parties with different ideological backgrounds. By early 1977 some other parties of these ideological families joined the coalition, renamed as Democratic Centre (CD). The co-operation of the moderates and former reformers was in the making.

At that stage of the party development, Prime Minister Adolfo Suárez appeared in the centre-right political arena as a popular reformist leader of the post-Franco National Movement government since July 1976. Suárez himself served under Franco as director general of the state-run television network, but remained relatively unknown to the public. As Prime Minister he skilfully convinced the corporatist Parliament to accept his Reform Law in October 1976, which opened the way to institutional reforms, including democratic parliamentary elections. In this respect, destroying the old regime, Suárez played a similar role to that of Portuguese 'liberals' in 1974, or Miklós Németh and the Hungarian reform communists in October 1989. His political reforms supported by the December 1976 referendum made him a credible moderate personality: a politician with Franquist past who committed himself to democracy.[22]

Suárez was a popular politician without a party, while the Democratic Centre (CD) became a non-ideological catch-all party without a strong, attractive leader. As a Prime Minister, he was afraid that without party backing the democratic elections proposed by him would sweep him out of power. He joined the CD in late April 1977, which gave birth to a 'new' party under the name of Democratic Centre Union (UCD). Nevertheless, the acceptance of Suárez as party leader occurred not without strong internal tensions. Suárez brought a considerable number of 'independents' to the party who had a Franquist past. Although they had government experience which was important at that time, their commitment to democratic change was questionable. Some UCD leaders resigned when Suárez significantly reshaped the party's electoral list, putting these 'independents' onto it. Some of the rank-and-file party members described the UCD as nothing more than a 'syndicate of power', claiming that the UCD was 'an official party led by a government'.[23]

The success of Suárez and the UCD made the internal critics silent. In the 15 June 1977 elections the UCD came out victorious, gaining 34.7 per cent of the popular vote, securing 165 seats in the Parliament out of 350, i.e. 47.1 per cent of the seats.[24] Suárez formed a minority government, rejecting any co-operation with the right wing Popular Alliance (AP). His government was quite successful, following the strategy of compromise, renovation and pact-making in the fields of (1) the establishment of a constitution, (2) managing economic hardships, and (3) institutionalising regional autonomies. Suárez's most famous attempt to ensure social peace and economic development was the Moncloa Pact in September 1977. 'It was signed by the government, parliamentary parties, and trade unions, giving the government authority to freeze salaries, reduce public spending, restrict credit, and increase fiscal pressure. In exchange, the government promised to carry out a progressive tax reform, to make the social security system more efficient, to reorganise the financial system, and to put into practice a series of urgent political reforms.'[25] Despite these successes the government had not been able to carry out its promises given in the Moncloa Pact, and, although the 1979 elections confirmed the government position of the UCD, by the turn of the decade its legitimacy and political support weakened.

In a particular historical situation, at the first, crucial period of democratic transformation, the UCD as a moderate centre-right force could provide the best choice for those who hoped for political change but feared Marxist radicalism. However, by 1980–1, it became more and more unlikely that the UCD would survive its second term. The heterogeneity of the party could be attractive at the beginning, but it became a heavy burden in the governing period. The UCD, unlike the Italian Christian democrats, lacked a unifying negative criterion for legitimation which could have served as an ideological cement, i.e. anti-Fascism, anti-Communism, resistance, etc.[26] As a centre coalition it slowly lost its electoral basis; it became too rightist for the centre-left voters, and too leftist for those who wished to vote right.

Finally, the UCD fell apart. The right wing Christian democrats had left the party and founded their own Popular Democratic Party (PDP) and joined an electoral coalition with the AP led by Manuel Fraga. The social democrats had also split off and later moved to the Spanish Socialist Workers' Party (PSOE) led by Felipe González. Adolfo Suárez, who had been forced to resign as Prime Minister in 1981, also moved out of the UCD to create a rather centre-left formation, the Social and Democratic Centre (CDS). In the historic elections of 1982, the UCD was electorally crushed, receiving only just over 7 per cent of the votes. About 75 per cent of the electoral support it had in 1979 was, in 1982, transferred to other parties.[27] At the same time, the renewed PSOE, with a more moderate, social democratic image, virtually doubled its electoral strength, almost winning an absolute majority of votes and obtaining a strong majority in both chambers of Parliament. Later, the UCD, as a 'syndicate of power' ceased to exist, and the PSOE utilising the electoral discontent and the popularity of its young leader, Felipe González, could keep power from 1982 onwards. As a socialist party, the PSOE was able to sell its social-liberal policy to the voters, for whom the 1982 change symbolised a final break with the Franquist legacy.

József Antall and the Hungarian Democratic Forum

The history of the Hungarian Democratic Forum (MDF) has different epochs. In the *first* period (September 1987–October 1988) the organisation had a rather centre-left populist character with strong commitment to the countryside poor and the Hungarian minorities outside the borders in the neighbouring countries. This stage can be also characterised from an organisational point of view as a formation of a political party from a friendly 'movement–intellectual' community. In the *second* period (October 1989–August 1992) the 'movement–intellectuals' were replaced by some newly arrived politicians which made the party fit to govern, and, at the same time gave it a predominantly Christian–conservative right of centre character. The *third* period (August 1992–June 1993) was the time of the counter-attack of the former populist intellectuals from a radical right direction, which brought the most heated debates and finally a merciless power struggle between the conservatives and the radicals. This internal fight ended in June 1993, when some exponents of the radical wing led by István Csurka were expelled from the MDF, and later formed a new, small right-wing party. The *fourth* epoch began in June 1993, when the 'reshaped' MDF is continuously struggling with itself in order to find a way back to its previous moderate style.

The starting point of the MDF clearly differs from that of the UCD. It was made by intellectuals as amateur politicians. As a movement it had its cultural–political roots, from the 1930s onwards, in the past. A circle of populist writers, following their tradition of 'Third Way' between Western-type liberalism and Soviet-type socialism emphasised the importance of national identity and the collective rights of the Hungarian minorities. They never called themselves 'opposition', unlike those underground intellectuals who edited samizdat journals in the 1980s; they had no 'avant-garde' or 'revolutionary' character. Their strategy was one of bargaining with the officials as well as the samizdat opposition. They could promise cautious, step-by-step change, which made them attractive for average citizens as viable moderate opposition. It was certainly not created 'by the people', but compared to the Spanish UCD it was still a bottom-up organisation. When the 'founding fathers' of the Forum met Imre Pozsgay in the village of Lakitelek on 27 September 1987, they only wished to form a party-like political pressure group and establish a co-operation with the reform wing of the ruling Communist Party. Their first self-definition suggested that the MDF was *both* party and movement, which stood politically neither on the side of the Party-state, nor the opposition.[28]

The logic of the sharpening political competition had forced the group to become a party, and the dynamics of political change quickly outdated the prospects of a reformist–moderate marriage. The fall of Pozsgay as a potential President and the emergence of radical opposition forced the MDF leaders to change the image of the party. József Antall, an old-fashioned but skilful politician was elected as party chairman in October 1989, and it was he who started to reshape the party, giving it an anti-communist, centre-right conservative character.

József Antall appeared first in the MDF during the Summer 1989 tri-lateral negotiations. His widely accepted political skills helped the MDF to break the stalemate of the Autumn of 1989 and make a successful electoral campaign. Occupying the centre-right position, Antall could successfully push his main rival party, the Free Democrats, to the left of centre political field. As a son of a Smallholder politician of the 1940s, his style and appearance equally made credible the MDF's distance from the communists, as well as the commitment of the party to deliberate, not-so-radical systemic change.[29]

In the first round of the first free elections, on 25 March 1990, when voters voted not only for individual candidates but for regional party lists, MDF gained 24.71 per cent of the votes. In the second round, on 8 April, the former MSzP electorate joined in voting for the MDF, as a result of which the party enjoyed a landslide victory in the individual constituencies. Finally, the MDF representatives occupied 165 seats out of 386 in the Parliament, which was 42.5 per cent of all seats.[30] Unlike the Spanish UCD, the Antall-led MDF had not intended to form a minority government, instead they created a centre right coalition with the Smallholders and Christian Democrats as 'natural allies'. This coalition had a majority in the Parliament with 59.3 per cent of the seats. The MDF leader József Antall became the first Prime Minister of the new democracy.

Despite Antall's successes, which had taken the MDF to power, the 'founding fathers' of Lakitelek remained suspicious towards the newcomer Prime Minister.[31] Antall rather trusted in his friends, coming from different circles, who did not belong to the semi-opposition of populist writers of the Kádár era. They rather occupied second line positions in the former regime representing the then existing passive neutrality of the society. (For instance, the Interior Minister Péter Boross, a key figure in the Antall government and later the successor to Antall, had formerly served as an influential official in the catering trade.) The MDF now turned into the party of capitalist enterprise, of the Christian middle classes and of future property owners, as would befit any conservative party. The former left-populist movement had moved towards the centre and legitimised itself as a Christian democratic conservative party. Meanwhile, the talk of a smooth transition did not frighten off former Communist Party members. The provincial elite that had joined the Communist Party purely to boost their careers flooded into the MDF.

As a newcomer, Antall's problem was similar to that of Suárez: to integrate his party from the top. It had proved to be extremely difficult, so he decided to create three ideological families inside the party (the populist, the Christian democrat, and the 'national liberal') in order to institutionalise and balance them from the top. Antall's aim was to follow the ancient logic of 'divide et impera' and, in this way to maintain a broad coalition from the centre to the extreme right. But the MDF lost the local elections in the Autumn of 1990, so the party was not able to provide administrative positions to its members in local governments, it could not satisfy their claims. Under the same flag, the party has been clearly divided between two groups: those who did have jobs in the government administration, and those angry rank-and-file members who did not. The gap between the party and its government had been broadening. The suspicious 'founding fathers', this time taking right-populist and anti-liberal arguments, efficiently used this popular dissatisfaction against the Prime Minister trying to control him from the party headquarters. They utilised the issues of compensation, decommunisation, and retroactive justice for the purpose of membership mobilisation against the government regarded by them as not only conservative but 'liberal'. They played with the emotions of the grassroots, demanding the government 'complete the systemic change' (i.e. the radical change of the elites), even beyond the framework of the rule of law.

Antall himself tried to take the wind out of the sails of his party's radicals till the last minute, and even beyond that. On the other hand, under pressure, he also used these demands for attacking the opposition, the President of the Republic, and to dismiss the Presidents of the Hungarian Radio and Television during the so-called 'media war'. Nevertheless, the power balance inside the party was shaken by the populist radicals, and the MDF image was changing again. This was no longer the voice of conservatism, but that of right radicalism. This was not the calm guardian of tradition, of thoughtful progress, reform, or organic bourgeoisification, but the voice of revenge, demanding a new tabula rasa.[32] After the anti-government (and in some points: neo-Fascist) attack of the MDF vice president István Csurka in August 1992, József Antall became a prisoner of the extremes of his own party. One of the 'natural allies', the Smallholders Party, had split into several parts over the issue of land reform and the following tensions, while the MDF, as a result of this radical turn, started to disintegrate. The majority of the governing coalition was not shaken, but it became more and more difficult to keep the diverging trends in one camp.

After long internal fights, the Csurka wing was ousted during the Spring of 1993. For the sake of this success Antall sacrificed those 'national liberals' of the party too, who were the most vehement opponents of the extreme right. Antall had to give up his governing philosophy which was based on keeping all of the rightist trends in one bloc. The 'founding fathers' were divided, most of them remained ambivalently 'faithful' to the Prime Minister. Csurka and his followers formed a new movement ('Hungarian Road') and a party, called Hungarian Justice and Life Party (MIÉP), while other ex-MDF deputies founded the national protectionist Hungarian Market Party (MPP). The 'national liberals' were not able to create a party: some of them joined other liberal parties, while others remained in the MDF. After the death of Prime Minister Antall in December 1993, it was mostly the government position of the party elite of the MDF that kept the party politicians together. Before the May 1994 elections the MDF lost its cohesiveness and former social support: it was only a little more than 'the syndicate of power'. The party received only 11.7 per cent in the first round of the elections, and finally occupied only 38 seats out of 386 in the new parliament. The MDF had lost its former attractiveness and become a relatively small party in the parliament being in the opposition.

The rise and fall of the first winners

The history of the UCD and the MDF, as first governing parties, has many differences: the UCD had no intellectual-ideological past, while the MDF had.

The UCD was formed from the top in order to create a leadership position for Suárez, while the MDF was rather an organic, bottom-up movement of populist intellectuals.[33] The UCD was a purely political phenomenon, while the kernel of the MDF was cemented by long friendship, common cultural background and co-operation of amateurish politicians. The Suárez-led UCD excluded the possibility of co-operation with the more rightist AP, while the Antall-led MDF aimed to embrace all the rightist colours from the moderate centre to extreme radicalism. With the same proportions of seats, the UCD governed from a minority position, while the MDF picked up two smaller parties on an ideological basis in order to form a majority government. The UCD leadership was able to make social pacts (Moncloa Pact), while the MDF leadership could only make political pacts (MDF-SzDSz agreement).

Nevertheless there are telling similarities too. Both parties were able to win the first free elections in a centre right position; both parties had promised a compromise between continuity and radical change. Both parties promised a less painful transition offering an opportunity for people compromised in the old regime to support them. Both parties were led by outstanding personalities compared to other party leaders, and they played a definite role in the victory of the party. However, both Suárez and Antall soon found themselves in a situation in which they were not able to harmonise the different political interests any longer. In the case of Suárez, the different political wings, from 'falangist populists' to social democrats, could not merge in the longer run; in the case of Antall, he was alienated from the grassroots and some radical party leaders working against him. The heterogeneity of these parties was, or became, so high that it made them difficult to classify. Both parties had the same proportion of seats in the Parliament, and spent a considerable period of their time in power at the first stage of democratic consolidation. Their middle-of-the-road policy was attractive to the voters: in Spain the citizens who voted for the UCD equally wanted to avoid Franquist continuity and the radical break of the Marxist left; in Hungary those people have chosen the MDF who equally refused the Kádárist Communism and the Thatcherite neo-liberalism. Both parties clearly expressed the wish of the majority of people at the first stage of change, after the collapse of an authoritarian regime. Their fate reflects the disappointment of society because of the widening gap between their expectations and the social reality. Despite their own mistakes, both were victims (and products) of the negative legacy of the authoritarian past. This legacy was rejected by the voters in the 1982 elections in Spain and in the 1994 elections in Hungary.

PLUS ÇA CHANGE

If any lesson is to be drawn from the two studies that make up the present chapter it is that the outcome of political change is very rarely in accord with the intentions and aspirations, let alone the ideologies, of political actors. This should, nevertheless, not be taken as a prescription for pessimism, for if well-intentioned actions can have undesired and unfortunate consequences, less well-intentioned actions may have more fortunate ones.

This paradox has been astutely recognised, in regard to transitions to democracy, by Samuel Huntington who contends that 'the crusaders for democratic principles, the Tom Paines of this world, do not create democratic institutions', but rather political leaders who view democracy not as a desirable goal in itself but as 'a means to other goals, such as prolonging their own rule, achieving international legitimacy, minimising domestic opposition, and reducing the likelihood of civil violence'.[34]

In the case of the reformers in Hungary and Portugal, a double paradox can be observed. The very forces that first sought to liberalise the old regime, and so helped to set in motion the process of transition, were swept aside and temporarily eclipsed by the fall of the dictatorship. Their very success had led to their defeat. Yet their opponents' success, in turn, prepared the ground for their return. Initially, they had been the ones who wanted to reform in order to preserve the old system, yet the consolidation of a new system has led to a resurgence of their fortunes.

In the case of the first parties to come to power in Hungary and Spain, they had won the first free elections, but in the government they were not able to respond to the revolution of 'rising expectations'. In spite of their promise of 'smooth transition' they were made responsible for the shortcomings of democracy, social security and economic performance. In spite of the different promises about 'a radical break' and 'shock therapy' of the various Solidarity governments of Poland, their fate was similar to their Hungarian and Spanish counterparts. It seems, the judgment of voters was pre-established, independently from the different promises of the political elites. As the Portuguese 'liberals' and the Hungarian reformist communists were replaced by the voters on the basis that they had belonged to the old regime, so the first parties to come to power had to go, whatever they had said, because they were regarded as responsible for not meeting the expectations concerning systemic change.

These paradoxes of transition characterise not only political elites but also the wider political and social system, and the recognition of this can often cause surprise. For instance, Adam Przeworski remarks of the Spanish transition to democracy that: 'It is astonishing to find that those who were satisfied with the Franco regime are also likely to be satisfied with the new democratic government.'[35] The same would probably be true in Hungary, though in both cases it is likely to reflect not a change in political beliefs but a change of strategy for the defence or promotion of material interests. Certainly in the case of Hungary, it has been convincingly argued that the exceptionally peaceful nature of the transition was due to the fact that 'many people from the major beneficiary groups of the old regime' were able 'to join the new system as net gainers'.[36]

The other side of the coin, a topic that merits a separate study, is the fate of the former dissidents, advocates of human rights and civil society, who at first, in 1989, appeared the victors in some east European countries in the early days of post-communist euphoria, but whose initial successes seem equally to have paved the way for their subsequent decline.[37] If this article has argued that many of those who enjoyed positions of power and privilege under the old regimes have come to benefit equally from the new ones, it can be predicted with even greater confidence that those who were the most passionate critics of the old regimes will be equally discontented with the new ones.

NOTES

1   Witney Schneidman, 'Bibliography: Sources for the Study of Contemporary Portugal', in Kenneth Maxwell (ed.), *Portugal in the 1980s*, New York, Greenwood Press, 1986, pp. 233–43.
2   László Bruszt, '1989: The Negotiated Revolution in Hungary', in György Szoboszlai (ed.), *Democracy and Political Transformation*, Budapest, Hungarian Political Science Association, 1991, pp. 213–25.
3   Bill Lomax, 'Ideology and Illusion in the Portuguese Revolution: The Role of the Left', in L.S. Graham and D.L. Wheeler (eds), *In Search of Modern Portugal: The Revolution and its Consequences*, Madison, University of Wisconsin Press, pp. 105–33.
4   Bill Lomax, 'From Death to Resurrection: The Metamorphosis of Power in Eastern Europe', *Critique*, 1993, no. 25, pp. 47–84.
5   E.R. Vilar and A.S. Gomes (eds), *Sedes: Dossier 70/72*, Lisbon, Moraes, 1973.
6   Francisco Sá Carneiro, *A Liberalização Bloqueada*, Lisbon, Moraes, 1972.
7   Richard Robinson, *Contemporary Portugal*, London, Allen & Unwin, 1979, p. 170; Tom Gallagher, *Portugal: A Twentieth Century Interpretation*, Manchester, Manchester University Press, 1983, p. 170.
8   Robinson, op. cit., p. 171.
9   F.Sá Carneiro, M. Guerra and O. Dias, *Vale a Pena ser Deputado?*, Lisbon, Jornal de Fundão, 1973.

10 O. Dias, M. Mota and J. Silva, *Encontro da Reflexão Política*, Lisbon, Moraes, 1973.
11 António Spínola, *Portugal e o Futuro: Análise da Conjunctura Nacional*, Lisbon, Arcádia, 1974.
12 Henrique Barrilaro Ruas (ed.), *A Revolução das Flores: vol I*, Lisbon, Aster, 1974, p. 63.
13 Bill Lomax, 'Hungary from Kádárism to Democracy: the Successful Failure of Reform Communism', in D.W. Spring (ed.), *The Impact of Gorbachev*, London, Pinter, 1991, pp. 154–74.
14 M. Bihari, Z. Bíró, L. Lengyel and Z. Király, *Kizárt a Párt*, Budapest, Primo, 1988.
15 Imre Pozsgay, *1989*, Budapest, Püski, 1993, pp. 123–8.
16 Partido Popular Democrático, *Programa do Partido Popular Democrático: A Social-Democracia para Portugal*, Lisbon, 1974, p. 13.
17 Sá Carneiro, *Por uma Social-Democracia Portuguesa*, Lisbon, Dom Quixote, 1975, p. 39.
18 Kenneth Maxwell, 'Spain's Transition to Democracy: A Model for Eastern Europe?', in Nils H. Wessell (ed.), *The New Europe: Revolution in East–West Relations*, Montpelier, Capital City Press, pp. 35–49.
19 András Bozóki, 'The Hungarian Transition in a Comparative Perspective', in A. Bozóki, A. Körösényi, G. Schöpflin (eds), *Post-Communist Transition: Emerging Pluralism in Hungary*, London, Pinter, New York, St. Martin's Press, 1992, pp. 181–5.
20 Joseph M.Colomer, 'Transitions by Agreement: Modelling the Spanish Way', *American Political Science Review*, 1985, no. 4, pp. 1283–302.
21 R. Gunther, G. Sani and G. Shabad, *Spain After Franco: The Making of a Competitive Party System*, Berkeley – London – Los Angeles, University of California Press, 1988, p. 37.
22 John F. Coverdale, *The Political Transformation of Spain after Franco*, London and New York, Praeger, 1980, pp. 44–53.
23 Gunther, Sani, Shabad, op. cit., p. 102.
24 Coverdale, op. cit., p. 73.
25 J.M. Maravall and J. Santamaria, 'Political Change in Spain and the Prospects for Democracy', in G. O'Donnell, P. Schmitter and L. Whitehead (eds), *Transitions from Authoritarian Rule: Southern Europe*, Baltimore, John Hopkins University Press, 1986, p. 86.
26 Ibid., p. 94.
27 José Amödia, 'Union of the Democratic Centre', in David S. Bell (ed.), *Democratic Politics in Spain: Spanish Politics after Franco*, London, Pinter, 1983, p. 24.
28 Magyar Demokrata Fórum, 'A Magyar Demokrata Fórum Alapítólevele', *Hitel*, 2 Nov 1988, p. 50.
29 T. Kolosi, I. Szelényi, Sz. Szelényi, and B. Western, 'The Making of Political Fields in Post-Communist Transition', in Bozóki, Körösényi, Schöpflin, op. cit., pp. 152–5.
30 András Körösényi, 'The Hungarian Parliamentary Elections', in Bozóki, Körösényi, Schöpflin, op. cit., pp. 77–9.
31 László Lengyel, 'Alapító atyák', *Kritika*, 1993, no 9, pp. 3–9.
32 András Bozóki, 'The Metamorphoses of the Hungarian Democratic Forum', *East European Reporter*, 1992, vol. 5, no. 2, p. 66.
33 András Bozóki, 'Intellectuals and Democratisation in Hungary', in C. Rootes and H. Davis (eds), *A New Europe? Social Change and Political Transformation*, London, 1994.
34 Samuel P. Huntington, 'Will More Countries Become Democratic?' *Political*

Science Quarterly, 1984, no. 2.
35 Adam Przeworski, 'Some Problems in the Study of the Transition to Democracy', in G. O'Donnell, P. Schmitter, and L. Whitehead (eds), *Transitions from Authoritarian Rule: Comparative Perspectives*, Baltimore, John Hopkins University Press, 1986, p. 63.
36 László Urbán, 'Why was the Hungarian transition exceptionally peaceful?', in Szoboszlai, op. cit., p. 309.
37 Federigo Argentieri, 'From Opposition to Opposition: the Successful Failure of Former Dissidents in East-Central Europe', paper presented to the conference *In Transition*, Bloomington, Indiana Memorial Union, 26–28 September 1993.

9 The emergence of new party systems and transitions to democracy

Romania and Portugal compared

Tom Gallagher

INTRODUCTION

Portugal and Romania have acquired markedly different forms of democracy following lengthy periods of authoritarian rule. In Portugal there has been a clear break with the past and a political system has emerged that fully corresponds to existing west European norms, one in which there has been regular alternation of parties in office in a context where basic rights and liberties are not in question. Meanwhile, in Romania, the emphasis has been on continuity as much as change, real doubts exist about how strongly entrenched individual and group rights are, and a ruling party whose personnel is largely drawn from the defunct Communist Party has largely shaped the political transition and filled most of the available political space.

THE LEGACY OF THE PAST

In both countries, the nature of the authoritarian regime helps to explain the weakness of competing parties in the important early stages of the transition process. A monolithic party (The Romanian Communist Party: RCP) or political association (the National Union in Portugal where the party concept was rejected), controlled all political activity. Formal political opposition was disallowed and sanctions of varying degrees of severity were imposed on any citizens who defied the ban. Cautious reformers whose counterparts in other right-wing authoritarian or Marxist states were able to plan a gradual transition towards open politics, sometimes in tandem with moderate opposition forces, were marginalised, or else existed only in small numbers.

Portugal and Romania are, of course, scarcely comparable in terms of the intensity of repression and the way that the dictatorship sought to transform society. The Portuguese 'New State' was not overtly political; citizens were not required to shape their public or private lives around its political demands. Many citizens were able to remain autonomous and engage in a range of social and economic activities that were independent of the state.

By way of contrast, Romanian communism was always keen to assert its leading role in society and unwilling to tolerate unsupervised individual or group behaviour. Except for Albania, no other east European country experienced such a deep-seated form of Stalinist repression. No autonomous social groups were permitted to exist within which tendencies of political opposition could develop. As a result there was no grassroots experience of political opposition of the kind to be found in Poland, Hungary or Spain during the latter stages of authoritarianism in those countries.

Unlike Portugal, the authoritarian regime in Romania engaged in ambitious experiments of social engineering which transformed the country and were bound to alter political culture in important ways. A large working class was created out of an overwhelmingly peasant population in the space of little more than one generation. The political elite, drawn from ambitious and talented individuals also of mainly peasant background claimed to rule on behalf of this peasant-derived proletariat and, in the search for legitimacy, proved adept at manipulating national symbols. Under Nicolae Ceausescu (leader from 1965 to 1989), a Stalinist commitment to a centrally-planned economy and collective agriculture was combined with traditional themes of the extreme right which had been influential in pre-1945 Romania (the myth of a homogeneous nation, Romania's medieval greatness, the need for social discipline and political uniformity to defeat external conspiracies).[1]

In neither country were there strong democratic traditions to draw upon. It should not be forgotten that both Portugal and Romania had enjoyed long periods of uninterrupted constitutional rule (Portugal: the liberal monarchy of 1851–1910; Romania: the constitutional monarchy of 1881 to 1938), but the oligarchy was reluctant to widen the political process to include other social groups. Eventually, the extension of the franchise exacerbated social and political divisions that became marked in both cases during and after World War I. Parties were not based on coherent ideologies or programmes but on personalities and clans. Rigged elections and the intimidation of opponents bred political extremism and a desire to overthrow government by force. The numerically dominant peasantry was regarded as a force to manipulate and nationalism was used in order to bridge a vast social chasm in both countries.

In Romania, there was a tradition of dominance by the collective over the individual, of the state over the citizens, which the communists were able to turn to their advantage. A degree of arbitrariness was accepted in political behaviour which left little room for bargaining or compromise. In both countries the absence of an autonomous or civically-minded middle class based on commerce or industry had important consequences; intellectuals and members of the state bureaucracy played important roles in politics, using the resources of the state to gain economic protection or advancement, a practice much intensified under Communism and to a lesser degree under Salazar in Portugal.

In Portugal, the pre-1926 royalist and republican parliamentary regimes were not an important reference point during the democratic transition. New parties looked to foreign models (European Social and Christian democracy) for guidance in building organisations and formulating programmes. But Romania's isolation meant that foreign models had little meaning for the bulk of the population. In comparison with the rest of eastern Europe, new political forces preferred to single out the pre-1945 past as a source of inspiration in order to reduce the impact of the communist era on the popular consciousness. But, as has been pointed out, traditional symbols and patterns of political behaviour were largely authoritarian or anti-democratic in character and hardly likely to reinforce democratic norms.

THE FORMATION AND PERFORMANCE OF NEW ELITES

The violent removal of the authoritarian regime was a feature of the transition in both Portugal and Romania which set them apart from most other European countries emerging from right or left authoritarianism. The level of force employed varied markedly in both cases but the abrupt rather than controlled character of the change influenced the nature of subsequent developments.

Dissidents from within the ruling power structure (high-ranking ones in Romania, much more junior in Portugal) toppled a discredited leadership. Spontaneous popular protest was an important feature of the changeover in Romania at the end of 1989. But, in both countries, the democratic opposition or dissident groups were either non-existent or too weak to play an important role in events.

The sets of plotters had different agendas. The available evidence suggests that in Romania the aim of those who overthrew and quickly executed Ceausescu was to abolish the personal rule of the discredited chief executive and not to fundamentally change the system of government.[2] The policy failures of the 1980s were blamed on the dictator, his family, and close associates rather than on the system of centralised power and state ownership. In Portugal, the plotters were initially cautious in their programme owing to disunity within their ranks but dismantling the repressive system was an agreed aim. Marcelo Caetano, a colourless and self-effacing dictator, was quickly sent into exile. Soon, the provisional junta was radicalised by pressure of public opinion in the cities and by a communist party which emerged from clandestinity with important organising ability and a credibility which nascent parties had still to acquire. By contrast, no such societal influences obliged the provisional government in Romania to alter course.

Civic groups and associations and nascent parties lacked the experience or strength to place their demands for a complete and swift break with the communist past on the agenda. Moderate communists whose credibility rested on their opposition to Ceausescu's idiosyncratic policies quickly smothered the spontaneous revolt that had preceded the putsch against the dictator.

Therefore, in Romania political insiders retained the initiative. Experience, unity, and control over key state institutions counted massively in their favour. The army remained obedient and did not side with anti-communist radicals. The power vacuum was quickly filled when a National Salvation Front was formed which appointed a provisional government and head of state. The new acting President, Ion Iliescu was a veteran communist who had been minister of youth and secretary of the party's central committee in charge of ideology before being dropped by Ceausescu in 1971 for 'petit-bourgeois liberalism'. He disagreed with increasingly doctrinaire policies but had never engaged in public criticism of the regime and could not be described as a dissident in the sense of a Havel or a Wałęsa. He formed an effective twenty-month partnership with Petre Roman, his Prime Minister who represented younger technocrats less reluctant to experiment with pluralism and dismantle the command economy than Iliescu would later prove to be.

The National Salvation Front quickly acquired important popular support by lightening the burdens of daily life for much of the population. Supplies of heat and electric light were restored; peasants were promised access to state land; rationing was scaled down; and a full television service was provided which offered entertainment as well as coverage of the exploits of those in power. Iliescu promised to shield the working-class from the effects of a transition to a market economy. He offered to revive the welfarist programme which in south-eastern Europe had won support for Tito, Zhivkov, as well as the early Ceausescu and which would enable ex-communists in Bulgaria, Romania as well as parts of Yugoslavia to be significant players in politics during the 1990s.

For Romanians, with traditionally low expectations for whom a benevolent ruler was a rarity, Iliescu's concern for the popular welfare was seen as a significant advance that quickly translated into massive support when the National Salvation Front became an electoral challenger. The ruling Armed Forces Movement in Portugal lacked an equivalent clearcut sense of direction or unity; it had fewer inducements to offer more politically restive and aware voters whose living standards had in most cases been rising steadily and who, it soon became clear, were not content with the prospect of benevolent paternalism exercised by military reformers who claimed legitimacy from the success of their anti-dictatorial coup.

To differing degrees both Romania's and Portugal's transitional rulers showed themselves uncomfortable with unsupervised, free-wheeling democracy. Their respective Communist Party and military backgrounds meant that they were likely to be ill-at-ease with debate, popular consultation, and other aspects of an open political system. Indeed, early in the lifetime of both transitions, doubts were expressed about whether competing parties could provide the answers for the deep-seated problems that were the legacy of tyrannical rule. Iliescu's speech of 28 January 1990 in which he expressed the hope that the FSN would not be 'a party formation' but instead would be permitted to work out 'a platform of national unity around objectives that are not party objectives but national objectives' found echoes among Portugal's military rulers in 1974–5.[3] Sylviu Brucan, a former communist who publicly broke with Ceausescu before 1989, argued afterwards that pluralism in post-Stalinist countries did not mean the building of a multi-party system but merely the development of democratic mechanisms within the ruling party.[4] He saw the NSF operating as 'an enlightened vanguard' which acted as a national pedagogue, a role that was not without appeal to sections of the MFA who also disparaged the multi-party concept. Brucan's further argument that the Romanian transition to democracy would take at least two decades, during which a paternalistic regime was necessary to hold the nation together, also had its Portuguese advocates in the mid-1970s as did his claim that the revolution in his country was so original that its aftermath must be different from other countries which had recently emerged from authoritarian rule.[5]

Both the MFA and the FSN showed a propensity to co-opt parties and different interest groups within the structures set up to administer their countries. For at least a year, Portuguese parties were prepared to accept the tutelage of army officers given the legitimacy the latter had obtained by unseating the dictatorship. But in Romania, nascent democratic forces refused to recognise the NSF which they saw as a formation of ex-communists building a limited democracy in order to preserve the power and privileges of groups comprising a still intact communist establishment. Facing vocal opposition from anti-communist groups which enjoyed limited support at home but had some backing in the west, the NSF moved quickly to consolidate its authority. Early elections were announced, which led to accusations that the NSF was seeking to impose a neo-communist solution by holding a poll less than twenty weeks after Ceausescu's overthrow and before its competitors had a chance to organise themselves. Certainly the NSF enjoyed crucial advantages over a weak and fragmented opposition. Its position as the dominant force in government gave it control over state assets from access to printing presses and transportation, to the uncontested use of radio and television. The last advantage was a crucial one in a society where television had shaped the outlook of millions of people, particularly poorly educated ones living in small towns and villages in those remoter areas which received few other sources of information about the outside world.[6]

Accusations of pre-electoral fraud were made by the main opposition parties which (leaving aside the united and well-organised movement of the Hungarian minority) were throwbacks to pre-communist times. The two main pre-1945 parties, the National Liberals (NLP) and the National

Peasant and Christian Democratic Party (NPCDP) reconstituted themselves. But the 'historic parties', as they were known, proved incapable
of deriving advantage from the fact that they had shaped national politics
in the decades when Romania had been an independent kingdom, whose
size and importance had grown as a result of the collapse of imperial rule
in eastern Europe after 1918. Decades of state propaganda had discredited the NLP and NPCDP in the eyes of impressionable citizens (the
Salazar regime, in its turn, also having portrayed the period of electoral
competition preceding its own rise to power in lurid terms).

The two opposition figures who challenged Iliescu in the presidential
elections were emigrés whose wealth and foreign connections enabled
government supporters in the media to depict them as intruders ready
to import brutal forms of capitalism whose effect would be to revive the
sharp inequalities characteristic of the prewar period. The emphasis on
anti-Communism in opposition campaigning was a major tactical blunder:
the FSN's opponents failed to make a distinction between crying 'Down
with Communism' and 'Down with the Communists'. The first slogan had
to do with the destruction of a system while the second one implied a
clear threat to the welfare of millions of Romanians who had joined the
party out of convenience rather than conviction.[7] The parties also dented
their credibility by failing to run a single presidential candidate against
Iliescu; many Romanians asked the obvious question that if they couldn't
unite on candidates how could they govern the country together.[8]

The disunity and incoherence of the Romanian opposition in the first
elections of the transition period is in sharp contrast to the co-operation
displayed by those Portuguese parties committed to liberal democratic
politics which sank their differences to lobby for elections to be held within
a year of the 1974 coup, offering a clear programmatic alternative to the
Marxism of the PCP and the radical populism of the MFA. The National
Salvation Front had a vested interest in holding early elections while the
Armed Forces Movement preferred to postpone them because it lacked
the equivalent means to shape the result. On 20 May 1990 Ion Iliescu was
elected President of Romania with 85 per cent of the votes cast, the NSF
receiving 65 per cent of the votes on an 86 per cent turnout. Despite
voting irregularities which probably inflated the winning margin, it is
clear that the FSN enjoyed the backing of important social formations
and interests: its strongest support was to be found among the peasantry,
sections of which in several other east European countries had endorsed
ex-communist parties to a greater or lesser extent; industrial workers,
particularly in large workplaces and in unprofitable and wasteful indus-
tries, gravitated to the FSN for social protection; the party and state
bureaucracy, from which the FSN had emerged, also understandably
endorsed it.[9]

Meanwhile, in parts of rural Romania where the opposition found
campaigning difficult, it was possible to encounter first-time voters who

declared that 'one party is enough for us here'. Especially in the villages, where the pattern of life left little space for private initiative, the notion of permanently-organised rivals with its overtures of conflict and competition, could easily seem menacing and disruptive. Authoritarian conditioning lasting forty-five years meant that many Romanians existed who, at least in 1990, were more at ease with a single political grouping along the lines of a one-party arrangement to be found in post-colonial Africa: dissent might be tolerated provided it was contained under the large umbrella of the single party.

In Portugal, military radicals who envisaged a supervisory role in a neutral and radical state failed to receive the popular endorsement for their 'third way' that Iliescu obtained from workers and peasants in Romania. The mandate for non-communist parties was sufficiently hefty to place Portugal on the road to becoming a conventional west-European democracy, although it would be one with several detours. Returned emigrés like Mario Soares, the Socialist Party leader, were able to build effective political machines based on urban professionals and parts of the working class. Young professionals with genuine skills whose status had been devalued under Ceausescu also swung behind Romanian liberal democrats returning from exile. But owing to the social changes witnessed under Communism this proved to be a flimsy electoral base; even if economic reform alters the social composition of the electorate, probably many years will need to elapse before the emergence of an autonomous civically-minded middle class able to sustain parties interested in building democracy from below.

Two other factors which swung the balance in favour of mainstream democratic forces in Portugal were the practical assistance from west-European governments and the deep-seated opposition to ruling radicals from regional interests in the north which the authorities in Lisbon were unable to subdue. Neither condition applied in Romania; questionable government behaviour was occasionally condemned in western Europe but no active steps were taken by governments to redress the balance in favour of beleaguered liberal democrats. Regional differentiation existed in Romania, a country that is far less ethnically homogeneous than Portugal; there is evidence that in 1990 the NSF feared a challenge to its authority from Transylvania, a large ethnically-mixed province that had become part of Romania only in 1918. It promoted ultra-nationalism in areas where it needed local help to contain the reformist opposition, helping to legitimise elements of the former Ceausescu power structure who have since damaged majority–minority relations in Transylvania.

In order to entrench itself in office, the NSF showed a readiness to exploit anti-democratic elements in political culture rather than encourage voters to become familiar with the expression of differences and the arranging of compromises to minimise them. A frustrated opposition transferred the struggle for democracy to the streets of the capital and other large cities after the elections. The state responded with violence in June 1990: vigilante workers were allowed to deal brutally with anti-communist protesters in Bucharest and indeed with any elements regarded as oppositional who had the misfortune to stray into their path. By contrast anti-communist violence unnerved the revolutionary elite in Portugal. It was unable to draw upon the popular support available to the NSF in a bid to deflect the popular challenge and pragmatic radical officers were persuaded to arrange a series of compromises with the political parties that led to a process of political normalisation after the revolutionary excitement of 1974–5.

In summary, there is a great deal to support the claim that a clash of two sets of authoritarian values was witnessed in Romania at the end of 1989: orthodox communists and some reformers in the Gorbachev mould versus the brand of doctrinaire personal communism associated with Ceausescu. A struggle between democratic and non-democratic values then ensued in 1990, but those who stood unambiguously for the former were very feeble and proved unable to influence the course of events. The continuity in personnel, rhetoric, reliance upon nationalism, and restrictions on the ability of citizens to influence public affairs seen in the early 1990s strengthens the view that Romania witnessed a power struggle within the communist establishment won by the least illiberal factions but groups whose commitment to genuine pluralism remains open to doubt. Iliescu and his entourage remain sceptical democrats whose preference is for a plebiscitary autocracy where individual and group rights remain ill-defined and where the manipulative organs of the dictatorship (the admittedly revamped intelligence service and television) are used to restrict political competition.

The contrast with Portugal is unmistakable; far fewer office-holders in the authoritarian system were able to play a role in politics after the 1974 coup. Their democratic successors were careful to behave in ways that would not suggest continuity with previous political practices. Commitment to democratic structures and procedures went much further. Portugal's adherence to international pacts and conventions concerning human rights and pluralism was seen as genuine, while similar steps by Romania stemmed more from a desire to acquire respectability abroad than to press ahead with the democratisation of the country.

NEW PARTY ELITES AND REGIME CHANGE

Given the institutional advantages which the National Salvation Front mobilised on its behalf, Romania possessed a dominant party system from 1990 to 1992. Parties opposed to the NSF were not in a position to challenge or block its plans for drawing up the constitution which was meant to lead the country towards a non-totalitarian future.

The NSF lacked a clearcut ideology. Attempts by Iliescu to define the party as a 'social democratic' one ready to follow a 'South Korean'

developmental model suggested opportunism or an inadequate understanding of developments in the non-communist world.[10] Critics have
described the party as 'neo-communist' but this description may be of
limited usefulness; it should be recalled that the Romanian Communist
Party in its heyday stood less for ideology and more for the advancement
of well-placed elements at local and national level who could exploit the
ruling system for their own sectional ends.[11]

A case can be made for describing the NSF as essentially a non-
ideological grouping which had emerged from the party apparatus with
the aim of protecting a set of caste interests in an altered set of circumstances. Those leading the NSF were motivated by a desire for survival
which enabled them to secure the loyalties of political functionaries used
to being directed from above. The requirements of survival, rather than
any deep-seated loyalty to the communist system which Iliescu publicly
admitted had been a failed experiment, helps to explain important features
of NSF behaviour. Once it was clear that liberal democrats were not
prepared to join a platform of national unity, Iliescu did not hesitate to
marginalise them. Recycled members of the nomenklatura dominated the
NSF – the chairman of the senate, was Alexandru Barladeanu, a former
politburo member and top economic planner, while the chairman of the
chamber of deputies had been a close Iliescu ally in the communist youth
movement. But there were also young technocrats (mostly from a nomenklatura background) who wished to move significantly faster in the
direction of economic reform than the old guard. Their presence in
Premier Roman's cabinet was much stronger than in the party at large.
In the summer of 1990 Roman and his ministers started to borrow much
of their economic rhetoric from the opposition, whose pro-capitalist policies had been denounced as an economic sell-out in the spring election.
But Roman's advocacy of 'economic shock-therapy' isolated him from
President Iliescu who exercised important sway in the NSF despite the
constitution which barred him from membership of any political party.
The split in the NSF was formalised in March 1992 when the bulk of party
activists formed a Democratic National Salvation Front (DNSF) explicitly loyal to Iliescu, a rump retaining the NSF title forming around Roman.

This split reduced the disparity in strength between government and
opposition. So did the propensity of opposition parties to bury their differences and form an electoral alliance called the Democratic Convention.
Common lists of candidates were presented in the winter 1992 local elections in which the DC came within a few percentage points of overtaking
the NSF. Rather belatedly, opposition forces in Romania had embarked
upon the path of co-operation taken by the Portuguese parties much earlier
in the transition process but they secured far fewer concessions from the
provisional government.

The 1991 Romanian constitution, ratified by a referendum on 9 December, was largely the work of the NSF's parliamentary party whose

membership was largely drawn from ex-communist party and state officials. Opposition deputies were included in committees deciding the shape
of the document and occasionally they were able to modify certain clauses
providing the government side had no objections. But constitution-
making – the main task of the 1990–2 parliament – did not narrow the
gulf between government and opposition or make co-operation possible
on other fundamental issues. Naturally, the NSF enjoyed considerable
advantages from having shaped the constitutional order according to its
preference for a powerful head of state exercising leverage over centralised
institutions; no Portuguese party enjoyed an equivalent role, the Portuguese constitution being a compromise between civil and military interests.

The Romanian constitution of 1991 displays a number of obvious
similarities to the Portuguese one adopted fifteen years earlier. Under it
Romania became a semi-presidential republic in which the head of state
is elected by universal suffrage and the powers invested in the office are
quite extensive. Almost no other successful post-communist east-European
leader sought the position of head of state rather than that of leader of
a political party. The President rather than parliament designates the
Prime Minister, and dismisses ministers and designates their successors,
albeit 'at the suggestion of the Prime Minister'.[12] The president can initiate
referenda and attend cabinet meetings which he is allowed to chair and
he has powers to appoint senior judges.

Portugal's own semi-presidential system was modified in the constitutional revision of 1982 after President Eanes used his presidential
prerogative in ways that Iliescu in Romania seems disposed to do. In
Iliescu's own words, the Romanian President would be 'an active president, who can be a factor of permanent action and co-operation with the
three elements of power: the legislative, judicial, and executive branches'.
But, unlike Portugal, the constitution was placed before the voters for
approval in a referendum, on 9 December 1991: 77.3 per cent voted in
favour on a 69.2 per cent turnout.

The inability of the parties to reach an understanding about the division of power between the different branches of government was reflected
in the new system of local government. In July 1990, Premier Roman
imposed NSF loyalists as interim mayors in cities where the party had got
well under 50 per cent of the vote. Soon there were well-documented
examples of state property being sold to members of the communist elite
on terms which enabled them to emerge as a new business class. In
Portugal, the new system of local government included important elements
of central direction, but accusations of partisanship by the government
were heard far less frequently than in Romania.[13]

Altogether there was no shortage of contentious issues which enven-
omed relations between government and opposition in Romania, and little
or no effective conflict regulation machinery. The most prominent disputes
included the role of the monarchy, which the communists had abolished

by force in 1947 (the ex-king going into exile), and the role of the Securitate or secret police, which was given a new name (the Romanian Information Service) in 1990 but whose staff were drawn largely from its controversial predecessor. Disputes over the nature and scope of land privatisation also kept the NSF and its chief opponents far apart.

In Portugal, the chief cleavage had been between revolutionary officers and their civilian allies who acquired their legitimacy from the 1974 anti-Fascist coup and civilian parties that had been endorsed by voters in the 1975 constituent assembly elections. Compromises – between the upholders of revolutionary purity and constitutional legitimacy – proved easier to secure in Portugal than in Romania. A pact drawn up in 1976 allowed civilian parties to govern the country, albeit under a degree of military tutelage.

The swift return of normal inter-party competition in Portugal could be interpreted as a sign that the danger to democracy from extra-legal forces was largely over. But the non-communist parties co-operated in 1982 to provide the two-thirds majority needed to abolish the military council which had veto power over important parliamentary legislation, while the President was also required to cede some of his office's most important powers. So in Portugal there were early examples of major players with rival agendas being able to bargain and negotiate in contrast to the intense partisanship that remained a feature of each stage of the Romanian transition.

Partisanship was temporarily diminished in Romania by the caretaker government presided over by independent technocrat Theodor Stolojan between October 1991 and October 1992. Several National Liberal deputies occupied ministerial portfolios but without being able to alter the direction of policy. The participation of NLP members in a government which, despite its appearance of independence, remained under the control of the NSF, weakened attempts at forging opposition unity. It stands in instructive comparison with the willingness of the small right-wing Centre Social Democratic Party (CDS) in Portugal to resolve the crisis arising from the collapse of the first constitutional government at the end of 1977 by forming an alliance with the Socialist Party.

Political alliances in Romania have been short-term and have involved a restricted group of players. With the exception of the NPCDP, all the major parties have experienced debilitating splits which lowered their standing in the eyes of an already sceptical electorate. Undoubtedly, the most contentious internal party dispute was that between Iliescu and Roman whose partnership dissolved in fierce acrimony in 1991. Roman's government fell on 26 September 1991 as a result of striking miners converging on the capital and seizing parliament. He had been unable to mobilise popular support against his extra-parliamentary foes in the way that Boris Yeltsin had managed to do in Moscow in August 1991 or King Juan Carlos had done in Spain on 13 February 1981 when Colonel Tejero had seized parliament. If, during his twenty-one months in office, Roman had combined his modernising rhetoric with an attempt to create an accessible democracy based on clear adherence to the rule of law, his government might not have collapsed in such an ignominious way.

President Iliescu's refusal to annul the resignation and reinstate Roman, once the miners had been removed from Bucharest, fuelled speculation about their invasion having been part of an internal power struggle within the FSN. 'Under circumstances of violence', Roman affirmed, 'there can be no resignation' and he criticised Iliescu's willingness to negotiate under the threat of force as 'an act of cowardice' bound to prove disastrous for democracy.[14] But personal as well as policy disagreements seem to have been at the heart of this dispute, which was also the case in Portugal with the first internal convulsions to rock both the Social Democratic Party (PSD, known as the Popular Democratic Party until 1976) and later the Socialist Party in 1980–1, both cases stemming from dissatisfaction with the personal leadership styles of the party founders. But Portuguese party disputes never spilled over into the streets or involved the occupation of the country's parliament. Having been summoned to Bucharest to act as pro-government shock troops in 1990, it is not surprising that Romanian miners were left with the impression that they had the right to intervene in the political process even against the government itself if it was felt to have abandoned its promise to offer social protection to groups made vulnerable by economic change.

Petre Roman's enforced removal was the most worrying example of the failure of a spirit of compromise to mitigate sharp conflicts of interest. It raised the danger that Romania might once again grow accustomed to coercion and brute force being used to resolve power struggles, and constitutional mechanisms being overridden. At least the parliamentary and presidential elections of 27 September 1992 were free of the violence and undisguised abuse of power that marked the first outing to the polls in 1990. Nevertheless, the campaign did not revolve around rival programmes and their efficacy but old political controversies. An opposition campaign dominated by charges of anti-Communism and calls for a monarchist restoration was countered by a government one accusing the Democratic Convention of intending to restore a landed elite and introduce social exploitation as part of a 'sell-out' to Western big business. In opinion polls, these ideological issues were ranked in importance by electors far less highly than policies to arrest the decline in living standards, and the reformist opposition may have lost an important opportunity to strengthen its credentials in the eyes of sceptical voters.[15] President Iliescu was re-elected but the parliamentary contest produced a stalemate in which the governing DNSF lost its absolute majority. Rather than seriously negotiate with its mainstream opponents, it formed an informal alliance with extremist parties. Nicolae Vacaroiu, a civil servant close to Iliescu became Prime Minister. He is not a member of the DNSF but his actions in subsequent months showed that he enjoyed the backing of extreme nationalist parties that held the balance of power.

Here the contrast with Portugal is obvious. In Romania, the non-communist opposition, although it occupied over 40 per cent of parliamentary seats after 1992, was increasingly marginalised as the government party drew closer to forces that drew their inspiration from the authoritarian era. Anti-democratic parties in Portugal never possessed equivalent influence. The only one which counted as an electoral player, the communist PCP, after 1975 remained consistently out of office (although it enjoyed influence in several ministries). All the main non-communist parties had experience of office soon after the 1976 constitution became law. A tradition of coalition governments involving parties ready to bridge the left–right divide ended with the election of the first single-party government with an absolute majority in 1987. However, a political balance was preserved owing to the fact that the head of state is drawn from the largest opposition party. There has been a diffusion of power between the executive, the president and parliament and President Soares has been able to block attempts by Prime Minister Cavaco e Silva to enhance the powers of his own office.

In neither Portugal nor Romania has parliament played an important role in generating respect or loyalty for democratic institutions. The fact that Portugal had ten governments between 1976 and 1987 does not attest to the ability of parliament to elicit consensus or co-operation from the major party blocs. The PCP's willingness to discard its vanguard role suggests that parliament's role as an agent integrating the country's diverse political forces has met with greater success. Whether the Assembly of the Republic would have succeeded in integrating parties which drew their inspiration from the ancien regime, if they had gained significant representation, remains less clear.

The two-chamber Romanian parliament resembles the Assembly of the Republic in the period from 1978 to 1980 when the Portuguese prime minister owed his/her appointment to a superior executive and not to parliament. Portugal, in what was the most uncertain period of its post-revolutionary transition, then enjoyed what Ulricke Liebert has described as 'an indeterminate' type of parliament. Such 'a parliament displays a pattern of interaction with the executive which is highly fragile and threatened by immobilisation, due to a lack of structures and values necessary to stabilise executive–legislative relations'.[16]

In 1992, four party blocs of differing sizes emerged from the first parliamentary elections held under the 1991 Romanian constitution. Parliament's legislative output has been limited, slowed up by the two-chamber arrangement, the exact division of responsibility between the two chambers never having been clearly demarcated. Limited co-operation across party lines has taken place in parliamentary committees, but the Vacaroiu government has shown a disinclination to co-operate with parliament on major issues. It has been very reluctant to allow parliament a supervisory role over the state media or the security services, two areas which are regarded as crucial for the maintenance of political authority.[17]

The conduct of the Romanian parliament has failed to enhance the standing of the country's fragile democracy in the eyes of the public. Frequent chaotic scenes recall the disorderly parliament of the Portuguese 1st Republic (1910–26). The disruptive role played by ultra-nationalist deputies elected for the first time in 1992 suggests that they have been capable of bending the rules of parliament to their own advantage and using both chambers as an arena for advancing populist ideas. The Romanian parliament's inability to make hardline deputies conform to accepted forms of behaviour suggests that it was ill-equipped to play the role of conflict regulator.

In summary, Romanian parties have shown no propensity for bargaining or pursuing consensus approaches unlike the Portuguese parties during the main phases of the democratic transition there. The interests of the National Salvation Front have taken precedence over the need to construct a political system with checks and balances that could enable the opposition to play a constructive role in mainstream politics. Similarly, the reformist opposition has been more concerned with doctrinal purity (rigid anti-Communism) than with exploring ways of reaching an accommodation with the more enlightened sectors of the government party. The shortlived presence of National Liberal deputies in the Stolojan cabinet contributed to the break-up of that party and the Democratic Convention, an umbrella grouping of the main reformist parties, might face similar strains if a pact with the government became a serious option. Within the NSF and its successors and the mainstream opposition, compromises between leaders and their colleagues and between larger and smaller parties have been practised more or less successfully, but the cleavage between the government party and its rivals remains an enormous one which is likely to prevent Romanian politics becoming stabilised for some time to come. So far, there is little sign of that close interaction between rival parties in the Romanian parliament that could reduce the level of partisanship between them.

PARTIES AND SOCIETY

Despite sharply contrasting programmes and even conceptions of democracy, Romanian opposition parties and that based on government office, share a number of basic traits. Perhaps chief among them is their weak implantation in society; membership is low even for the ruling party (which in 1992 claimed a 40,000 strong membership).[18] Although it inherited part of the machinery and personnel of the RCP, this was not an effective base from which to create a powerful nationwide movement given the manner in which the Communist Party had been marginalised under Ceausescu.

In both Romania and Portugal elitism and personalism have been distinguishing features of political parties over a long historical period. As a result, a low value has been placed on grassroots involvement in party affairs with internal democracy or even sporadic consultation not being a prominent hallmark of party life. In Portugal, for a brief period, the critical choices presented by the revolution of 1974–5 resulted in parties springing up which enjoyed a mass membership. But active participation and party identification declined in the late 1970s as parties succumbed to splits or else courted unpopularity when in charge of government on account of their inefficiency or financially restrictive policies. Parties lost the mobilising capacity in society which they had briefly possessed during the revolution and levels of membership soon sank below what was customary in many longer-established European democracies.

In Romania, the younger generation played a conspicuous role in the brief popular upsurge against tyranny in 1989 but thereafter they largely absented themselves from politics. The reluctance of the veterans who resuscitated the 'historic' parties to make room at the top for able younger people produced generational conflicts which further reduced the ability of parties like the NPCDP and the NLP to break out of their isolation. Hopes that a new party, the Civil Alliance Party, would acquire a modern image that would attract the young were dashed when ambitious Bucharest intellectuals split it in 1993 for short-term motives.

A severe problem for the opposition in general has been its failure to establish a presence in the countryside and smaller towns of Romania where the bulk of the population still resides. Excepting Hungarian-speaking areas, these remain a reservoir of support for the governing party and its nationalist allies. Those parties emphasising varying degrees of continuity with the past rely on traditional authority figures such as the local priest, doctor or police chief who may place obstacles in the way of the opposition campaigning in villages (something that certainly happened in 1990).

Television is also a vital instrument that the majority party possesses for communicating with voters outside the big cities. There is a high level of trust in information spread through television.[19] Citizens whose mentality and outlook were particularly influenced by totalitarian conditioning came to accept the veracity of officially disseminated information, and television was the key source of information for a regime which insisted that it possessed the monopoly of truth.

In Portugal, the MFA and its allies likewise regarded control of television as necessary for consolidating their authority. However, it had never been such an important weapon for an authoritarian regime which had refrained from systematic political indoctrination of the population, and the clumsy use which radicals made of television arguably was one of the catalysts which stoked up opposition to them. In both Portugal and Romania, during the most tense moments of the initial transitions, opposition claims that the state was subverting democracy by monopolising control of the media increased polarisation considerably, the difference being that the claims were widely believed in Portugal while in Romania they failed to shake the NSF's hold over the majority of the population. In Romania, an opposition newspaper described the electronic media as being one of the three pillars of presidential power, (the other two being control of the security services and of the investigating magistracy).[20] Undoubtedly, the proven ability of television to shape political attitudes and preferences in Romania makes it a key political weapon. In Portugal it has been a less serious source of friction since 1975, but the limited opportunities parties have of influencing public opinion other than through the media means that disputes are bound to recur over control of television.

The Romanian opposition parties have failed to acquire strong social bases, which reduces the likelihood of the ruling party voluntarily handing over power at an early stage. Parties committed to market economics have found it difficult to acquire backing from newly private companies that would enable them to mount more effective electoral campaigns. If anything, the first wave of Romanian capitalists have been inclined to support the ruling party and the nationalists, which may shed light on the way that state holdings have been sold off and who has benefited. Again, excepting the Hungarian minority party which has strong ties with the main minority faiths, religion has not been a source of opposition support even though a religious revival has got underway. The limited reach of parties implies that in Romania they are hardly in a position to act as agents of social integration during a period in which few citizens can escape harsh adjustments in their lives owing to the collapse of one social system and understandable uncertainty about what will replace it.

There is no sign that a new civic culture is emerging in Romania in which citizens become used to some aspect of regular political participation, even if they do not normally avail themselves of it. Memories of the systematic repression of dissent in the communist period and of the dangerous turbulence which marked the 1989–91 years in Romania has understandably impeded greater participation in Romanian politics. Of course, many citizens have been too absorbed by the battle for material survival to engage in an activity which offers few psychological rewards or practical incentives for those outside the governing party.

NATIONALISM AS A SUBSTITUTE FOR SOCIAL INTEGRATION

As in earlier periods of Romanian history, nationalism has become a source of legitimacy for a ruling elite which finds it difficult to appeal convincingly to citizens on the basis of its domestic socio-economic record or fidelity to democratic principles. A clear contrast can be drawn with Portugal where neither the radical nor moderate forces seeking to direct the political process used nationalist symbols arising from the dictatorship to strengthen their appeal. One of the aims of the Portuguese revolution which raised the least opposition was that of drastically reducing the size of the national territory by withdrawing from Africa. Later, all the major parties except the Communists endorsed Portugal's accession to the European Community, a decision approved by public opinion.

In Romania, the impact of xenophobic Communism was revealed by the ability of ultra-nationalist parties to acquire over 10 per cent of the seats in the 1992 general election which left them holding the balance of power. Ceausescu's goal of creating a strong, highly centralised, and ethnically homogeneous state was not one that perished with its architect. The administrative elite that he imposed on Hungarian-speaking areas to hasten the assimilation of an inconvenient minority formed an important pressure group after 1989 designed to block the granting of minority rights. Vatra Romaneasca (Romanian Cradle) is an example of an important local interest, fearing a loss of status, mobilising effectively to lobby the state on its behalf. Unfortunately, there are few counter examples of religious, occupational, or social groups committed to democratic values organising effectively to advance their interests before those of the state.[21]

The Romanian government has used or tolerated nationalist demagogues who offer simple and immediate solutions to complex problems by focusing attention on a range of internal enemies. Something similar happened in the 1930s when the extremist Iron Guard was courted and used by traditional parties seeking to neutralise one another. The Iliescu regime looks less tainted before international opinion if it can point to extremist forces beside whom it looks moderate even if their strength partly stems from its patronage. Although it is doubtful if Iliescu shares the chauvinism and anti-semitism of the ultra-nationalists, like them he has no interest in replacing a passive political culture in which a low value is placed on participation with an active one in which voters acquire the information and confidence to sceptically assess demagogic appeals. His regime has placed nationalists in top jobs in order to block attempts to create the autonomous space necessary for genuine pluralism to flourish. His critics allege that he is also ready to mobilise one social group against another (like the miners against students and intellectuals in 1990) in order to reinforce his own power-base and prevent serious alternatives to his rule emerging. In Portugal, nostalgia for the extreme right may exist but no serious political competitor has dared to revive the symbols of the authoritarian era. Indeed, the extreme right in Portugal is weaker than almost anywhere else in Europe, though scope for an authoritarian revival exists if economic progress is reversed.[22]

The strength of populist nationalism, the ability of the President to exercise major influence over the daily political process extending beyond his normal constitutional prerogatives, and the failure of political institutions to acquire widespread respect gives Romanian democracy a provisional character even after the constitutional machinery of the new state has largely been put in place. In the event of a major crisis, Iliescu's semi-presidential regime would appear to have as much chance of being removed by force as through the ballot box, and there is the danger that if the ballot-box proved decisive, power might still pass to anti-democratic forces.

In a 1993 poll, 27 per cent of Romanian respondents when asked what sort of government they would like, expressed a preference for 'an authoritarian, iron-fisted leadership'.[23] Later, in the same year, a different poll found that 58.8 per cent of respondents had no confidence in the ability of the government to solve outstanding national problems while 66.8 per cent felt that a government reshuffle would make no difference. To make matters worse, 39 per cent of respondents in a further 1993 poll doubted the ability of the reformist opposition to rescue the country, 50 per cent of respondents had no confidence in any party, and 60 per cent were disenchanted with the performance of both parliament and government.[24]

Romania's future as a fledgling democracy appears problematic when such a high level of disenchantment exists about the role of political institutions and office-holders, a feeling that extends to an opposition which has not been given the chance to reveal its administrative capacities. As Romania has lurched from fragile and inadequate democratic rule to long periods of dictatorship, most citizens seem to have grown very sceptical about the ability of political institutions to improve their lives.[25] This means that political expectations are low which can be a boon in a transition process where rulers can offer few economic rewards in the short-term. However, it also means that many citizens may be predisposed to believe in personalities as agents of salvation rather than parties or programmes. The name assumed by Ceausescu's successors, the National Salvation Front, perhaps revealed that their instinct was to appeal to voters on populist grounds rather than on more orthodox criteria. 'Salvation' was not dropped from the title until 1993 when the party was renamed the Party of Romanian Social Democracy, one that was a personal platform for a president who is consulted on all major internal decisions by its leaders.[26]

In Portugal, strong disenchantment was also expressed with the performance of political institutions at an equivalent point in the transition. Four years after the 1974 coup, 2,000 respondents when asked in a survey which government or regime governs or governed the country best, put the 1968–74 Caetano regime at the top of the list with 28 per cent, only 9 per cent opting for the first constitutional government of 1976–7, and 31 per cent answering with a 'don't know'.[27] But in Portugal there was none of the continuity in structures and personnel that in Romania make a reversal to some form of open authoritarian politics a distinct possibility at some point in the future. Popular disillusionment with parties in the Portugal of the late 1970s led to apoliticism rather than active endorsement for right or left authoritarianism. While bad for the long-term health of democracy, the flight of citizens from party activism probably helped to lower the political temperature during a period of declining living standards in the wake of several years of political mobilisation.

In Romania, citizens have remained spectators of a remote political game. A civic culture in which citizens feel able to participate in politics even if they rarely make use of the opportunity, has not emerged. Instead, at different points in the early 1990s citizens were mobilised at carefully-selected moments to endorse populist appeals or harsh anti-opposition measures, which suggests there is a risk of a plebiscitary democracy taking root in Romania.

Of course, a halt to declining living standards and the prospect of economic reconstruction in the context of regional stability in south-eastern Europe would be a powerful inducement for political normalisation. Portugal seems to have gone from a weakly-implanted democracy in the first decade after the 1974 coup to being an increasingly robust one, thanks to the conjuncture of favourable external circumstances. The consolidation of democracy next door in Spain, the substantial economic rewards that flowed from joining the European Community, and the way that global economic changes benefited the Portuguese economy, lowered dissatisfaction with the shortcomings of the democratic process during the second decade of political transition.

No renewal in Portuguese parties has occurred that can be measured in terms of the quality of leadership, the size of memberships, or growing popular prestige. But their defects are less visible and significant owing to developments, largely external in origin, that have increased living standards and ensured a less critical attitude towards politics on the part of the electorate. It is worth noting that the onset of prosperity after years of austerity have given Portuguese parties more opportunity to acquire social influence by distributing resources. But the healthy economic climate has reduced divisions as the ruling party (since 1987 the Social Democrats) has allowed the opposition parties to benefit from the expansion of state funding. Such restraint makes it likely that Portuguese parties will act as agents of social integration rather than division as democracy becomes consolidated, something which can only promote the legitimacy of the new democratic system.

Meanwhile, in Romania with its permanent shortage economy and bleak economic prospects, the ruling party has chosen to monopolise resources and offices in its gift right down to village level. It seems to have inherited the view prevalent under Communism that the dictates of political survival require power to be monopolised by a tight-knit group conforming to a restricted political agenda. Staunch conservatives whose political careers were shaped during the authoritarian era have modified the political system to allow important elements of pluralism such as a free press, competitive elections, and freedom of association. But many of their actions and statements suggest that they are reluctant democrats who have bowed to prevailing circumstances rather than voluntarily dropped authoritarian behaviour and embraced pluralism.

CONCLUSION

In Romania, it was a party whose origins can be traced to the authoritarian era which created an alternative political system that was sufficiently pluralistic to enable Romania to enter the Council of Europe and obtain other forms of external recognition. But the continuity, in terms of personality and structures, with the past places Romania apart from other post-communist east-European states; in them it has been customary for a range of political forces to co-operate in working out the ground rules for the switch from despotism to pluralism and it has been normal for parties to form wide-ranging coalitions or else to substitute one another in office at quite an early stage.

Portugal offers some useful comparisons with Romania, due allowance being made for the very different natures of their authoritarian systems and the much more difficult task of implanting democracy in Romania. In Portugal, parties were initially slow to play a defining role in the transition process. The rigours of the authoritarian regime and the abrupt and violent nature of its demise, delayed their emergence and placed the limelight on military officers who had abandoned their allegiance to the dictatorship. External factors and the vitality of civil society in some parts of the country soon enabled parties to play a greater role in the transition and to ensure that it complied with democratic criteria, features that did not come into play in Romania. However, in both countries a semi-presidential system was established, the role of parliament being downplayed. This proved to be an interlude (albeit a long one) in Portugal's transition as parties assumed greater control over the democratic process; in Romania, the constitution drawn up re-affirmed a historical trend whereby a powerful individual has exercised control over a set of centralised institutions.

Following the 1982 and 1989 revisions of the Portuguese constitution which removed powers from the presidency, Portuguese parties have shown unwavering commitment to a democracy which has moved from a transitional phase to one of consolidation. Romania is far from such a stage. The constitution, allowing for a semi-presidential system, was only installed at the end of 1991 and, although it was endorsed in a referendum, it remains contested by opposition parties whose vote increased sharply in the 1992 elections.

Romania's political system permits competition and places limits on the powers of the state but it does not retain the loyalty of important elements of the mainstream opposition; they regard it as illegitimate because of its architects' links with the pre-1989 regime. The ruling party showed no inclination to devise a constitutional formula that would win backing from the opposition. Instead it prefers to make short-term pacts with extremist parties whose nostalgia for the dictatorship is undisguised. Such compromises with undemocratic forces scarcely help to enhance democratic values and they raise suspicions that the liquidators of the communist dictatorship have only a limited commitment to democracy and prefer a hybrid system in which power can be exercised sometimes arbitrarily without international hostility.

In Portugal, the commitment of the major parties (the PCP: Communist Party being the sole exception) to democratic politics was not in doubt after the short revolutionary interlude. Parties did not distinguish themselves when in government during the first decade of democracy and were also prone to split when in opposition. Nevertheless, the maintenance of stability and the avoidance of sharp inter-party disputes enabled the democratic transition to proceed without interruption or challenge.

The political transition in Romania has been far more disturbed and offers less hope that behaviour patterns and values are being promoted which will be conducive for the survival of representative institutions. The conduct of the ruling party (and at times the opposition also) has not fostered respect for democratic processes, nor encouraged the citizenry to become actively involved in the process in order to remove abuses from the communist era that still remain in place. Government–opposition clashes in 1990 and the manner in which Premier Roman was removed from office by a violent mob which seized parliament in 1991, were incidents which dented the prestige of democracy in the formative period of the transition.

So, although the Portuguese and Romanian transitions showed some similarities in their initial phases which set them apart from other post-authoritarian regimes in southern and eastern Europe, the contrasts quickly became more important. Portuguese parties may never have been powerful enough to become active promoters of civic values and political participation, but their strength was enough to frustrate attempts in 1974–5 to revive autocratic politics. In Romania, the parties lack the cohesion and strength to be able to bar the way towards an authoritarian revival. Indeed, the questionable commitment of the ruling party to liberal democratic values is one of the greatest perils Romanian democracy faces in the years ahead.

NOTES

1 Vladimir Tismaneanu, 'The Quasi-Revolution and its Discontents: Emerging Political Pluralism in Post-Ceausescu Romania', *East European Politics and Societies*, 1993, vol. 7, p. 317.

2 Mary Ellen Fischer, 'The New Leaders and the Opposition', in Daniel Nelson (ed.), *Romania After Tyranny*, Boulder, Colorado, Westview Press, 1992, p. 46.

3 Fischer, op. cit., p. 51.

4 M. Calinescu and V. Tismaneanu, 'The 1989 Revolution and Romania's Future', *Problems of Communism*, 1991 (Jan.–April) p. 52, n. 38.

5 Calinescu and Tismaneanu, op. cit., p. 52.

6 Assessments of the 1990 Romanian elections were provided by Daniel Nelson, 'No Longer Tyranny, Not Yet Democracy', *Electoral Studies*, 1990, vol. 9; and T. Gallagher, 'Romania: The Disputed Election of 1990', *Parliamentary Affairs*, 1991, vol. 44, pp. 79–93.

7 Tom Gallagher, 'Obstacles To Political Participation in Romania'. Seminar on 'Disillusionment with Democracy', Council of Europe, Human Rights Centre, Essex University, Essex, July 1993.

8 Mark Almond, 'Romania Since The Revolution', *Government and Opposition*, 1990, vol. 25, p. 493.

9 For electoral and pre-electoral irregularities, see Human Rights in Romania Since the evolution, Helsinki Watch Report, 1991 and International Delegation Report (of Election Observers), *The May 1990 Elections in Romania*, National Republican Institute for International Affairs/National Democratic Institute for International Affairs, USA 1991.

10 See Dan Ionescu, 'In Quest of a Model: Development Strategies under Discussion', *Report on Eastern Europe*, 28 September 1990.

11 See Steven Sampson, 'Romania Today', *International Journal of Romanian Studies*, 1981–83, vol. 3, nos. 1–2, passim.

12 Michael Shafir, 'Romania's New Institutions: the Draft Constitution', *Report on Eastern Europe*, 20 September 1991, p. 27.

13 For Portuguese local government, see W. Opello, 'Local Government and Political Culture in a Portuguese Rural County', *Comparative Politics*, 1981, vol. 13; and T. Gallagher, 'The Portuguese Communist Party', in B. Szajkowski, (ed.), *Marxist Local Governments in Western Europe and Japan*, London and Boulder, Pinter & Reinner, 1986, pp 45–66.

14 *Report on Eastern Europe*, Digest of Weekly Events, 20 October 1991.

15 See Tismaneanu, 'The Quasi-Revolution . . .', pp. 312–14.

16 Ulrike Liebert and Maurizio Cotta (eds), *Parliament and Democratic Consolidation in Southern Europe*, 1990, Frances Pinter, London, p. 260.

17 The opposition parties won a rare victory in parliament by obtaining a majority for the setting up of a commission that would control the intelligence services, but the deputy later appointed as its head turned out to be the President's closest parliamentary ally, Senator Vasile Vacaru. *ARPRESS*, Selective Daily Bulletin, no. 693, 18 June 1993, no. 698, 24 June 1993.

18 Tismaneanu, op. cit., p. 317.

19 Ioan Mihailescu, 'Mental Stereotypes in Post-Totalitarian Romania', *Government and Opposition*, 1993, vol. 28, p. 318.

20 *22*, (Bucharest weekly newspaper), 8 July 1993.

21 See Tom Gallagher, 'Vatra Romaneasca and resurgent nationalism in Romania', *Ethnic and Racial Studies*, 1993, vol. 15; and T. Gallagher, 'The Rise of the Party of Romanian National Unity', *RFE-RL Research Report*, 18 March 1994, vol. 3.

22. See T. Gallagher, 'Portugal', in P. Hainsworth (ed.), *The Extreme Right In Western Europe and North America*, London, Pinter, 1992.
23 M. Shafir, 'Romanians and the Transition to Democracy', *RFE/RL Research Report*, 30 April 1993, p. 47.
24 The findings from the various opinion surveys cited here were taken from the Bucharest political magazine, *Sfera Politicii*, no. 10, October 1993.
25 Trond Gilberg, 'Romanians and Democratic Values: Socialisation After Communism', in Daniel Nelson (ed.), *Romania After Tyranny*, Boulder, Colorado, Westview Press 1992, pp. 83–4.
26 Dan Ionescu, 'Has Romania's Ruling Party Become Stronger or Weaker', *RFE-RL Research Report*, 27 August 1993, vol. 2, p. 15.
27 Ken Gladdish, 'Portugal: an open verdict', in Geoffrey Pridham (ed.), *Securing Democracy: political parties and democratic consolidation in Southern Europe*, London, Routledge, 1990, p. 119.

Main problem: The people cannot have the power that is there from the collapse (the vacuum) unless they enter the pol process; not, parties properly. They won't do this as there is still distrust — The next generation.

Can't say what is going to happen but can describe a lot and make presumptions

* It filled the space (vacuum) that maybe other oppositional parties might have done if they had been given the chance.

One of the major probs: problem of alienation.

10 The formation of political parties in post-communist Poland

Włodzimierz Wesołowski

Motto:
Parties from *principle*,
especially abstract speculative
principle, are known only to
modern times and are, perhaps,
the most extraordinary and
unaccountable *phenomenon* that has
yet appeared in human affairs
    David Hume (*Of Parties in General*)

HISTORICAL OVERVIEW

Political parties have not had a smooth take-off since the outbreak of the anti-communist revolution. This general statement is probably truer for Poland than it is for countries like Hungary. So we may be able to gain a particular understanding of the barriers to party system development within the emerging east-central European democracies by analysing the evolution of political parties in Poland between 1989 and 1994. Some of these barriers have not been overcome in Poland to this day, leaving its democracy unconsolidated and facing the prospect that future evolution may lead to the establishment of a system only partly operating in accordance with democratic criteria.[1]

The initial difficulties varied in nature. The old regime had completely discredited the Communist Party – which had identified itself as a party despite the fact that it had not fulfilled the basic characteristic functions of such an institution. Hence the deep-rooted resentment against political parties as such. The emergence of 'Solidarity', the powerful nation-wide civil movement, also had a negative effect on the formation of political parties. This movement was perceived initially as a substitute for all manner of democratic institutions, and virtually came to represent 'the general will of the sovereign people'. Both workers and intellectuals fell prey to this Rousseau-like illusion.[2] Of course, the latter were aware of the diversity of economic interests, ideologies and practical options it represented. Yet they believed that the powerful movement had more instrumental value in this form than if it fragmented into several parties. In effect, the process of party formation within the great Solidarity movement took place unexpectedly and spontaneously, not following any specific plan. Parties began to emerge largely on the basis of personal animosities between different leaders. Lech Wałęsa, in particular, contributed significantly to the conflict-ridden dissolution of Solidarity.

A second factor which contributed to the difficulties encountered in the development of what might be termed a normal party structure in Poland was the conviction, maintained by many social groups, that their immediate and long-term interests could be adequately articulated and effectively defended by the NSZZ Solidarity trade union which had survived the dissolution of the political unity of Solidarity as a civil movement. This conviction was still expressed in 1994, when the current leaders of the NSZZ Solidarity trade union launched an all-encompassing critique of every possible political institution (the president, government, parliament, political parties) and suggested that the trade union was better able to promote popular interests.[3]

These circumstances, generally unfavourable for the establishment of political parties on the basis of former opposition forces, led to a peculiar state of affairs. Between 1989 and 1993 the country was in fact ruled by Solidarity-derived parties which initiated all the market and democratic reforms of that period but which were organisationally very weak, highly fragmented and without social roots or strong ties with specific groups or social classes. Parliamentary deputies had been known to attempt to establish 'local party units', but had little success. On the other hand, those parties which had existed under the previous regime – the Polish Peasant Party (PSL) and the reconstituted Communist Party (SdRP) retained their local organisational infrastructure. Despite being politically marginalised at the outset the two parties nevertheless survived. Their existing organisational infrastructures were a significant condition of their return to power in September 1993, although equally important for this development, if not more so, was increasing popular discontent with the various policies of the post-Solidarity parties which impinged on different areas of society. Among them the most detrimental were those which led to deteriorating standards of living and rising unemployment among the working class, peasants and agricultural labourers.

THE PARTY SYSTEM AND CONSOLIDATED DEMOCRACY

Much of Poland's political elite and most of society are aspiring to develop a consolidated, liberal, representative democracy. But inherent in the notion of a 'consolidated democracy' is the assumption that there are also less consolidated democracies. Indeed, the emergence of an unconsolidated but lasting democracy seems to be a real threat in Poland and, while the transition to democracy may be judged to have finished, the political order established may be a tentative and potentially unstable one. In the country's new geopolitical setting such an unconsolidated democracy could even prove to be viable. Immature political parties would be one characteristic feature of such a deficient democracy.

It is evident from the experience of all modern states that democracy must be anchored in political parties in order to function properly. Pluralism in complex societies requires free expression of diversity, including the articulation of a range of public interests and aspirations. It also requires the reduction of complexity to a level which permits systematic thinking and the instigation of concrete action. Many public organisations and institutions serve the functions of articulating public interests and reducing social diversity. The accomplishment of this without political parties, however, is inconceivable under contemporary social conditions.

In Poland, the weakness of the party structure as a whole is confirmed by the failure of political parties to perform the following four functions:

- First, they fail to articulate any comprehensive model of social life; such models should be the subject of permanent discussion, otherwise politics degenerates into naked struggles for power; in other words, the existing political parties fail to fulfil their ideological functions in the deeper sense of the word.
- Second, they are poor in constructing alternatives to practical governmental policies; in other words they fail to perform adequately programmatic functions, i.e., to develop practical options and structure alternatives for the society and government. This is particularly true of economic matters.
- Third, they fail to mediate between government programmes and decisions on the one hand, and social interests, aspirations and options on the other; therefore they do not perform articulation and leadership functions (also known as the 'linkage' function).
- Fourth, they have not developed to the stage where they can provide the framework for various levels of political activity; in other words they do not fulfil their mobilisation functions.[4]

I do not want to be misunderstood: I am not saying that there are no manifestations whatsoever of these four functions. What I am saying is that they are not crystallised features of the party system as a whole. Deficiencies in this respect are particularly obvious in the case of the post-Solidarity parties, though to varying degrees. The transformed parties of the former regime which came to power in the 1993 elections have been somewhat more successful in performing mobilisation functions but they are still weak in the performance of the remaining three functions. The post-communist party has become very heterogeneous and is held together rather by memories of the past than by common ideology or a shared programme. The Polish Peasant Party on the other hand has functioned since 1989 as a typical pressure group, focusing almost entirely on the current interests of the peasantry. It has been unable to choose definitively between two seductive images which present themselves as alternatives, namely agrarianism and the social teaching of the Catholic Church. It has oscillated between them and at times has even evoked some version of socialism.

The poor performance of the party system has led to two highly unfavourable outcomes. The first is governmental instability caused by the lack of stable and sufficiently strong parliamentary support. A second consequence is the increasing political apathy of the common citizen. He or she still believes that democracy has its good side but is, on the other hand, becoming increasingly critical of democratic mechanisms and, if the chaotic situation persists, may be prepared to tolerate solutions of a dictatorial or strongly corporate nature.[5]

The recent political victory (September 1993) of parties rooted in the old regime has spurred on integrative tendencies within the post-Solidarity parties. But it has also increased centrifugal tendencies in the post-communist party. At the same time, the pressure to choose between different ideological commitments has encouraged fission within the Polish Peasant Party. All in all, the political arena is far from crystallised. The various political parties still lack programmatic unity; the post-Solidarity parties are organisationally weak; the electorate continues to view political parties sceptically. It criticises the fact that there are too many parties and that they seem to show no interest in the matters which most concern ordinary people.[6]

ORGANISATIONAL FRAGMENTATION AND INTEGRATION: PROBLEMS OF PARTY COALITION MAINTENANCE

The 1989 elections led to the establishment of a 'Contract Parliament' with three centres of gravity. The minority 'Solidarity block' (one third) formed the government and was virtually in power from the outset. This block was supported by the two former satellite parties (the Polish Peasant Party and the Democratic Party, which represented tradespeople and certain white-collar groups). It soon managed to marginalise the Communist Party, which was undergoing a rapid transformation. There were at this stage few signs of the process of fragmentation that was about to begin.

However, tendencies of fragmentation were insidiously creeping into political life. They could be attributed to the convergence of several factors which pointed to the same outcome. The first factor was the emergence of profound political and personal differences within the Solidarity block (which had previously been the point of convergence for all manner of ideological and political orientations). These differences had to surface sooner or later. A second factor was the existence of various groups of anti-communist opposition outside Solidarity. These groups soon began openly to demand their share of power. The largest was Leszek Moczulski's Confederation for Independent Poland (KPN), established underground before the emergence of Solidarity. The third factor was the great urge which inspired various small, often purely informal groups, to make their presence felt on the political scene: history was giving them a chance to make their mark.

If we view the situation from yet another perspective, we soon find that a number of unrealistic beliefs were held by several prominent intellectual Solidarity leaders. They had an opportunity to counteract spontaneous splitting but they did not take advantage of it. They believed that the leaders of the political wing of the Solidarity movement would keep co-operating in spite of their divergent tendencies.[7] They did not foresee that once internal disputes flared up they would acquire a dynamic of their own which would destroy the movement's unity and create divisions which it would be hard to overcome. According to another of their irrational beliefs democracy should encompass all possible manifestations of pluralism, even those of an extreme nature, because only an initial commitment to pluralism could guarantee the emergence of more coherent social forces, including strong political parties. No one foresaw that this fragmentation, by force of its own dynamic, could deepen and form rigid divisions. It was also mistakenly believed that the post-communist party had been marginalised more or less for good.

These beliefs went hand in hand with a conviction that the great transformation required strong government rather than strong parties.[8] Nobody asked what types of political organisation were supposed to act as the link between the political class and the broader society. Some people thought the NSZZ Solidarity Trade Union would perform this function, because – after all – at the beginning of the transformation, i.e. when the Mazowiecki and Bielecki governments were in office, it had agreed to act as a 'protective umbrella' and shield the economic and political reforms from potential opposition.

As a result of progressive fragmentation 111 'electoral committees' formed by parties and political groups presented voting lists in the 1991 elections – the first fully democratic elections in post-communist Poland.[9] The adoption of a proportional electoral law also reflected the advanced state of party fragmentation. In all, twenty-four different electoral groups effectively gained parliamentary representation. There were three parties in favour of a decidedly neo-liberal economic policy in general and of a strict financial policy in particular (The Democratic Union – UD, the Liberal Democratic Congress – KLD, and the Polish Beer-Lovers' Party – PPPP, later renamed the Polish Economic Programme, PPG); four parties which claimed themselves to follow a Christian line (The Christian Democratic Party – PChD, the National-Christian Union – ZChN, the

Centre Alliance – PC, and the Christian Democratic Party – PChD); one of the peasant parties also adopted a Christian vocabulary (Peasant Alliance – PL).

During the term of office of this parliament (1991–3), there were further divisions of existing parties into various official factions and many deputies began a pilgrimage around the political arena, changing parties as they went.[10] In effect, this fragmentation led to even deeper antagonism between the leaders of the Solidarity block and to a persistent instability on the part of the governments and the governing coalitions that were formed. The different coalitions which came to power strove to maintain the course of reform adopted by the first non-communist government under Mazowiecki, especially the principle parameters of the economic strategy adopted by Balcerowicz (i.e. strict budget control, reduction of inflation, continuing pressure for economic integration with Europe). However, because successive governments were so unstable and because they were formed as coalitions, and were therefore forced to compromise, the reforms (e.g. the popular privatisation programme) slowed down and social and industrial policy suffered from a persistent lack of clarity. This situation further antagonised those social groups who were losing because of the reforms – particularly the urban and rural working class and the unemployed. This in turn caused increasing deterioration of the social climate and aggravated dissatisfaction with those in power. The very dispersed distribution of the electorate's sympathies between 1991 and 1993 was also a significant factor in this. In parallel, there was a tendency of declining support for the parties that had grown out of the Solidarity movement.[11]

The fact that the political stage was greatly fragmented by no means implied that a range of political programmes was properly articulated or spelt out in any detail. Neither did it imply that the majority of the parties (particularly the small ones) were rooted in any specific social group. They wanted to be catch-all parties, but they actually caught very few votes. They even ignored the need to penetrate at least a few specific social environments and to establish sustained political linkages with them. The largest parties had a membership of 50 to 200 thousand. Small parties had from 500 to 5000 members (see Table 10.1).

A self-reinforcing complex of factors also began to operate. This complex first gave birth to and then sustained processes of organisational fragmentation, exacerbating the tendencies towards inconsequentiality and superficiality in the various political programmes. This organisational fragmentation by no means facilitated the penetration of specific social groups by the different parties, if only because they lacked the necessary strength and resources; ordinary people could no longer discern the minute differences between the programmes of the various parties. All they knew was that their leaders had quarrelled over something and this nourished criticism of the entire political elite.

Table 10.1 Reported party membership, 1991–3

Party	1991	1992	1993
Democratic Union	15,000	10,000	15–20,000
Social Democracy of the Polish Republic (SdRP)	60,000		65,000
Polish Peasant Party	180,000	200,000	200,000
Confederation for Independent Poland	21,000		35,000

Source: Adapted from Paul G. Lewis, *Party Factionalism and Democratisation in Poland.* See also note 10, p. 253, this volume.

Table 10.2 The Polish elections 1991–3 – numbers of seats in parliament

Party	1991	1993
UD – The Democratic Union	62	74
SLD – The Democratic Left Alliance[1]	60	171
PSL – The Polish Peasant Party	48	132
ZChN – The National-Christian Union	49	–
KPN – Confederation of Independent Poland	46	22
KLD – Liberal-Democratic Congress	37	–
PC – Centre Alliance	44	–
Solidarność – Solidarity Trade Union	27	–
PL – Peasant Accord	28	–
Polish Party of Beer Lovers	16	–
The German Minority	7	4
UP – Labour Union	4	41
PChD – The Party of Christian Democrats	4	–
ChD – Christian Democracy	5	–
UPR – Union of Real Politics	3	–
Party X	3	–
BBWR – Non-Party Block for Reforms	–	16
Representatives of other organisations[2]	17	–
Total	460	460

Sources: *Monitor Polski* no 41, 5 Dec. 1991, position 288; *Monitor Polski* no 50, 4 Oct. 1993, position 470 (official results of elections on 27 October 1991 and on 23 September 1993 respectively)

Notes:
1 SLD includes post-communist SdRP – Social Democracy of the Polish Republic and OPZZ – post-communist trade unions
2 Some of them joined larger parties after the election

The return to the left has more to do with *electoral* laws & the split up of Solidarity than anything else

TRagic

NB

The post-Solidarity parties recognised the detrimental effects of fragmentation even before the 1993 elections. At face value, the downfall of the Suchocka government was engineered by deputies of Solidarity trade union and to some extent supported by the post-communist and peasant parties. It was a sign that no government could operate any longer with so fragmented a parliament. Yet, despite this painful lesson, post-Solidarity parties were unable to overcome the exorbitant ambitions of their 'leaders' – each of whom wanted a party of their own. They decided to stand separately in the coming elections. The outcome was devastating. The qualified majority electoral law, favouring stronger parties in the allocation of seats, eliminated small parties from the new parliament. The net result was that the 'ancien regime' regained power: the post-communists and the Polish Peasant Party emphatically won the elections (see Table 10.2 above: 1991 and 1993 election results).

Polish experience thus suggests that party leaders must first be devastatingly defeated before they can learn to think rationally. Having lost the elections the post-Solidarity parties now began to unite. Two previously leading parties, the Democratic Union (UD) and the Liberal Democratic Congress (KLD) united in May 1994 and formed a new party, the Freedom Union (UW). However, the Democratic Union brought to the new party its own internal division (into libertarians, Christians and the social liberals). On the whole, the fusion strengthened the liberals' position on the political arena. The 'unionists' agree on one thing: pro-capitalist and pro-market reforms should be accelerated and government control of the economy reduced.

Catholic and national-Catholic parties also joined in the integration movement. In June 1994, following long talks and negotiations, two confederations were established. The first one, called the 'Covenant for Poland', gathered up the following parties: the Christian-National Union, the Centre Alliance, the Popular Alliance, the Movement for the Third Republic, and the group calling itself the Conservative Coalition. The architect of this fusion was Jarosław Kaczyński, leader of the Centre Alliance. The entire 'Covenant' stresses its Christianity, Polish nationalism and anti-Communism. As far as economic matters are concerned, it adheres to the social teaching of the Catholic Church, particularly to John Paul II's encyclical. It is quite evident that existing differences over economic policy tended to be ignored during the negotiations which preceded the union. The continuing independence of the different allied parties was emphasised by the procedure whereby each month a different party leader chaired the meeting of the confederation. The formation of the confederation bore fruit almost immediately, during the local self-government elections held on 19 June 1994. It managed to win local government seats in many towns and villages (in some localities as many as one third). In many places it was able to forge rightist coalitions with politically independent former local councillors. They claimed that this would reduce the influence of post-communists and of PSL in the country as a whole.

A second confederation, the Agreement of 11 November, was formed by the following parties: the Conservative Party, the Union of Real Politics, the Christian-Democratic Party, the Peasant-Christian Alliance, and the National-Democratic Party. Its architect was Aleksander Hall, a prominent intellectual and leader of the Conservative Party. This coalition was more oriented towards a long-run political strategy of winning over people who adhered to tradition in the cultural sphere, to Catholic values and who were also in favour of the unlimited rights of private property. They were conservative-liberals, whose views are close to those of British Conservatives. This coalition fared poorly in the local elections. The Freedom Union, the Covenant for Poland, and the Agreement of 11 November increasingly expressed the conviction that it would be necessary to contest the coming 1995 presidential elections together, in opposition to the post-communist party and the Polish Peasants' Party. At the time of writing, whether they will be able to select and support a single candidate remains to be seen.

A rearrangement of the political scene that will be different from that seen in Hungary thus became feasible in Poland. Economic and radical, secular liberals were poised to enter into coalition with right-wing nationalists and Christians. The 1993 victory of the post-communist parties could prove to be short-lived if the liberal, national and religious right did in fact unite forces. As far as our analysis is concerned, the main conclusion must be that we have witnessed the beginning of integration of the political scene and the formation of larger political blocks, at least at the organisational level. This integration was triggered by the victory of post-communist parties and organisations in the 1993 elections.

PROGRAMMATIC DISPERSION AND CONCENTRATION: PROBLEMS OF POLITICAL IDENTITY

Between 1990 and 1993 neither the small parties, nor the larger ones such as the Democratic Union, the Social Democracy of the Polish Republic (the political core of the SLD coalition) and the Polish Peasant Party crystallised their ideologies or clearly formulated long-term programmes. Several parties also avoided taking any definite stand-point on particularly controversial issues. In my opinion this tendency to hide behind clichés had significant roots. The most profound, intellectual reason was that serious theoretical and ideological discourse had not yet started. This was detrimental to overall processes of systemic transformation.[12] The post-communist party avoided the adjective 'socialist' in all its programmatic enunciations, just as the liberal party avoided the adjective 'capitalist'. The communists wanted to present themselves as a new political formation as rapidly as they could, despite their lack of any new theory or ideology. On their side, during the 1989–92 period economic liberals avoided the word 'capitalist'. The future model was described as 'market economy'. It was only later that they overcame their shyness and referred to the 'capitalist economic model' as a desired one.

It was symptomatic, too, that Catholic intellectuals and politicians also tended to avoid any theoretical-axiological presentation of their desired model of social life. They were not even encouraged to do so by John Paul II's elaboration of the social teaching of the Catholic Church. They merely repeated that socio-economic arrangements should be based on a social market economy, social justice, equal concern for capital and labour. Any theoretical commentary stopped short at asking whether the Pope was equally critical of socialism and capitalism or whether liberalism was perhaps closer to Christian solutions. Nationalist leaders were just as reluctant to theorise. In pre-war Poland the dominant concept in this political milieu was that of the strong state. Its power was to be measured, amongst other things, in terms of citizens' sacrifice and obedience toward the regime, the ability to stand up to neighbouring countries, and criteria of economic independence. These themes did not fit well with the task of post-communist transformation.

Jarosław Kaczyński, reflecting on recent political experiences, self-critically assessed the intellectual activity of the right in the following words:

> Various elements of popular naive thinking, especially in the economic sphere . . . remnants of various obsolete political ideas, remnants of the pathological thinking of Catholic circles formerly collaborating with the communist regime, the legacy of national insurrections, traditions of 'October 1956' – all these have been mixed together and have confused right-wing thought today.[13]

Janusz Lewandowski, one of the leaders of the Liberal Democratic Congress and Minister of Privatisation in the governments both of Bielecki and of Suchocka, and a dedicated advocate of the transfer of a 'normal' model of contemporary Western-type capitalism to Poland, wrote retro-spectively in 1994:

> What Poland needs is a clear developmental strategy. Society, in its transition from one system to another, needs a compass, a global vision that will make the separate steps meaningful . . . It is the duty of the Freedom Union to formulate a long-term, comprehensive vision of the 'second step' of the Polish reforms. The reformers grouped in the Democratic Union and the Liberal Democratic Congress failed to prepare such a vision in 1989–93 because they had merely been responding to various pressures.[14]

Only recently, under its new leader Ryszard Czarnecki, did the Christian-National Union set up ten thematic groups to draft a detailed party programme.[15] It was difficult to formulate comprehensive programmes when specific models and visions of the future were lacking. Party programmes, guided by no definite theoretical or ideological principles, tended to drift and became variegated and imprecise. They only reached a concrete level when called upon to solve specific problems relating to day-to-day policy. The documentation of the pre-election programmes is extremely revealing in this respect as they were full of clichés and third-rate detail.[16] The programmatic carelessness shown by many post-Solidarity parties was probably rooted in a conviction that the direction of political and economic transformation was predetermined by the very logic of pro-capitalist development and that there was very little room for variation and deliberate choice. Consequently it was felt that the government rather than political parties should take the responsibility for formulating goals of systemic transformation. In this fashion parties resigned, especially during the initial phase of the transformation, from the 'structuring of alternatives' – one of the basic functions of any political party.

To be more precise: the post-Solidarity parties which entered the governing coalitions (there were four such multi-party coalitions in 1989–93) always expressed a specific alternative when they formulated their set of goals. However, the awareness that there may exist different developmental pathways was relatively undeveloped in the party system as a whole. The ability to think in terms of developmental pathways presupposes the ability to think in terms of theory and social philosophy. This ability was lacking. My claim that party programmes have a very weak rooting in more general political theory or philosophy refers to three features of these programmes: they are superficial, fragmentary and internally inconsistent. I am not saying that they lack theoretical concepts and ideological slogans entirely. Political discourse in Poland, though superficial, is replete with general concepts. The same may be said of party programmes. These general concepts, which are however merely used as slogans, make it possible to detect some basic differences between parties' perceived realities.

Six major dimensions cut across the Polish party system. These are the following: 1 national and universal; 2 confessional and secular; 3 authoritarian and democratic; 4 laissez-faire and interventionist; 5 elitist and populist; and 6 communist-purging and communist-forgiving.

1 The national/universal dimension refers to the parties' approach to the icons of nationhood and to proclaimed national interests. At one extreme we find parties proposing strict adherence to national symbols, bringing up children with respect for traditional national culture, and suggesting that the national economic interest is endangered by foreign capital. At the other extreme are parties which favour the integration of Poland with Europe, bringing Polish culture closer to west European

universalistic patterns, and favouring the active role of foreign capital in rescuing the Polish economy.

2   The confessional/secular dimension has some affinity with the national/ universalistic one, although it nevertheless appears as an autonomous factor. There are many leaders who argue for the privileged role of Catholic principles and the Catholic moral code in public life. They have won important battles in parliament. According to new regulations, Polish mass media must respect Christian values. The anti-abortion bill forbids and punishes the killing of unborn children. At the other extreme are leaders and parties who are in favour of a neutral secular state in which the Catholic Church has no privileges. They want the Catholic Church to restrict its activity to purely religious affairs.

3   The laissez-faire/interventionist dimension is related to programmatic differences between parties which are primarily concerned with economic issues, although they do not exclude from their domain such matters as citizen rights and cultural development. This is, for example, true of both the liberal party (Liberal Democratic Congress) and the post-communist Social-Democratic Party. What separates these parties, however, along the laissez-faire/interventionist dimension, is their conception of the role of the state in the economy: whether it should be reduced to the lowest possible level of intervention or whether it should lead the transformation process and then control the functioning of the new system.

4   The authoritarian/democratic dimension refers to a discussion of what constitutes the most desirable political order for Poland; a strong presidential system with concentrated executive and legislative powers on the one hand and, on the other, a parliamentary-cabinet system are suggested as alternative solutions.

5   The elitist/populist dimension refers to opposing perceptions of where ultimate sovereignty resides: in the masses or with the elite. Populists would claim that the people are the supreme sovereign in politics, and so they should not be restricted in their articulations and actions; they have a right to the expression of their will, ignoring any institutional setting or legalistic framework. Elitists tend to emphasise the need to obey the law and act within established institutions; moreover, they tend to believe that established leaders know better than the masses what is in the best interest of the country (in extreme cases: what is in the interest of the masses as well). The populist strand is becoming steadily stronger in the NSZZ Solidarity trade union and the 'Samoobrona' (Self Defence) social movement.

6   The communist-purging/communist-forgiving dimension refers to the role of former communist functionaries and members of the Communist Party in public life today. Should they be eliminated and prevented from taking an active part in public life? Some political

leaders see this as a very important issue and try to use it as a vehicle for their own popularity and political career.

These dimensions, differentiating both party quasi-programmes and slogans, are mutually autonomous. In some parties they incline toward a certain level of logical convergence, e.g. confessionalism and nationalism, or laissez-faireism and democratism. However, the distinct feature of the situation in Poland is the existence of a large number of parties with different combinations of programmatic characteristics. This has made the emergence of anything like a coherent party system a slow and uncertain process, particularly as the electoral mechanisms in operation in 1991 and 1993 were very different. Some parties, for instance, propagate the need for a strong and punitive state authority and at the same time argue for the maintenance of a cabinet-parliamentary order and are opposed to a strong presidency. Some nationalist parties are not confessional. The programme of one of the significant parties (Centre Alliance – PC) underscores this party's attachment to the Christian-national tradition and also postulates the rapid development of strong capitalism, a full opening up to and integration with Europe. It therefore combines traditionalism and universalism. Two significant parties with a liberal orientation which have recently merged (the Democratic Union and the Liberal Democratic Congress) have both Catholics and libertarians among their leaders.

Is it possible that a more logical political structure will emerge from this mosaic? The fusion of several parties into federations such as the Covenant for Poland, the Agreement of 11 November and the Freedom Union may indicate that certain processes have been set in motion which may gradually force party leaders, activists and party members to adopt more homogeneous approaches. The direction which this new homogeneity will take in the different parties and confederations is not yet clear. These processes may induce some party members to quit their parties in the short run. They may also trigger further shifts of whole groups between parties.

It is possible that one particular process may prove to have particular significance for the further evolution of the party system relating to which programmatic element will take precedence: economic, political or cultural (religious, national). Since the programmes of Polish political parties are poorly crystallised, priority may be given either to economic reform, the form of the future political system, or to relations between the state and the Catholic Church. A new constitution will be drafted and voted on in 1995, the popular privatisation programme will be implemented and possibly improved, and attempts at amending the abortion law will be renewed. All three topics are ideologically and politically loaded and all three have the chance of gaining priority over others and mustering their own supporters. Potential political interest in these priorities is difficult to predict because parties may, to a certain extent, steer public psychology

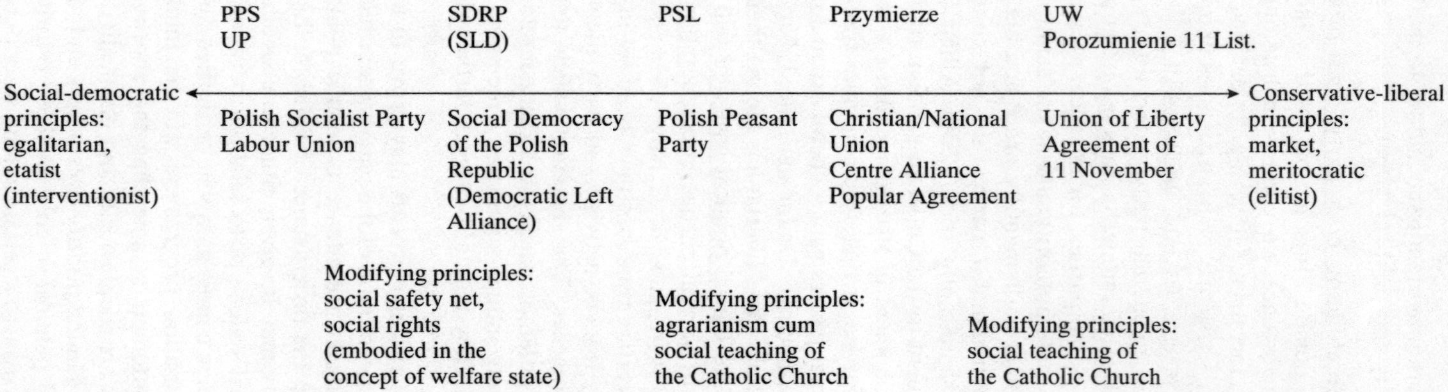

Social-democratic ←——————————————————————————→ Conservative-liberal
principles: principles:
egalitarian,   market,
etatist   meritocratic
(interventionist)   (elitist)

PPS UP	SDRP (SLD)	PSL	Przymierze	UW
Polish Socialist Party Labour Union	Social Democracy of the Polish Republic (Democratic Left Alliance)	Polish Peasant Party	Christian/National Union Centre Alliance Popular Agreement	Union of Liberty Agreement of 11 November Porozumienie 11 List.
	Modifying principles: social safety net, social rights (embodied in the concept of welfare state)	Modifying principles: agrarianism cum social teaching of the Catholic Church		Modifying principles: social teaching of the Catholic Church

Figure 10.1 Typology of parties in Poland: consolidated left–right axis (economic matters in the forefront of politics)

toward prolonged concern for the structure of the democratic system, the nature of state/Church relationships or privatisation issues.

In terms of typologies it is possible to see three possible structures toward which the party system in Poland may evolve. The first is the traditional right–centre–left continuum. The second I call the 'sectoral party system'. A third may be called a 'mixed party system'. The first type assumes that economic issues will come to the fore in the programmes of the different parties and their federations. The poles of the axis I define as social-democratic and conservative-liberal respectively. Going from left to right, i.e. from the social-democratic end, we find the following parties (see Figure 10.1): Polish Socialist Party and Labour Union; then the Social Democracy of the Polish Republic (Democratic Left Alliance). The Polish Peasant Party is in the very centre. To its right are two confederations: the Covenant (embracing the Christian/National Union, Centre Alliance and others), next comes the Agreement of 11 November. Close to the right pole is the Freedom Union.

Typologically pure parties on the extreme left should be egalitarian and étatist. However, no such parties exist in Poland. No pure liberal party exists either (i.e. there is no party propagating unrestricted market and meritocratic principles), although the Liberal-Democratic Congress came very close to this pole. To the right of the centre, pure liberal economic assumptions were modified by the social teachings of the Catholic Church, including the principle of equal concern for capital and work. The Polish Peasant Party, situated right in the middle, hints at a mixture of market-egalitarianism mediated by agrarianism and the social teaching of the Catholic Church. Between the centre and the left pole, party programmes are mediated by the secular doctrine of the welfare state.

Let us call the second typology of the party system a 'sectoral party system'. In suggesting this concept, I draw my inspiration from Herbert Kitschelt's article, 'A Silent Revolution in Europe?'[17] This typological model of the party system assumes that political parties and their electorates undergo a specific evolution. In this model, parties function as representatives of specific employment or ownership sectors. In this case the Social Democracy of the Polish Republic (Democratic Left Alliance) becomes the party representing people employed in industry, the Labour Union represents people employed in the state sector and services (education, health service, social welfare, central and local administration), the Polish Peasant Party represents individual farmers, and the Freedom Union represents small, medium and large entrepreneurs. The evolution of the different parties in this direction cannot be excluded in Poland and peasant parties, for example, have always been associated with specific sectors. Support for the same party, the Social-Democrats, by both industrial managers and industrial workers would be a novelty, however, although there are some indications of development toward such an alliance. Managers of state enterprises undergoing commercialisation have

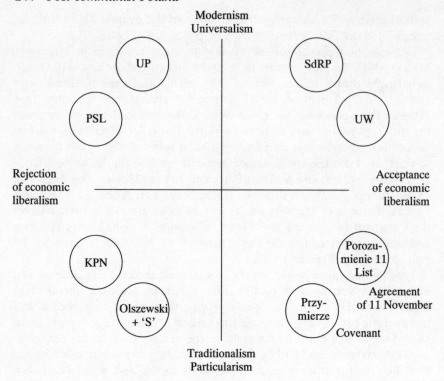

Figure 10.2 Hypothetical locations of the Polish electorates: a 'balanced' distribution

Note: See Table 10.2 for explication of acronyms. Olszewski was the Prime Minister, December 1991–June 1992. In the spring 1994 jointly with NSZZ Solidarność (acronym S) he started forming 'Political Clubs' and wrote the project of the new constitution propagated by the NSZZ Solidarność

been known to support some workers' postulates. Is this merely a transient phenomenon? It seems that future developments will depend on the form taken by the programme of popular privatisation. Some models of it may lead to the emergence of new common interests between technocrats and the workers. Under the umbrella of privatisation

The third typological outline of the party system in Poland is presented in Figure 10.2. Two equally important aspects have been involved here: economical and cultural (mainly religious). At the extremes of two orthogonal axes we have economic liberalism/anti-liberalism and modernism/traditionalism. By modernism I mean primarily the rejection of the Catholic Church's claims to the right to co-develop state legislation and participate in the official life of state institutions. Traditionalists, on the contrary, claim that the Catholic Church has the right to such privileges because of its moral and cultural role in the society. In this figure

Restricting Church influence

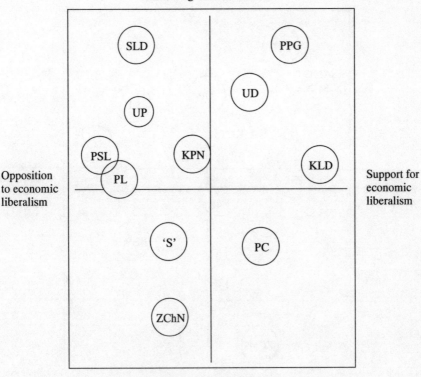

Promoting Church authority

Figure 10.3 Location of the electorates of Polish political parties, October 1991

Note: Adapted from Tomasz Żukowski, Wybory 1993: wyniki i ich uwarunkowania (Election 1993: its results and causes) Wydzial Dziennikarstwa i Nauk Politcznych, Uniwersytet Warszawski, 1994, mimeographed

liberalism and anti-liberalism mean much the same as the conservative-liberal and social-democratic extremes in Figure 10.1. A hypothetical 'balanced' distribution in terms of eight main ideological orientations is given in Figure 10.2.

Tomasz Zukowski's analyses of the real ideological orientations of the electorates of the various parties in 1991 and 1993 derived from survey data are given in Figures 10.3 and 10.4. Comparison of these two diagrams reveals that the attitudes of the followers of the different parties are only relatively stable.[18] The changing attitudinal locations of supporters may be linked to the low crystallisation of party programmes.

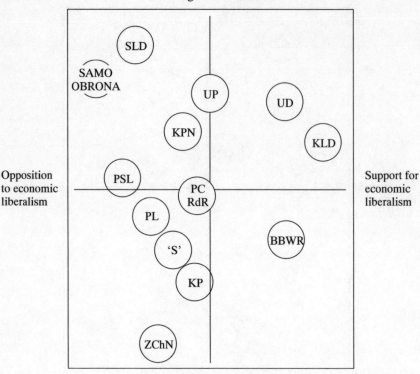

Figure 10.4 Location of the electorates of Polish political parties, June 1993

Note: Adapted from Tomasz Żukowski, Wybory 1993: wyniki i ich uwarunkowania (Election 1993: its results and causes) Wydzial Dziennikarstwa i Nauk Politcznych, Uniwersytet Warszawski, 1994, mimeographed

CRISIS AND REINTEGRATION OF POLITICAL CONSCIOUSNESS

After 1989 the institutions and principles of political democracy were introduced smoothly and effortlessly. Even the 'Contract Parliament' proved to be semi-democratic and, when Jaruzelski resigned and Wałęsa was elected president in 1991, democratic principles could operate without restraint. However, the political scene then began to evolve in a direction quite unexpected by the nation. The democratic authorities – the president, parliament and the government – seemed to forget society and go about their own business.

In their attempts to formulate specific reform programmes, the state authorities became alienated 'thematically' from popular thinking because no mechanism had been developed to enable them to consult with

Table 10.3 Opinions about democracy and political parties

Do you agree with the opinion that democracy is the best among the known forms of government? (voters undifferentiated)

Response	Percentage
strongly yes	30
rather yes	44
rather no	10
strongly no	3
difficult to say	13

Voters differentiated by

Level of education				Socio-economic category			
	Response(percentage)				Response(percentage)		
	yes	no	no response		yes	no	no response
elementary	64	13	23	managers and			
occupational	69	19	12	professionals	93	7	–
secondary	84	9	7	white collar			
higher	91	9	–	workers	77	13	10
				factory workers	71	18	11
				farmers	60	14	26
				entrepreneurs	88	12	–
				pensioners	72	12	16
				housewives	76	8	16
				students	81	8	11
				unemployed	62	22	16
				others	89	4	7

Source: Survey by OBOP, July 1994, see note 20, p. 253

social groups about the content of reform programmes. Conflicts between the various political leaders grew increasingly acrimonious and finally led to a situation where political controversies became split off from socio-economic interests and controversies. In effect, hardly anybody associated the 'war at the top', and later the 'quarrels in parliament' with his or her own vital interests. Democracy – allegedly the best instrument for resolving social problems – proved to be instrumentally useless for ordinary people. Since they had no previous experience in civil initiative people became passive, especially locally, despite the fact that by taking the initiative they might have had a lot to win. On the other hand, national political leaders in no way inspired group and civil activity – an accusation strongly voiced recently by Jacek Kuroń who admitted that he too was guilty of this sin.[19]

It is characteristic that, despite this general situation, society has continued to remain convinced that democracy is 'the best among the known forms of government' (Table 10.3 above). Just as characteristic, however,

Table 10.4 Opinions about leaders and political parties

Do you agree with the opinion that nobody needs political parties except their leaders and activists? (voters undifferentiated)

Response	Percentage
strongly yes	24
rather yes	29
rather no	29
strongly no	8
difficult to say	10

Voters differentiated by

Level of education				Socio-economic category			
Response(percentage)					*Response(percentage)*		
	yes	no	no response		yes	no	no response
elementary	60	24	16	managers and			
occupational	55	29	6	professionals	33	67	–
secondary	48	44	12	white collar			
higher	33	64	3	workers	49	46	5
				factory workers/			
				miners	57	36	7
				farmers	61	23	16
				entrepreneurs	40	57	3
				pensioners	61	27	12
				housewives	44	37	19
				students	43	43	14
				unemployed	45	44	11
				others	48	44	8

Source: Survey by OBOP, July 1994, see note 20, p. 253

[handwritten: How Democratic is Poland — Realistically speaking]

is another belief: that party performance is very mediocre. Over half the respondents (53 per cent) accepted the statement that 'nobody needs political parties except their leaders and activists' (Table 10.4 above).[20]

Other surveys have revealed the probable deeper sources of these negative opinions concerning political parties. People do not feel that these parties represent them. In his empirical theory of democracy, Sartori wrote that: 'democratic government ... is a responsive government, a government attentive to and influenced by the voice of the people'.[21] For a considerable proportion of Poles this version of democracy has not yet materialised. In 1993 47 per cent of the people investigated responded negatively to the query: 'Do any parties in Poland represent people like you?' In 1994 even more people responded negatively to the same question (65 per cent). The feeling that 'one is not being represented' correlates strongly with formal education: the lower the level, the greater the feeling of representative deprivation (Table 10.5).[22]

[handwritten: They were really (maj) of the ones that brought about the rev.]

Table 10.5 Popular opinions about political parties: representation

Are there any political parties in Poland which represent people like you?

Whole sample	October 1993 (percentage)	April 1994 (percentage)
Yes	40	22
No	47	65
Difficult to say	13	13

Level of education	Response(percentage)					
	yes		no		difficult to say	
	Oct. 1993	Apr. 1994	Oct. 1993	Apr. 1994	Oct. 1993	Apr. 1994
elementary	32	19	50	68	18	13
occupational	42	23	49	62	9	15
secondary	47	23	43	68	10	9
higher	59	38	37	52	3	10

Source: Both surveys (1993 and 1994) by 'Demoscop'. See note 22, p. 253

It is interesting that the feeling of political deprivation intensified after the elections of 19 September 1993. Directly after the elections, several surveys showed that people had expected the government to move closer to the masses and to listen more carefully to the voice of the masses. The data show that this expectation was short-lived. The alienation of political parties and the entire political class thus emerges as a virtually unquestionable truth according to Polish political analysts. Politicians themselves also openly admit it.

At least three factors contribute to the depreciation of the 'stratum of the professional politicians', to use Max Weber's concept. One is the low status of governmental institutions over the last forty years. Without going into the (multiple) reasons for this, one can say that this low status is constantly manifested in public opinion polls which elicit rankings of official institutions. For three years, parliament, the government, political parties and the president have systematically ranked lower than the army, police, and the ombudsman.[23] Although many institutional malfunctions spring from the immature behaviour of politicians themselves, these low ratings of 'their' institutions provide negative feedback and undermine their self-esteem.

Individuals without obvious party affiliations are preferred to those closely identified with party activities. A survey was commissioned by the weekly 'Polityka' in June 1994, in which two questions were asked: 'In your opinion who of the listed politicians should be given more power and who should be given less power?' Calculations of the net rankings consisted in subtracting the negative from the positive responses. The three first positions in the overall ranking went to people with no formal status in any political party. Rank one was obtained by Tadeusz Zieliński, the ombudsman (46.6 per cent net indications), rank two by Jacek Kuroń, perceived rather as a social activist than an ex-minister (33.9 per cent net indications), and rank three to Leszek Balcerowicz, perceived rather as an economist-theoretician than an ex-minister (27.1 per cent net indications). Such typical party politicians as Pawlak, Kwaśniewski, Oleksy, Bugaj, and Mazowiecki trailed far behind (25–19 per cent net). Lech Wałęsa had 19 per cent net indications.[24] This preference was further demonstrated in a later poll, which suggested that nearly half of all Poles thought the personal qualities of power-holders were more important than their party affiliation (only 15 per cent thought that this was the most important factor).[25]

A third factor is the politicians' unfortunate lack of leadership qualities (which should include political skills as well as a high moral standing). This does not permit them to serve as personality models for party activists as well as politically active citizens. This deficiency, along with the fragmentation of the parties, is probably an extremely important, purely political determinant of the difficulties currently experienced in achieving a mature democratic stage of development in Poland. In a study of parliamentary deputies in office in 1991–3 which I supervised, a symptomatic finding emerged: many outstanding Polish parliamentarians indicated the dramatic need for personality models in Polish politics. Top parliamentarians themselves self-critically recognised the fact and my thesis accorded precisely with their views. The credibility and popularity gap produced the crisis of political consciousness in Poland that had become apparent. A cry for democratic but strong leadership was heard within parties and the politically aware citizenry.[26]

The problem centred on the concept of political identity, both at the leadership and citizen level. Poland, and I would venture to say some other countries of the region, need to crystallise political identities. For that to happen, parties need to develop clear-cut political programmes and their leaders need to develop attractive personality features. In consequence, the average citizen would show more interest in politics. In one sense, nothing is more important in times of political transition than political identity.

Political analysts draw attention to the fact that in Western Europe the distinctions between different parties are becoming increasingly obliterated due to reduced programmatic differences: a similar process is being observed at the civil level where prosperity and rejection of the great ideologies have led to fluctuations in political opinion. It seems that in eastern Europe in general, and Poland in particular, democratic consolidation will not be possible if tendencies contrary to those observed in Western Europe today do not emerge. The whole of eastern Europe needs to formulate stable programmatic visions, a process that has to be developed by political parties. In order for these visions to emerge, it is necessary to refer to specific ideas as to how the social world should be arranged. These elements can be formulated by referring to theoretical knowledge concerning global social processes, including processes of inter-systemic transformation. It may be assumed that Poland could equally well develop a liberal, Christian, national, or socialist political identity. The building blocks for the formulating of these identities already exist in the form of fragmentary ideologies, human attitudes or even group activities. Nascent forms of ecologism and feminism are also present.

When we look back on the political history of Western European countries, we inevitably notice that liberal political identity emerged step by step, parallel to the strengthening of legal order and the development of the institutions of representative democracy. In Poland this process should be accelerated. However, the circumstances are unfavourable. Social reality is evolving very slowly. The transformation of class structures and the development of new interests will take a long time because the economic structure is changing very slowly. Clearly, there is a contra-diction between the need to develop a liberal identity and existing contingencies. It is also noteworthy that the active political citizen is only mildly attracted to a liberal political identity as a model personality because this identity has nothing exciting to offer in the immediate future. In order to deliberately develop such an identity, one must 'work hard'. It is not yet clear which groups are prepared to accept the challenge.

If a liberal identity is difficult to develop, it is much easier to develop 'in oneself' and 'for oneself' a Christian or national identity. Patterns of 'silent heroism' displayed by the ordinary person, heroism based on religious faith or faith in one's nation, are ubiquitous in Polish art and literature. These patterns of silent heroism are passed down from generation to generation within the family. People are familiar with definite incarnations of national or national-Christian leaders, and contemporary politicians can easily refer to them. Neither, as in the case of a liberal identity, is it easy to build a socialist identity. What was called real Socialism discredited socialist ideology, and any social practice now wishing to refer to Socialism must prove its novel character. Only then will the social identity referred to here as 'socialist' have the chance to develop. There is a potential for developing a 'socialist-communitarian' type of attitude among Polish workers and employees who are active politically.[27] For that to happen, however, more imaginative programmatic work is needed on the part of leaders, both of the Labour Union and the Social Democracy of the Polish Republic. There may emerge a new trend toward 'modern Christian' political identity-building. This type could deliberately combine the acceptance of most tenets of liberalism with adherence to core values of the Christian religion. Such an identity could overcome the traditionalism of Polish Catholicism, as well as its strong nationalistic and confessional tendencies. The idea of having in Poland a party which will be similar – at least in crucial dimensions – to the German CDU has attracted some circles of intellectuals and politicians from time to time.[28] Such a party would have a large reservoir of recruits to draw on from the Polish liberal-Catholic intelligentsia.

I have referred to the above identities very loosely. If political reality takes any definite path at all, it is likely to foster the development of one of them. They will probably not be as simple as the above-mentioned types. I do think, however, that it will not be possible to overcome the excessive fragmentation of the political scene if two parallel processes for the construction of political identity do not get under way: one among the political leaders, the other among the citizens – and, in particular, those exemplars of homo politicus who participate in the political life of the country persistently and meaningfully. If this goal is to be reached, political parties with distinct programmes are essential.

NOTES

1   Cf. Guilermo O'Donnell, Delegative Democracy, *Journal of Democracy*, vol. 5, no. 1, January 1994; Philippe C. Schmitter, Dangers, 'Dilemmas and Prospects for the Consolidation of Democracy' (manuscript).
2   Włodzimierz Wesołowski, 'The Significance of Political Elites in Post-Communist Poland'. The Woodrow Wilson Centre, Occasional Papers no. 32, Washington, DC, 1991.
3   Cf. 'Krzaklewski: Chodzi o ustrój' (Krzaklewski: The political system is the issue). Report on his speech in *Rzeczpospolita*, 7–8 May, 1994; ABC Marketing Research Agency, report 'Podłoże konfliktu' (The source of the conflict), *Rzeczpospolita*, 4 May 1994.
4   In defining the functions of political parties I draw, among others, on the following works: Maurice Duverger, *Political Parties: Their Organisation and Activity in the Modern State*, London: Methuen, 1954; Seymour M. Lipset and Stein Rokkan (eds), *Party Systems and Voter Alignments: Cross-National Perspective*, New York: The Free Press, 1967; Giovanni Sartori, *Parties and Party Systems*, vol. 1, Cambridge: CUP, 1976; Klaus von Beyme, *Political Parties in Western Democracies*, Aldershot: Gower, 1985; Alan Ware, *Citizens, Parties and the State: A Reappraisal*, Cambridge: Polity Press, 1987; B. D. Graham, *Representation and Party Politics: A Comparative Perspective*, Oxford: Blackwell, 1993; Peter Mair (ed.), *The West European Party System*, Oxford: OUP 1990; Ferdinand Muller-Rommel and Geoffrey Pridham, *Small Parties in Western Europe: Comparative and National Perspectives*, London: Sage Publications, 1991.
5   CBOS (Public Opinion Poll Centre), Serwis informacyjny (Information bulletin), 1993, no. 7, Warsaw.
6   CBOS, Społeczna wizja systemu politycznego Polski (Social vision of the political system in Poland). Research Report, February 1994, Warsaw.
7   Kozłowski, Maciej, 'Rzeczpospolita bezpartyjna?' (A Non-party Republic?), *Tygodnik Powszechny*, 18 March 1990; Grabowska, Mirosława, and T. Szawiel, *Anatomia elit politycznych: partie politycznych w postkomunistycznej Polsce* (The Anatomy of Political Elites: Political Parties in Post-communist Poland), Instytut Socjologii Uniwersytetu Warszawskiego, Warsaw 1993, chs 1 and 10.

8   *Rok 1989: Bronisław Geremek odpowiada, Jacek Żakowski pyta* (The Year 1989: Bronisław Geremek Responds, Jacek Żakowski Asks), Plejada, Warsaw, 1990, pp. 311–16, 361–2. Balcerowicz, Leszek, *800 dni: szok kontrolowany* (800 Days: A Controlled Shock), Polską Oficyna Wydawnicza BGW, Warsaw 1992.

9   *Monitor Polski* no. 41, 5 December 1991, position 288, Obwieszczenie Państwowej Komisji Wyborczej z dnia 30 października 1991 roku o wynikach wyborów do Sejmu Rzeczpospolitej Polskiej, przeprowadzonych w dniu 27 pazdzierniku 1991 roku (Announcement of the State Electoral Committee on the Results of Elections to the Polish Diet of the Polish Republic held on 27 October 1991).

10 On factionalism in Polish political parties see Paul G. Lewis, 'Party Factionalism and Democratization in Poland', Paper prepared for ECPR Workshop on Party Factionalism and Democratization, Madrid, 17–22 April 1994.

11 Ranking of political parties, Demoskop, Review, April–May 1994, Warsaw.

12 Stefan Bratkowski, 'Katastrofa intelektualna' (Intellectual catastrophe), *Rzeczpospolita*, 4–5 December 1993.

13 Jarosław Kaczyński. Pierwsze przykazanie: Jednoczmy sie (The first commandment: Let us unite). *Gazeta Polska*, 24 March 1994.

14 Janusz Lewandowski, 'Kapitalizm z polską twarzą' (Capitalism with a Polish face). *Gazeta Wyborcza*, 17 May 1994.

15 Cf. 'Dobre imię Polski i ZChN' (The Good Name of Poland and the ZChN), *Gazeta Wyborcza*, 7 October 1994.

16 'Programy polityczne partii' (Party political programmes). *Rzeczpospolita*, 17 September 1993.

17 Herbert Kitschelt, 'A Silent Revolution in Europe?' in Jack Hayward and Edward Page (eds), *Governing the New Europe*, Polity Press, Cambridge 1995.

18 Figures adjusted from Tomasz Żukowski, 'Wybory 1993 i ich uwarunkowania' (The 1993 elections and their determinants). Warsaw: Department of Journalism and Political Science, University of Warsaw, 1994 (manuscript).

19 'Jacek Kuroń, Rynek z ludzka twarzą' (The market with a human face). *Gazeta Wyborcza*, 20–21 November, 1993; Jacek Kuroń, 'Rzeczpospolita dla kazdego: Mysli o programie dzialania' (The Republic for all: Some considerations concerning the programme of action), *Życie Gospodarcze*, 22 May, 1994.

20 OBOP, 'Opinie o demokracji i alternatywnych formach rzadzenia: Komunikat z badań' (Opinions on democracy and alternative forms of rule: Research report), Warsaw: July 1994.

21 Sartori, Giovanni, *Parties and Party Systems. A Framework for Analysis*. vol. 1 Cambridge: CUP, 1976, p. 20.

22 Demoskop, Przeglad (Review). October, 1993; April–May, 1994, and supplementary materials received by the author from Demoskop.

23 CBOS, Serwis informacyjny (Information bulletin) no. 5, Warsaw, 1993.

24 'Gallup dla Polityki: Kto pociaga za sznurki?' (Gallup for Polityka: Who is pulling the strings?) *Polityka*, 16 July 1994.

25 *Rzeczpospolita*, 29 August 1994.

26 Lukasz Mazurkiewicz. 'Wizje przywodztwa politycznego w opiniach parlamentarzystow' (Visions of political leadership in parliamentary opinions), (manuscript).

27 Wesołowski, Włodzimierz, 'The Nature of Social Ties and the Future of Postcommunist Society: Poland after Solidarity', in John A. Hall (ed.), *Civil Society: Theory, History, Comparison*, Polity Press, Cambridge 1994.

28 Micewski, Andrzej, 'Katolicy zdezorientowani?' Trwale wartosci (Catholics disoriented? Enduring values), *Polityka*, 2 October 1993.

11 Bulgaria's new party system

Georgi Karasimeonov

Bulgaria's transition from communist dictatorship to democracy and party pluralism bears the traits of a specific development which makes Bulgaria a deviant case not only in comparison with the central European countries, but also with those in the Balkan region. Unlike the ruling parties of the first group, Bulgaria's communist regime, even in the wake of the 'palace coup' against the Zhivkov clique on 10 November 1989, did not face any real challenge from forces or political groups prepared to take power from the communists. Bulgaria's political development during the decades of communist rule which followed the brutal oppression of the anti-communist opposition in the late 1940s, bore no imprint of drawn out struggles or protests against the regime. There were outbursts from time to time which were mostly confined to inter-party factional conflict and strife. The most important of these took place in 1956 and 1964, between groups associated with Stalinist and Maoist leanings and those supporting the post-Stalinist liberalisation of the communist system.

The reasons why Bulgaria followed that kind of development lie not only in the effectiveness of the repressive institutions or in Sofia's almost total allegiance to the Soviet regime. Without going too deeply into an analysis of that phenomenon it is impossible to avoid mentioning some historical facts which aid a better understanding of the post-communist development in Bulgaria. First of all, communist rule had a psychological advantage in the almost mythical pro-Russian sentiments of the population dating from the time before Bulgaria's liberation from five centuries of Ottoman oppression. Russia and Russians are until today revered as the liberators of Bulgaria who left thousands of dead in the bloody Russian–Turkish war of 1877–8 which led to the revival of an independent Bulgarian state. These feelings in a large part of the population helped to legitimise the Soviet political model in a country whose ruling communities boasted of being Moscow's privileged allies. Consequently, anti-sovietism never played a role as a catalyst of anti-communist political attitudes or actions more typical of the central European nations which had been, at one time or another in the course of history, victims of Russian and Soviet imperial designs.

Second, the communist regime succeeded in effecting the rapid modernisation of the country, which had been one of the most backward nations of Europe. Massive industrialisation, advances in agriculture in the first stage of the formation of co-operatives, the elimination of illiteracy and urbanisation, for example, brought about a rapid rise in living standards and at the same time created a new middle class and intelligentsia loyal to the regime. The Communist Party and the network of its satellite organisations became a much sought-after instrument for achieving a rise in social status and the privileges that accompanied it. In the 1960s the Communists had an uncontested grip on political power without any fear of oppositional sentiments. They were able to keep their hold over a society still dominated by patriarchal, communal attitudes, a society which had never had sufficient time in its short history as an independent state after 1878 to create a viable civil society and affirm liberal democratic values. Even in the short periods of democratic rule, left-wing or populist agrarian political parties and orientations dominated the political landscape.

Thirdly, the regime followed a carrot and stick policy towards different social groups and especially towards the intellectuals, who remained in general loyal to or only partly critical of the regime. Last but not least the crisis of the system, especially in the economic field, was only seriously felt late in the 1980s, which limited any serious discontent based on material needs. Criticism of the regime, stimulated chiefly by perestroika in Russia, was mostly confined to demands for a more liberalised form of socialism and rarely crossed into the ranks of the Communist Party. The few dissidents became the core of the new-born democratic opposition in the late 1980s, but it never seriously challenged the Party's hegemony.

These circumstances explain why the change of power and the dethroning of party leader Zhivkov took the form of a palace coup supported by Gorbachev. In the aftermath of 10 November 1989 the Communist Party retained all the resources needed to decide the course of events and control the process of change. Having reintegrated into its ranks some of the most popular dissidents it was left practically on its own, without a real opposition to give legitimacy to the changes. Immediately after the 'palace coup' there came one of the crucial moments of Bulgaria's transition, and it was to have a serious impact on the future course of events in the country, including the formation of the new post-communist party system. The communists were faced with a choice – either to allow and stimulate a process of slow disintegration of the Communist Party into two or more parties, or to create an opposition partly from its own known supporters, and in this way to pull the strings from behind the scenes. The first option was seriously envisaged at the beginning, but later the second was preferred and was realised at the time when the round table discussions were about to start at the beginning of 1990. Having held its first session in December 1989, the Union of Democratic

Forces was created as the main democratic opposition. At the start of the 'round table' in January 1990 it was the Communist Party that had the final say in who should be the participants facing it on the opposing side. Those parties and groups that later were to represent the nucleus of the new party system received their credentials by the explicit 'permission' of the Communist Party. For their part, the communists held their first congress after the changes and the party only avoided a split by integrating into its leadership a new wave of younger personalities (Chavdar Kyuranov, Nikolai Vasilev, Petar Emil-Mitev, Stefan Prodev) known partly for their criticism of the Zhivkov regime. It allowed the existence of factions and made important changes in its statute and programme on a bearing towards social democracy.

These circumstances left their imprint on the new parties that came into existence. Those formations that received a place on the round table with the implicit permission of the Communists not only had the advantage of being the first at the starting line, but they were also able to acquire legitimacy through the televised sessions of the 'round table'.

These considerations should not give the false impression that every event was manipulated by the Communist Party. As the history of politics shows, especially in the great periods of democratic transition, events and the actions of people find their own dynamic, very often frustrating the plans of the most talented political players. Once established and legitimised, the new opposition in Bulgaria slowly started to play its own game. With its growing confidence and strength, supported more and more by a reviving civil service and by massive street actions, it became less and less a pawn, and more and more an actor in the new politics, although it had a long way to go to come close to being an equal opponent of a Communist Party (renamed 'Socialist' late in March 1990) which was very powerful and capable of adapting to the new situation. Its manifold resources, including a string of capable leaders, gave it great advantages in Bulgaria where the opposition had in many ways to start from scratch to create its first party formations.

THE FORMATION OF THE NEW PARTIES – OR THE COST OF NEGOTIATED TRANSITIONS

Coping with the past is one of the chief problems encountered in transitions from authoritarian rule, and offers a variety of experiences on which informative comparative judgements can be based. Options followed elsewhere frequently cast light on outcomes in east-central Europe, and this is as true in the case of party formation as in other spheres. In Germany, for example, the political space was left free and open after the ban of the Nazi Party and the re-establishment of the party structure more or less in its traditional form. A more recent development – in Spain, for example – is characterised by the so-called negotiated transition to democracy where 'political institutions that organise the democratic compromise must be designed in such a way as to protect the interests of the forces associated with the authoritarian regime and thus to minimise the extent of eventual transformations' so that 'political democracy is possible only at the cost of limiting social and economic transformations'.[1]

Most post-communist transitions took the form of 'negotiated transitions' or 'negotiated revolutions' which left an imprint on the whole political process, including in part party formation. The round table served as an extra-constitutional mechanism which defined the rules and the tempo of the changes, as well as the parameters of the compromises.[2] They also defined the framework of party pluralism and the scope of party formation. Post-communist negotiated transitions to democracy experienced in general two main models of party formation. One of them was the Central European model, where the anti-communist forces had a clear advantage over the former communists and were able to marginalise them in the first stage. This was accompanied in Hungary and Poland by either the self-dissolution of the communist party or its division into two main currents – one social-democratic and the other neo-communist and Marxist. In that way opposition to the reforms on the part of conservative forces and parties associated with the communist party was limited in the early stages, and the process of party formation crystallised faster and had clearer contours.

In Bulgaria, however, as noted, the negotiated transition was strongly influenced by the dominant post-communist party which used a piecemeal policy of slowly ceding political terrain to the newly founded parties which were very weak at the start. It neither broke up, nor experienced serious rifts, suffering rather a slow erosion of influence and support. On the whole it was able to keep its core supporters. It tried to preserve its identity and its historical roots while at the same time slowly transforming its image from a totalitarian to a parliamentarian, social-democratically oriented party, a process which was expected to be crowned with the adoption of a new party programme. The party's course was clearly set towards joining the democratic left forces in Europe. In the project for a new programme it is stated that the BSP is a 'modern socialist party of the democratic left'.[3] In its first four years the BSP was able relatively successfully to preserve its electoral strength in the face of very aggressive attempts on the part of the opposition to marginalise it by resorting to the use of the organs of repression (as was the Albanian experience). At the same time it witnessed periodical attempts by certain party members and groups to look for other party identifications.[4] Like other parties linked to the former regime its main problem has been in gaining credibility. This can only come after it passes the test of a party in power and this will certainly take time. The negative inheritance here plays a major role, since in Bulgaria, unlike in certain other post-communist countries, the Communist Party did not take the road of radically cutting its links with the communist past, trying to accommodate past and recent experiences. To that extent its change of identity remains untested and, for many, unclear.

The real strength of former communist parties in the region as a whole, but especially in Bulgaria, came not from the inheritance of past ideological traditions, but chiefly from organisational continuity. This might prove an important advantage over all newcomer parties who first have to learn the art of organisation. This becomes more pressing as the euphoria of the first days of the transition, which gave them a great mass following, gives way to apathy, disillusionment and abstention.

The strength and adaptability of the post-communists in Bulgaria deradicalised the transformation process and also delayed the process of party differentiation. First, the anti-communist coalition represented by the UDF was unable to establish a clear advantage or win a majority in parliament sufficient to force through the reforms, nor had it the resources (financial and organisational) to assert itself as the leading political force. Quite the contrary, it suffered itself a process of erosion, losing supporters and allies. Much of this was the result of the weaknesses of the parties that initially founded the UDF. Their fear of falling apart and the relative electoral weakness of most of them (some of them being only 'label' parties) delayed the formation of viable parties outside the field of the communists.

This was the case with the so-called historic parties, who tried to regain a foothold in the new political space opened by the democratic changes and the new pluralism – the Social-Democratic Party, the Agrarian Union and the Democratic Party. All of these, but especially the Agrarians, had played an important role in Bulgarian political life before the communist takeover. While the communists had a relatively stable social base and identity, from the new parties only the Agrarians and Social Democrats had a small constituency of an ageing group of people. All other party formations faced an ideological choice. It was the 'liberation myth' (Waller's term, used above) that was the main mobilising and binding factor. That is why the UDF was able to bring together such a coalition of divergent groups and leaders, each with different historical and individual experiences and traditions, and varying motivations – from deeply moral to opportunistic. The fact that anti-communist protest traditions had a very limited influence in Bulgaria compared with other countries rendered the newly-formed anti-communist coalition very fragile and susceptible to early contradictions and processes of disintegration, leaving the post-communists ample political space to use their advantages. Traditional linkages were almost lost, and it was ideological and moral reasons that determined people's choices and orientations. And since the UDF was set almost solely on an anti-communist orientation it drowned in it all other currents. When some member parties of the coalition tried to show a different profile from that of the aggressive anti-communists they were marginalised or even excluded from the UDF (as was the case with the Social Democrats, the Greens, those Agrarians who were in the UDF and so on). As soon as they tried to reassert themselves with their own profile they were marginalised by the radical anti-communists in the elections of 1991. A radical, mostly opportunistically motivated anti-communism and the lack of real roots in the population based on past services worked against the historic parties as they tried to assert their traditional profile.

This demonstrates that past identities and linkages played a very minor role in the re-establishment of the historical parties. Political interests or similar experiences that give a party substance as an association were missing for too long for them to play a decisive role in party formation. The changes that Bulgarian society had undergone in its forty years of communist rule were at least as radical as elsewhere in east-central Europe, and arguably more so. Consequently the rebirth of old parties had a very small effect on the affirmation of new democratic principles. Leaving aside a very small number of surviving old members of these parties, the post-communist parties had to create new identities in a society that was radically different from the past economic and political reality, and moreover in a new international context. In that sense the Bulgarian experience confirms even more than in other countries the conclusion of Berglund and Dellenbrant that 'all the parties with ideological and histor-ical roots in a distant but glorious past returned to find their constituencies changed almost beyond recognition by more than half a century of dictatorial or communist rule'.[5]

The heritage of the past has a different meaning for each of the major parties. For the post-communist Socialist Party it is a question of over-coming the negative past as part of gaining democratic credibility. For the 'new old' parties the revival of the past has a limited effect and concerns a marginal electorate of the older population. With the passing of time the majority of the electorate is less and less concerned with the past since they were not directly involved in it and they were being overwhelmed by new problems, many of them of an existential nature. The appeal to past loyalties and services in the struggle against Communism has had a relevance only to a dwindling minority of the population.

The past will still for a certain time affect the fortunes of both new and old parties which are slowly being overtaken by new challenges that post-Communism poses. The extent to which they can confront those challenges in practical terms will determine their fate and future role in political life, and the citizens' political attitudes and behaviour. 'Realpolitik' will increasingly determine the fate and electoral strength of all parties.[6]

In this connection it is to be noted that most parties have tried to gain legitimisation and a clear profile through the intermediation of some of the major international party formations. That is why their inclusion in one of the Internationals remains one of their major targets, especially in the case of the former communists. But how much this will have an effect on creating a stable electorate and create mass parties is doubtful because of the lack of salience of traditional cleavages that influenced the formation of the large classical party families. The fate of the social democratic, Christian democratic and liberal parties in Bulgaria demonstrates this clearly. International links play a role in that they might promote the 'import' of democratic values and engagements.

In that context the left–right dimension has lost its traditional relevance in party identification, though it is being revived in the new situation as a point of defining a party's place in the political system. At present this is more a matter of the political lexicon than of real substance, but certainly it might gain relevance as new and more stable social and political interests develop after the major part of the road to the market economy has been travelled. The future viability of political parties is a question that remains to be resolved in the context of current competitive appeals.

ELITES AND PARTY POLITICS

There is already an abundant literature on elites in the process of democratic transformation including that in post-communist societies. Most authors agree that post-communist elites have to be characterised as transitional, Ágh subdividing them into four main types.[7] The elite structure is still fluid and very unstable and it would be premature to discern a political elite in the sense of an established distinct group with its typical socio-professional characteristics, style of life and channels of influence.

Post-communist development is characterised by three distinct types of political elite formation. One is typical for the more advanced former socialist countries with a history of opposition to the communist regime (Hungary, Czechoslovakia, Poland). There the post-communist elite could be recruited to a great extent from the opposition groups. This yielded an elite that was relatively well educated and prepared to take over the tasks of government and keep the former *nomenclatura* in check. In these countries a real elite recomposition and the displacement of the old elite took place.

The second type of elite formation (in Albania, Romania and Russia, where the police state totally subdued civil society and left almost no islands of relative liberty) was characterised mainly by the transformation of the old communist elite.

A third, intermediate, type of elite formation – in Bulgaria – bore the imprint of a relatively weak civil society, lack of strong opposition to the old regime and dominance of the communist party in the transitional period. There the new elite was formed both through a transformation of the *nomenclatura* and through an influx of newcomers, some of them connected to the parties of the pre-communist period.

Bulgaria's anti-communist opposition lacked a well-educated group of people prepared for full participation in politics and government. This is why it relied mostly on 'turncoats' from the communist party or newcomers, the latter mostly social outsiders. Many of those who were most prepared for a political career were engaged in the professions, and these soon came under fire, accused of being too loyal to the old system.[8] At the same time those who were 'clean' of direct links to the old regime, mostly from the fields of the natural sciences or engineering, lacked the competence and the vision necessary for politics. Many were politicians by chance. This is why gross incompetence accompanied their activity in the first years following change of regime.

On the other hand the former Communist Party had abundant reserves of relatively well prepared and experienced professionals in all fields. The elimination of the old guard opened the road for newcomers from the younger generation, many of them well educated and pragmatically oriented, freed from the ideological burden and deficiencies of the former leading group. This gave them great advantages over the anti-communists and explains to a great extent the influence of the BSP and other offspring of the former Communist Party. There was a certain subdivision in their ranks. Most of the former *nomenclatura* formed the new economic elite, another part of the media elite and partly the political elite. In other words they had the indirect support of most other major elite groups. The transformed and newly formed elite from the ranks of the former communists will predominate in the new political system changing its identity according to their new social roles. And this will ultimately determine their political and party identification. The former communist elite has dissolved into new groups, each of them forming their own specific interests and political allegiances.

The dichotomous division of the political elite and the struggles within it on the basis of *pro* and *contra* communism is to a great extent artificially forged for opportunistic purposes.[9] Behind the facade, the integration of the newcomers into the ruling elite actually creates new links based on interests and a struggle for a bigger slice of the cake rather than on real ideological-political motivations.

Bulgaria finds itself to a large extent under the dominance of communal, even patriarchal, attitudes and dispositions due to a very short history of democratic politics and civil society in the pre-communist period, followed by an atomisation and pseudo-collectivism under communism. These legacies together are now forging a fracturing of society into new 'feuds' based on family, local and even criminal interests. This creates circumstances propitious for the establishment of a corrupt and uncontrolled political elite, a new type of *clientura*.[10] In a state of flux and in conditions close to anarchy, with a lack of traditions and civil service laws, and a declining authority of the state, the chances for the formation of corrupt elite groups are very great. Unstable economic and political conditions motivate a political behaviour typical of the 'Italian' syndrome. And most apt to be contaminated by it are the newcomers brought to the forefront of political life by the first wave of democratisation.

These negative tendencies are produced by the persistence of bureaucratic state structures and the lack of strong autonomous centres based in civil society. The formation of 'cultural democrats' in the elite instead of 'functional' ones will be a protracted process and a consequence of several interconnected factors.[11] Among the most important of them are the consolidation of democracy, a certain stability in the rotation of elites having the trust and confidence of the population, the formation of 'professional politicians' coming from the younger generation and the adoption of civil service and other laws directed against corruption. Political parties will have to play a very special role in that process by recruiting responsible political leaders and creating stable linkages with civil society. If they fail in that respect, the trust in democracy itself will be put in the balance. The growing lack of confidence and distrust in the new political elite in Bulgaria is confirmation of the fact that for the time being political parties are failing to fulfil one of their major functions, which should include promoting stability of the political system by both educating the electorate and learning from its responses.

INTERPARTY RELATIONS

Bulgaria's delayed party differentiation and the hegemony of the communists at the start of the democratic transformation forged a bipolar model of party relations. On one side was the powerful ex-communist Socialist Party and on the other a coalition of over ten parties and organisations united in the Union for Democratic Forces.[12] The anti-communist bloc was supported in the early years of transition by the Movement for Rights and Freedoms, whose electoral base is in the ethnic Turkish population and Islamised Bulgarians – the so-called 'Pomaks'. The first founding elections of 10 June 1990 produced a majority for the socialists in the Constituent Assembly, but they were faced by a strong anti-communist opposition. The latter retained the initiative, being backed not only by mass extra-parliamentary actions, but also by the president, the leader of the opposition Zhelyn Zhelev, elected to that position in the after-math of the forced resignation of the former Communist president Mladenov. This created a unique situation where neither side had a clear advantage. Although the ex-communists had the formal majority in parliament they were constantly under pressure to make concessions, which resulted in the formation of the first non-communist, de facto coalitional government in December 1990 which was supported by all parliamentary parties.

That governmental formula helped alleviate growing tensions in the country and introduced a precarious stability which facilitated the initiation of the first major reforms and helped the Constituent Assembly to achieve its major task – the adoption of a new constitution. The latter was an important step on the path of consolidating the democratic political framework. Only a small fraction of the UDF and the MRF failed to sign the constitution.

This precarious stability was to be followed by a growing political instability in the aftermath of the next (and the first regular) elections in October 1991. They were won by the radical wing of the UDF. The UDF as a whole underwent its first serious internal division into three blocs in the run-up to the elections. Besides the radicals two moderate coalitions of the UDF were formed, but they failed by a very small margin to overcome the 4 per cent threshold and remained outside parliament.

The new majority was formed by the UDF and the MRF which together embarked on an uncompromising confrontational course, trying to marginalise the socialists, although the latter remained a powerful opposition with almost half of the seats in parliament. The new majority which formed the government – without the direct participation of the MRF – declined any compromise with the Socialists and a situation of confrontation ensued which was to divide the political elite and the country into two irreconcilable blocs. The result was bitter fights and accusations. The former relative consensus achieved during the work on the constitution was replaced by a 'confrontational bipolar model' of party relations close to Sartori's 'polarised pluralism'.[13]

This party model was based on several antagonisms – ideological, generational, socio-professional, but also purely opportunistic. One party, the BSP, wanted to guarantee its survival and its positions in the new democratic system while its major opponent, the UDF, aimed at a radical change of the system. The relative strength of the ex-communists had the effect of generating an aggressive anti-communism on the part of the UDF, which tried to use it as a mobilising agent and as a compensation for its relative weakness, with a view to totally displacing the elite connected to the old regime. This stereotype of confrontational politics – the distance between embattled camps being promoted by the prominence of symbols such as the colour that each party adopted as its sign – had a major impact on political life, and on the reform process in particular, until 1992.

The major political players found themselves in a warlike confrontation with no real dialogue between them, and with one of the sides intent on the political demise of its opponent.[14] The danger of a 'tyranny of the majority' or what Ludzhev, a participant in the UDF government later called 'bureaucratic dictatorship', ensued.

It was prevented only by the fact that the UDF did not have an absolute majority. But that situation was to change when the MRF withdrew its support from the UDF in the autumn of 1992. At that point the growing internal conflicts in the UDF, and the interference of the popular president, led to the UDF government's losing its parliamentary support and to its being replaced by a new government. This was supposed to be a transitional government until the holding of new elections, one based on a new majority made up of the Socialists, part of the UDF (which formed their own group) and the MRF. But its activity was hampered by the continuing confrontation and by parliamentary sabotage on the part of the UDF, which made use of its positions in the chairmanship of the parliament and the major committees, and in the courts. Trying to force early elections, the UDF based its tactics on blocking the work of parliament. Indeed it partially succeeded in blocking the Socialists' attempts at reversing some bills and delaying the adoption of others, using its right to call for a vote of no confidence five times in just a few months.

This highly confrontational relationship between the major parliamentary parties had a detrimental effect on the introduction of new reforms, blocking the whole transitional process, especially in the economy. At the same time the fear that new elections would not change much in the overall situation guaranteed a longer life to an unstable and easily manipulated government which did not have a solid backing from the political parties.

Although Bulgaria avoided the fragmented party situation that Poland, for instance, experienced between 1991 and 1993, the lack of political dialogue and the presence of a highly confrontational relationship blocked major reforms and delayed the consolidation of democracy. It was expected that new elections would bring a modification of the party system because trends in public opinion clearly favoured a change in the paradigms of the current political course and a return to moderate, consensually oriented politics. Extremist tendencies based on the antinomy between Communism and anti-Communism are losing their motivating power as the deep economic and political crises bring ever more to the forefront the need for compromises in the quest for stability and national renaissance. It was expected, as public opinion polls showed, that new political formations and coalitions critical of the confrontational style of politics would gain strength and displace extremist tendencies in the major political blocs.

Bulgaria's evolution stands as no exception among the countries finding themselves on the road to democratic transition and trying to realise the principles of liberal democracy. As Ortega y Gasset so excellently put it in his *Revolt of the Masses*, the essence of liberal democracy is 'the proclamation of a resolve to live together with the opponent, even more – with the weak opponent'.[15] In that process the role of political parties and party relationships are of major importance in forging the new political culture of real pluralism based on compromise, political dialogue and tolerance. Their failure in that respect will delay and eventually endanger the whole process of transition, and later consolidation, of democracy. The political parties in the post-communist system are in crisis even before they have established themselves. They have before their eyes both the Weimar syndrome and the consequences of the Fourth French Republic's weak governments. One could lead to authoritarian regimes, the other to constitutional changes leading to presidential regimes.

One positive conclusion that can be drawn from the Bulgarian experience is that, in spite of the confrontational relationship between the major parties, the fabric of social peace was preserved. Several changes of government and two rounds of elections showed that at least for the time being the major players in political life saw no alternative to parliamentary politics and party pluralism. And that is no minor achievement after decades of totalitarian rule. But a continuation of the confrontational situation could easily turn the positive credit amassed in the first years of transition into a growing disappointment with party politics as a whole. Then the road will be open for authoritarian politicians and parties who are waiting on the sidelines.

NOTES

1 Przeworski, Adam, 'Democracy as a Contingent Outcome of Conflicts', in Jon Elster and Rune Slagstad (eds), *Constitutionalism and Democracy*, Cambridge: CUP, 1988, p. 80.
2 Waller, Michael, *The End of the Communist Power Monopoly*, Manchester: Manchester University Press, 193, p. 220.
3 Programa na BSP (Proekt), *Duma*, 19 March 1994.
4 The signing in March 1994 of an agreement for political partnership leading eventually to an electoral coalition between the newly founded Civil Alliance for the Republik (GOR) led by former BSP activist Aleksandar Tomov, which claims to be left of centre, and the Bulgarian Social-Democratic Party is seen as one of the most successful attempts to break the bi-polar party configuration dominated by the UDF and the BSP.
5 *The Journal of Communist Studies*, vol. 8, no. 1, 1992, p. 156.
6 It is also noted that most newcomers to the political scene, such as Aleksander Tomov's GOR (Civil Alliance for the Republic), as well as Dimitar Ludzhev's New Centre for Politics put a major accent on pragmatic politics and platforms.
7 See Attila Ágh's contribution to this collection.
8 This was the case in particular of the members of the Alternative Social-Liberal Party, which was the first splinter to leave the former Communist Party and later joined the UDF.
9 Wesełowski, Włodzimierz, 'The Autonomy of Political Elites in Transition from Communism to Democracy', conference paper presented in Blagoevgrad, Bulgaria, May 1992.
10 This is developed in Attila Ágh's chapter above.
11 Pridham, G, in *Securing Democracy: political parties and democratic consolidation in Southern Europe*, Routledge, 1991, p. 14.
12 For more details on the history and current development of political parties, see Karasimeonov, Georgi, in *Gesamt Europa, Analysen, Probleme und Perspektiven*, Opladen, Leske and Budrich, 1993, pp. 258–72 and in Wightman, Gordon (ed.), *Party Formation in Eastern Europe*, Aldershot: Edward Elgar, 1995.
13 Sartori, G, *Parties and Party Systems*, New York, 1976; also Roskin, Michael, 'The Emerging Party Systems of Central and Eastern Europe', *East European Quarterly*, March 1993, and Dellenbrandt, Jan Åke (ed.), in *Developments in East European Politics*, Basingstoke: Macmillan, 1993, p. 158.
14 One of the bills introduced by the UDF was to ban the Socialist Party; this was followed by various so-called decommunisation laws and clauses, some of which were adopted, the most notorious being the so-called Panev Law concerning the institutions engaged in education and science.
15 Ortega y Gasset, *The Revolt of the Masses*, Bulgarian edition, Sofia, 1993, p. 86.

Index

Provide Conceptual Context and Theoretical Analyses and also the facts and figures, — graphs stats and also the individual Perspective — My own opinion, their own experiences impressions.

The Power-holders of today —> The Return of the former communists to power.

The Re-draft of Power in the period of Democratic Transition in Poland.

Ambiguous Nature of the Democratic Transition in Eastern Europe.

After the Radical Transformation of the communist system — Consolidation Must occur.